Paul Robert Magocsi
A Bibliography and Commentaries

Paul Robert Magocsi
A Bibliography and Commentaries

FOURTH REVISED AND EXPANDED EDITION

Edited by Ksenya Kiebuzinski

Introductions by
Bohdan Budurowycz
John-Paul Himka
and
Ksenya Kiebuzinski

Distributed by the University of Toronto Press
for the Chair of Ukrainian Studies
University of Toronto
2021

Publication of this volume was made possible
by the generous support of the
Jackman Foundation (Toronto) and the
John and Helen Timo Foundation (Pittsburgh)

Library and Archives Canada Cataloguing in Publication

Title: Paul Robert Magocsi : a bibliography and commentaries / edited by Ksenya
   Kiebuzinski ; introductions by Bohdan Budurowycz, John-Paul Himka and
   Ksenya Kiebuzinski.
Names: Kiebuzinski, Ksenya, editor, writer of introduction. | Himka, John-Paul, 1949-
   writer of introduction. | Budurowycz, Bohdan B. (Bohdan Basil), 1921-2007, writer
   of introduction. | University of Toronto. Chair of Ukrainian Studies, issuing body.
Description: Fourth revised and expanded edition. | Previous editions edited by Luba
   Penzey, Gabriele Pietro Scardellato, Ksenya Kiebuzinski.
Identifiers: Canadiana 20210121351 | ISBN 9780772724991 (hardcover)
Subjects: LCSH: Magocsi, Paul R.—Bibliography. | LCSH: Ruthenians—Bibliography.
   | LCSH: Carpatho-Rusyns—Bibliography. | LCSH: Ruthenian Americans—
   Bibliography. | LCGFT: Bibliographies.
Classification: LCC Z8542.44 .P48 2021 | DDC 016.9477/9—dc23

Cover design: John Beadle

ISBN 978-0-7727-2499-1

Preface

Back in 2011, I had the honor to edit the third edition of Paul Robert Magocsi's bibliography. In my introduction, I wrote how Professor Magocsi's publications have facilitated the work of librarians in the area of Slavic and East European Studies, particularly his contributions to bibliography, cartography, encyclopaedias, historical guides, and his magisterial histories.

These scholarly compendia and narratives serve as pathways to discover lesser known geographies and historical events, figures, and peoples. They make it easier for me and my colleagues to support researchers and students. In 1991, for instance, when I started working as a librarian at the Harvard Ukrainian Research Institute, I would have been lost trying to help patrons (who were eager to learn about and to travel to the newly independent state) navigate the complex administrative and political changes in the territories of Ukraine without *Ukraine: A Historical Atlas*. Years later, when I moved to Canada, I found Professor Magocsi's guides to Ucrainica and the Peter Jacyk collection of Ukrainian serials invaluable for understanding and managing the University of Toronto Library's Ukrainian holdings.

These are just two examples of why I consider Professor Magocsi a librarian's friend. My use of the word 'friend' serves as an identifier. It also defines our relationship in which we share topical interests not only related to Ukraine (both our senior-year undergraduate research projects focused on Alsace: he focused on French foreign policy and I on the origin of the province's toponyms), as well as being fans of once perennial baseball losers (he the Brooklyn Dodgers, I the Boston Red Sox). We also have in common a mid-Atlantic love-hate relationship with the New Jersey Turnpike, both its marshes and industrial charm, about which Bruce Springsteen sings, "deliver me from nowhere." Let us imagine, for a moment, Professor Magocsi's people from nowhere, beginning with Andy Warhol, headed somewhere thanks to this celebrated road.

Professor Magocsi has spent a lifetime thinking, theorizing, and writing about issues of identity as they relate to individuals, ethno-cultural groups, and nations (often people from nowhere). It is thus appropriate that the newest edition of his *Bibliography*, updated for the period 2012 to 2020, also includes a new and extensive section of commentaries where a range of professionals (fellow historians, political scientists, philologists, Slavists, journalists) and civic activists turn the table and try to "identify" who is Professor Magocsi. They focus more on the individual rather than describing the significance of his publications (the over 840 reviews listed following many entries in the bibliography offer ample evidence of his scholarship's impact). The commentaries highlight what at first may be perceived as a paradox, the 'Magocsi question'. Who is he?

On the one hand, Paul Robert Magocsi is coined a political trickster, master intriguer, pseudo-imperialist, filthy ideological falsifier, loyal Magyar (Magyarone), and a stubborn Ukrainophobe by his detractors. Critics that are even more strident accuse him of being an agent of the Czechoslovak Security Services and the KGB. Others elevate his status from historian to an authoritarian. He is the "Godfather" of Lemko separatists, a Rusyn tsar or emperor, or, even, a new Stalin, albeit a Rusyn one. Professor Magocsi even transcends gender. Vasyl Markus calls him the "mid-wife of the Rusyn movement of the new nationality." (p. 228) From quibblers to vilifiers, those who oppose Professor Magocsi's ideas, scholarship, and teachings, accuse him of advancing Rusyn separatism with the aim of destroying the State of Ukraine.

On the other hand, those individuals who hold Professor Magocsi in high regard compare him to nineteenth- and twentieth-century national awakeners and innovators. He has been likened to the national awakener of Carpatho-Rusyns Aleksander Dukhnovych (1803–1865), the Ukrainian historian and statesman Mykhailo Hrushevs'kyi (1866–1934), the Czechoslovak philosopher and statesman Tomáš Garrigue Masaryk (1850–1937), and the Rusyn-American activist and first governor of Subcarpathian Rus', Gregory I. Zhatkovych (1886–1967). Professor Magocsi's champions consider him a liberal humanist and cosmopolitan, who is the objective chronicler, as well as a "new Messiah" (pp. 182 and 199), a "newly-arisen apostle" ("the prophet Moses," p. 222) of Carpatho-Rusyns, *and* a towering and prolific figure in Ukrainian studies. For his admirers, there are no conflicts of interest or contradictions between his scholarly work in Ukrainian studies and his engagement in Rusyn or Carpatho-Rusyn issues. George G. Grabowicz writes that Magocsi's scholarship on "the ethnic diversity and multicultural fabric of Ukraine's history . . . is animated by transnational, comparative, and inclusive values and criteria." (p. 251) There is no reason a scholar cannot be at once a leading historian of Ukraine and of Carpatho-Rusyns.

Some of the paradoxical characteristics described above come by way of hearsay, secondary sources, or the superficial reading of his publications on Carpatho-Rusynism. Those who meet the historian in person come away with a different and, often, lasting impression. He cuts a striking figure. A summer encounter with Professor Magocsi left one writer from Ukraine with the vision of a dandy, dressed in a white summer suit and bare-footed in sandals, "the image of a Hollywood star." (p. 239)

Other in-person meetings with him dispel negative preconceptions about his character. A group of university students in Chernivtsi discovered, during a book-signing visit for Professor Magocsi's *A History of Ukraine*, a friendly scholar quick to pass on a warm word and to shake hands with each one of them, thus outwardly displaying the characteristics of someone who has "the sense of democratic equality" (p. 254) when interacting with future colleagues. Senior colleagues perceive this same openness too. When the Ukrainian historian-ethnographer Ivan Krasovs'kyi visited Toronto in 1991, he described his meeting with Professor Magocsi as being marked by deep respect towards him. Despite the two holding contrary views, Professor Magocsi demonstrated humaneness, tact, and openness to compromise. Others who have had opportunities to visit Professor Magocsi at his University of Toronto office are quick to note his work ethic.

The qualities of friendliness, respect, and diligence are ones that I discovered, and have come to know, since arriving in Toronto in 2006 to serve as the Head of the Petro Jacyk Central and East European Resource Centre, and Slavic Resources Coordinator, for the University of Toronto Libraries. Professor Magocsi was the first faculty member to greet me on arrival and take me out to lunch at his favourite haunt, the downstairs pub of the Faculty Club, for its excellent fish.

Collegially, Professor Magocsi provided me a generous and thorough reading of a manuscript on a relative of mine who served as the first Galician Ruthenian to head the general hospital of Przemyśl in the 1890s. Research on this manuscript involved tracking down print and digitized resources described in Professor Magocsi's historical and bibliographic guide to Galicia. My discussion of identity politics in late nineteenth-century Zasiannia (westward beyond the San River) region benefited from Professor Magocsi's reconceptualization of the entrenched binary found in current scholarship of Russophiles (or Muscophiles) versus Ukrainian populists. His article on "Old Ruthenianism and Russophilism" opened up new pathways to think about individuals and groups who held ambivalent national allegiances. Many historians write them out of history for being anti-Ukrainian. Thinking I would receive a perfunctory commentary, instead, Professor Magocsi returned to me a carefully and thoroughly edited manuscript, with encouraging words about the need for more micro-histories such as mine.

Professor Magocsi is also someone who observes academic decorum. Handwritten thank-you notes are sent for services rendered beyond the ordinary, or to congratulate individuals for the completion of a noteworthy project or new publication. With a nod to the twenty-first century, these written comments *sometimes* are attached to an email sent from the Office of the John Yaremko Chair of Ukrainian Studies at the University of Toronto. Such electronic communications relayed on his behalf are a rare acknowledgment of the electronic and technological age in which we live and which dominates most of our present personal and professional lives. Professor Magocsi records his thoughts, ideas, and writings in cursive format. His adherence to a way of life from before the Information Age leads colleagues to joke that Professor Magocsi is a throwback not to the mid-20th century but to the preceding one, from around the mid-nineteenth-century Spring of Nations.

Nevertheless, there are the advantages of being a scholar off the grid. While Canada and much of the world shut down during the early months of the Covid-19 pandemic, sending faculty, librarians, and students home to teach, study, and learn from home, glued to their computer screens, Ukrainian studies at the University of Toronto carried on as before, albeit in a socially-distanced bubble. Professor Magocsi went daily to his office at the Jackman Humanities Building, carried out research and wrote, telephoned colleagues and conducted business with them, and, even, received mail and parcels by picking them up in person at the university's central mail facilities. In fall 2020, Professor Magocsi taught as before, showing up in his regularly scheduled classroom, with maps, and moved about the room, while a dedicated technician captured and transmitted the lecture to students. Meanwhile, the rest of us interacting virtually suffered Zoom or screen fatigue.

The pandemic complicated my editorial task. Rather than verifying bibliographic references and reviews *de visu*, I relied on what I could find and read online, whether through online library catalogues, journal article databases, open-source collections, or Googling the Internet. Gone were the pleasures of visiting the John P. Robarts Library and browsing the shelves of books and periodicals in its stacks, or thumbing through reference works in the Petro Jacyk Central and East European Resource Centre. Lost were the impromptu visits from Professor Magocsi and other friends and colleagues to the Centre.

Let us hope that 2021 and beyond will bring students and scholars back in face-to-face encounters. Let us assemble once again inside brick-and-mortar libraries to enjoy the services they offer, and to read from physical copies of books and journals, whether Professor Magocsi's works listed in this bibliography, or those by others, friends or colleagues, in whatever fields we wish to explore.

Ksenya Kiebuzinski
University of Toronto
December 2020

Contents

Preface—Ksenya Kiebuzinski   v

Introduction to the First Edition—Bohdan Budurowycz   xiii

Introduction to the Second Edition—John-Paul Himka   xviii

Introduction to the Third Edition—Ksenya Kiebuzinski   xxiv

Statistical Notes   xxx

Bibliography   1

Writings about Paul Robert Magocsi   157

Commentaries in Periodicals and the Media   167

Subject Index   279

Personal Name Index   292

Introduction to the First Edition

It was with a feeling of genuine pleasure that I accepted the invitation to write an introduction to Professor Magocsi's impressive bibliography, which reflects so well his manifold activities and scholarly interests. Its publication marks three important milestones in his life: his fortieth birthday, two decades of his published work, and the fifth anniversary of the establishment of the Chair of Ukrainian Studies at the University of Toronto, of which he became the first holder and which, under his imaginative and dynamic leadership, has helped to make this university one of the leading centres in that field on the North American continent.

A native of New Jersey, Professor Magocsi was educated at Rutgers and Princeton universities, receiving from the latter institution his Ph.D. degree in History in 1972. He continued his education in the School of Slavonic Studies at Charles University in Prague, the School of Hungarian Language and Civilization at Lajos Kossuth University in Debrecen, and at Harvard University where he was appointed for three years (1973-1976) to the prestigious Society of Fellows, which, in the words of Carl Kaysen, the former director of the Princeton Institute for Advanced Studies, is the "highest compliment Harvard pays to a young man."

Professor Magocsi's research, teaching, and administrative activities have been equally diversified. He worked, among other things, as a research specialist for the United States Office of Education and the University of Minnesota project entitled "Emigration, Education, and Social Change"; he participated in the United States Department of State academic exchange (IREX) with Czechoslovakia; he was an inventory consultant to the Bakhmetieff Archive of Russian and East European Civilization at Columbia University; he taught courses on the Habsburg Empire and its successor states and on linguistic and cultural minorities at Harvard University; and he acted as managing editor of the Harvard Series in Ukrainian Studies.

Professor Magocsi's earliest publications date from the 1960s and range from letters to the editors of newspapers (including, even in his student days, the prestigious *New York Times*—see items **1**, **5** and **16**) and reviews of films and plays to probing attempts to discover the truth behind the controversial events of the present and the past (e.g., the invasion of Czechoslovakia in 1968 and Khmel'nyts'kyi's uprising of 1648—see items **6-8** and **13**)—in other words, to find a response to the classical and yet almost unanswerable question, "wie es eigentlich gewesen." In addition, already during his years of apprenticeship Magocsi demonstrated a keen interest in two interrelated issues to which he was to devote over half of all his publications: the history of the country of his maternal ancestors, Subcarpathian Rus', and the problems of the Carpatho-Rusyn community in the United States. While some (rather amateurish) attempts in that direction had been made by his predecessors, it was he who almost singlehandedly "put Subcarpathian Rus' on the map" *(St. Vladimir's Theological Quarterly,* XXVIII, 2, 1984, p. 137).

Many of Professor Magocsi's articles, seminar reports, bibliographical compilations, and even textbooks of the Rusyn language (items **33** and **64**) produced during the 1970s can be described as merely byproducts of *The Shaping of a National Identity: Subcarpathian Rus', 1848-1948* (item **42**) . This, his *magnum opus,* emerged as a result of many years of hard labour and it generated over fifty reviews and review articles in some nine languages. As critics were quick to point out, this first major work by a young but mature scholar—the book which "we all dream of writing" *(Slovakia, XXXI,* 1984, p. 130)—was also the first and the most comprehensive treatment of the subject in any western language. Almost encyclopedic in its design, supplied with copious footnotes, extensive biographical appendices, and a massive bibliography of over 2,200 titles, it transcended the limits of conventional history and developed into a case study, demonstrating, in the words of a perceptive critic, "the relevance of a seemingly irrelevant group," for in it "the Subcarpathian Rusyns, no matter how 'minuscule' they appeared to themselves and to many outsiders, are propelled into new prominence through [Magocsi's] thorough historical analysis" *(Canadian Journal of History,* XIV, 3, 1979, pp. 492-493).

Even the lively polemics which developed around the book (especially the spirited exchange of opinions between one of the reviewers, Professor Vasyl Markus, and the author—items **94** and **110**) helped to clarify some of the contentious issues surrounding the subject and contributed to a better understanding of the infinitely complex processes which determine the formation of national identity in border areas, where various political ideologies may be competing for the allegiance of an ethnic group which has not yet made a definite commitment to any single national orientation.

An outgrowth of *The Shaping of a National Identity* was Magocsi's brief survey of the Rusyn-Ukrainians of Eastern Slovakia (item **119**), outlining their history from earliest times to the present, as well as a series of articles dealing with various aspects of the history of Subcarpathian Rus', its most prominent personalities, the language question, and the literature produced by them both in their homeland and in the United States (items **43-44 46-56, 58, 62-63, 82, 87, 90, 95, 100, 104-106, 113-115, 121, 123, 128**). At the same time, Magocsi expanded his research interests to the problems of the Ukrainian immigration. He edited and provided with an illuminating introduction the symposium on the Ukrainian experience in the United States (items **59-61**), published by the Harvard Ukrainian Research Institute, where, from 1976 to 1980, he occupied the position of Senior Research Fellow. In addition, his future interest in Galicia was foreshadowed by a number of studies devoted mainly to sociolinguistic and bibliographical issues and their impact on the national movement in the future "Ukrainian Piedmont" (items **36, 65, 107, 108**).

Professor Magocsi's appointment to the Chair of Ukrainian Studies at the University of Toronto and his subsequent move to Canada in 1980 opened a new stage in his activities as a scholar and teacher and gave him for the first time in his career the opportunity to initiate major new projects that gave full play to his organizational abilities. It is no secret that his appointment was surrounded by considerable controversy and that his qualifications were challenged by some members of the university community. However, he went through that "baptism of fire" with admirable equanimity and self-control, emerging from it unscathed.

Incidentally, this dispute was also fruitful from the bibliographical point of view, since his name became a household word within and beyond University of Toronto circles, giving rise to numerous "Magocsiana" appearing in the Ukrainian press, student newspapers, university bulletins, and local dailies (in itself enough material for a separate bibliography or study).

Professor Magocsi's partial answer to his would-be detractors was his insightful lecture on national cultures and university chairs (items **88** and **89**). An even more eloquent and effective rebuttal was provided by the publication of his *Galicia: A Historical Survey and Bibliographic Guide (item* **129**). In this work, Magocsi has produced a detailed and informative guide that will undoubtedly remain the most authoritative and complete bibliography on the subject for many years to come. Based on documentary sources and scholarly literature in many languages, it presents and evaluates some 3,000 books and articles—a vast undertaking that reflects the author's knowledge, skill, and energy.

Of special value are brief chapter surveys of the history of Galicia from pre-historic times to the present written in a fresh and lucid style, yet at the same time with commendable impartiality and with critical and sophisticated judgement. One of the unique features of the book is the inclusion of separate chapters dealing with Galicia's national and religious minorities. Small wonder, then, that the reviewers have been unanimous in praising it as "a work of exceptional quality," distinguished by "its readability, organization of source material, objectivity, and painstaking scholarship" *(Canadian Journal of History,* XX, 2, 1985, p. 256)—in short, "a model of how historical bibliography can and should be written" *(Canadian-American Slavic Studies,* XVIII, 4, 1984, p. 494). Other critics referred to it as "the first historical survey of Galicia that has been written with an unprejudiced mind" *(Orientalia Christiana Periodica,* L, 1984, pp. 501-502), and "virtually a concise encyclopedia of the 'Galician problem' in the broadest sense of the word" *(Zeszyty Historyczne,* No. 66, 1983, p. 207).

In addition to completing the book on Galicia, Professor Magocsi has also proven himself a prolific and indefatigable scholar in other areas: editing and providing introductions to the exquisite *Wooden Churches in the Carpathians* (item **111**) and to several volumes in the series "Revolution and Nationalism in the Modern World" (items **96-99**), as well as writing on such diverse groups as the Frisians, Luxembourgers, Maltese, Russians, Ukrainians, and preparing 87 maps of ethnic homelands for the *Harvard Encyclopedia of American Ethnic Groups* (items **70-79**). Finally, in a veritable labour of love—the beautifully designed and lavishly illustrated *Our People* (item **138**)—he has told with great perception and sincere affection the moving and fascinating story of the Carpatho-Rusyn immigrants and their descendants in North America, accompanied by a unique "Root Seeker's Guide to the Homeland."

Among his original publications of a seminal nature, I would like especially to mention Professor Magocsi's "Old Ruthenianism and Russophilism" (item **127**), prepared in conjunction with the Ninth International Congress of Slavists held in Kiev in 1983. Written in an objective and refreshingly dispassionate fashion, this essay provides new insights and interpretations on the Old Ruthenian movement among Ukrainians in Galicia during the second half of the nineteenth century. In the same spirit, he is currently revising his thought-provoking survey of Ukrainian history from earliest times to the present (a university textbook still unpublished), which provides a welcome relief from the romanticized accounts of some of his predecessors.

It should be stressed, moreover, that Professor Magocsi has also played an active part in organizing or co-sponsoring a number of scholarly conferences and lectures. He was also instrumental in the acquisition by the University of Toronto Library of the valuable Peter Jacyk collection of Ukrainian serials on microfilm, for which he compiled an authoritative itemized guide (item **120**). Indeed, the entire record of his activities both before and since the inception of the Chair shows, as an astute reviewer has observed, that "Magocsi clearly knows the uses of history, not as the science of a dead past, but as the genetic illumination of the present through the study of its origins and evolution" (Robert Taft, *Diakonia, XIII,* 2, 1978, p. 172). This eminently pragmatic philosophy is also reflected in Professor Magocsi's two latest books—*Ukraine: A Historical Atlas* (item **157**) and the catalogue, *Ucrainica at the University of Toronto Library* (item **156**), the former being a superbly executed reference tool indispensable to anyone interested in Ukrainian studies, the latter a full inventory of one of the largest and best organized collections of Ukrainian materials in Canada. The simultaneous publication of these newest works is certainly the most appropriate way to celebrate the Chair of Ukrainian Studies' fifth anniversary and at the same time to inaugurate its second quinquennium—*quod felix, faustum, fortunatumque sit!*

Bohdan Budurowycz
University of Toronto
1985

Introduction to the Second Edition

The scholarly career of Professor Paul Robert Magocsi, represented by the list of over 540 publications that follows, can be divided into three phases. First there was an Ivy-League phase, roughly corresponding to the 1970s. During these years he worked on his doctorate at Princeton University (received 1972) and then went on to Harvard University, where he was a member of the Society of Fellows, a senior research fellow of the Ukrainian Research Institute, managing editor of the Harvard Series in Ukrainian Studies, and a member of the editorial board of the *Harvard Encyclopedia of American Ethnic Groups*. In this formative period, Professor Magocsi worked in all the dominant themes and genres that were to distinguish his career. The second phase commenced in 1980 with his appointment to the Chair of Ukrainian Studies at the University of Toronto. Events in Europe, namely the revolutions of 1989, created the conditions for a third phase, which was also marked by his engagement as director and CEO of the Multicultural History Society of Ontario (1990-1997).

Each of these phases witnessed a marked increase in his productivity. In the bibliography that follows, we might assign items **1-79** to the first phase, items **80-215** to the second, and items **217-559** to the third. Each phase also demonstrated qualitative change. For example, in phase one, he prepared maps for the *Harvard Encyclopedia of American Ethnic Groups* (item **79**), and in phase two he published a complete historical atlas of Ukraine (item **157**), but in phase three he produced a historical atlas for the entire, extremely complex east-central portion of Europe (item **342**). Similarly, if in phase one he was contributing to an encyclopedia of ethnic groups (items **70-79**), by phase three he was the editor-in-chief of one (item **516**). Let us look at some of the highlights.

It was in his years at Harvard that Professor Magocsi began to make an impact on the scholarly community through his publications. Perhaps the first major work to attract attention was his historiographical guide to Subcarpathian Rus', published in the *Austrian History Yearbook* (item **22**), which won a prize from the American Association for the Study of Hungarian History. He soon followed this up with a bibliography on Carpatho-Ruthenians in America (item **27**). It turned out that these were but the first installments of a long-term project, since he was to update these works every ten years in the form of book-length annotated bibliographies (items **195, 504**). Also in this period he published two linguistically different versions of a popular manual, *Let's Speak Rusyn* (items **33, 64**), reprinted several times, which heralded his interest in developing a standard Rusyn literary language. He also made strong forays at this time into the history of ethnic groups in America, editing conference proceedings on the Ukrainian experience in the United States (item **59**) and contributing entries on Carpatho-Rusyns, Russians, Ukrainians and others (items **70-78**) to the Harvard encyclopedia mentioned above.

But the most important fruit of those years was *The Shaping of a National Identity: Subcarpathian Rus', 1848-1948* (item **42**). This was in many ways a programmatic work. It proceeded from the premise that national identity in Subcarpathia was not a given, that the East Slavs of this region could have become Ukrainians, or Rusyns, or Russians. It was the first work to treat identity in the Carpathians in this up-for-grabs fashion. He concluded that the issue had been settled in favor of the Ukrainians by 1948, although he had earlier expressed doubts about the finality (and desirability) of this result in an article he wrote under the pseudonym Pavel Mačy (item **26**). *The Shaping of a National Identity* stirred up what must have been the liveliest controversy ever to visit Ukrainian studies, as many Ukrainian historians in the diaspora considered the book to be biased toward the Rusyn option. This controversy was only to intensify in later years. The book was also a microcosm of the kind of work Professor Magocsi was to pursue during the following decades. Although it contained an interpretive survey of the development of nationalism in Subcarpathian Rus' in the century after the Revolutions of 1848, this took up only about half of the tome's 600-plus pages. It also had a long appendix with comparative data on activists of the Russophile, Ukrainophile, and Rusynophile orientations, which amounted to a first draft for a dictionary of national biography. Another appendix presented the spectrum of the varieties of literary language used in the region. The bibliography took up a fifth of the volume, and there were six maps.

When, in 1980, Professor Magocsi was appointed to the newly established Chair of Ukrainian Studies at the University of Toronto, many elements in the Ukrainian community, which had raised money for the chair, expressed dissatisfaction. Those who were discontent felt that Professor Magocsi in his articles and major book on Carpatho-Rusyns was undermining the unity of their vulnerable nation and should not occupy the Toronto chair. Professor Magocsi responded in a number of ways, but the way that is relevant here is his major contributions to mainstream Ukrainian studies.

In the Toronto years he published a book-length historiogaphical guide to Galicia (item **129**), which won Harvard University's Cenko Prize in Ukrainian bibliography and became an indispensable tool for students of Ukraine. He published a historical atlas of Ukraine (item **157**). He wrote an oft-cited, seminal article outlining a new framework for conceptualizing the Ukrainian national revival (item **210** and **257**). And he organized a conference on the outstanding Ukrainian churchman Andrei Sheptyts'kyi; the collection of articles that emerged from that conference (item **211**) remains one of the best works on the subject. Few other scholars in the field could match such a record. In addition, he continued to write on Carpatho-Rusyns, producing four editions of a coffee-table history of the Rusyns in North America, *Our People* (items **138, 374, 623**). In these years, his works on ethnic studies began to assume a fully North American perspective, that is, he was integrating Canada into his narratives.

In 1989, the Communist regimes collapsed in Poland and Czechoslovakia. Professor Magocsi was quick to realize the implications for the Lemkos/Rusyns/Ukrainians of these countries and pleased to discover that there was considerable interest among these populations in defining for themselves a non-Ukrainian Rusyn national identity. Professor Magocsi plunged into the nation-building process with them, writing numerous articles in the press of North America and Central Europe about the Carpatho-Rusyns and their aspirations. Many of the longer articles are collected in the two volumes entitled *Of the Making of Nationalities There is No End* (items **535, 536**). Symbolic of the success achieved was the announcement in 1995 that "a new Slavic language is born" (items **393**, **435**), a reference to a conference that established norms for literary Rusyn. Professor Magocsi's advocacy of the Rusyn cause provoked even more heated resistance from certain Ukrainian scholars, but now no longer just in the diaspora. Not only did Ukrainian scholars (and community activists) in Czechoslovakia, Poland, and Ukraine voice their strenuous objections to his activities, some sought to undermine his reputation.

Yet in spite of all the furor around him, Professor Magocsi was able in this third period to publish several major works, including an 800-page history of Ukraine (item **452**). An achievement of the first magnitude was his historical atlas of East Central Europe (item **342**), which appeared as volume I in the excellent multivolume History of East Central Europe edited by Peter Sugar and Donald Treadgold. Perhaps equally impressive was his editorship of the *Encyclopedia of Canada's Peoples* (item **516**).

What can we expect him to publish in the first years of the new century? He is working on at least two large projects that are logical extensions of his previous oeuvre: a survey of the nationality question in Galicia from the 1830s to 1914 and an encyclopedia of Rusyn history and culture. He has prepared a thoroughly revised and expanded version of the slightly re-titled *Historical Atlas of Central Europe* (item **581**). And certainly there will a further installment in the decennial Carpatho-Rusyn bibliography (item **636**). It is probable also that there will be some surprises.

In surveying Dr. Magocsi's unusually productive career, two features seem to stand out: the themes on which he writes, and the genres that he favors. The central core of his interest is clearly the question of national identity among the East Slavs of the Carpathians. His multifaceted work on the Carpatho-Rusyns is particularly striking, but he has also made major contributions to the history of the Ukrainians in Galicia. Judging by the quantity and emotional engagement of his writings on each of the two cases, the Rusyns of Subcarpathia and the Lemko region are of driving interest to him, while the Galician Ukrainians are studied in detail because they both influenced developments among the Rusyns and they provide illuminating comparison on the formation of national identity in a context of competing orientations. Outward from this core are various concentric circles: one includes the Rusyns and ethnic groups in general in North America; the other leads from Ukraine to East Central

Europe as a whole. The case of the Rusyns invites certain comparisons to small nations in Western Europe, hence the occasional pieces on Monaco and Luxembourg. There is work too on the theory of nationality. All scholars strive to work in a context, but few have worked so productively and fundamentally in their "concentric circles" as has Professor Magocsi, producing entire textbooks, encyclopedias, and atlases which put their specialty in the larger context. It is an unusual, yet unusually fruitful, scholarly style.

Also unusual are Professor Magocsi's genres of choice. It is far more typical of historian, at least in our time, to concentrate on the monograph, that is, the detailed study of a particular, narrowly defined issue or incident, whether in book or article form. Such monographic studies are not unknown in Professor Magocsi's work (see for example items **272**, **344**), but they occupy a lesser place. Typically, the historian is supposed to produce several monographic studies which then lead to a work of synthesis. Professor Magocsi likes to work in synthetic genres, however, genres which both guide and facilitate the monographic work of others. What I have in mind are his edited collections, historiographical guides, annotated bibliographies, atlases, encyclopedias, surveys, and textbooks. These might be called the magisterial genres.

Professor Magocsi also works in engaged genres. He writes many discursive, interpretive, frequently provocative pieces for other scholars as well as educated laymen. He also writes the kind of pieces East Europeans call "popular-scientific" or even "publitsystyka"; for example, one might look at his numerous contributions to the quarterly *Carpatho-Rusyn American*. Nor does he shrink from forthright polemics, when they strike him as warranted. He is, in short, not just studying history, but taking part as actor in the historical process. In other words, he uses his knowledge of history to influence history. This is a feature of his work that is very distinctive.

The two types of genres in which he works, the magisterial and engaged, complement one another in an interesting way. Bibliographies, atlases, and the like are by no means value-free texts, but they frequently pose as such. Moreover, they restrict the play of subjectivity by comparison to monographic investigations. In the engaged genres, on the contrary, the subjective element is expected to play and does play a larger part than in the monograph. This is one of the things that makes

Professor Magocsi's work so interesting to read: he achieves balance by writing history in two diverse, yet complementary ways.

What we have here, then, is a scholar with a unique profile, who has made immense contributions to knowledge: about how national identity is formed, about the ethnic groups who make up North America, about east-central Europe, about Ukraine, and about the Carpatho-Rusyns.

John-Paul Himka
University of Alberta
2000

Introduction to the Third Edition

Professor Paul Robert Magocsi is a librarian's friend. We appreciate him as a bibliographer, cartographer, and encyclopaedist. His scholarly contributions to these fields are invaluable to us in answering reference queries and supporting the research needs of our students, faculty, and fellow scholars. We also value him for his enthusiasm for the printed word. As a bibliophilist, he has helped build one of the most outstanding Central and East European university library collections in North America, and he has assembled the most comprehensive Carpato-Ruthenica collection anywhere.

I will return to his bibliographic and bibliophilic achievements further on, but first a bit about the man himself. Paul Robert Magocsi was born and grew up in northern New Jersey. Despite his familial Carpatho-Rusyn and Hungarian roots, his first "national" allegiance was as a "died-in-the-wool" Brooklyn Dodgers fan. This choice of a "wait 'til next year" sports team set somewhat of a precedent in his academic interests, that is, groups either at the margins or waiting to realize themselves. As a senior at Rutgers University, he wrote an honour's thesis on Alsace, the ever-annexed, culturally distinct region between France and Germany. Then, upon the invitation of James Billington (a historian of Russia and the Soviet Union, and the thirteenth Librarian of Congress), Magocsi came to Princeton University with the intent of researching the Zaporozhian Cossacks. Again, his interest was in studying a group on a frontier—"beyond the rapids" (*za porohy*)—though now located on the southern steppes of Ukraine. His plans changed, however, when on a research trip to Czechoslovakia in 1968 he witnessed the Soviet-led invasion that crushed the Prague Spring. He chose to write his doctoral dissertation (Ph.D., 1972) on the Carpatho-Rusyns, a people who have traditionally lived in the border regions of present-day Poland, Slovakia, Ukraine, and Hungary. This research would lead to his first major monograph, *The Shaping of a National Identity: Subcarpathian Rus', 1848-1948*, 1978; 2nd reprinting 1979; Ukrainian translation 1994 (items **42** and **372**).

Professor Magocsi's Harvard University period began when he was invited in 1971 by Omeljan Pritsak to come to Cambridge as a research fellow. In all, he was awarded ten years of post-doctoral research appointments at Harvard's Center for Middle Eastern Studies, its Society of Fellows, and the newly established Ukrainian Research Institute, where he was a senior research fellow until 1980. At Harvard, Magocsi also served as the first managing editor of the Harvard Series in Ukrainian Studies, and a member of the editorial board of the *Harvard Encyclopedia of American Ethnic Groups*. With access to the fabulous library collections at Widener and Houghton Libraries, and with his frequent research trips to Prague, Vienna, and Ukraine, the decade of the 1970s was particularly productive for his research on the history of nineteenth-century Galicia. That research culminated in *Galicia: a Historical Survey and Bibliographical Guide*, 1983; 2nd printing 1985; 3rd printing 1990 (item **129**), which for the first time brought together references to literature and documents in fourteen languages that traced the historical development of this border region.

In July 1980, Professor Magocsi was appointed to the Chair of Ukrainian Studies at the University of Toronto. The appointment was officially inaugurated on 22 October 1980 with his lecture on "National Cultures and University Chairs" (items **88** and **89**). The Chair was renamed the John Yaremko Chair in Ukrainian Studies in 2010 to honour John Yaremko's two-million dollar gift to the university. As chairholder, Professor Magocsi teaches undergraduate and graduate courses, directs master's and doctoral studies in Ukrainian history, holds research seminars, sponsors international conferences, offers research fellowships, and promotes relations with Ukraine. Aside from this prestigious academic appointment, Professor Magocsi has also had a career of service to the Carpatho-Rusyns as founding president since 1978 of the Carpatho-Rusyn Research Center, and to the ethnic groups of his adopted country, Canada, from 1990 to 1998 as director of the Multicultural History Society of Ontario, where he oversaw the publishing of the *Encyclopedia of Canada's Peoples*, 1999 (item **516**). For his scholarly contributions, Magocsi has been recognized as Full Academician of the International Slavonic Academy of Sciences in Kyiv, Ukraine, and as Fellow of the Academy of Humanities and Social Sciences of the Royal Society of Canada.

Despite his demanding teaching and professional commitments, Professor Magocsi has published prolifically—the present bibliography numbers over 870 entries—on his various scholarly interests in Ukrainian, Carpatho-Rusyn, and central European studies, including bibliography, historical cartography, historiography, nationality- and language-identity issues, religion, and North American immigration. His book-length contributions and edited volumes on Galicia include the historiographical guide mentioned above, and a monograph and collected essays on the region, *The Roots of Ukrainian Nationalism: Galicia as Ukraine's Piedmont*, 2002 (item **579**), and *Galicia: A Multicultured Land*, 2005 (item **631**). In Ukrainian studies, Magocsi's monographs comprise, among others, an edited volume on the Ukrainian churchman Andrei Sheptytskyi, *Morality and Reality: The Life and Times of Andrei Sheptyts'kyi*, 1989 (item **211**); and two histories of Ukraine: *A History of Ukraine*, 1996 (item **452**), Ukrainian translation 2007 (item **654**), 2nd revised and expanded edition 2010, with the added subtitle *the Land and Its Peoples* (item **718**), Ukrainian translation 2012 (item **733**); and *Ukraine: An Illustrated History*, 2007 (item **661**), Ukrainian translation 2012 (item **735**).

No less important is his ground-breaking work on Rusyn or Carpatho-Rusyn history and culture. This includes academic studies, such as the encyclopaedia on Rusyns, 2002, 2nd revised edition 2005 (items **582** and **617**), Ukrainian translation 2010 (item **714**); *The Rusyns of Slovakia: A Historical Survey*, 1993 (item **341**), Rusyn-Slovak bilingual translation, 1994 (item **373**); five volumes of a "national bibliography": *Carpatho-Rusyn Studies: An Annotated Bibliography, 1975-2009* (items **195**, **504**, **636**, **721**, and **738**), as well as his publicistic, popular, and educational efforts, including: *Our People: Carpatho-Rusyns and Their Descendants in North America*, in four editions (items **138**, **374**, and **623**); *The People from Nowhere: An Illustrated History of Carpatho-Rusyns*, 2006 (item **641**) and in nine other language translations, 2006-09 (items **640**, **652**, **653**, **666**, **697**, **698**, **766**, **767**, **774**); and *Let's Speak Rusyn*, in four linguistic variants (items **33**, **64**, **48**, and **837**), the first two of which appeared in revised editions (items **781** and **815**).

For anyone who works in the classroom teaching, or in the library supporting, Central and East European studies, the essential books from Professor Magocsi's scholarly corpus are his *Ukraine: A Historical Atlas*,

1985, 2nd printing 1986, revised printing 1987, 2nd revised printing 1992 (item **157**), and *Historical Atlas of East Central Europe*, 1993, 2nd printing 1995 (item **342**), 2nd revised and expanded edition retitled *Historical Atlas of Central Europe*, 2002 (item **581**) and 3rd revised edition (item **848**). The Ukrainian atlas has been characterized as "a beautiful, valuable, and all too rare historical atlas," one that fills a void in scholarship "for a correct and unfalsified depiction of Ukraine." For myself, I have always found the map and section on minority populations in nineteenth-century Ukraine particularly useful. The atlas of east-central/central Europe, with nearly one hundred reviews, has been described as incomparable and of lasting influence in the fields of history and geography, variously applauded as "a marvellous conspectus," "a cartographic masterpiece," and "a jewel of a reference work."

Two other works edited by Professor Magocsi that are of superb and formidable scholarship, and go-to books for students and lay people, are his *Encyclopedia of Rusyn History and Culture*, 2002; revised edition 2005 (items **582** and **617**), Ukrainian translation 2010 (item **714**), and the *Encyclopedia of Canada's Peoples*, 1999 (item **516**). These last two volumes in some ways are the most important of his reference publications, as they document the histories, biographies, and cultural activities of ethnic groups that likely would not be included in the greater cultures of which they are a part. In the case of Carpatho-Rusyns, their cultural, political, and religious figures are often ignored in the historical encyclopaedias of the states in which they have lived, such as, for example, Austria-Hungary, Czechoslovakia, Poland, or Ukraine.

As for Professor Magocsi the bibliophile, his support of the library forms a basis for his (and all of our) scholarship. It is precisely his self-identification with being a research and publishing scholar that makes his own scholarship inseparable from the library, be it in Toronto, Prague, Vienna, or elsewhere. And, as someone who has worked as a librarian at two of the top five academic libraries in North America—Harvard University and the University of Toronto—I can attest to his having elevated the Slavonic collection, particularly its Ucrainica, to one that can support graduate and post-doctoral level research and attract international visiting scholars.

The establishment of the Chair of Ukrainian Studies in 1980 at the University of Toronto initiated the period when the University Library began intensively to expand its Ukrainian holdings. As the newly appointed chairholder, Professor Magocsi undertook the first systematic analysis of the Ukrainian collection at the University of Toronto Libraries (item **156**). The result was the "discovery" of over eleven-thousand titles, or approximately thirteen-thousand volumes, which by 1986 grew to twenty-thousand volumes. To give you a sense of the phenomenal growth of the library's Ucrainica collection, during the 1970s it grew on average by four-hundred volumes per year, while in the first five years after Professor Magocsi's appointment to the university it grew by 1,400 volumes per year.

The presence of the Chair of Ukrainian Studies attracted donations of significant private libraries, and also spurred the purchasing of invaluable research collections. In 1982, the University of Toronto Libraries acquired a valuable collection from the estate of John Luczkiw, with a focus on the literary, cultural, and political activities of Ukrainians in the diaspora, particularly those who immigrated to Canada in the first half of the twentieth century and those who found themselves in post-World War II Germany and Austria (so-called displaced persons). The following year, in 1983, the Chair of Ukrainian Studies with a grant from benefactor Petro Jacyk acquired on microfilm all western Ukrainian serials held at the Austrian National Library in Vienna, as well as some additional titles held by the Széchényi National Library in Budapest, the National Museum in Prague, the Pontifical Oriental Institute in Rome, and the Episcopal and Heritage Institute Libraries of the Byzantine Catholic Diocese of Passaic, New Jersey. As the special catalogue indicates (item **120**), the microfilm collection spans the years 1848 to 1918, and includes complete or nearly complete runs of 175 newspapers and journals issued in the historic regions of western Ukraine (i.e., Galicia, Bukovina, and Transcarpathia) that had been part of the Austro-Hungarian Empire.

A third major acquisition came in 1984 from the estate of the Canadian-born New York book collector Paul M. Fekula (1905-1982). The purchase was made possible through the Chair of Ukrainian Studies Foundation, with additional funds from a variety of individual sources. Known as the Millennium Ukrainian Collection, in commemoration of the decade-long celebrations marking one thousand years of Christianity in Ukraine-Rus', these twenty-one books comprise biblical texts, liturgies, and prayer books printed between 1614 and 1794, and produced on presses in the cultural centres of Lviv, Kyiv, and Pochaïv in present-day Ukraine. Other, smaller, collections followed the acquisitions of the Millennium and Jacyk material, and continue to this day.

And, I might add, that Professor Magocsi's support for the library collection does not apply only to Ucrainica. Every year he donates personally books and serials in Czech, English, German, Hungarian, Russian, Rusyn, and Slovak, among other languages, to the University of Toronto Libraries. Much more significant is his library of Carpatho-Ruthenica housed at the office of the Chair of Ukrainian Studies.

Presently, the collection consists of over 20,000 books and serials dating from the seventeenth century to the present that deal with the history, language, and culture of Carpatho-Rusyns in all regions where they reside in the European homeland as well as in the diaspora (especially the United States and Canada). The material is published in the various local Rusyn dialects as well as in Latin, Hungarian, Russian, Ukrainian, Czech, Slovak, Polish, German, Yiddish, French, English, etc. Included are works in the fields of bibliography, demography, history, biography, religion, language, ethnography, literature, art, and architecture. Among them are encyclopaedic and statistical guides, church schematisma, school texts, original literary works, atlases, maps, and complete runs of serials dating from the late nineteenth century to the present.

With this bibliography recognizing forty-seven years of Paul Robert Magocsi's publications, I, on behalf of my profession and the University of Toronto Libraries, salute him as a dedicated scholar, a meticulous bibliographer, and an enthusiastic bibliophile.

Ksenya Kiebuzinski
University of Toronto
2010

Statistical Notes

This bibliography is comprehensive in scope. It contains 878 title entries by Paul Robert Magocsi, of which there are 64 authored books, 13 edited books, 23 brochures, 3 catalogues of library collections, 115 chapters in books, 99 articles in scholarly journals, 350 articles in other periodicals, 573 encyclopedic entries, 1,290 individual maps, 15 works edited, 20 introductions/afterwords to books, 8 résumés/reports, 41 reviews, 3 audio lectures, 24 letters to the press, and 47 interviews. Several entries were written originally or were translated into twenty languages other than English: Chinese (1), Croatian (4), Czech (15), Danish (1), French (7), German (6), Hebrew (1), Hungarian (12), Italian (1), Macedonian (1), Polish (13), Romanian (8) Russian (6), Rusyn (143), Serbo-Croatian (2), Slovak (26), Slovenian (1), Turkish (1), Ukrainian (99), and Vojvodinian Rusyn (34).

The arrangement is chronological and the entries are numbered consecutively. Each title is presented in most cases by one entry only, which consist of a full bibliographic description followed by information, if applicable, about publication elsewhere, reprints, and translations. In addition, the bibliographical data indicates 844 reviews of Professor Magocsi's publications, which are cited under the entries of the titles to which they pertain.

The names Julian Galloway, Pavel Mačů, Philip Michaels, and Sanford White, which appear in brackets at the end of some titles, refer to pseudonyms used by the author for some of his works. Appended to the bibliography is a list of select writings about Professor Magocsi. The volume concludes with a subject index and an index of authors, commentators, editors, interviewers, reviewers, and translators mentioned in the entries.

Among Professor Magocsi's English-language publications, the five bestselling books (through 2020) are:

Title	No. of editions	No. sold
Historical Atlas of East-Central/ Central Europe	3	24,161
Ukraine: A Historical Atlas	2	13,621
History of Ukraine	2	10,805
Our People	4	7,447
Let's Speak Rusyn (3 variants)	2	7,146

The Shaping of a National Identity

Subcarpathian Rus', 1848–1948

Paul Robert Magocsi

Bibliography entry **42**.

ПАВЛО-РОБЕРТ МАГОЧІЙ

ПІДКАРПАТСЬКА РУСЬ:
ФОРМУВАННЯ НАЦІОНАЛЬНОЇ
САМОСВІДОМОСТІ
(1848–1948)

Bibliography entry **878**.
Cover design: Valerii Padiak

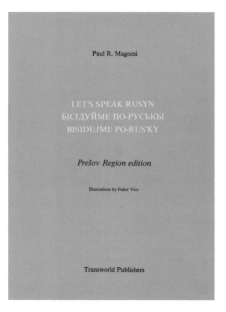

Paul R. Magocsi

LET'S SPEAK RUSYN
БІСІДУЙМЕ ПО-РУСЬКЫ
BISIDUJME PO-RUS'KY

Prešov Region edition

Illustrations by Fedor Vico

Transworld Publishers

Bibliography entry **33**. Cover design: author

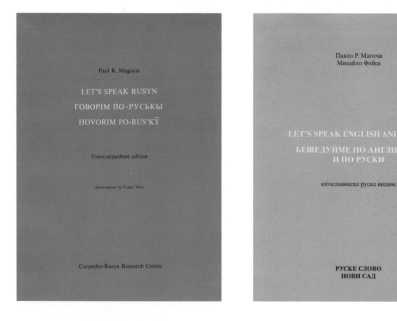

Paul R. Magocsi

LET'S SPEAK RUSYN
ГОВОРІМ ПО-РУСЬКЫ
HOVORIM PO-RUS'KӮ

Transcarpathian edition

Illustrations by Fedor Vico

Carpatho-Rusyn Research Center

Bibliography entry **64**.
Cover design: author

Павло Р. Магочи
Михайло Фейса

LET'S SPEAK ENGLISH AND RUSYN
БЕШЕДУЙМЕ ПО АНГЛИЙСКИ
И ПО РУСКИ

югославянске руске виданє

РУСКЕ СЛОВО
НОВИ САД

Bibliography entry **487**.

Paul Robert Magocsi

Let's Speak Rusyn

БІСЇДУЙМЕ ПО РУСИНЬСКЫ
BISYIDUIME PO RUSYN'SKŶ

Prešov Region Edition
Revised and Expanded

Bibliography entry **781**. Cover design: Nick Kupensky

Paul Robert Magocsi

Let's Speak Rusyn

ГОВОРЬМЕ ПО РУСИНЬСКЫ
HOVOR'ME PO RUSYN'SKŶ

Transcarpathian Region Edition
Revised and Expanded

Bibliography entry **815**. Cover design: Nick Kupensky

Paul Robert Magocsi

Let's Speak Lemko Rusyn

БЕСІДУЙМЕ ПО ЛЕМКІВСКЫ
BESIDUIME PO LEMKIVSKŶ

Lemko Region Edition

Bibliography entry **837**. Cover design: Nick Kupensky

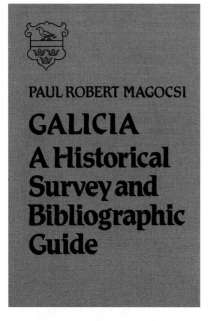

Bibliography entry **129**.

Bibliography entry **354**.
Cover design: Gerry Locklin

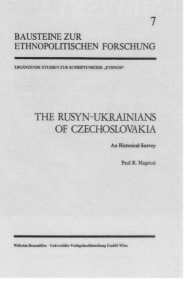

Bibliography entry **119**.

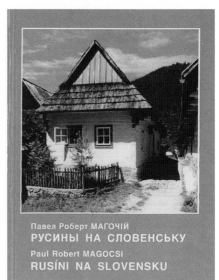

Bibliography entry **373**.
Cover design: Alexander Zozuľák

Our People
Carpatho-Rusyns and Their Descendants in North America

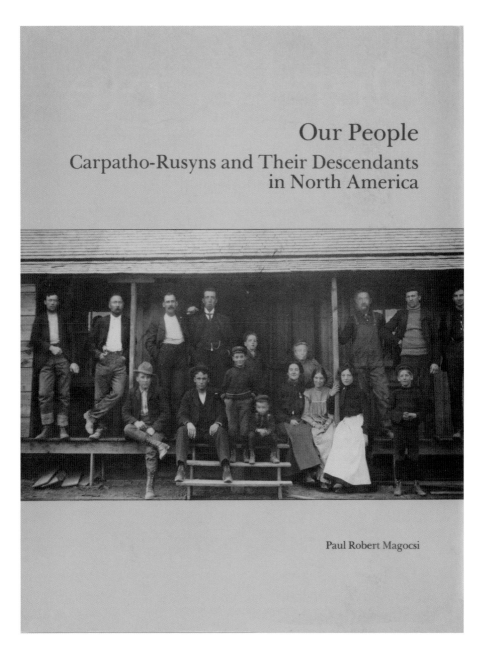

Paul Robert Magocsi

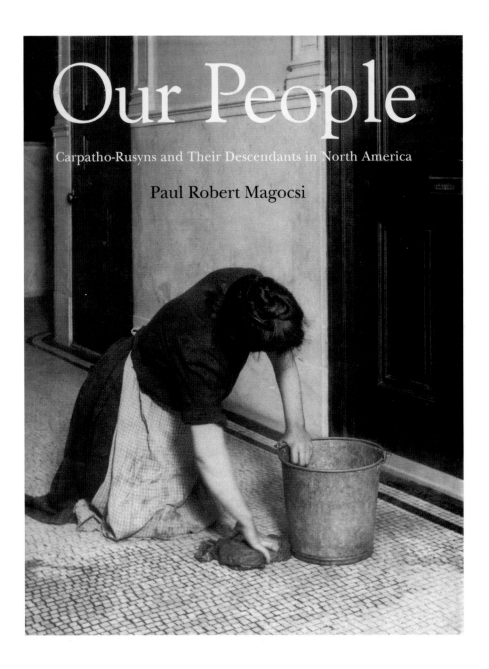

Our People

Carpatho-Rusyns and Their Descendants in North America

Paul Robert Magocsi

Bibliography entry **374**. Cover design: author

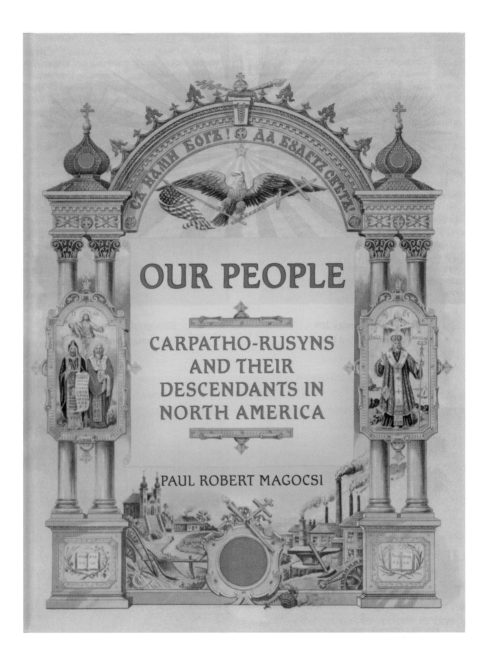

OUR PEOPLE

**CARPATHO-RUSYNS
AND THEIR
DESCENDANTS IN
NORTH AMERICA**

PAUL ROBERT MAGOCSI

Bibliography entry **623**. Cover design: Gabriele Scardellato

Historical Atlas of East Central Europe

Paul Robert Magocsi

Cartographic design by Geoffrey J. Matthews

A History of East Central Europe   Volume I

Bibliography entry **342**.

Historical Atlas of Central Europe

Paul Robert Magocsi

Revised and Expanded Edition

Bibliography entry **581**.

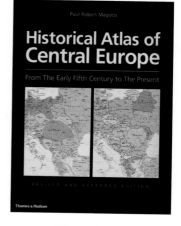

Paul Robert Magocsi

Historical Atlas of
Central Europe

From The Early Fifth Century to The Present

REVISED AND EXPANDED EDITION

Thames & Hudson

Bibliography entry **581**.

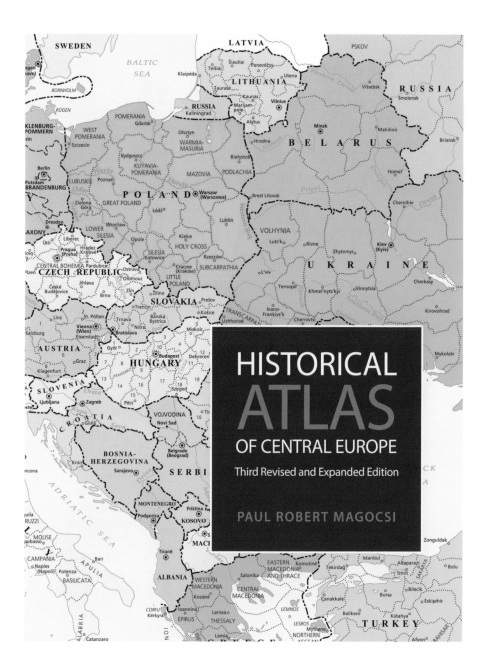

HISTORICAL

ATLAS

OF CENTRAL EUROPE

Third Revised and Expanded Edition

PAUL ROBERT MAGOCSI

ІСТОРІЯ УКРАЇНИ

Павло Роберт Маґочій

Bibliography entry **654**. Cover design: Andrii Shubin

A HISTORY OF
UKRAINE

PAUL ROBERT MAGOCSI

Bibliography entry **452**.

Україна

Історія її земель та народів

Друге видання

Павло-Роберт
МАГОЧІЙ

Bibliography entry **733**. Cover design: Valerii Padiak

Paul Robert Magocsi

A HISTORY OF
UKRAINE

The Land and Its Peoples

SECOND EDITION

Bibliography entry **718**. Cover design: author

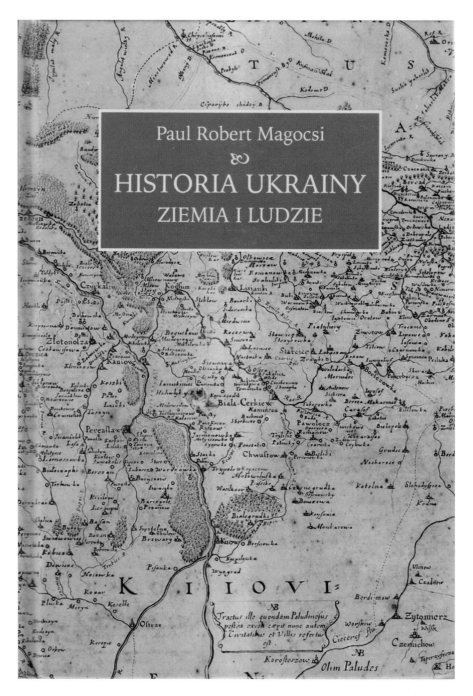

Paul Robert Magocsi
&
HISTORIA UKRAINY
ZIEMIA I LUDZIE

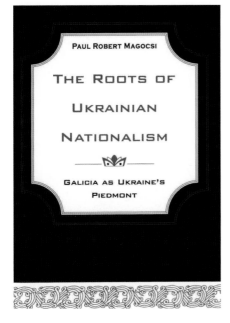

Bibliography entry **661**.
Cover design: Gabriele Scardellato

Bibliography entry **735**.
Cover design: Iaroslav Havryliuk

Bibliography entry **579**.

Bibliography entry **377**.

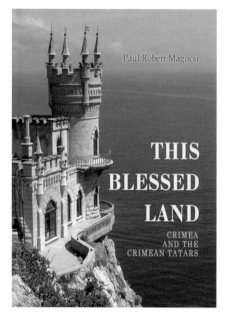

Bibliography entry **759**.
Cover design: author

Bibliography entry **831**.
Cover design: Mehmet Ulusel

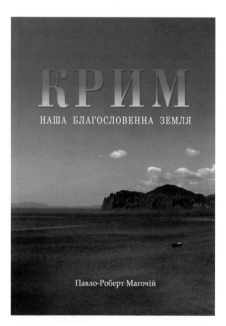

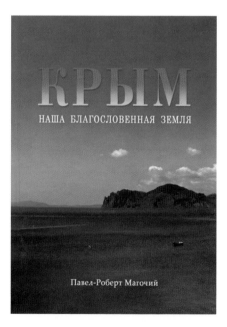

Bibliography entry **760**.
Cover design: Valerii Padiak

Bibliography entry **761**.
Cover design: Valerii Padiak

Bibliography entry **641** and **652**. Cover design: Valerii Padiak

Bibliography entry **640**, **653**, **666**, **697**, **698**, **766**, **767**, **774**. Cover design: Valerii Padiak

JEWS
and
UKRAINIANS
A MILLENNIUM OF CO-EXISTENCE

PAUL ROBERT MAGOCSI
YOHANAN PETROVSKY-SHTERN

Bibliography entry **799**. Cover design: John Beadle

ЄВРЕЇ
та
УКРАЇНЦІ
ТИСЯЧОЛІТТЯ СПІВІСНУВАННЯ

ПАВЛО-РОБЕРТ МАҐОЧІЙ
ЙОХАНАН ПЕТРОВСЬКИЙ-ШТЕРН

Bibliography entry **800**. Cover design: John Beadle

Павло-Роберт Магочій

КОЖЕН КАРПАТОРУСИН
Є РУСИНОМ...
але
НЕ КОЖЕН РУСИН
Є КАРПАТОРУСИНОМ

Bibliography entry **786**. Cover design: Valerii Padiak

Павел Роберт Магочій

НАША
ОТЦЮЗНИНА
Історія карпатськых русинӯв

Bibliography entry **621**.
Cover design: Valerii Padiak

Павел Роберт МАГОЧІЙ

"Я русин был,
єсмь и буду..."

Выступы на
Світовых конгресах русинӯв

НА ВАС БЫЛИ ПЫШНЫ - ДІВКЫ СЫНЫ
...ЖЕБЫ ПЛОДЫ НАШЫХ ОТЦӮВ НЕ
ПРОПАЛИ, ЖЕБЫ ГРОБЫ НАШЫХ
ПРЕДКӮВ НЕ ПЛАКАЛИ.

Bibliography entry **622**.
Cover design: Valerii Padiak

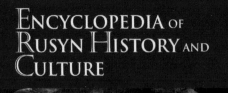

REVISED AND EXPANDED EDITION

Edited by Paul Robert Magocsi and Ivan Pop

Bibliography entry **617**. Cover design: author

Bibliography entry **714**.
Cover design: Valerii Padiak

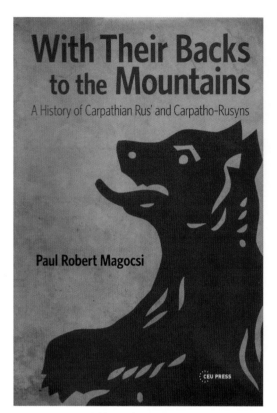

Bibliography entry **790**.
Cover design: Sebastian Stachowski

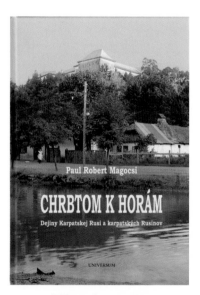

Bibliography entry **806**.
Cover design: Stanislav Šalko

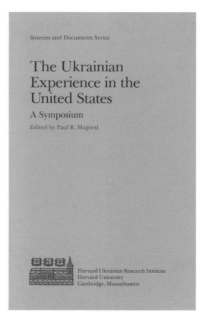

Sources and Documents Series

The Ukrainian
Experience in the
United States

A Symposium

Edited by Paul R. Magocsi

Harvard Ukrainian Research Institute
Harvard University
Cambridge, Massachusetts

Bibliography entry **59**.
Cover design: Jenny Bush

PAUL ROBERT MAGOCSI EDITOR

MORALITY
AND REALITY
The Life and Times of
Andrei Sheptyts'kyi

Bibliography entry **211**.
Cover design: Laurie Mazliach

Najnowsze dzieje języków słowiańskich

Русиньскый язык

Bibliography entry **608**.
Cover design: Adam Bagiński

БАБИН ЯР
באבּי׳יאר
BABYN YAR

Bibliography entry **801**.
Cover design: Anna Harasym

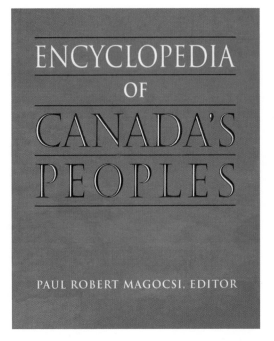

Bibliography entry **516**.

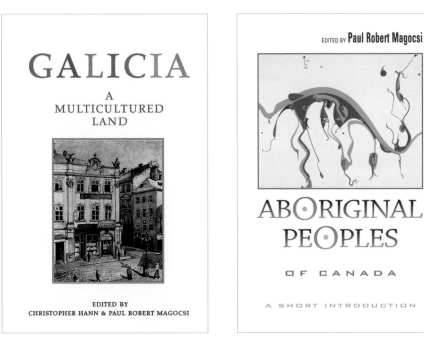

Bibliography entry **631**.

Bibliography entry **580**.

Bibliography entry **111**. Cover design: Ulrike Dietmayer

Bibliography entry **AAA**. Cover design: Valerii Padiak

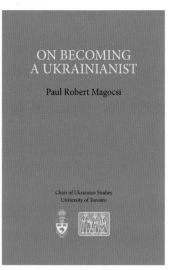

Bibliography entry **839**.
Cover design: John Beadle

ПАВЛО-РОБЕРТ МАҐОЧІЙ

ЯК
Я СТАВ
УКРАЇНОЗНАВЦЕМ

Bibliography entry **840**. Cover design: Valerii Padiak

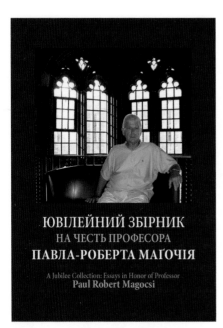

ЮВІЛЕЙНИЙ ЗБІРНИК
НА ЧЕСТЬ ПРОФЕСОРА
ПАВЛА-РОБЕРТА МАҐОЧІЯ

A Jubilee Collection: Essays in Honor of Professor
Paul Robert Magocsi

Bibliography entry **III**.
Cover design: Valerii Padiak

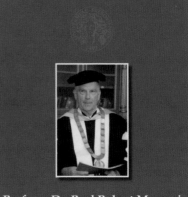

Profesor Dr. Paul Robert Magocsi
Doctor honoris causa
Prešovskej univerzity v Prešove

Bibliography entry **GGG**.

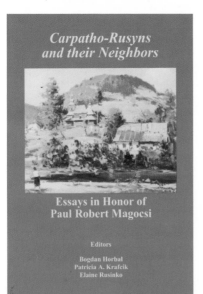

*Carpatho-Rusyns
and their Neighbors*

Essays in Honor of
Paul Robert Magocsi

Editors

Bogdan Horbal
Patricia A. Krafcik
Elaine Rusinko

Bibliography entry **II**.
Cover design: Jack Figel

Володимир Фединишинець

ІСТОРИЧНА МЕТАФОРА
ПРОФЕСОРА МАҐОЧІЯ

Bibliography entry **K**.
Cover design: Volodymyr Fedynyshynets'

Bibliography

1964

1   "They Like It": letter on Luxembourg, *The New York Times Magazine*, November 29, 1964, p. 42.

1966

2   Review of the Joseph Levine film, "The Carpetbaggers," *Rutgers Daily Targum*, November 1966, p. 2.

1967

3   "La Condition Artistique," *Rutgers Review*, II (New Brunswick, N.J., 1967), pp. 3-6.

1969

4   Review of the Brandon Thomas play, "Charley's Aunt," *The Daily Princetonian*, February 5, 1969, p. 2.

5   "Origin of Welsh Motto": letter on Prince Charles of Wales and Luxembourg, *The New York Times*, July 12, 1969, p. 26.

6   "The Communist Party of Luxembourg and the Soviet Invasion of Czechoslovakia," *Troater*, Nos. 4-5 (Echternach, Luxembourg, 1969), 4 p.

7   "Eyewitness Account of the Crackdown in Czechoslovakia," *University: A Princeton Quarterly*, No. 41 (Princeton, N. J., 1969), pp. 23-27.

1970

8 "Between the Hammer and the Anvil: Reflections on the Jewish-Cossack Problem of 1648," *Rutgers Review*, IV, 1 (New Brunswick, N. J., 1970), pp. 31-36.

9 "Glosa," *Druzhno vpered*, XX, 6 (Prešov, Czechoslovakia, 1970), p. 1.

1971

10 "The Nationality Problem in Subcarpathian Rus', 1919-1945" (résumé). In *Minutes of the Seminar in Ukrainian Studies held at Harvard University*, No. 1: *1970-1971*. Cambridge, Mass., 1971, pp. 28-30.

11 Chief Editor, *Recenzija: A Review of Soviet Ukrainian Publications*, II, 1 (Cambridge, Mass., 1971), 81 p.

1972

12 "Nationalism from the Historical Viewpoint" (résumé). In *Minutes of the Seminar in Ukrainian Studies held at Harvard University*, Vol. II. Cambridge, Mass., 1971-72, pp. 61-67.

13 "The View from Prague," *East Europe*, XXI, 5 (New York, 1972), pp. 14-16. [Pavel Mačů]

14 Review article of Mykola Shtets', *Literaturna mova ukraïntsiv Zakarpattia i Skhidnoï Slovachchyny pislia 1918*, in *The Annals of the Ukrainian Academy of Arts and Sciences*, XII, 1-2 (New York, 1969-72), pp. 247-252.

15 "Recent Documentary Publications," review article of *Shliakhom Zhovtnia: zbirnyk dokumentiv*, 6 vols., in *Recenzija*, II, 2 (Cambridge, Mass., 1972), pp. 58-86.

16 Letter on Kiev as "mother of Russian cities," *The New York Times*, June 3, 1972.

17   "The Ukrainians of Czechoslovakia." In *Dukla Ukrainian Dance Company from Prešov, Czechoslovakia*. New York: Hurok Publications, 1972, pp. 4-14.

Reviewed:
K. Krups'kyi in *Svoboda* (Jersey City, N.J.), November 16, 1972, p. 2 and 10.

18   Review article of Petro K. Smiian, *Zhovtneva revoliutsiia i Zakarpattia*, in *Recenzija*, III, 1 (Cambridge, Mass., 1972), pp. 61-72.

1973

19   "The Role of Education in the Formation of a National Consciousness," *East European Quarterly*, VII, 2 (Boulder, Colo., 1973), pp. 157-165.

20   "Immigrants from Eastern Europe: The Carpatho-Rusyn Community in Proctor, Vermont," *Vermont History*, XLII, 1 (Montpelier, Vt., 1973), pp. 48-52.

1974

21   "Rusyny v Iugoslaviï: moï vrazhinnia z podorozhi po Iugoslaviï," *Nova dumka*, III [8] (Vukovar, Yugoslavia 1974), pp. 116-118.

22   "An Historiographical Guide to Subcarpathian Rus'," *Austrian History Yearbook*, IX-X (Houston, Texas, 1973-74), pp. 201-265. Reprinted in Harvard Ukrainian Research Institute Offprint Series, No. 1. Cambridge, Mass., 1975; revised version in item **536**, pp. 323-408.

Reviewed:
Europa Ethnica, XXX, 3 (Vienna, 1976), pp. 147-148.
George Gajecky in *Ukraïns'kyi istoryk*, XIII, 1-4 (New York, 1976), p. 147.
M. Lacko in *Mária*, XVI, 6 (Toronto, 1976), p. 17.
Michał Lesiów in *Slavia Orientalis*, XXVI, 2 (Warsaw, 1977), pp. 238-239.

23   "The Present State of National Consciousness among the Rusyns of Czechoslovakia," *Europa Ethnica*, XXI, 4 (Vienna, 1974), pp. 98-110.

1975

24 "The Ruthenian Decision to Unite with Czechoslovakia," *Slavic Review*, XXXIV, 2 (Seattle, Wash., 1975), pp. 360-381. Reprinted in Harvard Ukrainian Research Institute Offprint Series, No. 3. Cambridge, Mass., 1975, and in item **535**, pp. 124-146.

Reviewed:
George Gajecky in *Ukraïns'kyi istoryk*, XIII, 1-4 (New York, 1976), p. 147.
Hungarian Studies Newsletter, No. 22 (New Brunswick, N. J., 1980), pp. 4-5.

25 "The Rusyns of Czechoslovakia," *The Cornish Banner*, I, 2 (Trelispan, Cornwall, 1975), pp. 4-6. [Pavel Mačiu]

26 "National Assimilation: The Case of the Rusyn-Ukrainians of Czechoslovakia," *East-Central Europe*, II, 2 (Pittsburgh, Pa., 1975), pp. 101-132. [Pavel Mačiu] Reprinted in item **535**, pp. 242-289.

1976

27 *Carpatho-Ruthenians in North America: A Bibliography.* Philadelphia, Pa.: The Balch Institute, 1976, 6 p.

28 "Carpatho-Ruthenians and the Bicentennial," *Eastern Catholic Life* (Passaic, N. J.), October 17, 1976, pp. 1 and 3; and *The Byzantine Catholic World* (Pittsburgh, Pa.), October 24, 1976, p. 2.

29 "Political Activity of Rusyn-American Immigrants in 1918," *East European Quarterly*, X, 3 (Boulder, Colo., 1976), pp. 347-365. Reprinted in Harvard Ukrainian Research Institute Offprint Series, No. 13. Cambridge, Mass., 1976, and in item **535**, pp. 394-415.

30 "Anthology of Documents." In Richard Renoff and Stephen Reynolds, eds. *Proceedings of the Conference on Carpatho-Ruthenian Immigration.* Harvard Ukrainian Research Institute Sources and Documents Series. Cambridge, Mass., 1976, pp. 20-24 *et passim*.

Reviewed:
Ewa Skulimowska-Ochyra in *Slavia Orientalis*, XXVII, 1 (Warsaw, 1978), pp. 42-44.
M. Lacko in *Mária*, XVIII, 7-8 (Toronto), p. 24.

31 "Istoriografiiny voditel' za Podkarpatsku Rus," *Nova dumka*, V [12] (Vukovar, Yugoslavia, 1976), pp. 121-129, and VII [17] (1978), pp. 91-108. Translation of item **22** into Vojvodinian Rusyn by Djura Herbut.

32 "The Historical Context of Subcarpathian Ruthenia," "Carpatho-Ruthenian Language and Literature," and "Carpatho-Ruthenian Art and Architecture." Three recorded lectures in *Cultural Seminar on Carpatho-Ruthenia*, 4 cassettes. Englewood, N. J.: Transworld Manufacturing Co., 1976. Re-released, Fairview, N. J.: Carpatho-Rusyn Research Center, 1984.

Reviewed:
Robert Taft in *Diakonia*, XIII, 2 (New York, 1978), pp. 168-175.

33 *Let's Speak Rusyn—Bisidujme po-rus'kŷ: Prešov Region Edition.* Englewood, N. J.: Transworld Publishers, 1976, xxii, 106 p., 1 map, 24 illustrations by Fedor Vico. Second printing, 1978. Third printing, 1989. Second revised edition, see item **781**.

Reviewed:
Bohdan Strumins'kyj in *Suchasnist'*, XVIII, 6 (Munich and New York, 1977), pp.116-117.
Richard Renoff in *Carpatho-Rusyn American*, I, 1 (Fairview, N. J., 1978), p. 4.
Volodymyr Nota in *Nova dumka*, VII [19] (Vukovar, Yugoslavia, 1978), pp. 52-53.
Wayles Browne in *Folia Slavica*, III, 3 (Columbus, Ohio 1979), pp. 354-361.
W. Fiedler in *Zeitschrift für Slawistik*, XXIV, 4 (Berlin, 1979), pp. 585-588.
Ivan Hainyk in *Sribna zemlia-fest* (Uzhhorod), May 8-14, 1997.

34 "Historical Background of the Ukraine," and "Ukrainians in the United States." In *Festival Bostonian's Ukrainian Celebration.* Boston: Mayor's Office for Cultural Affairs, 1976, pp. 5-11.

1977

35 "The Problem of National Affiliation among the Rusyns (Ruthenians) of Yugoslavia," *Europa Ethnica*, XXXIV, 1 (Vienna, 1977), pp. 5-8.

36 "Movne pytannia iak faktor natsional'noho rukhu u Skhidnii Halychyni XIX. stolittia," *Svoboda* (Jersey City, N. J.), July 1, 2, and 6, 1977.

37 "The First Carpatho-Ruthenian Printed Book," with Bohdan Strumins'kyj, *Harvard Library Bulletin*, XXV, 3 (Cambridge, Mass., 1977), pp. 292-309 and 5 plates. Reprinted in Harvard Ukrainian Research Institute Offprint Series, No. 17. Cambridge, 1977.

Reviewed:
Byzantine Catholic World (Pittsburgh, Pa.), August 14, 1977.
Hungarian Studies Newsletter, No. 22 (New Brunswick, N. J., 1980), p. 5.

38 *Ukrainian Heritage Notes*. Cambridge, Mass.: Ukrainian Studies Fund, 1977, 16 p., 6 illustrations.

Reviewed:
Harvard Librarian, XIII, 1 (Cambridge, Mass., 1978), p. 2.
Forum, No. 40 (Scranton, Pa., 1978-79), p. 33.

39 *Carpatho-Ruthenica at Harvard: A Catalog of Holdings*, with Olga K. Mayo. Englewood, N. J.: Transworld Publishers, 1977, 149 p. Second printing, Fairview, N. J.: Carpatho-Rusyn Research Center, 1983.

Reviewed:
A. Pekar, *Byzantine Catholic World* (Pittsburgh, Pa.), February 19, 1978 and *Eastern Catholic Life* (Passaic, N. J.), February 26, 1978, p. 1.
Harvard Librarian, XIII, 1 (Cambridge, Mass., 1978), p. 12.
College and Research Libraries News, XXXIX, 5 (Chicago, Ill., 1978), p. 294.
Victor Swoboda in *Slavonic and East European Review*, LVIII, 3 (London, 1980), pp. 455-456.

40 "Problems in the History of Ukrainian Immigration to the United States" (résumé). In *Minutes of the Seminar in Ukrainian Studies held at Harvard University*, Vol. VII. Cambridge, Mass., 1976-77, pp. 29-31.

41 "The Language Question as a Factor in the National Movement in Eastern Galicia during the Second Half of the Nineteenth Century" (résumé). In *Minutes of the Seminar in Ukrainian Studies held at Harvard University*, Vol. VII. Cambridge, Mass., 1976-77, pp. 78-81.

1978

42 *The Shaping of a National Identity: Subcarpathian Rus', 1848-1948.* Cambridge, Mass. and London, England: Harvard University Press, 1978, xvi, 640 p., 6 maps, 6 tables. Second printing, 1979.

Reviewed:
Marc Raeff in *Cahiers du monde russe et soviétique*, XIX, 4 (Paris, 1978), pp. 451-452.
Walter C. Warzeski in *East Central Europe*, V, 1 (Tempe, Ariz., 1978), pp. 160- 161.
Richard Renoff in *Diakonia*, XIII, 3 (New York, 1978), pp. 257-266.
Ivan L. Rudnytsky in *Eastern Catholic Life* (Passaic, N. J.), May 7, 1978; *Byzantine Catholic World* (Pittsburgh, Pa.), May 21, 1978; *Svoboda* (Jersey City, N. J.), June 8, 1978; and *Narodna volia* (Scranton, Pa.), May 17, 1979.
Volodymyr Komaryns'kyi in *Homin Ukraïny* (Toronto), October 4, 1978, pp. 6-7.
Donald Petyo in *Byzantine Catholic World* (Pittsburgh, Pa.), July 2, 1978.
Roger Krieps in *d'Letzeburger Land*, XXV, 47 (Luxembourg, 1978), p. 13.
Avhustyn Shtefan in *Ameryka* (Philadelphia), December 23, 1978.
John-Paul Himka in *Harvard Ukrainian Studies*, II, 3 (Cambridge, Mass., 1978), pp. 374-380.
Steven L. Guthier in *Russian Review*, XXXVIII, 1 (Stanford, Ca., 1979), pp. 105-107.
Keith Hitchins in *American Historical Review*, LXXXIV, 2 (Washington, D. C., 1979), p. 510.
Manuel B. García Alvarez in *Revista de la Facultad de derecho de la Universidad Complutense*, No. 55 (Madrid, 1979), pp. 201-203.
Mykhailo Fedorovych [Andreas Rebet] in *Khrystyians'kyi holos* (Munich,

1979), and *Vil'ne slovo* (Toronto), March 24, 1979.

M. Lacko in *Mária*, XIX, 2 and 3 (Toronto, 1979), p. 16 and pp. 15-16.

Choice, XV (Chicago, 1979), p. 1713.

Andrew Gregorovich in *Forum*, No. 41 (Scranton, Pa., 1979), p. 32.

Christine D. Worobec in *Journal of Ukrainian Graduate Studies*, IV, 1 [6] (Toronto, 1979), pp. 113-115.

M. Mark Stolarik in *Nationalities Papers*, VII, 2 (Charleston, Ill., 1979), pp. 221-222.

M. Lacko in *Slovenské hlasy z Ríma*, XIX, 8-9 (Rome, 1979), p. 31.

Béla K. Kiraly in *Canadian Slavonic Papers*, XXI, 2 (Ottawa, 1979), pp. 260-261.

Evan Lowig in *St. Vladimir's Theological Quarterly*, XXIII, 2 (Tuckahoe, N. Y., 1979), pp. 124-126.

M. Lacko in *Orientalia Christiana Periodica*, XLV (Rome, 1979), pp. 234-236.

Ukraïns'ke pravoslavne slovo, XXX, 3 (Bound Brook, N. J., 1979), pp. 21-22.

Europa Ethnica, XXXVI, 3 (Vienna, 1979), p. 206.

Emil Niederhauser in *Századok*, CXII, 6 (Budapest, 1979), pp. 1125-1126.

Günther Wytrzens in *Österreichische Osthefte*, XXI, 4 (Vienna, 1979), pp. 327- 328.

Peter Scheibert in *Zeitschrift für Ostforschung*, XXVIII, 2 (Marburg, West Germany 1979), pp. 313-315.

M. T. [Miroslav Tejchman] in *Slovanský přehled*, LXV, 6 (Prague, 1979), pp. 506- 507.

Manuel B. García Alvarez in *Revista de Estudios Políticos*, XXXIX, 12 (Madrid, 1979), pp. 226-228.

Stephen Fischer-Galati in *Canadian Review of Studies in Nationalism*, VI, 2 (Charlottetown, Prince Edward Island, 1979), pp. 258-259.

Alexander Fried in *Canadian Journal of History*, XIV, 3 (Saskatoon, Sask., 1979), pp. 491-493.

John S. Reshetar, Jr. in *Slavic Review*, XXXIX, 1 (Urbana, Ill., 1980), pp. 144-145.

Vasyl' Markus' in *Suchasnist'*, XXI, 6 (Munich, 1980), pp. 105-122.

Victor Swoboda in *Sobornost/Eastern Churches Review*, II, 1 (London, 1980), pp. 98-100.

M. Sulyma in *Novyi shliakh* (Toronto), June 21 and June 28/July 5, 1980, pp. 8-9 and 7-8.

Victor Swoboda in *The Slavonic and East European Review*, LVIII, 3 (London, 1980), pp. 455-456.

Emil Niederhauser in *Acta Historica*, XXVI, 1-2 (Budapest, 1980), pp. 213-214.

Michael V. Belok in *Journal of Thought*, XV, 4 (1980), pp. 103-105.

Geoff Eley in *Social History*, VI, 1 (London, 1981), pp. 83-107.

Vikentii Shandor in *Ukraïns'kyi istoryk*, XVII, 1-4 (New York, Toronto, and Munich, 1980), pp. 180-190.

Jiří Kovtun in *Svědectví*, XVI, 63 (Paris, New York, and Vienna, 1981), pp. 591- 592.

Hungarian Studies Newsletter, no. 27-28 (New Brunswick, N. J., 1981), p. 5.

V.M. [Vasyl Markus], "Natsionalne opredzel'ovanie rusynokh Karpatskei Rusy: gu knizhky Pavla Magochyia o ruskei ystoryi," *Nova dumka*, X [28 and 20] (Vukovar, Yugoslavia, 1981), pp. 71-75 and 88-92. Translation by Roman Miz of Markus review listed above.

Paul Wexler in *Language Problems and Language Planning*, V, 2 (Austin, Texas, 1981), pp. 200-204.

I.S. Khmil' in *Ukraïns'kyi istorychnyi zhurnal*, XXV, 2 (Kyiv, 1982), pp. 39-43.

hr [L'udovít Haraksim] in *Historický časopis*, XXX, 3 (Bratislava, 1982), pp. 484- 485.

Wolfdieter Bihl in *Austrian History Yearbook*, XVII-XVIII (Minneapolis, 1981- 82), pp. 461-462.

Ljubomir Medješi in *Rada vojvodanskikh muzeja*, XXVIII (Novi Sad, 1982-83), pp. 138-140.

Owen V. Johnson in *Slovakia*, XXXI [57] (West Paterson, N. J., 1984), pp. 130-132.

Ivan L. Rudnytsky in *East European Quarterly*, XIX, 2 (Boulder, Colo., 1985), pp. 139-159. Reprinted in Ivan L. Rudnytsky, *Essays in Modern Ukrainian History*. Edmonton, Alta.: Canadian Institute of Ukrainian Studies, 1987, pp. 353-374.

R. Polchaninov in *Novoe russkoe slovo* (New York), May 10, 1986, p. 10.

Maciej Koźmiński in *Studia z Dziejów ZSRR i Europy Środkowej*, XVII (Wrocław, Warsaw, Cracow, Gdańsk, and Łódź, 1981), pp. 215-217.

Conrad Grau in *Jahrbuch für Geschichte der sozialistischen Länder Europas*, XXVI, 2 (Berlin, 1983), pp. 189-190.

Paul J. Best in *Wierchy*, LIII (Cracow, 1984), pp. 344-345.

43 "Alexander Duchnovyč (1803-1865)," *Carpatho-Rusyn American*, I, 1 (Fairview, N. J., 1978), p. 3. [unsigned]

44 "Notes on the Geography of Subcarpathian Rus'," *Carpatho-Rusyn American*, I, 1 (Fairview, N. J., 1978), pp. 5-6. [unsigned]

45 *Ukrainian Heritage Notes: The Language Question in Galicia.*

Cambridge, Mass.: Ukrainian Studies Fund, 1978, 24 p., 9 illustrations.

Reviewed:
Forum, No. 40 (Scranton, Pa., 1978-79), p. 33.

46 "The Language Question Among the Subcarpathian Rusyns" (résumé). In *Minutes of the Seminar in Ukrainian Studies held in Harvard University*, Vol. VIII. Cambridge, Mass., 1977-78, pp. 42-46.

47 "Adol'f I. Dobrianskij (1817-1901)," *Carpatho-Rusyn American*, I, 2 (Fairview, N. J., 1978), p. 3. [unsigned]

48 "The Historical Context of the Carpatho-Rusyns," *Carpatho-Rusyn American*, I, 1, 2, 3, and 4 (Fairview, N. J., 1978), pp. 4-5, 4-5 and 4; II, 1, 2 and 3 (1979), pp. 5-6, 4, and 4-5.

49 "Rusyn-American Ethnic Literature." In Wolodymyr T. Zyla and Wendell M. Aycock, eds. *Ethnic Literatures Since 1776: The Many Voices of America*, Vol. II. Lubbock, Texas, 1978, pp. 503-520. Reprinted in Harvard Ukrainian Research Institute Offprint Series, No. 5. Cambridge, Mass., 1975, and in item **535**, pp. 430-445.

Reviewed:
Myron B. Kuropas in *Harvard Ukrainian Studies*, II, 4 (Cambridge, Mass., 1978), pp. 536-538.

50 "Le rôle de Sigismond de Luxembourg dans l'histoire des Rusines," *d'Letzeburger Land*, XXV, 47 (Luxembourg, 1978), pp. 13-14.

51 "Avhustyn I. Vološyn (1874-1945)," *Carpatho-Rusyn American*, I, 3 (Fairview, N. J., 1978), p. 3. [unsigned]

52 "Recent [Carpatho-Rusyn] Publications 1975," *Carpatho-Rusyn American*, I, 3 and 4 (Fairview, N. J., 1978), pp. 5 and 5; II, 1 and 2 (1979), pp. 7 and 5. [unsigned]

53 "Michail Baludjanskij (1769-1847)," *Carpatho-Rusyn American*, I, 4 (Fairview, N. J., 1978), p. 3. [unsigned]

54 "Carpatho-Ruthenian." In Heinz Kloss and Grant D. McConnell, eds. *The Written Languages of the World: A Survey of the Degree and Modes of Use*, Vol. I: *The Americas*. Québec: Les Presses de l'Université Laval, 1978, pp. 553-561.

1979

55 "Karpato-Rusyny u Ameryky," *Nova dumka*, VIII [20] (Vukovar, Yugoslavia, 1979), pp. 67-73; [21], pp. 97-100; [22], pp. 69-73. Translated into Vojvodinian Rusyn by Roman Miz.

56 *The Language Question Among the Subcarpathian Rusyns.* Fairview, N. J.: Carpatho-Rusyn Research Center, 1979, iv, 38 p. Second revised printing, including translation into Vojvodinian Rusyn (see item **152**), 1987, iv, 55 p.

Reviewed:
Harvard Librarian, XIII, 4 (Cambridge, Mass., 1979), p. 8.
Evan Lowig in *The Orthodox Church* (Syosset, N. Y.), February 1980, p. 8.

57 "Interv"iu z d-rom Pavlom Magochiiem," *Ameryka* (Philadelphia, Pa.), April 6, 1979, p. 4. Reprinted in *Ameryka* (Philadelphia, Pa.), May 29 and June 5, 1980; *Narodna volia* (Scranton, Pa.), May 29, 1980; *Vil'ne slovo* (Toronto), June 21 and 28, 1980. Interview conducted by Lidiia Stetsyk.

58 "Julian I. Revay (1899-1979)," *Carpatho-Rusyn American*, II, 2 (Fairview, N. J., 1979), p. 3. [unsigned]

59 *The Ukrainian Experience in the United States: A Symposium*, editor. Cambridge, Mass.: Harvard Ukrainian Research Institute Sources and Documents Series, 1979, xii, 205 p.

Reviewed:
Student (Edmonton), March-April, 1980.
Evan Lowig in *St. Vladimir's Theological Quarterly*, XXIV, 2 (Tuckahoe, N.Y., 1980), pp. 142-143.

Europa Ethnica, XXXVII, 3 (Vienna, 1980), p. 171.

Frances Swyripa in *Journal of Ukrainian Studies*, V, 2 [9] (Toronto, 1980), pp. 97-100.

Peter Scheibert in *Jahrbücher für Geschichte Osteuropas*, XXVIII, 4 (Wiesbaden, West Germany 1980), p. 639.

Bohdan Herasymiw in *Canadian Review of Studies in Nationalism*, VIII, 1 (Charlottetown, Prince Edward Island, 1981), p. 188.

A. Rawlyk in *Canadian-American Slavic Studies*, XV, 4 (Tempe, Ariz., 1981), pp. 638-639.

60   "Problems in the History of the Ukrainian Immigration to the United States," *ibid.*, pp. 1-20.

61   "Commentary on the Rise of Ukrainian Ethnic Consciousness in America during the 1890s," *ibid.*, pp. 64-67.

62   "Gregory I. Zsatkovich (1886-1967)," *Carpatho-Rusyn American*, II, 3 (Fairview, N. J., 1979), p. 3. [unsigned]

63   "Recent [Carpatho-Rusyn] Publications 1976," *Carpatho-Rusyn American*, II, 3 and 4 (Fairview, N. J., 1979), pp. 5 and 5; III, 1, 2, 3, and 4 (1980), pp. 6, 5, 5, and 7.

64   *Let's Speak Rusyn—Hovorim po-rus'kŷ: Transcarpathian edition.* Fairview, N. J.: Carpatho-Rusyn Research Center, 1979, xxii, 106 p., 1 map, 24 illustrations by Fedor Vico. Second revised edition, see item **815**.

Reviewed:
Mykhailo Popovych, *Hovorim po rusyns'kŷ*. Uzhhorod: Vyd-vo Grazhda, 2010, 32 p.

1980

65   "Nationalism and National Bibliography: Ivan E. Levyts'kyi and Nineteenth Century Galicia," *Harvard Library Bulletin*, XXVIII, 1 (Cambridge, Mass., 1980), pp. 81-109. Reprinted in Harvard Ukrainian Research Institute Offprint Series, No. 28. Cambridge, Mass., 1980, and in item **579**, pp.159-189.

66 "Travel to the Homeland," *Carpatho-Rusyn American*, III, 1 and 2 (Fairview, N. J., 1980), pp. 4-5 and 4-5. [Philip Michaels]

67 "Andy Warhol," *Carpatho-Rusyn American*, III, 2 (Fairview, N. J., 1980), p. 3. [unsigned] Reprinted in abridged form and with author attribution in *Eastern Catholic Life* (West Patterson, N. J.), March 15, 1987, pp. 7 and 9; *GCU Messenger* (Munhall, Pa.), March 26, 1987, p. 8; *Demokracie in exil* (Munich), April 1987, p. 4.

68 Review of *Mitteilungen*, Nr. 14, in *Slavic Review*, XXXIX, 1 (Urbana, Ill., 1980), pp. 145-146.

69 "Interview with Dr. Paul R. Magocsi," *New Perspectives*, IV, 5 (Toronto), June 28, 1980, pp. 1 and 12.

70 "Belorussians." In Stephan Thernstrom, ed. *Harvard Encyclopedia of American Ethnic Groups*. Cambridge, Mass. and London, England: Harvard University Press, 1980, pp. 181-184.

Reviewed:
Ia. Haleika in *Belaruski holas* (Toronto), November, 1980.

71 "Carpatho-Rusyns," In *ibid.*, pp. 200-210. Reprinted in *America* (Philadelphia), June 28, July 5, 12 and 19, 1982.

72 "Cossacks." In *ibid.*, pp. 245-246.

73 "Eastern Catholics." In *ibid.*, pp. 301-302.

74 "Frisians." In *ibid.*, pp. 401-403. [unsigned]

75 "Luxembourgers." In *ibid.*, pp. 686-689. Reprinted, see below, item **91**.

76 "Maltese." In *ibid.*, pp. 694-695. [unsigned]

77 "Russians." In *ibid.*, pp. 885-894.

Reviewed:

R. Polchaninov in *Novoe russkoe slovo* (New York), February 22, March 1 and 8, 1981.
R. Polchaninov in *Posev*, XXXVII, 10 (Frankfurt, 1981), pp. 60-61.
R. Polchaninov in *The Russian Review*, XL, 4 (Stanford, Calif., 1981), pp. 462- 464.

78   "Ukrainians." In *ibid.*, pp. 997-1009.

79   87 maps of ethnic homelands. In *ibid.*, pp. 3-1021 *passim*.

80   "Katedra ukraïns'kykh studiï v Toronts'kim universyteti: vyhliady na maibutnie," *Novyi shliakh* (Toronto), July 26, 1980, p. 8 and August 2, 1980, p. 7; *Vil'ne slovo* (Toronto), August 16/23, 1980, p. 3 and August 30/September 6, 1980, p. 5.

81   "Sandra Dee," *Carpatho-Rusyn American*, III, 3 (Fairview, N. J., 1980), p. 3. [unsigned]

82   "Carpatho-Rusyn Language and Literature," *Carpatho-Rusyn American*, III, 3 and 4 (Fairview, N. J., 1980), pp. 4-5 and 4-5; IV, 1, 2 and 4 (1981), pp. 4-6, 4-5, and 4-6.

83   "Vienna as a Resource for Ukrainian Studies: With Special Reference to Galicia," *Harvard Ukrainian Studies*, III-IV, pt. 2 (Cambridge, Mass., 1979-1980), pp. 609-626. Reprinted in item **575**, pp. 190-214.

84   "National Cultures and University Chairs," *The Ukrainian Weekly* (Jersey City, N. J.), November 9, 16, 23 and 30, 1980. Reprint of item **88**.

85   "Education Essential for Cultural Self-Defense: Guest Editorial," *The Newspaper* (Toronto), October 29, 1980.

1981

86   "Carpatho-Rusyn Ethnicity: Past Developments and Future Prospects," *Byzantine Catholic World* (Pittsburgh, Pa.), February 1, 8 and 15, 1981; *Eastern Catholic Life* (Passaic, N. J.), February 15,

22, March 1, 8, 15, 1981.

87 "Recent [Carpatho-Rusyn] Publications 1977," *Carpatho-Rusyn American*, IV, 1, 2, 3 and 4 (Fairview, N. J., 1981), pp. 6, 6-7, 7, and 6-7.

88 *National Cultures and University Chairs: An Inaugural Lecture, October 22, 1980.* Toronto: University of Toronto Chair of Ukrainian Studies, [1981], 23 p.

Reviewed:
Wolfgang Kessler in *Österreichische Osthefte*, XXXIV (Vienna, 1992), pp. 490- 491.

89 *Natsional'ni kul'tury i universytets'ki katedry: inavguratsiina lektsiia, 22-ho zhovtnia 1980.* Toronto: Toronts'kyi universytet, Katedra ukraïnoznavchykh studii, [1981], 23 p. Translation of item **88** into Ukrainian by Marco Carynnyk.

90 "Augustine Stefan," *Carpatho-Rusyn American*, IV, 2 (Fairview, N. J., 1981), p. 3. Reprinted in *Vil'ne slovo* (Toronto), October 17, 1981. [unsigned]

91 "Luxembourgers in America," *Luxembourg News of America*, XV, 1, 2, 6 (Mt. Prospect, Ill., 1981), pp. 2 and 5, 6, 7. Reprint of item **75**. [unsigned]

92 "Aleksander Pavlovyč (1819-1900)," *Carpatho-Rusyn American*, IV, 3 (Fairview, N. J., 1981), p. 3. [unsigned]

93 "Misreading History: A Reply" (conclusion), *Carpatho-Rusyn American*, IV, 3 (Fairview, N. J., 1981), pp. 5-6.

94 "Nepravyl'ne rozuminnia istoriï: vidpovid' retsenzentovi [Vasyl Markus]," *Suchasnist'*, XXI, 9 (Munich, 1981), pp. 65-82.

95 "Igor Grabar (1871-1960)," *Carpatho-Rusyn American*, IV, 4 (Fairview, N. J., 1981), p. 3. [Philip Michaels]

96 "Introduction" to Mykhailo S. Hrushevs'kyi, *The Historical Evolution of the Ukrainian Problem*. Revolution and Nationalism in the Modern World, No. 1. Cleveland: John T. Zubal, 1981, pp. v-ix.

Reviewed:
Walter Dushnyk in *Ukrainian Quarterly*, XXXVIII, 3 (New York, 1982), pp. 302- 304.

97 "Introduction" to Gustaf F. Steffen, *Russia, Poland and the Ukraine*. Revolution and Nationalism in the Modern World, No. 2. Cleveland: John T. Zubal, 1981, pp. v-viii.

Reviewed:
Walter Dushnyk in *Ukrainian Quarterly*, XXXVIII, 3 (New York, 1982), pp. 302- 304.

98 "Introduction" to *The Ukrainians and the European War*. Revolution and Nationalism in the Modern World, No. 6. Cleveland: John T. Zubal, 1981, pp. v-xi.

Reviewed:
Walter Dushnyk in *Ukrainian Quarterly*, XXXVIII, 3 (New York, 1982), pp. 302- 304.

99 "Introduction" to *Texts of the Ukraine 'Peace'*. Revolution and Nationalism in the Modern World, No. 3. Cleveland: John T. Zubal, 1981, pp. v-xi.

Reviewed:
Walter Dushnyk in *Ukrainian Quarterly*, XXXVIII, 3 (New York, 1982), pp. 302-304.

100 "Rusyns and the Slovak State," *Slovakia*, XXIX (West Paterson, N.J., 1980-81), pp. 39-44. Reprinted in item **533**, pp. 235-241.

101 Review of *Aufbruch und Neubeginn: Heimatbuch der Galizendeutschen*, Pt. 2, edited by Julius Krämer, in *Harvard Ukrainian Studies*, V, 4 (Cambridge, Mass., 1981), pp. 553-554.

1982

102 "Rusyn-Ukrainian Cooperation in the United States," *The Ukrainian Weekly* (Jersey City, N. J.), May 23, 1982, pp. 5 and 16; *America* (Philadelphia), May 24, 1982, pp. 2 and 4. Reprinted in item **536**, pp. 29-34.

103 "National Cultures and University Chairs," *An Baner Kernewek/ The Cornish Banner*, No. 28 (Trelispen, Cornwall, 1982), pp. 6-11. Reprint of item **88**.

104 "Fedir Korjatovyč (c. 1350-1414)," *Carpatho-Rusyn American*, V, 1 (Fairview, N. J., 1982), p. 3. [Philip Michaels]

105 "Recent [Carpatho-Rusyn] Publications 1978," *Carpatho-Rusyn American*, V, 1, 2, 3 and 4 (Fairview, N. J., 1982), pp. 7, 6-7, 7, and 6.

106 "Anatolij Kralyc'kyj (1835-1894)," *Carpatho-Rusyn American*, V, 2 (Fairview, N. J., 1982), pp. 2-3. [Philip Michaels]

107 "The Language Question as a Factor in the National Movement in Eastern Galicia." In Andrei S. Markovits and Frank E. Sysyn, eds. *Nationbuilding and the Politics of Nationalism: Essays on Austrian Galicia*. Harvard Ukrainian Research Institute Monograph Series. Cambridge, Mass.: Harvard University Press for HURI, 1982, pp. 220-238, and in item **579**, pp. 83-98.

108 "Bibliographic Guide to the History of Ukrainians in Galicia." In *ibid.*, pp. 255-320.

Reviewed (items **107** and **108**):
Thomas W. Simons, Jr. in *Russian Review*, XLII, 3 (Cambridge, Mass., 1983), pp. 327-328.
Richard Blanke in *Canadian Journal of History*, XIX, 1 (Saskatoon, Sask., 1984), pp. 130-131.
Nadia Diuk in *Journal of Ukrainian Studies*, IX, 1 [16] (Toronto, 1984), pp. 117-119.
Michael Hurst in *Slavonic and East European Review*, LXII, 3 (London, 1984), pp. 457-458.
Francis S. Wagner in *Nationalities Papers*, XII, 2 (Charleston, Ill., 1984), pp. 292-293.

Charles C. Herod in *Canadian Review of Studies in Nationalism*, XI, 2 (Charlottetown, Prince Edward Island, 1984), pp. 292-293.

Gary B. Cohen in *Canadian-American Slavic Studies*, XVIII, 1-2 (Irvine, Ca., 1984), pp. 213-214.

Charles K. Krantz in *East-Central Europe*, XI, 1-2 (Irvine, Ca., 1984), pp. 224-226.

A. Ka. in *Jahrbücher für Geschichte Osteuropas*, XXXIII, 1 (Stuttgart, 1985), p. 155.

Adam Galos in *Kwartalnik Historyczny*, XCII, 2 (Warsaw, 1985), pp. 445-446.

109 "Map of Galicia in the Austro-Hungarian Empire," In *ibid.*, p. 322.

110 "Ia rusin bil, iesm i budu: niepravilne pokhopenie istoriï Vasilia Markusa," *Nova dumka*, XI [32 and 33] (Vukovar, Yugoslavia, 1982), pp. 68-72 and 54-58. Translation of item **94** into Vojvodinian Rusyn by Roman Miz.

111 *Holzkirchen in den Karpaten: Die Fotografien Florian Zapletals/ Wooden Churches in the Carpathians: The Photographs of Florian Zapletal*, editor and introduction. Vienna: Wilhelm Braumüller Universitäts-Verlagsbuchhandlung, 1982, 176 p., 239 illustrations and end maps.

Reviewed:
Sviatoslav Hordyns'kyi in *Suchasnist'*, XXXIII (New York and Munich, 1983), pp. 331-334.

Hungarian Studies Newsletter, no. 37 (Washington, D. C., 1983), p. 3.

[Andrew Gregorovich] in *Forum*, no. 54 (Scranton, Pa., 1983), p. 33.

Pavlo Murashko in *Journal of Ukrainian Studies*, VIII, 2 [15] (Toronto, 1983), pp. 124-126.

Jack E. Kollmann in *Canadian Slavonic Papers*, XXV, 4 (Toronto, 1983), pp. 602-603.

S.B. in *Bauen mit Holz*, LXXXV, 10 (Karlsruhe, Germany 1983), p. 668.

J. A. Stupp in *Südostdeutsche Vierteljahrblätter*, XXXII, 4 (Munich, 1983).

Feliks J. Bister in *Nedelja*, No. 52 (Klagenfurt, Austria), December 26, 1982, p. 10.

Max Demeter Peyfuss in *Österreichische Osthefte*, XXV (Vienna, 1983), p. 439.

Vera Mayer, in *Österreichische Zeitschrift für Volkskunde*, LXXXVI, 4 (Vienna, 1983), pp. 267-269.

Evan Lowig in *St. Vladimir's Theological Quarterly*, XXVIII, 2 (Crestwood, N. Y., 1984), pp. 135-137.

Mojmír S. Frinta in *East Central Europe*, X, 1-2 (Irvine, Ca., 1983), pp. 265-266.

Josef Jančář in *Narodopisné aktuality*, XXI, 3 (Strážnice, Czechoslovakia, 1984), p. 215.

Myroslava M. Mudrak in *Harvard Ukrainian Studies*, VIII, 3/4 (Cambridge, Mass., 1984), pp. 540-542.

Igor Thurzo in *Architektúra a urbanizmus*, XVIII, 8 (Bratislava, 1984), pp. 119-120.

Marshall Winokur in *Slavic and East European Journal*, XXIX, 3 (Albany, N. Y., 1985), pp. 363-365.

Hans-Joachim Härtel in *Bohemia*, XXVI, 2 (Munich, 1985), pp. 461-464.

A. Jacobs in *Het Christelijk Oosten*, XXXVIII, 3 (Nijmegen, Netherlands, 1986), p. 228.

Z. Hudchenko in *Pam'iatnyky Ukraïny*, XVIII, 2 (Kyiv, 1986), p. 63. *Wald und Holz Rundschau*, XLIII, 6 (Vienna, 1987), p. 39.

Peter Maser in *Ostkirchliche Information*, No. 5 (Hannover, West Germany, 1988), pp. 13-14.

Michail Chološnjaj-Matjijov in *Ruski kalendar 1995* (Novi Sad, 1994), pp. 76- 82.

112 "There Is Another Way" [Russophiles and Identity], *The Ukrainian Weekly* (Jersey City, N. J.), October 10, 1982, p. 6. [unsigned]

113 "Jurij Venelin-Huca (1802-1839)," *Carpatho-Rusyn American*, V, 3 (Fairview, N. J., 1982), p. 3. [Philip Michaels]

114 "Our Center Replies," *Carpatho-Rusyn American*, V, 3 (Fairview, N. J., 1982), pp. 6-7. [unsigned]

115 "Vasyl' Grendža-Dons'kyj (1897-1974)," *Carpatho-Rusyn American*, V, 4 (Fairview, N. J., 1982), p. 3. [Philip Michaels]

116 Letter to the editor, *Annaly Lemkivshchyny/Annals of Lemkivshchyna*, III (New York, 1982), pp. 233-234.

117 Review of Alexander J. Motyl, *The Turn to the Right: The Ideological Origins and Development of Ukrainian Nationalism, 1919-1929*, in *Slavic Review*, XLI, 4 (Stanford, Ca., 1982), pp. 738-739.

118 Review of Robert A. Kann, *A History of the Habsburg Empire*,

1526- 1918, in *Harvard Ukrainian Studies*, VI, 4 (Cambridge, Mass., 1982), pp. 542-543.

1983

119 *The Rusyn-Ukrainians of Czechoslovakia: An Historical Survey.* Bausteine zur ethnopolitischen Forschung, Vol. VII. Vienna: Wilhelm Braumüller Universitäts-Verlagsbuchhandlung, 1983, 93 p., 2 maps, Second printing, 1985.

Reviewed:

[Joseph M. Kirschbaum] in *Bulletin of the Slovak World Congress*, XIII [58] (Toronto, 1983), p. 23.

[Andrew Gregorovich] in *Forum*, no. 56 (Scranton, Pa., 1983), p. 32. *Europa Ethnica*, XL, 4 (Vienna, 1983), p. 249.

M. T. [Miroslav Tejchman] in *Slovanský přehled*, LXIX, 5 (Prague, 1983), p. 423.

Oleh S. Fedyshyn in *Canadian Slavonic Papers*, XXVI, 1 (Toronto, 1984), p. 115.

W. B. in *Österreichische Osthefte*, XXV (Vienna, 1983), p. 453.

Evan Lowig in *St. Vladimir's Theological Quarterly*, XXVIII, 2 (Crestwood, N. Y., 1984), pp. 135-137.

Owen V. Johnson in *Slovakia*, XXXI (West Paterson, N. J., 1984), p. 132.

Gegenstimmen, V [17] (Vienna, 1984), p. 39.

Pavlo Murashko in *Journal of Ukrainian Studies*, IX, 2 [17] (Toronto, 1984), pp. 112-114.

Bohdan P. Procko in *East Central Europe*, X, 1-2 (Irvine, Ca., 1983), pp. 264-265.

John-Paul Himka in *Canadian-American Slavic Studies*, XVIII, 4 (Irvine, Ca., 1984), pp. 495-496.

Zdenek Suda in *Kosmas*, III, 1 (Pittsburgh, Pa., 1984), pp. 178-179.

Alexander Baran in *Slavonic and East European Review*, LXIII, 3 (London, 1985), pp. 452-453.

Stanley B. Kimball in *Canadian Review of Studies in Nationalism*, XII, 2 (Charlottesville, Prince Edward Is., 1985), p. 373.

Imrich Stolárik in *Kanadský Slovák* (Toronto), July 12, 1986, p. 7.

Hungarian Studies Newsletter, No. 50 (Washington, D. C., 1986-87), p. 4.

A. Burg in *Het Christelijk Oosten*, XXXIX, 2 (Nijmegen, Netherlands, 1987), p. 134.

Ruth Szamvaj in *Anthropology of East Europe Review*, VII, 1-2 (Ann Arbor, Mich., 1988), p. 30.

120 *The Peter Jacyk Collection of Ukrainian Serials: A Guide to Newspapers and Periodicals.* Toronto: University of Toronto Chair of Ukrainian Studies, 1983, 42 p.

Reviewed:
Hungarian Studies Newsletter, no. 37 (Washington, D. C., 1983), p. 5.
E. Kasinec in *Canadian Slavonic Papers*, XXVI, 2-3 (Toronto, 1984), pp. 266-267.
A. Ka [Andreas Kappeler] in *Jahrbücher für Geschichte Osteuropas*, XXXIII, 1 (Stuttgart, 1985), p. 155.

121 "Andrej Karabeleš (1906-1964)," *Carpatho-Rusyn American*, VI, 1 (Fairview, N. J., 1983), p. 3. [Philip Michaels]

122 "Rusyn Remnants in America [Cleveland, Ohio]," *Carpatho-Rusyn American*, VI, 1 (Fairview, N. J., 1983), pp. 4-5. Reprinted in *Karpatska Rus'* (Yonkers, N. Y.), July 19, 1985, p. 3.

123 "Recent [Carpatho-Rusyn] Publications 1979," *Carpatho-Rusyn American*, VI, 1, 2, 3, 4 (Fairview, N. J., 1983), pp. 6-7, 7, 7, 4-6.

124 "Emilij A. Kubek (1857-1940)," *Carpatho-Rusyn American*, VI, 2 (Fairview, N. J., 1983), p. 3. [Philip Michaels]

125 "Our Center Replies," *Carpatho-Rusyn American*, VI, 2 (Fairview, N. J., 1983), pp. 6-7. [unsigned]

126 "Slovo na iuvileinomu pryniatti [Dr-a Stepana Rosokhy]," *Vil'ne slovo* (Toronto), no. 28-29, July 9/16, 1983, p. 6.

127 "Old Ruthenianism and Russophilism: A New Conceptual Framework for Analyzing National Ideologies in Late 19th Century Eastern Galicia." In Paul Debreczyn, ed., *American Contributions to the Ninth International Congress of Slavists*, Vol. II: *Literature, Poetics, History*. Columbus, Ohio: Slavica Publishers, 1983, pp. 305-324. Reprinted in item **579**, pp. 99-118.

Reviewed:
Virginia M. Burns in *Canadian Slavonic Papers*, XXVII, 4 (Toronto, 1985), pp. 457-459.

Judith M. Mills in *Slavic and East European Journal*, XXX, 1 (Albany, N. Y., 1986), pp. 104-106.

128 "Vasyl' Dovhovyč (1783-1849)," *Carpatho-Rusyn American*, VI, 3 (Fairview, N. J., 1983), p. 3. [Philip Michaels]

129 *Galicia: A Historical Survey and Bibliographic Guide*. Toronto, Buffalo, and London, England: University of Toronto Press, 1983, xx, 299 p., 6 maps. Second printing, 1985. Third printing, 1990.

Reviewed:
[Andrew Gregorovich] in *Forum*, no. 55 (Scranton, Pa., 1983), p. 33.
Wasyl' Veryha in *Novyi shliakh* (Toronto), October 29, 1983, p. 9.
Benedykt Heydenkorn in *Zeszyty Historyczne*, No. 66 (Paris, 1983), pp. 206-209.
Bohdan Romanenchuk in *Ameryka* (Philadelphia), December 14, 1983, p. 3.
Roman S. Goliat in *Narodna volia* (Scranton, Pa.), February 16, 1984; reprinted in *Vil'ne slovo* (Toronto), March 24, 1984, p. 3.
Wilhelm Metzler in *Das heilige Band*, XXXVIII, 4 (Metzingen/Württemberg, West Germany, 1984), pp. 3-4.
Franz A. J. Szabo in *Slavic Review*, XL, 2 (Urbana-Champaign, Ill., 1984), pp. 331-332.
Stephen M. Horak in *American Historical Review*, LXXXIX, 4 (Washington, D. C., 1984), p. 1115.
Ukrainian Review, XXXII (London, 1984), p. 95.
Evan Lowig in *St. Vladimir's Theological Quarterly*, XXVIII, 2 (Crestwood, N. Y., 1984), pp. 131-132.
Jan Krajcar in *Orientalia Christiana Periodica*, L, 2 (Rome, 1984), pp. 501-502.
Evan Lowig in *Nova dumka*, XIII [41] (Vukovar, Yugoslavia, 1984), p. 41.
Philip Longworth in *The Slavonic and East European Review*, LXIII, 1 (London, 1984), pp. 121-122.
Dmytro M. Shtohryn in *Slavic Review*, XLIII, 3 (Urbana, Ill., 1984), p. 542.
Choice, XXI, 2 (Chicago, Ill., 1984), p. 806.
Lawrence D. Orton in *Canadian-American Slavic Studies*, XVIII, 4 (Irvine, Ca., 1984), pp. 493-495.
A. B. Pernal in *Canadian Journal of History*, XX, 2 (Saskatoon, Sask., 1985), pp. 255-257.
Stella Hryniuk in *Canadian Slavonic Papers*, XXVII, 3 (Toronto, 1985), p. 360.
Günther Wytrzens in *Wiener slavistiches Jahrbuch*, XXX (Vienna, 1984), pp. 191-192.

Bohdan S. Wynar in *American Reference Books Annual*, Vol. XVI (Littleton, Colo., 1985), p. 46.

Wolodymyr T. Zyla in *The Ukrainian Quarterly*, XLI, 3-4 (New York, 1985), pp. 251-252.

Hungarian Studies Newsletter, No. 46 (Washington, D. C., 1985-86), pp. 2-3.

[Theodor Vieter] in *A. W. R. Bulletin*, XXIV [33], 1-2 (Vienna, 1986), p.90.

Stanisław Grodziski in *Studia Historyczne*, XXIX, 2 (Wrocław, 1986), pp. 301- 304.

M. T. in *Slovanský přehled*, LXXII, 6 (Prague, 1986), p. 483.

Wolfgang Häusler in *Mitteilungen des Instituts für österreichische Geschichtsforschung*, XCIV, 1-2 (Graz and Vienna, 1986), p. 259.

Maciej Siekierski in *East Central Europe*, XIII, 1 (Irvine, Ca., 1986), pp. 98-99.

Claude Michaud in *Bulletin de la Société d'histoire moderne*, 16éme série, No. 31—supplement to *Revue d'histoire moderne et contemporaine*, LXXXV, 4 (Paris, 1986), p. 47.

Rudolf A. Mark in *Zeitschrift für Ostforschung*, XXXVI (Marburg, West Germany, 1987), pp. 126-128.

Keith P. Dyrud in *Modern Greek Studies Yearbook*, IV (Minneapolis, 1988), pp. 342-345.

Wolfdieter Bihl in *Austrian History Yearbook*, XXI (Minneapolis, 1985), pp. 201-202.

130 "Formuvannia natsional'noï ideolohiï v Halychyni pid kinets' dev"iatnadtsatoho stolittia: ne-ukraïns'ki oriientatsiï." In G.V. Stepanov, ed. *Reziume dokladov i pis'mennykh soobshchenii: IX mezhdunarodnyi s"ezd slavistov, Kiev, sentiabr 1983.* Moscow: Nauka, 1983, pp. 553-554.

1984

131 "The Language Question in Nineteenth-Century Galicia." In Riccardo Picchio and Harvey Goldblatt, eds. *Aspects of the Slavic Language Question*, Vol. II: *East Slavic.* New Haven: Yale Concilium on International and Area Studies, 1984, pp. 49-64.

132 "The Language Question Among the Subcarpathian Rusyns." In *ibid.*, pp. 65-86.

Reviewed (items **130** and **131**):

Henrik Birnbaum in *Die Welt der Slaven*, N. F., IX, 1 (Munich, 1985), pp. 119-145.

Tom Priestly in *Canadian Slavonic Papers*, XXVIII, 1 (Toronto, 1986), pp. 111-113.
V.M. Du Feu in *Slavonic and East European Review*, LXV, 2 (London, 1987), pp. 252-253.

133 "East Slavs in America," *Eastern Catholic Life* (Passaic, N. J.), June 17, 1984, pp. 7-8; *The Ukrainian Weekly* (Jersey City, N. J.), June 24, 1984, pp. 7 and 10; *Byzantine Catholic World* (Pittsburgh, Pa.), July 15, 1984, pp. 6-8. Reprinted in the *Carpatho-Rusyn American*, IX, (Fairview, N. J., 1986), pp. 6-8, and in item **534**, pp. 11-18.

Reviewed:
Orest Subtelny in *The Ukrainian Weekly*, July 15, 1984, pp. 4 and 13. Reprinted in *Carpatho-Rusyn American*, IX, 2 (Fairview, N. J., 1986), pp. 4-5.
Philip Yevics in *Eastern Catholic Life*, August 5, 1984, pp. 8-9.
R. Polchaninoff in *Novoe russkoe slovo* (New York), August 19, 1984.

134 "Ukrainian Opera in North America," *The Ukrainian Weekly*, July 1, 1984, p. 11; *New Perspectives*, VIII, 6 (Toronto, 1984), p. 4; *America* (Philadelphia), July 9, 1984, pp. 3-4.

135 Review of Kenneth C. Farmer, *Ukrainian Nationalism in the Post-Stalin Era*, in *Canadian Review of Studies in Nationalism*, XI, 1 (Charlottetown, Prince Edward Island, 1984), pp. 163-164.

136 "The Pope's Unionville Visit: Was it Really Unfortunate?," *The Catholic Register* (Toronto), October 13, 1984, p. 4; *Catholic New Times* (Toronto), October 14, 1984, p. 5; *America* (Philadelphia), November 12, 1984, p. 4; *Kanadský Slovák* (Ottawa), November 3, 1984, p. 4.

137 "The Congress of Slavists in Kiev: Some Recollections." In Ladislav Matejka and Benjamin Stolz, eds. *Cross Currents: A Yearbook of Central European Culture*, Vol III. Ann Arbor, Mich., 1984, pp. 49- 57.

138 *Our People: Carpatho-Rusyns and Their Descendants in North America*. Preface by Oscar Handlin. Toronto: Multicultural History Society of Ontario, 1984, xii, 160 p. 4 maps, 86 illustrations.

Second edition. Preface by Michael Novak, 1985. Third revised edition, see item **374**. Fourth revised edition, see item **623**.

Reviewed:
Eastern Catholic Life (Passaic, N. J.), December 16, 1984, p. 1.
The Church Messenger (Pemberton, N. J.), January 20, 1985, p. 1.
Byzantine Catholic World (Pittsburgh, Pa.), December 16, 1984, p. 1.
The Ukrainian Weekly (Jersey City, N. J.), March 17, 1985, pp. 7 and 15.
Hungarian Studies Newsletter, No. 43-44 (New Brunswick, N. J., 1985), p. 5.
Benedykt Heydenkorn in *Związkowiec*, No. 56 (Toronto), July 16, 1985, p 5.
Paul W. McBride in *Nationalities Papers*, XIII, 1 (North York, Ont., 1985), pp. 150-151.
Imrich Stolárik in *Kanadský Slovák* (Toronto), March 23, 1985, p. 7.
Bohdan S. Kordan in *Journal of Ukrainian Studies*, X, 2 [19] (Toronto, 1985), pp.119-121.
Franz H. Riedl in *Europa Ethnica*, XLII, 2-3 (Vienna, 1985), p. 183.
Serge R. Keleher in *Sobornost/Eastern Churches Review*, VII, 2 (London, 1985), pp. 62-64.
International Migration Review, XX [74] (Staten Is., N. Y., 1986), pp. 522-523.
Martha Bohachevsky-Chomiak in *Canadian Slavonic Papers*, XXVIII, 1 (Toronto, 1986), pp. 123-124.
Evan Lowig in *St. Vladimir's Theological Quarterly*, XXX, 2 (Crestwood, N. Y., 1986), pp. 182-184.
Joseph M. Kirschbaum in *Bulletin of the Slovak World Congress*, XV [no. 73] (Toronto, 1986), p. 24.
Robert Taft in *Orientalia Christiana Periodica*, LII, 2 (Rome, 1986), pp. 485-487. Reprinted in: *Jednota* (Middletown, Pa.), February 3, 1988, p. 20; *Eastern Catholic Life* (Lackawanna, N. J.), January 31, 1988, p. 1; *Byzantine Catholic World* (Pittsburgh), February 7, 1988, p. 1; *GCU Messenger* (Beaver, Pa.), February 11, 1988, p. 10-11; *Horizons* (Parma, Ohio), February 28, 1988, p. 8.
Tim Rusnak in *Social Education*, L, 9 (Arlington, Va., 1986), pp. 390-392.
John Lee in *Orthodox News*, IV, 4 (London, 1986), p. 3.
East European Anthropology Group, V, 2 (Ann Arbor, Mich., 1986), p. 7.
Orthodox Catholic Voice, V (Akron, Ohio, 1987), p. 6.
Roman S. Holiat in *Svoboda* (Jersey City, N. J.), May 14, 1987, pp. 2 and 4.
R. Polchaninov in *Novoe russkoe slovo* (New York), May 15, 1987, p. 10.
Vitaut Kipel in *Slavonic and East European Review*, LXV, 2 (London, 1987),pp. 252-253.
Andrzej A. Zięba in *Przegląd Polonijny*, XIII, 3 (Cracow, 1987), pp. 128-130.

Emil Niederhauser in *Világtörténet*, No. 4 (Budapest, 1987), pp. 145-146.
Henrietta Hansen in *Slovo: Sokol Minnesota Newsletter*, XII, 5 (Minneapolis, Minn., 1989), p. 9.
Robert Taft in *Nova dumka*, XVIII, 1 [71] (Vukovar, Yugoslavia, 1989), p. 50.
Liubomir Medieshi in *Shvetlosts*, XXVIII, 5 (Novi Sad, 1990), pp. 628-637.
A. S. Sh. [Andrei Shlepets'kyi] in *Narodný novynký* (Prešov), May 13, 1992, p. 2.
L'ubica Chorváthová in *Slovenský národopis*, XL, 2 (Bratislava, 1992), pp. 234-235.

139 Review of Engelbert Zobl and Hertha A. Zobl, *Holzbaukunst in der Slowakei*, in *Slovakia*, XXXI (West Paterson, N. J., 1984), pp. 145-146.

140 "Recent [Carpatho-Rusyn] Publications 1980," *Carpatho-Rusyn American*, VII, 1, 2, 3, 4 (Fairview, N. J., 1984), pp. 7, 6, 7-8, 5-6. [Philip Michaels]

141 "IX Mizhnarodnyi z" ïzd slavistiv u Kyievi: deiaki spohady," *Vidnova*, No. 2 (Munich, 1984-85), pp. 204-214.

142 "Alexis G. Toth (1853-1909)," *Carpatho-Rusyn American*, VIII, 1 (Fairview, N. J., 1984), p. 3. [Philip Michaels]

143 "From Our Center," *Carpatho-Rusyn American*, VIII, 1 (Fairview, N. J., 1984), p. 11. [unsigned]

144 "American Carpatho-Russian Orthodox Greek Catholic Church." In Volodymyr Kubijovyč, ed. *Encyclopedia of Ukraine*, Vol. I: A-F. Toronto, Buffalo, and London: University of Toronto Press, 1984, p. 62.

145 "*Amerikanskii russkii viestnik.*" In *ibid.*, p. 63.

146 "*Byzantine Catholic World.*" In *ibid.*, p. 338. [unsigned]

147 "Dziubai, Oleksander." In *ibid.*, pp. 777-778.

148 *"Eastern Catholic Life."* In *ibid.*, p. 782. [unsigned]

149 Review of Istvan Deak, *The Lawful Revolution: Louis Kossuth and the Hungarians, 1848-1849,* in *Harvard Ukrainian Studies,* VIII, 3/4 (Cambridge, Mass., 1984), pp. 511-513.

150 Review of Iuliian Khymynets', *Moï sposterezhennia iz Zakarpattia* in *Harvard Ukrainian Studies,* VIII, 3/4 (Cambridge, Mass., 1984), pp. 531-532.

151 "Baroque Choral Concert" [review], *Deer Park Church Magazine,* No. 1 (Toronto, 1984), p. 5.

152 "Pitanie iazika medzi podkarpatskima rusinami," *Tvorchosts,* X (Novi Sad, Yugoslavia, 1984), pp. 6-22. Translation into Vojvodinian Rusyn of item **56**.

1985

153 "Alexander Dzubay (1857-1933)," *Carpatho-Rusyn American,* VIII, 2 (Fairview, N. J., 1985), p. 3.

154 "Recent [Carpatho-Rusyn] Publications 1981," *Carpatho-Rusyn American,* VIII, 1, 2, 3, 4 (Fairview, N. J., 1985), pp. 9-10, 6-7, 7-9, 6-7.

155 "A Heritage Recalled: Prorocheskoe Svietlo/The Prophetic Light," *Rutland Historical Society Quarterly,* XV, 2 (Rutland, Vt., 1985), pp. 18-23.

156 *Ucrainica at the University of Toronto Library: A Catalogue of Holdings,* compiled with the assistance of Nadia Odette Diakun, 2 vols. Toronto, London, and Buffalo: University of Toronto Press, 1985, xviii, 1845 p.

Reviewed:
Forum, No. 65 (Scranton, Pa., 1986), p. 31.

Vitaut Kipel in *Canadian Slavonic Papers*, XXVIII, 4 (Toronto, 1986), pp. 462- 463.
Wolfdieter Bihl in *Österreichische Osthefte*, XXIX, 1 (Vienna, 1987), p. 132.
Alan Rutkowski in *Journal of Ukrainian Studies*, XII, 1 [23] (Edmonton, Alta., 1987), pp. 105-106.
ICEES International Newsletter, No. 24 (Paris, 1987), p. 24.
Bohdan S.Wynar in *American Reference Books Annual*, Vol. XIX (Englewood, Colo., 1988), pp. 62-63.
Yar Slavutych in *Papers in the Bibliographical Society of Canada*, XXVI (Toronto, 1987), pp. 169-170.
Dmytro M. Shtohryn in *Slavic Review*, XLVII, 4 (Austin, Tex., 1988), pp. 790-791.

157 *Ukraine: A Historical Atlas*, with cartography by Geoffrey J. Matthews. Toronto, London, Buffalo: University of Toronto Press, 1985, 62 p., 24 map plates. Second printing, 1986. Third printing, revised, 1987. Fourth printing, revised, 1992.

Reviewed:
Bohdan Stebel's'kyi in *Homin Ukraïny/Literatura i mystetstvo* (Toronto), March 12, 1986, pp. 2-3.
Ukrainian Canadian, XXXVIII, 5 (Toronto, 1986), p. 27.
John Switalski in *Gwiazda Polarna* (Stevens Point, Wisconsin), May 24, 1986.
[Andrew Gregorovich] in *Forum*, No. 67 (Scranton, Pa. 1986), p. 23.
Claude Michaud in *Bulletin de la Société d'histoire moderne*, 16ème série, No. 31— supplement to *Revue d'histoire moderne et contemporaine*, LXXXV, 4 (Paris, 1986), pp. 46-47.
E. Ostrowsky in *Choice*, XXIV, 5 (Middletown, Conn., 1987), p. 744.
Vasyl' Veryha in *Novyi shliakh* (Toronto), June 6, 1987, p. 5.
Ron Whistance-Smith in *Western Association Map Library Information Bulletin*, XVII, 2 (Santa Cruz, Ca., 1987), pp. 169-170.
Paul Labrecque in *Cahiers de géographie du Québec*, XXXI [no. 82] (Quebec City, 1987), pp. 115-116.
Wolfdieter Bihl in *Österreichische Osthefte*, XXIX, 1 (Vienna, 1987), pp. 131-132.
Serge A. Sauer in *Association of Canadian Map Libraries Bulletin*, No. 62 (Ottawa, 1987), pp. 25-26.
David MacKenzie in *Canadian Slavonic Papers*, XXIX, 1 (Toronto, 1987), pp. 118-119.
Lubomyr R. Wynar in *Slavic Review*, XLVI, 2 (Stanford, Ca., 1987), pp. 335-336.

Ihor Stebelsky in *Journal of Ukrainian Studies*, XII, 1 (Edmonton, Alta., 1987), pp. 101-105.

W. Rybotycki in *Geographical Journal*, CLIII, 2 (London, 1987), pp. 297-298.

Ian M. Matley in *The American Cartographer*, XV, 2 (Falls Church, Va., 1988), p. 219.

Ihor Stebelsky in *Ukraïns'kyi istoryk*, XXIV, 1-4 [93-96] (New York, Toronto, and Munich, 1987), pp. 174-178.

A. French in *Journal of Historical Geography*, XIV, 1 (London, 1988), p. 101.

Andrew B. Pernal in *Harvard Ukrainian Studies*, XI, 3-4 (Cambridge, Mass., 1987), pp. 538-543.

Senyk in *Orientalia Christiana Periodica*, LIII, 2 (Rome, 1987), pp. 492-493.

Cartenform, No. 135 (Budapest, 1989), pp. 1-2.

Carsten Goehrke in *Jahrbücher für Geschichte Osteuropas*, XXXVII, 1 (Munich, 1989), pp. 121-122.

Brenton M. Barr in *Cartographica*, XXVI, 2 (Toronto, 1989), pp. 114-115.

Ezra Mendelsohn in *Studies in Contemporary Jewry*, Vol. V (New York and Oxford, 1989), pp. 372-373.

A. Balabushevych and O. Ie. Markova in *Ukraïns'kyi istorychnyi zhurnal*, XXXIV, 1 (Kyiv, 1990), pp. 151-153.

Hugo Weczerka in *Zeitschrift für Ostforschung*, XXXVIII, 3 (Marburg, West Germany, 1989), pp. 465-466.

Wolfdieter Bihl in *Austrian History Yearbook*, XXI (Minneapolis, 1985), p. 201.

Edward G. Mathews, Jr. in *Diakonia*, XXIII, 3 (Scranton, Pa., 1990), p. 189.

Emil Niederhauser in *Századok*, CXXIV, 3-4 (Budapest, 1990), pp. 528-530.

David Saunders in *European History Quarterly*, XXI (London, Newbury Park and New Delhi, India, 1991), pp. 81-95.

George K. Epp in *Mennonite Historian*, XVIII, 3 (Winnipeg, Man., 1992), p. 8.

Walter C. Clemens, Jr. in *Conflict Quarterly*, XIII, 3 (Fredericton, New Brunswick, 1993), pp. 94-96.

Edmund Pries in *Mennonite Historian*, XXII, 1 (Winnipeg, 1996), pp. 11-12.

158 "Joseph P. Hanulya (1874-1962)," *Carpatho-Rusyn American*, VIII, 3 (Fairview, N.J., 1985), p. 3. [Philip Michaels]

159 "Tysiacholittia: interv"iu z prof. Magochym," *Svoboda* (Jersey City, N.J.), November 26, 27, 29, 30 - December 3 and 4, 1985, pp. 2, 2, 2- 3, 2, 2, and 2. Reprinted in *Novi dni*, XXXVII, 2 and 3 (Toronto, 1986), pp. 13-16 and 13-16. Excerpted in *Vil'na dumka* (Lidcombe, N.S.W., Australia), April 20-27 and May 4-11, 1986.

Reviewed:
Oleksander Dombrovs'kyi in *Svoboda* (Jersey City, N.J.), February 14 and 15, 1986, p. 2 and p. 2. Reprinted in *Bat'kivshchyna* (Toronto), February/ March 1986, pp. 8-9.

160 *Travel to the Homeland.* Fairview, N.J.: Carpatho-Rusyn Research Center, [1985], 6 p. [unsigned]

161 "Basil Takach (1879-1948)," *Carpatho-Rusyn American*, VIII, 4 (Fairview, N.J., 1985), p. 3.

1986

162 "Peter Ustinov's 'My Russia' is Uniquely His," *The Ukrainian Weekly* (Jersey City, N.J.), March 23, 1986, pp. 8 and 14; *Ukrainian Echo* (Toronto), April 22, 1986, pp. 2 and 7; *New Perspectives* (Toronto), May 17, 1986, pp. 4 and 6. Excerpted in *Ukraïns'kyi holos* (Winnipeg), August 15, 1988, p. 2.

163 "Orestes Chornock (1883-1977)," *Carpatho-Rusyn American*, IX, 1 (Fairview, N.J., 1986), p. 3. [Philip Michaels]

164 "From Our Center," *Carpatho-Rusyn American*, IX, 1 (Fairview, N.J., 1986), pp. 8-9. [unsigned]

165 "Recent [Carpatho-Rusyn] Publications 1982," *Carpatho-Rusyn American*, IX, 1, 2, 3, 4 (Fairview, N.J., 1986), pp. 9-11, 6-7, 8-10, 6-7.

166 "Mychail Pop-Lučkaj (1789-1843)," *Carpatho-Rusyn American*, IX, 2 (Fairview, N.J., 1986), p. 3. [Philip Michaels]

167 Review of George Luckyj, *Panteleimon Kulish: A Sketch of His Life and Times*, in *Canadian Review of Studies in Nationalism*, XIII, 1 (Charlottetown, Prince Edward Is., 1986), pp. 155-156.

168 "Ivan Franko i status ukrainskoi natsii v mnogonatsional'nom gosudarstve (konets XIX-nachalo XX vv." In M.V. Bryk et al., eds. *Ivan Franko i mirovaia kul'tura: tezisy dokladov mezhdunarodnogo simpoziuma*, Vol. II. Kyiv: Naukova dumka, 1986, p. 82.

169 "Literatura rusinokh z Podkarpatia u Ameryky," *Nova dumka*, XV [55 and 56] (Vukovar, Yugoslavia, 1986), pp. 34-37 and 23-27.

170 "Ivan S. Orlaj (1771-1829)," *Carpatho-Rusyn American*, IX, 3 (Fairview, N.J., 1986), p. 3. [Philip Michaels]

171 "The Carpatho-Rusyn Emblem and Flag," *Carpatho-Rusyn American*, IX, 3 (Fairview, N.J., 1986), pp. 7-8.

172 "Havrijil Kostel'nyk (1886-1948)," *Carpatho-Rusyn American*, IX, 4 (Fairview, N.J., 1986), pp. 3, 7. [Philip Michaels]

173 "In Memoriam" [Augustine Stefan and Stepan Rosocha], *Carpatho-Rusyn American*, IX, 4 (Fairview, N.J., 1986), p. 7. [unsigned]

174 "Greetings for the Patriarchal Blessing," *Nativity of the Mother of God Ukrainian Catholic Church, Niagara Falls, Ontario*. Niagara Falls, Ont., 1986, p. 7.

1987

175 "The Carpatho-Rusyn Press." In Sally M. Miller, ed. *The Ethnic Press in the United States: A Historical Analysis and Handbook*. New York, Westport, Conn., and London: Greenwood Press, 1987, pp. 15-26. Reprinted in item **535**, pp. 416-429.

176 "Famine or Genocide?: on Robert Conquest's *Harvest of Sorrow*," *The World and I*, II, 4 (Washinton, D.C., 1987), pp. 416-423.

Reviewed:
Petro Sulyma in *Svoboda* (Jersey City, N.J.), May 28, 29, 30, 1987, pp. 2, 2, 2.
B.K. in *Bat'kivshchyna* (Toronto), June-July 1987, p. 3.
Stepan Zhenets'kyi in *Ukraïns'kyi holos/Kanadiis'kyi farmer* (Winnipeg), September 14, 1987 and in *Nasha meta* (Toronto), September 30, 1987, pp. 3, 6.

177 "Are the Armenians Really Russians?—Or How the U.S. Census Bureau Classifies America's Ethnic Groups," *Government Publications Review*, XIV, 2 (Elmsford, N.Y., 1987), pp. 133-168.

Reviewed:
Simon Brězan in *Lětopis Instituta za serbski ludospyt*, Rjad D, No. 4 (Bautzen, East Germany, 1989), p. 87.
Vasyl' Markus in *Novyi shliakh* (Toronto), April 21, 1990, p. 7. Reprinted in *Anabazys*, XI, 1 [39] (Toronto, 1990), pp. 11-12
Oleh Wolowyna in *The Ukrainian Weekly* (Jersey City, N.J.) March 18, 1990, pp. 7 and 14.

178 "Julijan Kolesar," *Carpatho-Rusyn American*, X, 1 (Fairview, N.J., 1987), p. 3. [Philip Michaels]

179 "The Lemko Rusyns: Their Past and Present," *Carpatho-Rusyn American*, X, 1 (Fairview, N.J., 1987), pp. 5-12. Reprinted in item **533**, pp. 113-129.

Reviewed:
Volodymyr Boliubash in *Homin Ukraïny* (Toronto), September 16, 1987, p. 10.

180 "Ethnic Chairs: Success by Default," *University of Toronto Bulletin*, September 28, 1987, p. 10. Reprinted in *New Perspectives* (Toronto), November 1987, p. 4.

181 "On the Tenth Anniversary of the Multicultural History Society of Ontario," *Polyphony*, IX, 1 (Toronto, 1987), p. 95.

182 Series editor: Pavlo Markovyč, *Rusyn Easter Eggs from Eastern Slovakia*. Classics of Carpatho-Rusyn Scholarship, Vol. I. Vienna: Wilhelm Braumüller Universitäts-Verlagsbuchhandlung, 1987, 146 p., 1 map, 36 plates.

Reviewed:
Bohdan Medwidsky in *Canadian Slavonic Papers*, XXX, 1 (Toronto, 1988), pp. 159-160.
R.F. Taft in *Orientalia Christiana Periodica*, LIV, 1 (Rome, 1988), pp. 262-263.
Mykola Mušynka in *Carpatho-Rusyn American*, XI, 4 (Fairview, N.J., 1988), pp. 8-9.
Veneta Newall in *Slavonic and East European Review*, LXVIII, 2 (London, 1990), pp. 389-390.
Marianne Stössl in *Zeitschrift für Ostforschung*, XXXIX, 1 (Marburg/Lahn,

1990), pp. 130-132.

N-n in *Hermeneia: Zeitschrift für ostkirchliche Kunst*, VI, 1 (Dortmund, 1990), p. 46.

Wolfgang Kessler in *Österreichische Osthefte*, XXXII (Vienna, 1990), p. 174.

183 "In Remembrance: Ivan Macyns'kyj," *Carpatho-Rusyn American*, X, 3 (Fairview, N.J., 1987), p. 9-10.

184 "Our Condolences [on Peter G. Stercho]," *Carpatho-Rusyn American*, X, 3 (Fairview, N.J., 1987), p. 11.

185 "Recent [Carpatho-Rusyn] Publications 1983," *Carpatho-Rusyn American*, X, 1, 2, 3 and 4 (Fairview, N.J., 1987), pp. 12, 10, 11, and 9. [unsigned]

186 "Carpatho-Rusyns." In Dirk Hoerder, ed. *The Immigrant Labor Press in North America, 1840s-1970s: An Annotated Biblio-graphy*, Vol. II: *Migrants from Eastern and Southeastern Europe*. New York, Westport, Conn., and London: Greenwood Press, 1987, pp. 385-400.

187 "Ucrainica Collections and Bibliography in North America: Their Current Status," *Journal of Ukrainian Studies*, XII, 2 [23] (Edmonton, Alta., 1987), pp. 77-91.

188 "Piat' rokiv zasnuvannia katedry ukraïns'kykh studiï pry universyteti v Torontu u Kanady," *Nova dumka*, XVI [62] (Vukovar, Yugoslavia, 1987), pp. 33-36.

189 "Min Zu Wen Hua Yu Da Xue Jiao Xue," *Su Lian Wen Hua Jiao Yu*, II [3] (Wuhan, China), pp. 36-48. Translation of item **88** into Chinese, with a brief introduction about the author, by Shen Yun.

1988

190 "Dzekuiutsi Soiuzu i 'Novei dumki' zatsikavel som she za iuhoslavianskikh Rusinokh," *Nova dumka*, XVII [66] (Vukovar, Yugoslavia, 1988), p. 73. Interview conducted by Havriïl Takach.

191 "Rusinistika—detseniia dosiahokh i plan za buduchnosts," *Shvetlosts*, XXVI, 1 (Novi Sad, Yugoslavia, 1988), pp. 70-94.

192 "Religion and Identity in the Carpathians." In Ladislav Matejka, ed. *Cross Currents*, Vol. VII. Ann Arbor, Mich.: University of Michigan Department of Slavic Languages and Literatures, 1988, pp. 87-107.

193 "The Year of the Millennium," *PMC: Practice of Ministry in Canada*, V, 1 (Toronto, 1988), pp. 17-18.

194 "Millennium of Christianity: Clearing Up the Confusion," *The Ukrainian Weekly* (Jersey City, N.J.), March 13, 1988, pp. 7 and 12. Reprinted as "1988: the Year of the Millennium," in *Ethnocultural Notes and Events* [May-June] (Toronto, 1988), pp. 7-10; *Eastern Catholic Life* (West Patterson, N.J.), June 12 and 26, 1988, p. 5 and p. 5.

Reviewed:
Frank E. Sysyn in *The Ukrainian Weekly*, April 3, 1988, p. 7.
M. J. Dragan in *The Ukrainian Weekly*, June 5, 1988, p. 7.

195 *Carpatho-Rusyn Studies: An Annotated Bibliography*. Vol I: *1975-1984*. Garland Reference Library of the Humanities, Vol. 824. New York and London: Garland Publishing, 1988, viii, 143 p., 2 maps.

Reviewed:
Bohdan S. Wynar in *American Reference Books Annual*, Vol. XX (Englewood, Colo., 1989), pp. 190-191.
Dmytro Shtohryn in *Slavic Review*, XLVIII, 4 (Austin, Texas, 1989), pp. 718-719.
Patricia A. Krafcik in *Slavic and East European Journal*, XXXIV, 1 (De Kalb, Ill., 1990), pp. 125-127.
Edward G. Mathews, Jr. in *Diakonia*, XXIII, 3 (Scranton, Pa., 1990), p. 190.
Emil Niederhauser in *Századok*, CXXIV, 3-4 (Budapest, 1990), pp. 538-539.
R.E.J. [Robert E. Johnston] in *Canadian Slavonic Papers*, XXXII, 4 (Toronto, 1990), pp. 522-523.
Günther Wytrzens in *Wiener slavistisches Jahrbuch*, XXXVI (Vienna, 1990), p. 263.
Wolfdieter Bihl in *Austrian History Yearbook*, XXII (Minneapolis, Minn., 1991), pp. 172-173.

David Saunders in *European History Quarterly*, XXI (London, Newbury Park, and New Delhi, 1991), pp. 81-95.
L'ubica Chorváthova in *Slovenský národopis*, XL, 2 (Bratislava, 1992), p. 233.
Robert A. Karlowich in *Harvard Ukrainian Studies*, XVI, 3-4 (Cambridge, Mass., 1992), pp. 467-469.

196 "From Our Center" [The Lemko Question], *Carpatho-Rusyn American*, XI, 1 (Fairview, N.J., 1988), p. 8. [unsigned]

197 "Carpatho-Rusyn Studies: A Decade of Accomplishment and an Agenda for the Future." In Boris Christa et al., eds. *Slavic Themes: Papers from Two Hemispheres*. Neuried, West Germany: Hieronymus, 1988, pp. 175-193.

198 "Hanulia, Yosyf." In Volodymyr Kubijovyč, ed. *Encyclopedia of Ukraine*, Vol. II: G-K. Toronto, Buffalo, and London: University of Toronto Press, 1988, p. 123. [unsigned]

199 "From Our Center" [The Lemko Question: Response], *Carpatho-Rusyn American*, XI, 2 (Fairview, N.J., 1988), pp. 8-10. [unsigned]

200 "In Remembrance: Stephen B. Roman," *Carpatho-Rusyn American*, XI, 2 (Fairview, N.J., 1988), pp. 10-11.

201 "Recent [Carpatho-Rusyn] Publications 1984," *Carpatho-Rusyn American*, XI, 2 and 4 (Fairview, N.J., 1988), pp. 11 and 10; XII, 2 and 3 (1989), pp. 11 and 7. [unsigned]

202 "Carpatho-Rusyns in Ontario." In Lubomyr Y. Luciuk and Iroida L. Wynnyckyj, eds. *Ukrainians in Ontario*. In *Polyphony*, Vol. X. Toronto: Multicultural History Society of Ontario, 1988, pp. 177-190. Revised version published in item **533**, pp. 446-466.

203 "The Chair of Ukrainian Studies at the University of Toronto," *ibid.*, pp. 221-227.

204 Review of Raphael Mahler, *Hasidism and the Jewish Enlightenment*, in *American Historical Review*, XCIII, 5 (Washington, D.C., 1988), p. 1364.

205 "Rusinistika—decenija dometa i plan za budučnost." In Magdalena Veselinović Šulc, ed. *Folklor u Vojvodini*, Vol II. Novi Sad: Udruženje folklorista SAP Vojvodine, 1988, pp. 11-33.

Reviewed:
Roman Miz in *Nova dumka*, XVIII [74] (Vukovar, 1989), pp. 45-46.

206 "Our [C-RRC] Tenth Anniversary," *Carpatho-Rusyn American*, XI, 3 (Fairview, N.J., 1988), p. 10. [unsigned]

1989

207 *The Russian Americans*. The Peoples of North America Series. Introduction by Daniel Patrick Moynihan. New York and Philadelphia: Chelsea House Publishers, 1989, 112 p., 1 map, 69 illustrations. Second revised edition, 1996.

Reviewed:
Janet E. Gelfand in *School Library Journal*, XXXV (Marion, Ohio, 1989), p. 129.
Booklist, LXXXV, 11 (Chicago, 1989), p. 937.
R. Polchaninov in *Novoe russkoe slovo* (New York), May 18, 1990, p. 23.
Russkaia zhizn', August 7, 1991, p. 3.
Nasha strana (Buenos Aires), May 25, 1991, p. 4.
Oleg Łatyszonek in *Przegląd Polonijny*, XVII, 3 (Wrocław, Warsaw and Cracow, 1991), pp. 149-150.
Elizabeth Talbot in *School Library Journal*, XL, 1 (Boulder, Colo., 1996), p.135.
Children's Bookwatch, V, 12 (Oregon, Wisc., 1995), p. 8.

208 "Monaco Becomes Monégasque: Language Revival in a Country Rediscovering Itself," *The World and I*, IV, 7 (Washington, D.C., 1989), pp. 620-631.

209 *The Carpatho-Rusyn Americans*. The Peoples of North America Series. Introduction by Daniel Patrick Moynihan. New York and Philadelphia: Chelsea House Publishers, 1989, 112 p., 2 maps, 60 illustrations. Second revised edition, see item **560**.

Reviewed:
GCU Messenger (Beaver, Pa.), February 22, 1990, p. 1.

Sr. M. Demetria in *Eastern Catholic Life* (West Patterson, N.J.), February 4, 1990, p. 4.

M.B. [Mykhal Bytsko] in *Nove zhyttia/Holos Rusyniv* (Prešov, Czechoslovakia), May 11, 1990, p. 4.

Denise Wilms in *Booklist*, LXXXVI, 6 (Chicago, 1989), p. 664.

Idella Washington in *Book Report*, IX, 1 (Worthington, Oh., 1990), p. 63.

L'ubica Chorváthova in *Slovenský národopis*, XL, 2 (Bratislava, 1992), p. 234.

Miloslav Rechcigl Jr. in *Czechoslovak and Central European Journal*, X, 1 (New York, 1991, pp. 151-154.

210 "The Ukrainian National Revival: A New Analytical Framework," *Canadian Review of Studies in Nationalism*, XVI, 1-2 (Charlottetown, Prince Edward Is., 1989), pp. 45-62. Reprinted in item **579**, pp. 38-54.

211 *Morality and Reality: The Life and Times of Andrei Sheptyts'kyi*, editor. Introduction by Jaroslav Pelikan. Edmonton, Alta: Canadian Institute of Ukrainian Studies, 1989, xxvi, 485 p., 2 maps, 53 illustrations.

Reviewed:

Evan Lowig in *St. Vladimir's Theological Quarterly*, XXXIV, 2-3 (Crestwood/ Tuckahoe, N.Y., 1990), pp. 258-261.

Roman Holiat in *The Ukrainian Quarterly*, XLVI, 2 (New York, 1990), pp. 189-191.

Benedykt Heydenkorn in *Związkowiec* (Toronto), January 3, 1991, p. 5.

Theophilus C. Prousis in *Russian History*, XVII, 4 (Bakersfield, Calif., 1990), pp. 449-450.

Martha Bohachevsky-Chomiak in *Catholic Historical Review*, LXXVIII, 4 (Washington, D.C., 1992), pp. 677-679.

H.D.D. in *Jahrbücher für Geschichte Osteuropas*, XLI, 1 (Wiesbaden, 1993), pp. 156-157.

James T. Flynn in *Austrian History Yearbook*, XXV (Minneapolis, Minn. 1994), pp. 269-270.

Sophia Senyk in *Harvard Ukrainian Studies*, XV, 3-4 (Cambridge, Mass., 1991), pp. 454-456.

Stella Hryniuk in *Slavonic and East European Review*, LXXI, 3 (London, 1993), pp. 558-559.

Rudolf A. Mark in *Zeitscrift für Ostmitteleuropa-Forschung*, XLIV, 2 (Marburg, 1995), pp. 303-305.

212 "Dimitry Zarechnak," *Carpatho-Rusyn American*, XII, 3 (Fairview, N.J., 1989), p. 3. [Philip Michaels]

213 "Czechoslovakia Discovers Andy," *ibid.*, pp. 4-7.

214 "Robert Maxwell," *Carpatho-Rusyn American*, XII, 4 (Fairview, N.J., 1989), pp. 2-3. [Philip Michaels]

215 "Stand Up and Be Counted," *Carpatho-Rusyn American*, XII, 4 (Fairview, N.J., 1989), p. 4. Also in *Byzantine Catholic World* (Pittsburgh), March 18, 1990, p. 24; *Eastern Catholic Life* (West Patterson, N.J.), April 1, 1990, p. 9; *Church Messenger* (Portage, Pa.), March 18, 1990, p. 1 & 8.

216 "[Rusyns and] the Revolution of 1989," *Carpatho-Rusyn American*, XII, 4 (Fairview, N.J., 1989), pp. 5-9. Also in *Byzantine Catholic World* (Pittsburgh), March 18, 1990, pp. 8-13; *Church Messenger* (Portage, Pa.), February 18, 1990, pp. 3, 5, 7; *Ruske slovo* (Novi Sad, Yugoslavia), Nos. 18-22, May 5-June 8, 1990, p. 2 each issue; *Kalendár-Almanac National Slovak Society of the USA for the Year 1992*, ed. Joseph Stefka. Pittsburgh, Pa., 1992, pp. 43-48. Excerpted in *GCU Messenger* (Beaver, Pa.), February 8, 1990, pp. 1 and 4; "Holos rusyniv" in *Nove zhyttia* (Prešov), June 22 and 19, 1990, pp. 4 and 4; *Karpatska Rus'* (Yonkers, N.Y.), October 26 and November 2, 1990, pp. 3-4 and 3-4.

1990

217 "Rusyn-Americans, Slovak-Americans, and Czecho-Slovakia." In *Kalendár-Almanac: National Slovak Society of the USA*, ed. Joseph Stefka. Pittsburgh, Pa., 1990, pp. 59-62.

218 "Carpatho-Rusyns." In Francesco Cordasco, ed. *Dictionary of American Immigration History*. Metuchen, N.J. and London: Scarecrow Press, 1990, pp. 105-109.

219 "Ukrainians," *ibid.*, pp. 716-721.

220 "Natsionalni i kulturno-sotsiialni rozvoi Rusinokh-Ukraïntsokh Chekhoslovatskei," *Shvetlosts*, XXVIII, 1 and 2 (Novi Sad, 1990), pp. 77-96 and 213-235. Translation of item **26** into Vojvodinian Rusyn by Diura Latiak.

221 "Vshitko pro viriuchykh: pys'mo Karpato-Rusyns'koho Doslidnoho Tsentra (KRDTs) iepyskopovi hreko-katolyts'koi tserkvy v Chekhoslovakiï—Ivanovi Hirkovi," *Nove zhyttia* (Prešov), March 23, 1990, p. 4.

222 Translation from German of Günther Wytrzens, "Nikolaj Nagy-Nod' (1819-1862)," *Carpatho-Rusyn American*, XIII, 1 (Pittsburgh, Pa., 1990), p. 3.

223 "Revolution of 1989 Update," *ibid.*, XIII, 1, 2, 3 and 4, pp. 7-9, 4-6, 9 and 6-7. [unsigned]

224 "Greetings from the Carpatho-Rusyn Research Center to President Václav Havel, Czechoslovakia, and to Oleksandr Zozuljak, Chairman, Initiative Group of Rusyn-Ukrainians in Prešov, Czechoslovakia," *Carpatho-Rusyn American*, XIII, 1 (Pittsburgh, Pa., 1990), p. 9. [unsigned]

225 "John Sopinka," *Carpatho-Rusyn American*, XIII, 2 (Pittsburgh, Pa., 1990), pp. 3-4. [Philip Michaels]

226 "Greetings from the Carpatho-Rusyn Research Center to Bishop Ján Hirka, Greek Catholic Eparchy of Prešov, and Mychajlo Tomčanij, Society of Carpatho-Rusyns, Užhorod, *ibid.*, p. 7.

227 "Recent Publications 1985 [about Carpatho-Rusyns]," *ibid.*, XIII, 1, 2, 3 and 4, pp. 11, 10-11 and 11. [unsigned]

228 "Rusyny—narod po-hirs'komu krylatyi" [interview with P.R. Magocsi by Ivan Petrovtsii], *Nove zhyttia* (Irshava, Soviet Ukraine), September 27, 1990, pp. 1-2. Also in *Chervonyi prapor* (Berehovo, Soviet Ukraine), October 9, 1990, pp. 1-3; *Rusyn*, I, 3 (Prešov, 1991), pp. 25-26; and in Hungarian: "Büszke nép a ruszin," *Vörös*

zászlo (Berehovo), October 9, 1990, pp. 1-3.

Shorter version in *Otchyi khram* (Uzhhorod, Soviet Ukraine), September/October, 1990, pp. 4-5; *Zakarpats'ka pravda* (Uzhhorod), November 14, 1990, p. 2; and in Russian: "Narod po-gornomu krylatyi," *Zakarpatskaia pravda* (Uzhhorod), November 14, 1990, p. 2.

229 Review of Jan Kozik, *The Ukrainian Movement National Movement in Galicia, 1815-1849,* in *Canadian Review of Studies in Nationalism*, XVII, 1-2 (Charlottetown, Prince Edward Island, 1990), pp. 292-293.

230 Series editor: Alexander Bonkáló, *The Rusyns*. Classics of Carpatho-Rusyn Scholarship, Vol. III. New York: Columbia University Press/East European Monographs, 1990, xxii, 160 p., 2 maps.

231 "Joseph W. Tkach," *Carpatho-Rusyn American*, XIII, 3 (Pittsburgh, Pa., 1990), p. 3. [Philip Michaels]

232 "Religion and the Revolution of 1989: The Orthodox Perspective," *ibid.*, p. 4. [Philip Michaels]

233 "Every Language Needs Poets and Novelists," *ibid.*, p. 10. [Philip Michaels]

234 "Kul'turnye institutsii kak instrument natsional'nogo razvitiia v XIX v. v vostochnoi Galitsii." In V.I. Zlydnev, ed., *Slavianskie i balkanskie kul'tury XVIII - XIX vv.: sovetsko-amerikanskii simpozium.* Moscow: Akademiia Nauk SSSR/Institut Slavianovedeniia i Balkanistiki, 1990, pp. 132-143.

235 "Nation-Building or Nation Destroying?: Lemkos, Poles, and Ukrainians in Contemporary Poland," *Polish Review*, XXXV, 3/4 (New York, 1990), pp. 197-209. Reprinted in item **533**, pp. 316-331.

Reviewed:
Andrzej A. Zięba, "O Łemkach w Honolulu," *Tygodnik Powszechny*, XLIII, 12 (Cracow, 1989), p. 5.

Andrzej Chodkiewicz, "O Łemkach," *Ład*, VIII, 6 (Warsaw, 1990).
Ivan Krasovs'kyi, "Kil'ka dumok u spravi Lemkiv: z pryvodu statti A.
Ziemby 'O Lemkach w Honolulu'," *Nashe slovo* (Warsaw), July 30, 1989;
reprinted in *Lemkivshchyna*, XI, 3 (Clifton, N.J., 1989), pp. 14-15.
Ivan Lyko, "Lemko-rusyn—ukraïnets'-'lemko'!," *ibid*, XI, 4 (1989), pp. 12-
14.
Ivan Hvozda, "Podiï, iaki khvyliuiut' lemkivs'ku spil'notu, iak i vse ukraïns'ke
suspil'stvo," *Lemkivshchyna*, XII, 1 (Clifton, N.J., 1990), pp. 6-11; reprinted
in *Novyi shliakh* (Toronto), May 19, 26 and June 2, 1990; and *Nashe slovo*
(Warsaw), November 11, 18 and 25, 1990.
Myroslav Levyts'kyi, "Politychni ta suspil'ni napriamky sered lemkiv u XX
stolitti," *Nashe slovo* (Warsaw), January 21, 1990.
Vasyl' Mel'nyk, "Neorusynstvo i ioho interpretatory," *Zakarpats'ka pravda*
(Uzhhorod), esp. pt. 4, August 24, 1990.
Diura Latiak, "Ishche raz o Lemkokh u Honolulu," *Ruske slovo* (Novi Sad,
Yugoslavia), June 27, 1990.
Mar"ian Koval's'kyi, "Retsenziia na...," *Duklia*, XL, 3 (Prešov, 1992), pp. 53-59.

236 Review of Wolodymyr Kosyk, *L'Allemagne national-socialiste et
l'Ukraine*, in *American Historical Review*, XCV, 4 (Washington,
D.C., 1990), p. 1245.

237 "George J. Demko," *Carpatho-Rusyn American*, XIII, 4 (Pittsburgh,
Pa., 1990), p. 3. [Philip Michaels]

238 "The Rusyn-Ukrainian Debate in the Prešov Region," *ibid.*, pp. 4-5.
[Philip Michaels]

239 "The Rusyn-Ukrainian Debate in Soviet Transcarpathia," *ibid.*, pp.
5- 6. [Philip Michaels]

240 "Greetings from the Carpatho-Rusyn Research Center to Alexander
Veličko, Společnost přátel Podkarpatské Rusi, Prague, and to Djura
Papuga, Ruska Matka, Ruski Krstur," *ibid.*, p. 8.

241 "Rusyny i revoliutsiia 1989 roku." In *Dumki z Dunaiu*, Vol. II.
Vukovar, Yugoslavia: Soiuz Rusinoch i Ukraïntsokh Horvatskei,
1990, pp. 123-131. Translation of item **216** into Ukrainian by Marco
Carynnyk.

242 "Magyars and Carpatho-Rusyns: On the Seventieth Anniversary of the Founding of Czechoslovakia." In *Adelphotes: A Tribute to Omeljan Pritsak by his Students/Harvard Ukrainian Studies*, XIV, 3/4 (Cambridge, Mass., 1990), pp. 427-460. Reprinted in item **535**, pp. 147-187.

243 "Karpato-rusinische Untersuchungen: Ein Jahrzehnt der Errungenschaften und ein Plan für die Zukunft," *Der Donauraum*, XXX, 3 (Vienna, 1989-90), pp. 20-36.

244 "Rusyn-Americans and Czechoslovakia." In Bohomír Bunža, ed. *Rada svobodného Československa/Council of Free Czechoslovakia: Historie, program, činnost, dokumenty*. Toronto: Rada svobodného Československa, 1990, pp. 206-211.

245 "Lyst-vitannia iz-za okeanu," *Otchyi khram* (Uzhhorod, Soviet Ukraine), July, 1990, p. 2.

1991

246 "The Era of the Nation-State is Over," *Compass*, IX, 1 (Toronto, 1991), pp. 13-15.

247 "Lemkivs'kŷ rusynŷ kolys' i teper'," *Rusyn*, I, 1 and 3 (Medzilaborce, 1991), pp. 4 and 22. Translation into Rusyn of item **179**.

248 "Karpatorusyny: novyi chy vidrodzhennyi narod?," *Nove zhyttia* ("Holos Rusyniv") (Prešov, Czechoslovakia), April 2, 1991, p. 6; *Novyny Zakarpattia* (Uzhhorod), May 21, 1991, pp. 4-5.

Reviewed:
Vadym Dyvnych, "Bo svoï to za horamy. . .," *Slovo* (Kyiv), May 1991, pp. 5-7.
Volodymyr Fedynyshynets', "Buty Rusynom—buty Rusynam!," *Molod' Zakarpattia* (Uzhhorod), May 25, 1991, supplement 8 p. Reprinted in Rusyn, Slovak, and English translation in Volodymyr Fedynyshynets', *Myrna nasha rusyns'ka put'*. Prešov: Rusyns'ka obroda, 1992, pp. 4-19, 38-54, 72-91.

249 "Rusíni už nie sú v zátvorke," *Smena na nedel'u* (Bratislava), March 29, 1991, p. 5. Interview by Eva Čobejová. Excerpted in Vojvodinian Rusyn, "Rusini uzh nie u zagradzeniu," *Ruske slovo* (Novi Sad, Yugoslavia), May 3-10, 1991, p. 2.

250 "From the President of the C-RRC" [the C-RRC as a cultural, not political organization], *Carpatho-Rusyn American*, XIV, 1 (Pittsburgh, Pa., 1991), p. 3.

251 "Revolution of 1989 Update," *ibid.*, XIV, 1, 2, 3, and 4 (1991), pp. 6-8, 7, 7, and 6-7. [unsigned]

252 "Recent [Carpatho-Rusyn] Publications 1986," *ibid.*, XIV, 1 (1991), p. 9. [unsigned]

253 "Recent Events," *ibid.*, XIV, 1, 2, 3, and 4, pp. 11, 10-11, 8 and 7. [unsigned]

254 "Letter of Greeting." In *Ukrainian Canadian Centenary Souvenir Program*. Toronto: Association of United Ukrainian Canadians, 1991, p. 17.

255 "Rozmakh rusinskoho rukhu," *Ruske slovo* (Novi Sad, Yugoslavia), April 5, 1991, p. 4. Interview by Stevan Konstantinovich.

256 "Made or Re-Made in America?: Nationality and Identity Formation Among Carpatho-Rusyn Immigrants and Their Descendants," *Coexistence: A Review of East-West and Development Issues— Special Issue: The Émigré Experience*, XXVIII (Dordrecht, Netherlands, 1991), pp. 335-348. Reprinted in Paul Robert Magocsi, ed. *The Persistence of Regional Cultures: Rusyns and Ukrainians in their Carpathian Homeland and Abroad*. New York: Columbia University Press/East European Monographs, 1993, pp. 163-178.

257 "Ukraïns'ke natsional'ne vidrodzhennia: nova analitychna struktura," *Ukraïns'kyi istorychnyi zhurnal*, XXXV, 3 (Kyiv, 1991), pp. 97-107. Translation of item **210** into Ukrainian by Marco Carynnyk.

258 "First World Congress of Rusyns," *Carpatho-Rusyn American*, XIV, 2 (Pittsburgh, Pa., 1991), pp. 7-9. [Philip Michaels]

259 "A Unique Document," *ibid.*, p. 9. [unsigned]

260 "Ukraińcy Galicji pod rządami Habsburgów i Sowietów," *Zeszyty Historyczne*, XCVII (Paris, 1991), pp. 91-100. Translation of item **287** into Polish by Benedykt Heydenkorn.

261 "Domovina v Karpatoch: rusínski Američania, slovenskí Američania a Česko-Slovensko," *Historická revue*, II, 4 (Bratislava, 1991), pp.21-23. Translation of item **217** into Slovak by Elena Jakešová.

262 "From the President of the C-RRC" [greetings to Metropolitan Stephen J. Kocisko on his Jubilee Celebration], *Byzantine Catholic World*, June 23, 1991, p. 7.

263 "Pätnásť minút slávy—a dosť'!: narodnostné menšiny strednej a východnej Európy dnes a zajtra," *Kultúrny život*, XXV, 31 (Bratislava, 1991), p. 8. Translation of item **354** into Slovak by Elena Jakešová.

264 "Pravdivi informatsiï o Rusintsokh: Dr. Pavlo Robert Magochi o iaziku, pravokh menshinokh u Europi," *Ruske slovo* (Novi Sad, Yugoslavia), July 19, 1991, p. 7. Interview conducted by Havriï Koliesar.

265 "Magyars and Carpatho-Rusyns." In H. Gordon Skilling, ed. *Czechoslovakia, 1918-88: Seventy Years From Independence*. London and Oxford: Macmillan/St. Antony's College, 1991, pp. 105-129.

266 "1989 és Kelet-Közép-Európa nemzeti kisebbségei," *Regio*, II, 2 (Budapest, 1991), pp. 98-107. Translation of item **354** into Hungarian by D. András Ban.

267 "Ievropa narodiv, a ne derzhav," *Novyny Zakarpattia* (Uzhhorod), August 24, 1991, p. 8. Interview.

268 "Ivan Rakovs'kyj (1815-1885)," *Carpatho-Rusyn American*, XIV, 3 (Pittsburgh, Pa., 1991), p. 3. [Philip Michaels]

269 "Preface," in Lubomyr Luciuk and Stella Hryniuk, eds., *Canada's Ukrainians: Negotiating an Identity*. Toronto, Buffalo, and London: University of Toronto Press, 1991, pp. xi-xv.

Reviewed:
Stephen Carey in *Canadian Review of Studies in Nationalism*, XXII, 1-2 (Charlottetown, Prince Edward Is., 1995), pp. 191-192.

270 "Revoluţiile din 1989 şi minorităţile naţionale in Estul şi Centrul Europei," *Tribuna* (Cluj, Romania), June 27-July 3, 1991, pp. 9 and Translation of item **354** into Romanian by Aurel Sasu.

271 "O budoucnosti rusinů," *Podkarpatská Rus: zpravodaj*, No. 3 (Prague, 1991), pp. 7-8. Interview conducted by Agáta Pilátová.

272 "The Kachkovs'kyi Society and the National Revival in Nineteenth-Century East Galicia," *Harvard Ukrainian Studies*, XV, 1/2 (Cambridge, Mass., 1991), pp. 48-87. Reprinted in item **579**, pp. 119-158.

273 Review of Elemér Illyés, *Ethnic Continuity in the Carpatho-Danubian Area*, in *Slavic Review*, L, 3 (Austin, Texas, 1991), pp. 710-711.

274 "Robliat' tak zo zasadí?"—letter in response to the Position Paper of the Ukrainian Creative Intelligentsia in Czechoslovakia, *Narodnŷ novynkŷ* (Prešov, Czechoslovakia), October 30, 1991, p. 2. In Slovak translation: "Odozva z Kanady na stanovisko ukrajinskej tvorivej inteligencie," *Slovenský východ* (Košice, Czechoslovakia), October 30, 1991.

275 "Rusynŷ: novŷi tsy onovlenŷi narod?," *Rusyn*, I, 2 (Prešov, 1991), pp. 2-8. Translation of item **318** into Rusyn.

276 Review of N.F. Dreisziger and A. Ludanyi, eds., *Forgotten Minorities: The Hungarians of East Central Europe*, in *Canadian*

Slavonic Papers, XXXIII, 1 (Edmonton, Alta., 1991), pp. 77-78.

277 "Quindici anni di attività della Multicultural History Society of Ontario," *Altreitalie*, III, 6 (Rome, 1991), pp. 124-129. Interview conducted by Matteo Sanfilippo.

278 "Le nationalisme monégasque: contradiction terminologique ou réalité pratique?," *Europa Ethnica*, XLVIII, 4 (Vienna, 1991), pp. 187-197. Translation into French of item **280**.

279 "Rozdilinia na rusyniv i ukraïntsiv—treba pryiaty," *Narodnŷ novynkŷ* (Prešov), December 19, 1991, p. 1.

280 "Monégasque Nationalism: A Terminological Contradiction or Practical Reality?," *Canadian Review of Studies in Nationalism*, XVIII, 1-2 (Charlottetown, Prince Edward Is., 1991), pp. 83-94.

281 "From the President of the Carpatho-Rusyn Research Center" [remarks at the opening of the Museum of Modern Art in Medzilaborce, June 30, 1991], *Carpatho-Rusyn American*, XIV, 4 (Pittsburgh, Pa., 1991), p. 2.

282 "Fedir Vico," *ibid.*, p. 3. [Philip Michaels]

283 "Andy Uncovered," *ibid.*, pp. 4-5.

284 "Greetings from the C-RRC" [to Metropolitan Stephen J. Kocisko on his Jubilee Celebration], *ibid.*, p. 11. Reprinted in *Byzantine Catholic World* (Pittsburgh, Pa.), June 23, 1991, p. 7.

1992

285 "Rusini na Zapadu," *Dnevnik* (Novi Sad, Yugoslavia), January 14, 1992, p. 9. Interview conducted by I. Ch. Kovačević.

286 "The MHSO in the Service of Ontario and Canada," *Newsletter of the MHSO*, V, 2 (Toronto, 1992), p. 3.

287 "A Subordinate or Submerged People: The Ukrainians of Galicia Under Habsburg and Soviet Rule." In Richard L. Rudolph and David F. Good, eds. *Nationalism and Empire: The Habsburg Empire and the Soviet Union.* New York: St. Martin's Press in association with the Center for Austrian Studies, University of Minnesota, 1992, pp. 95-107. Reprinted in item **579**, pp. 55-64.

288 "Rusyns Regain Their Autonomy," *Ukrainian Canadian Herald* (Toronto), March 16, 1992, p. 7. Reprinted in *Carpatho-Rusyn American*, XV, 1 (Pittsburgh, Pa., 1992), pp. 10-11; *Association for the Study of Nationalities Analysis of Current Events*, IV, II (New York, 1993).

289 "The Society of Carpatho-Rusyns," *Carpatho-Rusyn American*, XV, 1 (Pittsburgh, Pa., 1992), pp. 3-5. [unsigned]

290 "Byzantine (Greek) Catholics in America and Europe [Letter to Bishop Basil H. Losten]," *ibid.*, pp. 6-7.

291 "Since the Revolution of 1989," *ibid.*, XV, 1, 2, 3, and 4 (1992), pp. 8, 11, 9-11, and 11. [unsigned]

292 "Recent Events," *ibid.*, XV, 1, 2, 3, and 4 (1992), pp. 11, 10-11, 11, and 10. [unsigned]

293 "Rusyns in Hungary," *ibid.*, XV, 3 (1992), p. 2. [Philip Michaels]

294 "Ruthenians or Ukrainians: Professor Magocsi Interviewed in Kiev for Paris Newspaper *Le Monde*," *Ukrainian Canadian Herald* (Toronto), September 14, 1992, p. 6; *Eastern Catholic Life* (West Patterson, N.J.), October 11, 1992, p. 5; *News from Ukraine* (Kyiv, Ukraine), No. 43, October 1992, p. 7; *Trembita*, V, 2 (Minneapolis, Minn., 1993), pp. 2-4.

295 "Interv"iu profesora Magochiia u Kyievi dlia paryz'koï hazety 'Le Monde'," *Molod'Zakarpattia* (Uzhhorod, Ukraine), October 3, 1992. Translation into Rusyn: "Magochii—agent abo ni?," *Narodnŷ novynkŷ* (Prešov, Czecho-Slovakia), September 16, 1992, pp. 1-2.

Translation into English: "Magocsi—Agent or Not," *Trembita*, IV, 5 (Minneapolis, Minn., 1992), pp. 9-10.

296 Series editor: Athanasius B. Pekar, *The History of the Church in Carpathian Rus'*. Classics of Carpatho-Rusyn Scholarship, Vol. IV. New York: Columbia University Press/East European Monographs, 1992, lii, 296 p.

297 Review of Julianna Puskás, *Overseas Migration from East-Central and Southeastern Europe, 1880-1940*, in *Journal of American Ethnic History*, XII, 1 (New Brunswick, N. J., 1992), pp. 114-115.

298 "Zadacha robochoho seminaria abo pershíi kongres rusyns'koho iazŷka," *Rusyn*, II, 5-6 (Prešov, 1992), pp. 4-5.

299 "Rusini Karpaccy—lud nowy czy odrodzony?," in *Magury '91*. Warsaw: Towarzystwo Karpackie/Studenckie Koło Przewodników Beskidzkich, 1992, pp. 52-73. Translation of item **318** into Polish by Tadeusz Andrzej Olszański.

300 "Carpatho-Rusyns: Their Current Status and Future Perspectives." In Jana Plichtová, ed. *Minorities in Politics: Cultural and Language Rights*. Bratislava: Czechoslovak Committee of the European Cultural Foundation, 1992, pp. 212-223. Reprinted in item **308**, revised in item **346**, and reprinted in item **535**, pp. 138-159.

Reviewed:
Mykola Mushynka, "Zakarpats'ki rusyny-ukraïntsi na mizhnarodnomu sympoziumi," *Zakarpats'ka pravda* (Uzhhorod, Ukraine), December 17, 1991, pp. 2-3.
Mykola Mushynka, "Vsuperech zdorovomu hluzdu: prof. Pavlo Mahochi radyt': 'rozdiliai i ... asymiliui!'," *Karpats'ka pravda* (Uzhhorod, Ukraine), January 23, 1992, pp. 4 and 6.
Mykola Mushynka, *Politychnyi rusynizm na praktytsi: z pryvodu vystupu prof. Pavla-Roberta Magochi na sympoziumi 'Natsional'ni menshosti Tsentral'noï i Pivdenno-Skhidnoï Ievropy, Bratislava-Chasta, lystopad 1991 r.* Supplement to *Nove zhyttia*, No. 47-48 (Prešov, 1991), 12 p. Reprinted— Prešov: Soiuz rusyniv-ukraïntsiv ChSFR, 1991; *Nashe slovo* (Warsaw), March 29, April 5 and 26, May 3 and 10, p. 4 each issue; *Homin Ukraïny* (Toronto), July 8, 22, 29, 1992, pp. 10, 10-11, 10; and Clifton, N. J.: Lemko

Research Foundation, [1992]; Toronto: Khrest, 1992. Polish translation, "Polityczny rusinizm w praktyce," in *Magury '91*. Warsaw: Towarzystwo Karpackie/Studenckie Koło Przewodników Beskidzkich, 1992, pp. 74-86.

301 "Karpats'ki rusyny: teperishnii status ta perspektyvy na maibutnie," *Podkarpats'ka Rus'* (Uzhhorod, Ukraine), July 30, August 13, September 10, 1992, pp. 2, 3, and 2. Excerpts translated into Ukrainian of item **308**.

302 "Stworzeni czy przekształceni w Ameryce? Narodowość i procesy świadomościowe wśród imigrantów karpacko-rusińskich i ich potomków w USA," *Przegląd Polonijny*, XVIII, 3 (Wrocław, Warsaw, and Cracow, 1992), pp. 5-17. Translation of item **256** into Polish by Andrzej A. Zięba.

303 "Ioannykij Bazylovyč (1742-1821)," *Carpatho-Rusyn American*, XV, 4 (Pittsburgh, Pa., 1992), p. 3. [Philip Michaels]

304 "Our Condolences [Julijan Kolesar]," *ibid.*, p. 7. [unsigned]

305 "Byzantine (Greek) Catholics in Europe and America [Letter to Bishop Basil H. Losten]," *ibid.*, p. 8.

306 "Scholarly Seminar on the Codification of the Rusyn Language," *Carpatho-Rusyn American*, XV, 4 (Pittsburgh, Pa., 1992), pp. 4-5; *Österreichische Osthefte*, XXXV, 1 (Vienna, 1993), pp. 182-185; *Scottish Slavonic Review*, XIX, 2 (Glasgow, 1992), pp. 145-147; *International Journal of the Sociology of Language*, No. 104 (Berlin and New York, 1993), pp. 119-123 with introduction and postscript by Joshua A. Fishman; *Europa Ethnica*, L, 3 (Vienna, 1933), pp. 147-149; *Revue d'études slaves*, LXV, 3 (Paris, 1993), pp. 597-599; *Canadian Review of Studies in Nationalism*, XX, 1-2 (Charlottetown, Prince Edward Is., 1993), pp. 193-195; *Slavia*, LXXII, 4 (Prague, 1993), pp. 550-552; *Slovanský přehled*, LXXIX, 2 (Prague, 1993), pp. 232-233; *Slavica Slovaca*, XXIX, 1 (Bratislava, 1994), pp. 88-89; *Zeitschrift für Slawistik*, XXXIX, 4 (Berlin, 1994), pp. 610-612. Excerpts in *CAS* [Canadian Association of Slavists] *Newsletter*, XXXIII [80] (Edmonton, Alta., 1993), p. 18.

307 Review of Bohdan S. Wynar, *Ukraine: A Bibliographical Guide to English-Language Publications*, in *Canadian Review of Studies in Nationalism*, XIX, 1-2 (Charlottetown, Prince Edward Is., 1992), pp. 196-197.

308 "Carpatho-Rusyns: Their Current Status and Future Perspectives," *The Polish Quarterly of International Affairs*, I, 1-2 (Warsaw, 1992), pp. 95-112.

309 "Karpato-Rusini: obecny status i perspektywy," *Sprawy Międzynarodowe*, XLV, 7-12 (Warsaw, 1992), pp. 95-110. Translation of item **308** into Polish.

310 "Ukránok-e a Ruszinok?," *Világszövetség* (Budapest), September 1, 1992. Interview conducted by Géza Gecse.

311 "Rusini na Zakarpatiu," *Shvetlosts*, XXX, 2-6 (Novi Sad, 1992), pp. 83-93. Translation of item **325** into Vojvodinian Rusyn by Mikola Skuban.

312 "Karpatskí Rusíni: súčasný stav a perspektívy v budúcnosti," *Slovenský národopis*, XL, 2 (Bratislava, 1992), pp. 183-192. Translation of item **300** into Slovak by L'ubica Babotová.

313 "Odpoved'," *Slovenský národopis*, XL, 3 (Bratislava, 1992), pp. 317- 322.

314 "The Birth of a New Nation, or the Return of an Old Problem? The Rusyns of East Central Europe," *Canadian Slavonic Papers*, XXXIV, 3 (Edmonton, Alta., 1992), pp. 199-223. Reprinted in item **486** and item **535**, pp. 332-360.

Reviewed:

V. Nimchuk in *XI. medzinárodný zjazd slavistov: Záznamy z diskusie k predneseným referátom* (Bratislava: Slovenský komitét slavistov/ Slavistický kabinet SAV, 1998), p. 553.

315 "Vidrodzhennia karpatoznavsta pislia 1975 roku." In Mykola Mushynka, ed. *Vid Naukovoho tovarystva im. Shevchenka do Ukraïns'koho Vil'noho Universytetu*. Kyiv, L'viv, Prešov, Munich, Paris, New York, Toronto, Sydney: Akademiia Nauk Ukraïny/ Instytut ukraïns'koï arkheohrafii, 1992, pp. 356-375.

316 "Naukovyi seminar z pytan' kodyfytsiï rusyns'koï movy," *Nova dumka*, XXI [96/97] (Zagreb, Croatia, 1992), pp. 32-24. Translation of item **306** into Ukrainian by Iryna Koropenko. [unsigned]

1993

317 "Rusyns to Have Their Own Language," *Eastern Catholic Life* (West Patterson, N. J.), January 31, 1993, pp. 1, 8, and 11; *Horizons* (Parma, Oh.), January 31, 1993, p. 7; *Ukrainian Canadian Herald* (Toronto), February 1, 1993, pp. 10 and 15; *Karpatska Rus'* (Yonkers, N. Y.), January 22, 1993, p. 3.

318 "Carpatho-Rusyns: A New or Revived People?" In *Kalendár-Almanac National Slovak Society of the USA for the Year 1993*, ed. Joseph Stefka. Pittsburgh, Pa., 1993, pp. 38-45. Reprinted in item **536**, pp. 249-274.

319 "Macedonians are Recognized in the U.S. Census: Remarks at the First Annual Banquet of the Canadian Macedonian Place Historical Society," *Macedonian Canadian News* (Toronto), April 1993, p. 7.

320 "The Rusyns Along the Danube—in Former Yugoslavia," *Carpatho- Rusyn American*, XVI, 1 (Pittsburgh, Pa., 1993), p. 2.

321 "Antal Hodinka (1864-1946)," *ibid.*, p. 3 [Philip Michaels].

322 "Recent Events," *ibid.*, XVI, 1, 2, 3, and 4 (1993), pp. 6, 11, 8-9, and 10. [unsigned]

323 "Since the Revolution of 1989," *ibid.*, XVI, 1, 2, 3, and 4 (1993), pp. 6, 11, 10-11, and 10-11. [unsigned]

324 "Fifteen Years of Service [of the Carpatho-Rusyn Research Center]," *ibid.*, XVI, 1 (1993), p. 11. [unsigned]

325 "The Rusyns of Transcarpathia." In *Minorities in Central and Eastern Europe*. Minorities Rights Group International Report 1993, No. 1. London: Minority Rights Group, pp. 23-26, 44.

326 "Rusyns'ka kultura i nauka: suchasna sytuatsiia i perspektyvŷ: z vístupu Pavla Roberta Magochiia na II. Svitovim Kongresi Rusyniv u Krynytsi," *Narodnŷ novynkŷ* (Prešov), June 2, 1993, p. 3. Excerpts of item **331** translated into Rusyn.

327 "Carpatho-Rusyns: A Tortuous Quest for Identity." In Ladislav Matějka, ed. *Cross Currents*, Vol. XII. New Haven, Conn.: Yale University Press, 1993, pp. 147-159.

328 *An Interview with Professor Paul Robert Magocsi/Interv'iu z profesorom Pavlom Robertom Magochim.* Orwell, Vt.: Carpatho-Rusyn Research Center, 1993, 19 and 22 p. Interview conducted by Oles Mušynka. Reprinted in *Trembita*, VI, 2 (Minneapolis, 1994), pp. 3-25, and in item **533**, pp. 228-248. Excerpts in *Podkarpats'ka Rus'* (Uzhhorod), October 7, 1993, p. 2; December 16 and 30, 1993, pp. 3 and 2; *Karpats'kyi krai*, IV, 1-2 (Uzhhorod, 1994), pp. 5-6.

Reviewed:
Serhii Fedaka in *Sribnia zemlia* (Uzhhorod), October 23, 1993.

329 "Josyf Sembratovyč (1821-1900)," *Carpatho-Rusyn American*, XVI, 2 (Pittsburgh, Pa., 1993), p. 2. [Philip Michaels]

330 "Religion and Identity in the Carpathians: East Christians in Poland and Czechoslovakia." In Boris Gasparov and Olga Raevsky-Hughes, eds. *Christianity and the Eastern Slavs*, Vol. I: *Slavic Cultures in the Middle Ages/California Slavic Studies,* Vol. XVI. Berkeley, Los Angeles, and Oxford: University of California Press, 1993, pp. 116- 138. Reprinted in item **535**, pp. 60-85.

331 "Rusyn Culture and Scholarship: Present Status and Future Perspectives," *Trembita*, V, 4 (Minneapolis, Minn., 1993), pp. 1-3,

9- 11. Reprinted in item **536**, pp. 275-286.

332 *Rusynŷ—narod zo svoïma kulturnŷma kharakteristykamy*. Prešov: Rusyns'ka obroda, 1993, 8 p. Excerpts from item **325** translated into Rusyn and published as an insert in *Narodnŷ novynkŷ* (Prešov), September 22, 1993.

333 "Persha svitova voina y revoluchní roky 1918-1919," *Podkarpats'ka Rus'* (Uzhhorod), September 9, 1993, p. 3.

334 "Die Russinen: Ihr gegenwärtiger Status und ihre Zukunftsperspektiven," *Osteuropa*, XLIII, 9 (Berlin, 1993), pp. 809- 824. Translation of item **300** into German by Annette Julius.

335 "Prešov region." In Danylo Husar Struk, ed. *Encyclopedia of Ukraine*, Vol. IV. Toronto, Buffalo, and London: University of Toronto Press, 1993, pp. 188-196.

336 "Slovaks." In *ibid.*, pp. 760-761.

337 "Supreme Ruthenian Council." In *ibid.*, p. 109.

338 *The Persistence of Regional Cultures: Rusyns and Ukrainians in Their Carpathian Homeland and Abroad/Tryvalist' rehional'nykh kul'tur: rusyny i ukraïntsi na ïkhnii karpats'kii batkivshchyni ta za kordonom*, editor. Classics of Carpatho-Rusyn Scholarship, Vol.V. New York: Columbia University Press/East European Monographs, 1993, x and 220 p., 4 maps.

Reviewed:
Liubomir Medieshi in *Ruske slovo*, August 26, 1994, p. 9.
Reference and Research Book News, IX [May] (Portland, Oregon, 1994), p. 7.
Martyn Rady in *Slavonic and East European Review*, LXXIII, 2 (London, 1993), pp. 354-355.
Iurii Kundrat in *Duklia*, XLIV, 4 (Prešov, Slovakia, 1995), pp. 83-85.
Constantin Simon in *Orientalia Christiana Periodica*, LXI, 2 (Rome, 1995), pp. 664-666.
Iurii (Juraj) Kundrat in *Journal of Ukrainian Studies*, XXI, 1-2 (Toronto, 1996), pp. 318-321.

Przemysław Żurawski vel Grajewski in *Kwartalnik Historyczny*, CIV, 1 (Warsaw, 1997), pp. 72-84.

Anna Veronika Wendland in *Jahrbücher für Geschichte Osteuropas*, XLV, 1 (Wiesbaden, 1997), pp. 158-159.

Rudolf A. Mark in *Zeitschrift für Ostmitteleuropa-Forschung*, XLV, 4 (Marburg, 1997), pp. 606-608.

Fred Stambrook in *Austrian History Yearbook*, XXX (Minneapolis, 1999), pp. 281-282.

Bertalan Pusztai in *Acta Ethnographica Hungaria*, XLV, 3-4 (Budapest, 2000), pp. 443-444.

339 "Made or Re-made in America? Nationality and Identity Formation Among Carpatho-Rusyn Immigrants and Their Descendants/ Stvoreni chy peretvoreni v Amerytsi?: narodnist' i protses samovyznachennia sered karpatorusyns'kykh imigrantiv i ïkhnikh nashchadkiv." In *ibid.*, pp. 163-178 and 166-181. Reprint and translation of item **256** into Ukrainian. English text reprinted in item **535**, pp. 467-482.

340 "Commentary"/"Komentar." In *ibid.*, pp. 191-202 and pp. 194-205.

341 *The Rusyns of Slovakia: An Historical Survey.* Classics of Carpatho-Rusyn Scholarship, Vol. VI. New York: Columbia University Press/East European Quarterly, 1993, xii and 185 p., 6 maps, 38 illustrations.

Reviewed:

Harm Ramkema in *Oost-Europa Verkenningen*, No. 132 (Amsterdam, 1994), pp. 50-52.

P.W. Knoll in *Choice*, XXXII, 2 (Middletown, Conn., 1994), p. 346.

Constantin Simon in *Orientalia Christiana Periodica*, LXI, 2 (Rome, 1995), pp. 666-668.

M.T. [Miroslav Tejchman] in *Slovanský přehled*, LXXXI, 2 (Prague, 1995), p. 124.

A.B. Pernal in *Canadian Journal of History*, XXXI, 1 (Saskatoon, 1996), pp. 119-120.

Anna Veronika Wendland in *Jahrbücher für Geschichte Osteuropas*, XLV, 1 (Wiesbaden, 1997), pp. 157-158.

Przemysław Żurawski vel Grajewski in *Kwartalnik Historyczny*, CIV, 1 (Warsaw, 1997), pp. 84-85.

Bogdan Horbal in *Canadian-American Slavic Studies*, XXX, 2-4 (Vancouver,

B.C., 1997), pp. 448-450.

Rudolf Mark in *Zeitschrift für Ostmitteleuropa-Forschung*, XLVI, 4 (Marburg, 1997), pp. 606-608.

Victor S. Mamatey in *Canadian Review of Studies in Nationalism*, XXIV, 1-2 (Charlottetown, Prince Edward Is., 1997), pp. 149-150.

Keith P. Dyrud in *Slovakia*, XXXVI [66-67] (Passaic, N.J., 1998), pp. 140-142.

Fred Stambrook in *Austrian History Yearbook*, XXX (Minneapolis, 1999), p. 282.

342 *Historical Atlas of East Central Europe*. A History of East Central Europe, Vol. I. Seattle, Wash.: University of Washington Press; and Toronto: University of Toronto Press, 1993, xiv and 219 p., 89 maps, 28 tables. Second revised and expanded edition, see item **581**. Third revised edition, see item **848**.

Reviewed:

Edward B. Cone in *Library Journal*, CXVIII, 19 (New York, 1993), p. 74.

Booklist, XC, 22 (Chicago, 1993), p. 777.

A. W. M. Gerrits in *NRC Handelsblad* (Rotterdam, Netherlands), March 26, 1994.

Newsletter of the Society for German-American Studies, XV, 1 (Northfield, Minn., 1994), p. 8.

The Bookwatch, XV, 4 (San Francisco, Calif., 1994), p. 8.

Elizabeth Shostak in *Wilson Library Bulletin*, LXVIII, 9 (Bronx, N. Y., 1994), p. 128.

The Bookseller, No. 4 (London, 1994), p. 33.

Shofar, XII, 2 (West Lafayette, Ind., 1994), p. 186.

Daniel Johnson in *The Times* (London), April 28, 1994, p. 38.

Angus Clarke in *The European* (London), April 29-May 5, 1994, "Élan," p. 13.

Christopher J. Walker in *Diplomat*, XLVIII (London, 1994), p. 27.

J. M. Alexander in *Choice*, XXXI, 10 (Middletown, Conn., 1994), p. 1558.

Tony Barber in *The Independent* (London), June 7, 1994.

Geographical: Royal Geographical Society Magazine, LXVI, 6 (London, 1994), p. 34.

Military Illustrated Past and Present, No. 73 (London, 1994), p 7.

Zev Ben-Shlomo in *Jewish Chronicle* (London), August 5, 1994, p. 22.

Bohdan S. Wynar in *American Reference Books Annual*, Vol. XXV (Englewood, Colo., 1994), pp. 214-215.

Iain Dickie in *Miniature Wargames and Military Hobbies* (Bournemouth, England, 1994), p.

Emil Niederhauser in *Századok*, CXXVIII (Budapest, 1994), pp. 780-783.

Neil Jordan in *LA [Library Association] Record*, XCVI, 8 (London, 1994), p. 451.

New Statesman and Society, VII [307] (London, 1994), p. 36.

Reference and Research Book News, IX (Portland, Oregon, 1994), p. 7.

Andrew Gregorovich in *Forum*, No. 90 (Scranton, Penn., 1994), p. 29.

Richard Mullen in *Contemporary Review*, CCLXV [1,544] (Surrey, England, 1994), pp. 167-168.

MultiCultural Review, III, 3 (Westport, Conn., 1994), p. 42.

Kurt W. Treptow in *Romanian Civilization*, III, 1 (Bucharest, 1994), pp. 128-131.

Susan V. Howard in *Reference Reviews*, VIII (Taunton, England, 1994), p. 8.

L'udovít Haraksim in *Historický časopis*, XLII, 4 (Bratislava, 1994), pp. 689-691.

Charles W. Ingrao in *International History Review*, XVI, 4 (Burnaby, B.C., 1994), pp. 856-857.

James Boxall in *Association of Canadian Map Libraries and Archives Bulletin*, No. 91 (Ottawa, 1994), pp. 35-36.

Antoni Mironowicz in *Białoruskie Zeszyty Historyczne*, II (Białystok, Poland, 1994), pp. 156-158.

Reference Book Review, XVI, 1 (Dallas, 1994).

Keith Sword in *Journal of Refugee Studies*, VII, 2-3 (Oxford, 1994), pp. 301-302.

Serge Keleher in *Religion, State and Society*, XXII, 4 (Oxford, 1994), pp. 419-420.

Bohuslav Litera in *Slovanský přehled*, LXXX, 4 (Prague, 1994), p. 404.

John-Paul Himka in *Journal of Ukrainian Studies*, XIX, 2 (Edmonton, 1994), pp. 99-101.

Murray Low in *SUC* [Society of Cartographers] *Bulletin*, XXVIII, 1 (Middlesex, England, 1994), pp. 51-52.

E. Sem. in *Český časopis historický*, XCII, 3 (Prague, 1994), p. 565.

John S. Hill in *Business Library Review*, XIX, 4 (Auburn, Ala., 1994), pp. 250-254.

R.H.S. [Robert H. Scott] in *College and Research Libraries*, LV, 5 (Chicago, 1994), pp. 421-422.

Ralph Hebden in *Geography*, LXXIX, 4 [345] (Sheffield, England, 1994), p. 374.

Hans B. Neumann in *Canadian Book Review Annual 1993* (Toronto, 1994), pp. 64.

Darrick Danta in *Harvard Ukrainian Studies*, XVIII, 3-4 (Cambridge, Mass., 1994), pp. 377-378.

Spyridon Sfetas in *Balkan Studies*, XXXV, 1 (Salonika, Greece, 1994), pp. 186-187.

T.D.B. in *Army Quarterly and Defence Journal*, CXXV, 1 (Tavistock, England, 1995), pp. 119-120.

László Veszprémy in *Hadtörténelmi közlemények*, CVIII, 1 (Budapest, 1995), pp. 209-210.

John S. Micgiel in *Slavic Review*, LIV, 2 (Philadelphia, 1995), pp. 504-505.

Anton Miranovich in *Belaruski histarychny ahliad*, II, 1 (Mensk, Belarus, 1995), pp. 100-104.

Rado L. Lencek in *Slovene Studies*, XV, 1-2 [1993] (Bloomington, Ind., 1995), pp. 191-196.

Vladimir I. Kusin in *Slavonica*, I, 2 (Keele, England, 1994-95), pp. 108-109.

Vlad Shurkin in *WAML* [Western Association of Map Libraries] *Informational Bulletin*, XXVI, 1-2 (Provo, Utah, 1994-95), pp.18-20.

Mehrdad Izady in *International Journal of Kurdish Studies*, VIII, 1-2 (Brooklyn, N.Y., 1995), pp. 127-130.

Paths to the Past: North San Diego County Genealogical Society, XXIV, 8 (Carlsbad, Calif., 1995), p.5.

Albert J. Schmidt in *Journal of Historical Geography*, XXI, 2 (London, 1995), pp. 221-222.

Andre Gunder Frank in *Political Geography*, XIV 8 (Oxford, 1995), p. 711.

Hans Renner in *Tijdschrift voor Geschiedenis*, CVIII, 3 (Groningen, Netherlands, 1995), pp. 436-437.

Stefan Troebst in *Südost-Forschungen*, LIV (Munich, 1995), pp. 279-280.

Hö. [Edgar Hösch] in *Jahrbücher für Geschichte Osteropas*, XLIII, 4 (Stuttgart, 1995), pp. 607-608.

H.R. in *Siebenbürgische Semesterblätter*, IX (Gundelsheim, Germany, 1995), pp. 90-91.

Mladen Klemenčić in *Boundary and Security Bulletin*, II, 4 (Durham, England, 1995), p. 101.

Harald Heppner in *Österreichische Osthefte*, XXXVII 3 (Vienna, 1995), p. 799.

William E. Wright in *Austrian History Yearbook*, XXVII (Minneapolis, Minn., 1996), pp. 319-320.

Andrew Dawson in *Geographical Journal*, CLXII, 1 (London, 1996), pp. 94-95.

Journal of Economic Literature, XXXIV, 1 (Nashville, 1996), p. 254.

Algirdas Jakubčionis in *Naujasis židinys*, No. 6 (Vilnius, 1996), pp. 433-434.

Martyn Rady in *Slavonic and East European Review*, LXXIV, 3 (London, 1996), pp. 534-535.

AB Bookman's Weekly, XCVII, 22 (Clifton, N.J., 1996), pp. 2120-2122.

Mladen Klemenčić in *Vjesnik* (Zagreb), November 28, 1996, p. 18.

Ivan Pop in *Slavianovedenie*, XXXII, 4 (Moscow, 1996), pp. 111-112.

Donald W. Buckwalter in *Professional Geographer*, XLVIII, 4 (Washington, D.C., 1996), pp. 474-475.

William H. Berentsen in *Canadian-American Slavic Studies*, XXX, 2-4 (Vancouver, B.C., 1996), pp. 447-448.

André van de Walle in *Contactblad, Oost-Europa*, No. 33 (Groningen, Netherlands, 1997), pp. 97-98.

Philip Longworth in *Polin: Studies in Polish Jewry*, X (London and Portland, Oregon, 1997), pp. 379-381.

H. Kandler in *HOMO*, XLVIII, 2 (Jena, Germany, 1997), p. 201.

Constantin Simon in *Orientalia Christiana Periodica*, LXIII, 1 (Rome, 1997), pp. 214-216.

Martin Schulze Wessel in *Bohemia*, XXXVIII, 2 (Munich, 1997), pp. 401-402.

Lawrence Klippenstein in *The Mennonite Historian*, XXXIII, 1 (Winnipeg, 1997), pp. 12-13.

George J. Demko in *Slovakia*, XXXVI [66-67] (Passaic, N.J., 1998), pp. 119-120.

Hermina G. B. Anghelescu in *Libraries and Culture*, XXXIII, 2 (Austin, Texas, 1998), pp. 219-221.

[Victor H. Mair] in *Sino-Platonic Papers*, No. 90 (Philadelphia, 1999), pp. 30-32.

Lidija Čehulić in *Politička misao*, XXXVI, 1 (Zagreb, 1999), pp. 258-260.

343 "Zrod novoho naroda, abo nachertania staroho problemu?" *Rusyn*, III, 4 (Prešov, 1993), pp. 1-3. Excerpts of item **314** translated into Rusyn by Anna Plishkova.

344 "The Ukrainian Question Between Poland and Czechoslovakia: The Lemko Rusyn Republic (1918-1920) and Political Thought in Western Rus'-Ukraine." *Nationalities Papers*, XXI, 2 (New York, 1993), pp. 95-105. Reprinted in item **535**, pp. 303-315.

345 "Vedecký seminář o kodifikaci rusínského jazyka," *Slovanský přehled*, LXXIX, 2 (Prague, 1993), pp. 232-233. Translation of item **306** into Czech.

346 "Carpatho-Rusyns: Their Current Status and Future Perspectives," *Slovakia*, XXXV (West Paterson, N.J., 1991-92 [1993]), pp. 36-57. Revised version of item **300**.

347 "Carpatho-Rusyns: Their Current Status and Future Perspectives,"

Carpatho-Rusyn American, XVI, 2 (Pittsburgh, Pa., 1993), pp. 4-9. Revised and slightly abridged version of item **300**.

348 "A Reply," *ibid.*, XVI, 4 (1993), pp. 6-9. Translation of item **313** into English.

349 Review of Evyatar Friesel, *Atlas of Modern Jewish History*, in *Studies in Contemporary Jewry*, XI (New York and Oxford, 1993), pp. 265- 267.

350 "Znanstveni seminar o kodifikaciji rusinskega jezika," *Slavistična revija*, XLI, 2 (Ljubljana, 1993), pp. 270-272. Translation of item **306** into Slovenian by Mira Hladnik.

351 "Preface." In Andrew Gregorovich, compiler. *A Bibliography of Canada's Peoples: Supplement I, 1972-1979*. Toronto: Multicultural History Society of Ontario, 1993, pp. ix-xiii.

352 "Ambasadorovi Levkovi Luk"ianenku Ambasada Ukraïny," *Novyi shliakh* (Toronto), August 7-14, 1993. Reprinted in *Podkarpats'ka Rus'* (Uzhhorod, Ukraine), January 27, 1994, p. 4.

353 "Podkarpatští Rusíni—jejich status a perspektivy," *Podkarpatská Rus*, IV, 4 (Prague, 1993), p. 5. Excerpt of item **300** translated into Czech.

1994

354 *The End of the Nation-State?: The Revolution of 1989 and the Future of Europe/La fin des états-nations?: La révolution de 1989 et le sort de l'Europe.* Royal Military College of Canada Distinguished Speakers Series in Political Geography. Kingston, v Ont.: Kashtan Press, 1994, 32 p. English-language version reprinted Kingston, Ont.: Kashtan Press, 1994, 32 p. Reprinted in item **365** and revised in item **535**, pp. 306-320.

355 "Foreword." In Lubomyr Luciuk, *Welcome to Absurdistan: Ukraine, the Soviet Disunion and the West*. Kingston, Ont.: Kashtan Press, 1994, p. iv. Reprinted 1995, p. iii.

356 "Alexis G. Toth (1853-1909)," *Carpatho-Rusyn American*, XVII, 1 (Pittsburgh, Pa., 1994), p. 3. [Philip Michaels]

357 "Safe Haven Exhibition—Opening Remarks," *Newsletter— Multicultural History Society of Ontario*, VII, 2 (Toronto, Ont., 1994), p. 3.

358 "Carpatho-Rusyns." In *Encyclopedia of World Cultures*, Vol. VI: *Russia and Eurasia/China*, ed. Paul Friedrich and Norma Diamond. Boston: G. K. Hall, 1994, pp. 69-71.

359 "Iak Rusyns'ku obrodu otsin'uie svit," *Narodnŷ novynkŷ* (Prešov, Slovakia), May 11, 1994, p. 4.

360 "Interviu zoz Profesorom Pavlom Robertom Magochiiom," *Shvetlosts*, XXXII, 1 (Novi Sad, 1994), pp. 26-42. Interview conducted by Oles Mushynka. Translation of item **328** into Vojvodinian Rusyn by Mikhailo Feisa.

361 "Karpato-rusyns'kí Amerychane/Carpatho-Rusyn Americans," *Rusyn*, IV, 2 (Prešov, 1994), pp. 27-28.

362 "Since the Revolution of 1989," *Carpatho-Rusyn American*, XVII, 2, 3 and 4 (Pittsburgh, Pa., 1994), pp. 11, 11 and 10.

363 "Recent Events," *ibid.*, XVII, 2, 3 and 4 (1994), pp. 11, 10 and 10-11.

364 "Religion and the Nationality Question in the Ukraine." In Valeria Heuberger et al., eds. *Nationen, Nationalitäten, Minderheiten*. Schriftenreihe des Österreichischen Ost- und Südosteuropa-Intstituts, Vol. XXII. Vienna and Munich.: Verlag für Geschichte und Politik/R. Oldenburg Verlag, 1994, pp. 232-235.

365 "The End of the Nation-State?: The Revolution of 1989 and the National Minorities of East Central Europe," *ibid.*, pp. 259-268.

366 "Le rôle de Sigismond de Luxembourg dans l'histoire des Rusines."

In Josef Macek, Ernő Marosi, and Ferdinand Seibt, eds. *Sigismund von Luxembourg: Kaiser und König in Mitteleuropa 1387-1437*. Warendorf, Germany: Fahlbusch Verlag, 1994, pp. 83-86.

367 "Nazva 'Karpats'kŷ rusynŷ'/The Name 'Carpatho-Rusyn'," *Rusyn*, IV, 3 (Prešov, 1994), p. 28.

368 "The Carpatho-Rusyn Research Center and Czecho-Slovakia," *Carpatho-Rusyn American*, XVII, 3 (Pittsburgh, Pa., 1994), pp. 8-9.

369 "Jews in Subcarpathian Rus' Today," *ibid.*, p. 7. [unsigned]

370 "Remarks at the Canadian Macedonian Human Rights Committee," *Human Rights Monitor Newsletter*, I, 1 (Toronto, 1994), p. 4.

371 "Paul Magocsi on Scholarly and Ethnic Diversity," *Austrian Studies Newsletter*, VI, 3 (Minneapolis, Minn., 1994), pp. 12-13. Interview conducted by Daniel Pinkerton.

372 *Formuvannia natsional'noï samosvidomosti: Pidkarpats'ka Rus' (1848-1948)*. Polychka Karpats'koho kraiu, No. 3-6. Uzhhorod: Karpats'kyi krai, 1994, 296 p., 6 tables. Translation of item **42** into Ukrainian.

Reviewed:
Ihor Kercha in *Edinstvo-plius* (Uzhhorod), October 22, 1994.
I. Iuryk in *Rusyns'ka hazeta* (Chust), January 3, 1995, p. 4.
Mykhailo Almashii in *Novyny Zakarpattia* (Užhorod), February 9, 1995, p. 6. Reprinted in Mykhayl Almashii, *Evoliutsiia svitozora*. Uzhhorod: Karpats'ka vezha, 2016, pp. 435-437.
AP [Agáta Pilátová] in *Podkarpatská Rus*, IV, 1 (Prague, 1995), p. 2.
Luca Calvi in *Annali di Ca'Foscari*, XXXV, 1-2 (Venice, 1996), pp. 504-511.
Emil Niederhauser in *Századok*, CXXX, 1 (Budapest, 1996), pp. 192-193.

373 *Rusynŷ na Slovens'ku/Rusíni na Slovensku*. Prešov: Rusyns'ka obroda, 1994, 214 p., 6 maps, 38 illustrations. Translation of item **341** into Rusyn by Anna Plishkova and into Slovak by Elena Jakešová.

Reviewed:

A.P. [Anna Plishkova] in *Narodnŷ novynkŷ* (Prešov), November 2, 1994, pp. 3-4.

István Udvari in *Klió*, IV, 2 (Nyíregyháza, 1995), pp. 56-58. Reprinted in István Udvari, *Tallózások ukrán, ruszin és szlovák könyvek körében.* Nyíregyháza, 1995, pp. 237-242, and *Studia Russica*, XVI (Budapest, 1997), pp. 355-358.

Ruske slovo (Novi Sad), January 26, 1996, p. 12.

G. Székely in *Historický časopis*, XLIX, 4 (Bratislava, 2001), pp. 709-710. Translation into Rusyn: *Narodnŷ novynkŷ* (Prešov), 30, VI, 2004, p.1— reprinted in Vasyl' Iabur and Anna Plishkova, *Rusyn'skŷi iazŷk pro 3. klasu serednikh shkol.* Prešov: Rusyn i Narodnŷ novynkŷ, 2004, pp. 49-50.

374 *Our People: Carpatho-Rusyns and Their Descendants in North America.* Third revised edition. Toronto, Ontario: Multicultural History Society of Ontario, 1994, xii and 220 p., 4 maps, 101 illustrations. Fourth revised and expanded edition, see item **623**.

Reviewed:

Teresa Tickle Mahowald in *Ethnic Forum*, XV, 1-2 (Kent, Ohio, 1995), pp. 226-227.

Alberta History, no. 2 (Edmonton, 1995), p. 27.

Bishop Roman in *Orthodox Catholic Voice*, XIII, 4-5 (Akron, Ohio, 1995), p. 22.

F. Michael Perko in *Church History*, LXV, 2 (Chicago, 1996), p. 347.

M. J. Okenfuss in *Jahrbücher für Geschichte Osteuropas*, XLIV, 2 (Wiesbaden, 1996), pp. 308-309.

Fred Stambrook in *Slavic Review*, LV, 3 (Cambridge, Mass., 1996), pp. 680-681.

Gregory Woolfenden in *Eastern Churches Journal*, III, 3 (Fairfax, Va., 1996), p. 161.

Thomas F. Sable in *Diakonia*, XXIX, 1 (Scranton, Pa., 1996), p. 74.

Carol Skalnik Leff in *Canadian Review of Studies in Nationalism*, XXIV, 1-2 (Charlottetown, Prince Edward Is., 1997), pp. 150-151.

N.F. Dreisziger in *Histoire sociale/Social History*, XXX [60] (Ottawa, 1997), pp. 479-481.

A. Karger in *Osteuropa*, XLVIII, 7 (Stuttgart, 1998), p. 746.

R. F. Taft in *Orientalia Christiana Periodica*, LXV, 1 (Rome, 1999), p. 208.

375 Review of George O. Liber, *Soviet Nationality Policy, Urban Growth, and Identity Change in the Ukrainian SSR, 1923-1934*, in *Canadian Journal of History*, XXIX (Saskatoon, Sask., 1994), pp. 598-600.

376 "Karpatsko-rusínské výskumne centrum a Československo," *Podkarpatská Rus*, IV, 4 (Prague, 1994), pp. 4 and 7. Translation of item **368** into Slovak by L'ubica Babotová.

377 *Halychyna: istorychni ese.* L'viv: [Svit], 1994, 322 p. Translation of item **579** into Ukrainian.

Reviewed:
Emil Niederhauser in *Századok,* CXXX, 5 (Budapest, 1996), pp. 1338-1340.
Luca Calvi in *Ricerche Slavistiche*, XLIII (Rome, 1996), pp. 659-665.
M.T. [Miroslav Tejchman] in *Slovanský přehled*, LXXXII, 3-4 (Prague, 1996), p. 338.
Iaroslav Hrytsak in *Journal of Ukrainian Studies*, XXII, 1-2 (Edmonton, 1997), pp. 167-168.

378 "Rusyn Renaissance Society (Rusyns'ka Obroda)," *Carpatho-Rusyn American*, XVII, 4 (Pittsburgh, Pa., 1994), pp. 4-7.

379 Review of David Little, *Ukraine: The Legacy of Intolerance*, in *Slavic Review*, LIII, 4 (Stanford, Calif., 1994), pp. 1138-1140.

380 Series editor: Aleksander Dukhnovych, *Virtue is More Important than Riches*. Translated with an introduction by Elaine Rusinko. Classics of Carpatho-Rusyn Scholarship, Vol. VII. New York: Columbia University Press/East European Monographs, 1994, xliv, 85 p.

Reviewed:
David Saunders in *Slavonic and East European Review*, LXXV, 1 (London, 1997), p. 130.
Larissa Onyshkevych and L'ubica Babotová in *Ukrainian Quarterly*, LIII, 1-2 (New York, 1997), pp. 109-111.

381 Review of Keith P. Dyrud, *The Quest for the Rusyn Soul*, in *Catholic Historical Review*, LXXX, 1 (Washington, D.C., 1994), pp. 125-127.

382 "Koniec Československa: rusínska perspektíva." In *Idea Československa a střední Evropa*. Brno: Doplněk, 1994, pp. 220-223.

1995

383 Review of Michael F. Hamm, *Kiev: A Portrait, 1800-1917*, in *American Historical Review*, C, 2 (Washington, D. C., 1995), pp. 556- 557.

384 "Pozdravní slova kodifikatsiï," *Narodnŷ novynkŷ* (Prešov), February 8, 1995, p. 2. Translation of item **394** into Rusyn.

385 "Dilo Rusyniv progresuie," *Narodnŷ novynkŷ* (Prešov), February 15, 1995, p. 1.

386 "K uzákoneniu rusínskeho spisovného jazyka na Slovensku," *Pravda* (Bratislava), February 17, 1995. Excerpts of item **394** into Slovak.

387 "Rusinske iazichne pitanie znova postavene," *Shvetlosts*, XXXIII, 1 (Novi Sad, 1995), pp. 117-134. Shorter version of item **436** translated into Vojvodinian Rusyn by Helena Medješi.

Reviewed:
Mikhailo Kovach, "Popatrunki vel'kikh priiatel'okh rusnatsokh na ruski iazik." In Iuliian Tamash and Slavko Sabo, eds. *Rusnatsi/Rusini*. Novi Sad: Filozofski fakultet, Katedra za rusinski jezik književnost, 1996, pp. 199-209.

388 *Carpatho-Rusyns*. Orwell, Vermont: Carpatho-Rusyn Research Center, 1995, 24 p. Revised second edition. Ocala, Florida: Carpatho-Rusyn Research Center, 1997, 24 p. Excerpts reprinted in item **535**, pp. 3-11. Third revised and expanded edition. Ocala, Florida: Carpatho-Rusyn Research Center, 2004, 32 p. Fourth revised edition, 2012, 34 p. Fifth revised edition, 2020, 32 p.

389 *Karpats'ki rusyny*. Prešov, Slovakia: Karpats'ko-rusyns'kyi doslidnyts'kyi tsentr, 1995, 24 p. Translation of item **388** into Ukrainian by Iryna Koropenko. Reprinted in *Rusnats'kyi svit*, Vol. I, pt. 1 (Uzhhorod, 1999), pp. 54-67.

Reviewed:
M. Rusnak in *Karpats'ka Ukraïna* (Uzhhorod, Ukraine), June 20, 1995, p. 1. Reprinted in *Nove zhyttia* (Prešov, Slovakia), September 2, 1995, p. 5.

390 *Karpatskí Rusíni*. Prešov, Slovakia: Karpatorusínske výskumné centrum, 1995, 24 p. Revised second edition, 2000. Third revised and expanded edition, 2006, 32 p. Translation of item **388** into Slovak by L'ubica Babotová.

Reviewed:
Jan Časlavka in *Podkarpatská Rus*, V, 3 (Prague, 1995), p. 2.

391 *Karpato-Rusini/Karpato-Rusini/Carpatho-Rusyns*. Novi Sad: Ruske slovo, 1995, 64 p. Translation of item 388 into Vojvodinian Rusyn by Gabrijela Hudak, into Serbian by Frederika Pavlovich, followed by English original.

Reviewed:
Glas/Holos Soiuzu, No.1 (Novi Sad, 1997), pp. 23-24.
I. H. Kovachevich in *Ruske slovo* (Novi Sad, Yugoslavia), August 4, 1995, p. 7.
Roman Miz in *Dzvoni*, II, 6 (Novi Sad, Yugoslavia, 1995), p. 17.

392 "A ruszinok 'nagykövete'," *Kelet-Magyarország* (Nyíregyháza, Hungary), May 27, 1995, p. 11. Interview by Csilla Páll.

393 "A New Slavic Language is Born," *Carpatho-Rusyn American*, XVIII, 1 (Fairfax, Virginia, 1995), pp. 4-5; *Slovak Studies Association Newsletter*, XVIII, 1 (Urbana, Ill., 1995), pp. 14-16; *Austrian Studies Newsletter*, VII, 3 (Minneapolis, 1995), p. 17; *Europa Ethnica*, LII, 2- 3 (Vienna, 1995), pp. 105-107; *Carpatho-Rus'* (Yonkers, N.Y.), September 29, 1995, p. 3, *East European Politics and Societies*, IX, 3 (Berkeley, Calif., 1995), pp. 534-537; *Association internationale pour la défense des langues menacées— magazine de presse et d'information*, bulletin de décembre (Liège, Belgium, 1995), pp. 17- 21; *Revue des études slaves*, LXVII, 1 (Paris, 1995), pp. 237-239; *Österreichische Osthefte*, XXXVII, 3 (Vienna, 1995), pp. 779-782; *Canadian Review of Studies in Nationalism*, XXII, 1-2 (Charlottetown, Prince Edward Is., 1995), pp. 195-196; *Contact Bulletin of the European Bureau for Lesser Used Languages*, XII, 3 (Baile Átha Cliath, Ireland, 1995), p. 1; *Slavonica*, II, 1 (Keele, England, 1995-96), pp. 131-133; *Slavia Orientalis*, XIV, 2 (Warsaw, 1996), pp. 287-289.

Reviewed:
V.M. [Vasyl Markus] in *Novyi shliakh* (Toronto), June 24, 1995, pp. 8-9.

394 "Greetings [from the C-RRC] on the Codification of the Rusyn Language in Slovakia," *ibid.*, p. 5.

395 "Codification: Another Viewpoint," *ibid.*, pp. 7-8. [unsigned]

396 "Recent Events," *ibid.*, XVIII, 1, 2, 3 (1995), pp. 8, 9, 10-11. [unsigned]

397 "Since the Revolution of 1989," *ibid.*, XVIII, 1, 2, 3 (1995), pp. 9, 9, 9-10. [unsigned]

398 "The Carpatho-Rusyns: Geography, Economy, and Religion," *Carpatho-Rusyn American*, XVIII, 2 (Fairfax, Virginia, 1995), pp. 7- 8.

399 "Recent Publications in English About Carpatho-Rusyns, 1986-1987," *ibid.*, p. 11.

400 "A New Slavic Language for a Distinct Slavic People," *ASN* [Association for the Study of Nationalities] *Analysis of Current Events*, VI, 9 (New York, 1995), pp. 5-6; reprinted in *Kalendár-Almanac 1996*. Pittsburgh, Pa.: National Slovak Society of the USA, 1996, pp. 71-72.

401 "Carpatho-Rusyn Americans." In Judy Galens, Anna Sheets, and Robyn V. Young, eds. *Gale Encyclopedia of Multicultural America*, Vol. I (New York, 1995), pp. 252-261. Reprinted in second edition. Edited by Jeffrey Lehman. Farmington Hills, Mich.: Gale Group, 2000, pp. 345-354, and in item **535**, pp. 379-393.

402 "Russian Americans." In *ibid.*, Vol. II, pp. 1159-1172. Reprinted in second edition, Vol. III, pp. 1520-1533.

403 "Bretons." In Kenneth T. Jackson, ed. *Encyclopedia of New York City*. New Haven, Conn. and London: Yale University Press, 1995, p. 136.

404 "Carpatho-Rusyns." In *ibid.*, p. 182.

405 "Kerensky, Alexander (Feodorovich)." In *ibid.*, p. 634.

406 "Russians." In *ibid.*, pp. 1029-1030.

407 "Tsy rusynŷ pryhotovlenŷ do novoho s'vita?" *Besida*, VII, 3-4 (Krynica and Legnica, Poland, 1995), pp. 13 and 16. Translation of item **412** into Lemko Rusyn.

408 "Zrodil sa nový slovanský jazyk," *Československý týdeník* (Glen Cove, N.Y.), June 15, 1995, p. 9; *Slovanský přehled*, LXXXI, 2 (Prague, 1995), pp. 159-160. Translation of item **393** into Slovak by L'ubica Babotová.

409 "Profesor dr Robert Pavel Magochi o trokh otrimanikh kongresokh rusnatsokh shveta" (interview), *Ruske slovo* (Novi Sad, Yugoslavia), June 15, 1995, p. 31.

410 "Interpelatsiia proty diskriminatsiï rusyniv," *Narodnŷ novynkŷ* (Prešov), October 18, 1995, pp. 1 and 3. [unsigned]. Translation of item **412** into Rusyn.

411 "Podkarpatska literatura priselientsokh," *Literaturne slovo*, No. 11—*Ruske slovo* (Novi Sad), November 24, 1995, p. 18. Translation of excerpts of item **49** into Vojvodinian Rusyn by Nataliia Dudash.

412 "An Inquiry to the Present Government of Slovakia Concerning National Discrimination Against Rusyns, *Carpatho-Rusyn American*, XVIII, 3 (Fairfax, Va., 1995), pp. 4-5. [unsigned]

413 "Are Rusyns Ready to Enter the New World?," *ibid.*, pp. 6-7. Reprinted in item **535**, pp. 287-291.

414 "The Carpatho-Rusyns: Language, Identity, and Culture," *ibid.*, pp. 8- 9.

415 "Rusyns'ke pytannia," *Politychna dumka*, III, 2-3 (Kyiv, 1995), pp. 105-115. Translation of item **300** into Ukrainian by Iryna Koropenko.

Reviewed:
Mai Panchuk, "Politychne rusynstvo v Ukraïni," in *Politychna dumka*, III, 2-3 (Kyiv, 1995), pp. 116-123.
I. Ia. [Ivan Iatskanyn] in *Nove zhyttia* (Prešov), March 29, 1996, pp. 1 and 3.

416 "The Hungarians in Transcarpathia (Subcarpathian Rus')," *A Kárpátaljai Magyar Tudományos Társaság Közlemenyei*, II (Uzhhorod, 1995), pp. 40-51.

417 "Emylijan Bokšaj, 1889-1976," *Carpatho-Rusyn American*, XVIII, 4 (Fairfax, Va., 1995), p. 3. [Philip Michaels]

418 "The Carpatho-Rusyns: History." *ibid.*, pp. 6-7; XIX, 1 and 2 (1996), pp. 4-5 and 4-6. Reprinted in item **535**, pp. 11-25.

419 "Rodil se je novi slovanski jezik," *Slavistična revija*, XLIII, 3 (Ljubljana, 1995), pp. 408-410. Translation of item **393** into Slovenian.

1996

420 "Rusini rovnopravni hrazhdanie ziedinienei Evropi: diskusiia Liubomira Mediesha zoz profesorom Pavlom R. Magochiiom." In Diura Pap, ed. *Ruski kalendar 1996*. Novi Sad: Ruske slovo, 1996, pp. 50-55. Reprinted in Liubomir Medieshi, *Ruska traditsiia*. Novi Sad: Druzhtvo za ruski iazik, literaturu i kulturu, 2007, pp. 73-82.

421 "Language and National Survival," *Jahrbücher für Geschichte Osteuropas*, XLIV, 1 (Wiesbaden, 1996), pp. 83-85.

422 "The Rusyn Language Question Revisited," *International Journal of the Sociology of Language*, No. 120 (Berlin and New York, 1996), pp. 63-84.

423 *Rusíni a jejich vlast*. Edice Podkarpatská Rus, No. 13. Prague: Společnost přátel Podkarpatské Rusi, 1996, 70 p.

424 "Adaptation without Assimilation: The Genius of Greek Catholic Eparchy of Mukachevo," *Eastern Catholic Life* (West Paterson, N.J.), May 19 and June 2, 1996, pp. 4-6 and 9-10.

425 "Adaptatsiia bez asimilatsiï: genialnost' grekokatolyts'koï ieparkhiï Mukacheva," *Rusyn*, VI, 3-4 (Prešov, Slovakia, 1996), pp. 13-14. Translation of item **424** into Rusyn.

426 "Prystosovanstvo bez asymiliatsiï," *Karpats'kyi krai*, VI, 1-4 (Uzhhorod, Ukraine, 1996), pp. 11-12. Translation of excerpts of item **424** into Ukrainian by Iryna Koropenko.

427 *A ruszinok.* Budapest: Magyarországi Ruszinok Szervezete, 1996, 24 p. Translation of item **388** into Hungarian by János Borisz.

428 *Rusini Karpaccy.* [Orwell, Vermont]: Carpatho-Rusyn Research Center, 1996, 24 p. Translation of item **388** into Polish by Helena Duć-Fajfer.

429 "Recent Publications in English About Carpatho-Rusyns, 1988," *Carpatho-Rusyn American*, XIX, 1 (Fairfax, Va., 1996), p. 11.

430 "Ukrainian Scholars Recognize Rusins," *Trembita*, VIII, 3 (Minneapolis, Minn., 1996), p. 4 [unsigned]

431 Translation from Rusyn into English of "The World Congress of Rusyns: An Interview with the Chairman," *Carpatho-Rusyn American*, XIX, 2 (Fairfax, Va. 1996), pp. 7-8. [unsigned]

432 "Update on the Rusyn Language," *ibid.*, XIX, 2, pp. 8-9.

433 "Since the Revolution of 1989," *ibid.*, XIX, 2, 3 (1996), pp. 10-11, 10- 11. [unsigned]

434 "Recent [Carpatho-Rusyn] Events," *ibid.*, XIX, 2, 3 (1996), pp. 11, 9. [unsigned]

435 *A New Slavic Language is Born: The Rusyn Literary Language of Slovakia/Zrodil sa nový slovanský jazyk: Rusínsky spisovný jazyk na Slovensku*, editor. Introduction by Nikita I. Tolstoj. Classics of Carpatho-Rusyn Scholarship, Vol. VIII. New York: Columbia University Press/East European Monographs, 1996, xvi and 96 p.

xiv and 68 p., 15 illustrations.

Reviewed:

M.T. [Miroslav Tejchman] in *Slovanský přehled*, LXXXIII, 4 (Prague, 1997), pp. 413-414.

Mikhail Kapral' in *Studia Slavica Hungarica*, XLII (Budapest, 1997), pp. 193-195.

Wiesław Witkowski in *Slavia Orietnalis*, XLVI, 3 (Cracow, 1997), pp. 499-501.

Grace E. Fielder in *Slavic and East European Journal*, XLII, 2 (Tucson, Ariz., 1998), pp. 347-348.

David Short in *Slavonic and East European Review*, LXXVI, 1 (London, 1998), pp. 120-121.

Michael Moser in *Wiener slawistisches Jahrbuch,* XLIV (Vienna, 1998), pp. 225-229.

L'udovít Haraksim in *Historický časopis*, XLVI, 2 (Bratislava, 1998), pp. 339-340.

T. Mills Kelly in *Austrian History Yearbook*, XXX (Minneapolis, 1999), pp. 311-313.

Catherine V. Chvany in *Language in Society*, XXVIII, 4 (Cambridge, 1999), pp. 621-624.

Kerstin S. Jobst in *Jahrbücher für Geschichte Osteuropas*, XLVII, 4 (Stuttgart, 1999), pp. 611-612.

Bertalan Pusztai in *Acta Ethnographica Hungarica*, XLV, 3-4 (Budapest, 2000), pp. 443-444.

T. R. Carlton in *Canadian Slavonic Papers,* XLIV, 3-4 (Edmonton, 2002), pp. 290-292.

436 "The Rusyn Language Question Revisited." In *ibid.*, pp. 19-47. Reprinted in item **535**, pp. 86-111.

437 "Rusínska jazyková otázka znovu nastolená." In *ibid.*, pp. 15-40. Translation of item **436** into Slovak by L'ubica Babotová.

438 *Carpatho-Rusyn Settlement at the Outset of the 20th Century with Additional Data from 1881 and 1806 / Rozselenia karpat'skikh rusyniv na zachatku XX stolitia z dalshymy dannŷmy z 1881-ho i 1806-ho roku: Map and Placename Index.* [Orwell, Vermont]: Carpatho-Rusyn Research Center, 1996. Second revised edition, 1998. Third revised edition, 2011.

Reviewed:
Liubomir Medieshi in *Ruske slovo* (Novi Sad), May 10, 1996, p. 12.
Mykola Mushynka, "Skil'ky nas bulo pered 190 rokamy?," in *Nove zhyttia*, (Prešov), June 7, 1996, p. 6.
Volodimir Fedinisinec in *Kárpáti igaz szó* (Uzhhorod), June 8, 1996.
László Sasvári, "Térképkiegészítés," in *Rusynskŷi zhŷvot* (Budapest), May 8, 1997, p. 2.
Paul J. Best in *Karpatska Rus'/Carpathian Rus'*, XCI, 1 (Higganum, Conn., 2020), p. 14.

439 "Karpats'ki motyvy kanads'koho profesora: interv'iu z komentarem," *Novyny Zakarpattia* (Uzhhorod), June 22, 1996, p. 14. Interview conducted by Iaroslav Iadlovs'kyi; commentary by Mykhailo Tyvodar.

440 "Another Slavic Language in the Making," *Slavonic and East European Review*, LXXIV, 4 (London, 1996), pp. 683-686.

441 "The Hungarians in Transcarpathia (Subcarpathian Rus')," *Nationalities Papers*, XXIV, 3 (Oxfordshire, England, 1996), pp. 525-534. Reprinted in item **416** and item **535**, pp. 290-302.

442 "Zrodil sa nový slovanský jazyk," *Slavia*, LXV, 1-2 (Prague, 1996), pp. 225-227. Translation of item **393** into Slovak.

443 "Promises, Promises: Chaos or Deception in Slovakia," *Carpatho-Rusyn American*, XIX, 3 (Fairfax, Va., 1996), p. 2. Reprinted in *Trembita*, IX, 1 (Minneapolis, 1997), p. 3.

444 "Volodymyr Fedynyshynets'," *ibid.*, p. 3. [Philip Michaels]

445 "Olena Šinali Mandyč," *Carpatho-Rusyn American*, XIX, 4 (Fairfield, Va., 1996), p. 3. [Philip Michaels]

446 Review of André Liebich and André Reszler, *L'Europe centrale et ses minorités: vers une solution europeéene?*, in *Slavic Review*, LV, 4 (Cambridge, Mass., 1996), p. 891.

447 "Universytets'ki kafedry ukraïnistyky v Ievropi ta Pivnichnii

Amerytsi," *Naukovyi visnyk Chernivets'koho universytetu*, No. 6-7: *istoriia* (Chernivtsi, 1996), pp. 266-274. Translation of item **508** into Ukrainian by Iryna Koropenko.

448 "Ukrainians and the Habsburgs." In Stefania Szlek Miller, ed. *Ukraine: Developing a Democratic Polity—Essays in Honour of Peter J. Potichnyj. Journal of Ukrainian Studies*, XXI, 1-2 (Toronto, 1996), pp. 55-66. Reprinted in item **579**, pp. 73-82.

449 Review of Orest Subtelny, *Ukraine: A History*, in *ibid.*, pp. 249-252.

450 "A ruszinok." In Ernő Eperessy, ed. *Tanulmányok a magyarországi bolgár, görög, lengyel, ormény, ruszin nemzetiség néprajából.* Budapest: Mikszáth kiadó, 1996, pp. 167-174.

451 "The Rusyns." In *ibid.*, pp. 176-183.

452 *A History of Ukraine.* Toronto: University of Toronto Press and Seattle: University of Washington Press, 1996, xxvi and 784 p., 42 maps, 19 tables. Second revised and expanded edition, see item **718**.

Reviewed:
Robert Legvold in *Foreign Affairs*, LXXVI, 2 (New York, 1997), p. 192.
Marta Dyczok in *The Ukrainian Weekly* (Jersey City, N.J.), February 2, 1997, p. 9.
Ljubomir Medješi in *Ruske slovo* (Novi Sad), March 28 and April 4, 1997, pp. 23 and 10 Republished in *Rusyn*, VII, 3-4 (Prešov, 1997), pp. 25-26.
ICCEES *International Newsletter*, No. 38 (Melbourne, Australia, 1997), p. 6.
Nestor Gula in *Zdorov* (Toronto), spring 1997.
Steve Pona in *Winnipeg Free Press* (Winnipeg), March 23, 1997 and in *Sunday Free Press* (Brandon, Manitoba), March 23, 1997.
Reference and Research Book News, XII (Portland, Oregon, 1997).
Volodymyr Fedynyshynets' in *Rio-inform* (Uzhhorod, Ukraine), July 22, 1997.
Journal of Economic Literature, XXXV, 3 (Pittsburgh, 1997), pp. 1504-1505.
G.E. Snow in *Choice*, XXXIV (Middletown, Conn., 1997), p. 189.
Jean-Bernard Dupont-Melnyczenko in *Revue des études slaves*, LXIX, 3 (Paris, 1997), pp. 468-469.
Virginia Quarterly Review, LXXIII, 3 (Charlottesville, Va., 1997), p. 79.
Dennis R. Papazian in *History: Reviews of New Books*, XXVI, 1 (Washington, D.C., 1997), p. 30.

Andreas Gottsman in *Österreichische Osthefte*, XXXIX, 2 (Vienna, 1997), pp. 314-316.

George Knysh in *The Ukrainian Quarterly*, LIII, 3 (New York, 1997), pp. 268-273.

Nicholas V. Riasanovsky in *Journal of Ukrainian Studies*, XXII, 1-2 (Edmonton, 1997), pp. 165-166.

Andrew Wilson in *Europe-Asia Studies*, XLIX, 8 (Glasgow, 1997), pp. 1552-1554.

Thomas M. Prymak in *Forum*, No. 97 (Scranton, Pa., 1997), pp. 27, 30-31.

J. Jurijčuk in *Historický časopis*, XLV, 2 (Bratislava, 1997), pp. 352-353.

Emil Niederhauser in *Századok*, CXXXI, 6 (Budapest, 1997), pp. 1432-1434.

William J. Parente in *Diakonia*, XXX, 2-3 (Scranton, Penn., 1997), pp. 176-177.

Paul S. Pirie in *Slavic and East European Journal*, XLII, 2 (Tucson, Ariz., 1998), pp. 339-340.

Mark Raeff in *Novyi zhurnal*, No. 211 (New York, 1998), pp. 281-286.

Hans-Joachim Torke in *Historische Zeitschrift*, CCLXVI, 1 (Oldenbourg, Germany, 1998), pp. 138-140.

Andreas Kappeler in *Jahrbücher für Geschichte Osteuropas*, XLVI, 3 (Stuttgart, 1998), pp. 440-441.

Myroslav Shkandrij in *Canadian Book Review Annual 1997* (Toronto, 1998), pp. 305-306.

James Urry in *Journal of Mennonite Studies*, XVI (Winnipeg, 1998), pp. 265-268.

Andrew Sorokowski in *Austrian History Yearbook*, XXIX (Minneapolis, 1998), pp. 291-293.

Peter Galadza in *Logos*, XXXIX, 1 (Ottawa, 1998), pp. 133-135.

Ezra Mendelson in *Studies in Contemporary Jewry*, Vol. 14 (New York: Oxford University Press, 1998), pp. 294-297.

[Victor H. Mair] in *Sino-Platonic Papers*, No. 90 (Philadelphia, 1999), pp. 28-30.

Tadeusz Andrzej Olszański in *Więź*, XLII, 2 [484] (Warsaw, 1999), pp. 209-213.

Mark von Hagen in *Journal of Modern History*, LXXI, 1 (Chicago, 1999), pp. 257-259.

Fedir Myshanych in *Rusnats'kyi svit*, Vol. I, pt. 1 (Uzhhorod, 1999), pp. 145-157.

Michael F. Hamm in *Russian History/Histoire russe*, XXVI, 1 (Idyllwild, Calif., 1999), pp. 123-124.

Anna Veronika Wendland in *Zeitschrift für Ostmitteleuropa-Forschung*, XLIX, 1 (Marburg, 2000), pp. 130-132.

Taras Kuzio in *Nationalism and Ethnic Politics*, VI, 4 (London, 2000), pp. 106-109.
Yaroslav Hrytsak in *Slavic Review*, LX, 3 (Champaign, Ill., 2001), pp. 637-638.
Roman Solchanyk in *The Russian Review*, LXI, 4 (Columbus, Ohio, 2002), pp. 638-639.
K. Hoshovs'ka in *Ukraïna na mizhnarodnii areni u XX stolitti.* Uzhhorod: Patent, 2000, pp. 153-156.
M. V. Dmitriiev in *Canadian Slavonic Papers*, XLIV, 3-4 (Edmonton, 2002), pp. 287-290.
Volodymyr Potul'nyts'kyi in *Eidos: al'manakh teoriï ta istoriï istorychnoï nauky*, No. 1. Kyiv: Natsional'na akademiia nauk Ukraïny, Instytut istoriï Ukraïny, 2005, pp. 379-382.

1997

453 "Adaptation without Assimilation: The Genius of the Greek Catholic Eparchy of Mukachevo." In *Kalendár-Almanac 1997 of the National Slovak Society of the USA*. Pittsburgh, Pa.: National Slovak Society, 1997, pp. 61-64.

454 "Ivan Harajda (1905-1944)," *Carpatho-Rusyn American*, XX, 1 (Fairfax, Va., 1997), p. 3. [Philip Michaels]

455 "Stalinism or Tsarism in Present-Day Ukraine," *ibid.*, pp. 4-5. Also published in *A.I.D.L.C.M. [Association internationale pour la défense des langues et des cultures menacées] Bulletin de presse et d'information* (Liege, 1998), pp. 14-17. [Julian Galloway]

456 Translation from Rusyn of Jevhenij Župan, "The Humanitarian and Socioeconomic Situation in Subcarpathian Rus' Today," *ibid.*, pp. 7- 9. [unsigned]

457 Translation from Ukrainian of Mychajlo Tomčanij, "Grandfather's Memories." *ibid.*, p. 10. [unsigned]

458 "Publications in English about Carpatho-Rusyns, 1990 and 1991," *ibid.*, p. 11.

459 "Literatura kraianokh z Karpatskei Rusi." In Nataliia Dudash, ed. *Rusinski/ruski pisnï*. Novi Sad: Ruske slovo, 1997, pp. 235-241. Abridged translation of item **49** into Vojvodinian Rusyn by Nataliia Dudash.

460 "Rusynŷ sut' i budut'," *Narodnŷ novynkŷ* (Prešov), May 28, 1997, pp. 1-2. Translation of item **465** into Rusyn by Anna Plishkova.

461 "Chi rusini porikhtani za ukhod do novoho shveta?" In Mikhailo Varga, ed. *Zbornïk robotokh zoz Tretsoho Shvetovoho Kongresa Rusinoch (Rusnatsokh, Lemkokh)*. Ruski Kerestur, Yugoslavia: Ruska Matka, 1997, pp. 71-75. Translation of item **413** into Vojvodinian Rusyn by Ljubomir Medješi.

462 "Aktivnosts Naukovei komisiï Shvetovoho kongresa rusinokh." In *ibid.*, pp. 153-154.

463 "Rusinokh iest i budze: priznachki za IV Shvetovi kongres Rusinokh," *Rusynskŷi zhŷvot* (Budapest), June 5, 1997, pp. 2-3. Translation of item **465** into Vojvodinian Rusyn by Ljubomir Medješi.

464 "Preshli zme dalieku drahu," *Ruske slovo* (Novi Sad, Yugoslavia), June 6, 1997, p. 5. Excerpts of translation of item **463** into Vojvodinian Rusyn by Ljubomir Medješi.

465 "Rusyns Are, and Will Be: Remarks at the IV World Congress of Rusyns," *Carpatho-Rusyn American*, XX, 2 (Fairfax, Va. 1997), pp. 7-8. Reprinted in *Trembita*, IX, 2 (Minneapolis, 1997), pp. 13-15, and in item **536**, pp. 292-297.

466 "Aleksej L. Petrov (1859-1931)," *Carpatho-Rusyn American*, XX, 2 (Fairfax, Va., 1997), p. 3. [Philip Michaels] Reprinted in *Carpatho-Rus'* (Yonkers, N.Y.), October 23, 1998, p. 4.

467 Translation from Rusyn of Myron Sysak, "The Difference between Us," *ibid.*, pp. 4-5. [unsigned]

468 "Since the Revolution of 1989," *ibid.*, XX, 2 and 4 (1997), pp. 9 and 12-13. [unsigned]

469 "Recent [Carpatho-Rusyn] Events," *ibid.*, XX, 2 and 4 (1997), pp. 10 and 7. [unsigned]

470 "To barz vel'ki uspikh: o nainovshei antologiï ruskei poeziï," *Ruske slovo* (Novi Sad, Yugoslavia), June 27, 1997, p. 13. Interview conducted by M. Zazuliak.

471 "Oznacheni dosiahi rusinskei kulturi/Rusini realnosts dvatsetspershoho viku," *Ruske slovo*, July 27 and July 4, 1997, pp. 19 and 10. Translation of item **465** into Vojvodinian Rusyn by Helena Skuban and Ljubomir Medješi.

472 "Anketa na IV. Svitovíi kongres Rusyniv v Budapeshti," *Rusyn* VII, 3-4 (Prešov, 1997), p. 2.

473 "Prystosuvannia bez asymiliatsiï: henial'nist' hreko-katolyts'koï ieparkhiï Mukacheva." In *Uzhhorods'kii Uniï—350 rokiv: materialy mizhnarodnykh naukovykh konferentsiï, Uzhhorod, kviten' 1996 r.* Uzhhorod: Uzhhorods'kyi derzhavnyi universytet,1997, pp. 72-77. Translation of item **424** into Ukrainian by Iryna Koropenko. Reprinted in *Kovcheh: naukovyi zbirnyk iz tserkovnoï istoriï,* IV (L'viv, 2003), pp. 162-169.

474 "Une nouvelle nationalité slave: les Ruthènes de l'Europe du centre-est," *Revue des études slaves*, LXIX, 3 (Paris, 1997), pp. 417-428.

475 Review of Peter Faessler et al, eds., *Lemberg—Lwow—Lviv: Eine Stadt im Schnittpunkt europäischer Kulturen*, in *Polin: Studies in Polish Jewry*, Vol. X (London and Portland, Oregon, 1997), pp. 360-362.

476 "Ioho pero ne znaie kordoniv: vstupne slovo do zbirnyka Volodymyra Fedynyshyntsia 'Shch ne vmerla karpato-rusyns'ka tsyvilizatsiia'," *Aino*, No. 1 (Uzhhorod, 1997), pp. 65-67.

477 "Rusyny sut' i budut': vystup na Svitovomu konhresi rusyniv," *ibid.*, pp. 12-17. Translation of item **465** into Ukrainian by Mykhailo Fedynyshynets'.

478 "Amerikából jöttem ...," *Rusynskŷi zhŷvot* (Budapest), October 9, 1997, p. 4. Interview conducted by Judit Kiss.

479 Translation from Rusyn, "Resolutions and Recommendations of the Fourth World Congress of Rusyns," *Carpatho-Rusyn American*, XX, 3 (Fairfax, Va., 1997), p. 11.

480 "Carpatho-Rusyns." In David Levinson and Melvin Ember, eds. *American Immigrant Cultures: Builders of a Nation*, Vol. I. New York: Macmillan Reference USA/Simon and Schuster Macmillan, 1997, pp. 141-148.

481 "Rusyn Catholics in America." In Michael Glazier and Thomas J. Shelley, eds. *The Encyclopedia of American Catholic History*. Collegeville, Minn.: Liturgical Press, 1997, pp. 1221-1224.

482 Foreward to Raymond Herbenick. *Andy Warhol's Religious and Ethnic Roots: The Carpatho-Rusyn Influence on His Art*. Lewiston, N.Y., Queenston, Ontario and Lampeter, Wales: Edwin Mellen Press, 1997, pp. i-ii.

483 "Nová slovanská národnost'?: Rusíni stredovýchodnej Európy." In Marian Gajdoš and Stanislav Konečný, eds. *Etnické minority na Slovensku*. Košice: Spoločenskovedný ústav SAV, 1997, pp. 251-263. Translation of item **529** into Slovak by L'ubica Babotová.

484 Series editor: Maria Mayer, *The Rusyns of Hungary: Political and Social Developments, 1860-1910*. Classics of Carpatho-Rusyn Scholarship, Vol. IX. New York: Columbia University Press/East European Monographs, 1997, xiv and 320 p., map.

Reviewed:
Anthony J. Amato in *H-Net Reviews in the Humanities and Social Science* (September 1999) http://www.h-net.org/reviews/showrev.php?id=3417
Hugo Lane in *Nationalities Papers*, XXXIX, 4 (Oxfordshire, England, 2001),

pp. 689-696.

485 "Biography of Maria Mayer." In *ibid.*, pp. ix-xiii.

486 "The Birth of a New Nation, or the Return of an Old Problem?: The Rusyns of East Central Europe," *Acta Etnografica Hungarica*, XLII, 1-2 (Budapest, 1997), pp. 119-138.

487 *Let's Speak English and Rusyn: Yugoslav Rusyn Edition/ Besheduime po angliiski i po ruski: iuhoslavianske ruske vidanie*, with Mikhailo Feisa. Novi Sad: Ruske slovo, 1997, 120 p., 24 illustrations by Fedor Vico.

Reviewed:
Mikhailo Feisa in *Shvetlosts*, XLIII, 4 (Novi Sad, 2005), pp. 518-521.

488 "Adaptace bez asimilace." In Jaromír Hořec, ed. *Střední Evropa a Podkarpatská Rus*. Podkarpatská Rus, Vol. XVI. Prague: Společnost Podkarpatské Rusi, 1997, pp. 17-22. Translation of item **424** into Czech by Bohumil Svoboda.

489 "Our [Carpatho-Rusyn Research Center] Twentieth Anniversary." *Carpatho-Rusyn American*, XX, 4 (Fairfax, Va., 1997), pp. 4-6.

490 Translation from Ukrainian of "Our Rusyn Truth: Declaration of the Rusyn Scholarly and Enlightenment Society," *ibid*, pp. 8-9. [unsigned]

491 "Library of Congress Recognizes Carpatho-Rusyns," *ibid.*, p. 11. [unsigned]

492 "Mapping Stateless Peoples: The East Slavs of the Carpathians," *Canadian Slavonic Papers*, XXXIX, 3-4 (Edmonton, 1997), pp. 301-331, 7 maps. Reprinted in item **535**, pp. 26-59; and with additions, 2018.

1998

493 "Novŷi slavian'skŷi narod?: Rusynŷ serydnëvostochnoi Evropy,"

Rusyns'ka bysida, II, 1, 2 and 4 (Uzhhorod, 1998), pp. 3, 2, and 2. Translation of item **529** into Rusyn by Ivan Petrovtsi.

494 "Adaptatsiia bez asymiliatsiï: henial'nist' hreko-katolyts'koï ieparkhiï Mukacheva." *Acta Hungarica*, VII-VIII (1996-1997). Uzhhorod and Debrecen, 1998, pp. 103-108. Revised version of item **473**.

495 "Nova slavian'ska narodnost'?," *Rusyn*, VIII, 1-2 (Prešov, 1998), pp. 27-30. Translation of item **529** into Rusyn by Anna Plishkova.

496 Review of Kevin Hannan, *Borders of Language and Identity in Teschen Silesia*, in *Slavic Review*, LVII, I (Champaign, Ill., 1998), pp. 181-182.

497 Series editor: Aleksei L. Petrov, *Medieval Carpathian Rus': The Oldest Documentation about the Carpathian-Rusyn Church and Eparchy*. Classics of Carpatho-Rusyn Scholarship, Vol. II. New York: Columbia University Press/East European Monographs, 1998, xxxii and 209 p., 2 maps.

Reviewed:
Hugo Lane in *Nationalities Papers*, XXXIX, 4 (Oxfordshire, England, 2001), pp. 689-696.
Bertalan Pusztai in *Magyar egyháztörténeti vázlatok* [1989], XVI, 3-4 (Budapest, 2004), pp. 223-225.

498 "The Icon-Breaker: Aleksei L. Petrov as Historian" and "Works by and about Aleksei L. Petrov on Carpatho-Rusyns." In *ibid.*, pp. ix-xxvii.

499 "East Slavs South of the Carpathians: Settlement Patterns from the Late Eighteenth Century to the Present" (resumé). In Jerzy Rusek, Janusz Siatkowski, Zbigniew Rusek, eds. *XII Międzynarodowy Kongres Slawistów: streszczenia referatów i komunikatów—Językoznawstwo*. Warszawa: Wyd-wo Energeia, 1998, pp. 106-107.

500 "The Icon Breaker: Aleksei L. Petrov as Historian." In A.D. Dulichenko, ed. *Iazyki malye i bol'shie: In Memoriam Acad. Nikita*

I. Tolstoi/Slavica Tartuensia, Vol. IV. Tartu: Universitas Tartuensis, Slaavi filoloogia öppentool, 1998, pp. 289-300.

501 "Karpatskí Rusíni." In Božena Jacková and Ivan Latko, eds. *Náš kultúrno-historický kaléndár*. Uzhhorod: Vyd-vo Zakarpattia, 1998, pp. 36-42.

502 "EU gavner regioner og mindretal," *Berlingske Tidende* (Copenhagen, Denmark), August 24, 1998. Interview on regionalism and national minorities in European Union conducted by Kim Bach.

503 "Unormuie sia status Rusyniv v Ukraïni?," *Narodný novynký* (Prešov), September 30, 1998, p. 2. Interview conducted by Anna Plishkova.

504 *Carpatho-Rusyn Studies: An Annotated Bibliography*, Vol. II: *1985-1994*. New York: Columbia University Press/East European Monographs, 1998, viii and 280 p., 2 maps.

Reviewed:
M.T. [Miroslav Tejchman] in *Slovanský přehled*, LXXXVI, 4 (Prague, 2000), p. 548.
Wiesław Witkowski in *Slavia Orientalis*, L, 1 (Cracow, 2001), pp. 153-154.
Kerstin S. Jobst in *Jahrbücher für Geschichte Osteuropas*, L, 1 (Wiesbaden, 2002), p 134.
Tomasz Kamusella in *Canadian-American Slavic Studies*, XXXVI, 1-2 (Idyllwild, Calif., 2002), pp. 230-233.

505 "Status Rusinokh u Ukraïni," *Ruske slovo* (Novi Sad, Yugoslavia), October 16, 1998, p. 12. Translation of item **503** into Vojvodinian Rusyn.

506 Series editor: Pëtr Bogatyrëv, *Vampires in the Carpathians: Magical Acts, Rites, and Beliefs in Subcarpathian Rus'*. Classics of Carpatho-Rusyn Scholarship, Vol. X. New York: Columbia University Press/East European Monographs, 1998, xxii and 188 p.

Reviewed:
Natalie Kononenko in *Slavic and East European Journal*, XLIII, 4 (Tucson, Ariz., 1999), pp. 737-738.

E.A. Warner in *Slavonic and East European Review*, LXXVII, 4 (London, 1999), pp. 744-746.

507 Review of Ann Lencyk Pawliczko, ed., *Ukraine and Ukrainians throughout the World*, in *Slovakia*, XXXVI [66-67] (Passaic, N.J., 1998), pp. 142-144.

508 "Ukrainian University Chairs in Europe and North America." In Ilona Slawinski and Joseph P. Strelka, eds. *Glanz und Elend der Peripherie: 120 Jahre Universität Czernowitz.* Bern, Berlin, Frankfurt am Main, New York, Paris, Vienna: Peter Lang/ Österreichische Ost- und Südosteuropa-Institut, 1998, pp. 135-144.

509 "Shto sia mozhe Evropa nauchity od Pidkarpatia," *Rusyn*, VIII, 5-6 (Prešov, 1998), pp. 13-15. Translation of item **531** into Rusyn by Anna Plishkova.

510 "Mapovania narodiv bez shtatu: Vŷkhodnŷ Slavianŷ v Karpatakh," *ibid.*, pp. 19-20. Excerpts of item **492** translated into Rusyn by Anna Plishkova.

511 "Shcho mozhe Ievropa navchytsia vid Zakarpattia," *Aino*, No. 2-5 (Uzhhorod, 1998), pp. 42-46. Also in *Khrystyians'ka rodyna* (Uzhhorod), No. 15 [47], September 17, 1998, pp. 12-13; and in *Rusnats'kyi svit*, Vol. I, pt. 1 (Uzhhorod, 1999), pp. 109-114. Translation of item **531** into Ukrainian by L'ubica Babotová.

512 "Laboratorne vyproshchuvannia natsional'noï svidomosti," *Krytyka*, II, 10 [12] (Kyiv, 1998), pp. 4-6. Translation of item **208** into Ukrainian.

513 "Adaptacja bez asymilacji: fenomen greckokatolickiej eparchii w Mukaczewie." In Stanisław Stępień, ed. *Polska-Ukraina 100 lat sąsiedztwa*, Vol. IV. Przemyśl: Południowo-wschodni instytut naukowy, 1998, pp. 233-238. Translation of item **424** into Polish.

1999

514 "Khronolohiia istorii Pidkarpats'koï Rusi," *Khrystyians'ka rodyna* (Uzhhorod), March 4, 1999, pp. 4-5. [unsigned]

515 *Karpats'ka mantiia amerykans'koho profesora, abo subota— rusyns'kyi den': interv"iu.* Sad zhurnalu "Aino," No. 4. Uzhhorod: Mystets'ka liniia, 1999, 24 p. Interview conducted by Mykhailo Fedynyshynets'.

516 *Encyclopedia of Canada's Peoples*, editor. Toronto, Buffalo, and London: University of Toronto Press, 1999, xxvi and 1339 p., 1 table.

Reviewed:
Devin Crawley in *Quill and Quire*, LXV, 6 (Toronto, 1999), p. 51.
Robert Fulford in *The Globe and Mail* (Toronto), September 11, 1999, p. D-11.
Michah Rynor in *University of Toronto Bulletin* (Toronto), September 13, 1999, p.15.
Pauline Comeau in *Canadian Geographic*, CXIX, 7 (Ottawa, 1999), p. 72.
Canadian Scene, Issue 1519 (Toronto, 1999), pp. 6-7.
Michah Rynor in *University of Toronto Magazine*, XXVII, 1 (Toronto, 1999), p. 6.
Shanon M. Graff in *American Reference Book Annual*, Vol. XXXI (Englewood, Colo., 2000), p. 132.
Elena Jakešová in *Historický časopis*, XLVIII, 2 (Bratislava, 2000), pp. 371-374.
Patricia Morley in *Canadian Book Review Annual 1999* (Toronto, 2000), p. 13.
Alan B. Anderson in *Canadian Ethnic Studies*, XXXII, 3 (Calgary, Alberta, 2000), pp. 111-119.
Eliott Robert Barkan in *Journal of American Ethnic History*, XX, 3 (New Brunswick, N. J., 2001), pp. 144-147.

517 "Bosnian Muslims [in Canada]." In *ibid.*, pp. 270-273.

518 "Carpatho-Rusyns [in Canada]." In *ibid.*, pp. 340-343.

519 "Adaptation without Assimilation: The Genius of the Greco-Catholic Eparchy of Mukachevo," *Logos*, XXXVIII, 1-4 [1997] (Ottawa, 1999), pp. 269-282. Reprinted in item **536**, pp. 194-204.

520 "Zadachi pered II. seminarom rusyn'skoho iazyka," *Narodnŷ novynkŷ* (Prešov), April 28, 1999, p. 4.

521 "Dar od Karpatorusyn'skoho nauchnoho tsentra," *ibid.*, p. 6.

522 "Rusynistika na univerzitakh Evropy," *Rusyn*, IX, 1-2 (Prešov, 1999), pp. 34-35.

523 "Mynule desiat'richa bŷlo naislavnishe pro Rusyniv: vŷstup na 5. Svitovim kongresi Rusyniv," *Narodnŷ novynkŷ* (Prešov), July 7, 1999, p. 3. Translation of item **526** into Rusyn by Anna Plishkova.

524 "Mame svoio chesne ruske meno: Akademik Pavlo Robert Magochi na piiatim Shvetovim kongresu rusinokh (rusnatsokh, lemkokh)," *Ruske slovo* (Novi Sad, Yugoslavia), July 30, 1999, p. 6.

525 "Zauvazhennia, predstavleni na V-omu Svitovomu konhresi rusyniv," *Khrystyians'ka rodyna*, No. 9 [64] (Uzhhorod, 1999), pp. 4-5. Reprinted in *Rusnats'kyi svit*, Vol. II (Uzhhorod, 2001), pp. 21-24. Translation of item **526** into Ukrainian by Yana Filippenko.

526 "Remarks at the Vth World Congress of Rusyns," *Trembita*, XI, 3 (Minneapolis, 1999), pp. 3-6. Excerpts reprinted in *The New Rusyn Times*, VII, 1 (Pittsburgh, 2000), p. 5.

527 "Adaptace bez asimilace." In *Náš česko-rusínský kalendář/Nash ches'ko-rusyns'kŷi kalendar 2000*. Compiled by Ivan Latko. Uzhhorod: Společnost české kultury J.Á. Komenského/Klub T. G. Masaryka, 1999, pp. 98-99. Translation of item **519** into Czech by Bohomíl Svoboda.

528 "Rusínski američania, slovenskí američania a Česko-Slovensko." In *Náš kultúrno-historický kalendár 2000*. Compiled Ivan Latko, Božena Jacková, and Vasil Paňkovič. Uzhhorod: Užhorodský spolok Slovákov, 1999, pp. 38-44. Translation of item **217** into Slovak by Elena Jakešová.

529 "A New Slavic Nationality?: The Rusyns of East Central Europe." In Tom Trier, ed. *Focus on the Rusyns*. Copenhagen: Danish Cultural Institute, 1999, pp. 15-29. Reprinted in item **535**, pp. 361-375.

530 "Nova slavians'ka narodnost'?: Rusynŷ serednёvŷkhodnoi Evropŷ." In *ibid.*, pp. 13-35. Translation of item **527** into Rusyn by Anna Plishkova.

531 "What Can Europe Learn from Transcarpathia?" In Tom Trier, ed. *Inter-Ethnic Relations in Transcarpathian Ukraine.* ECMI Report, No. 4. Flensburg, Germany: European Centre for Minority Issues, 1999, pp. 63-69. Reprinted in item **536**, pp. 298-305.

532 "Utváření národní identity: Podkarpatská Rus, 1848-1948," *Střední Evropa*, XV [91 and 92-93] (Prague, 1999), pp. 87-99 and 114-129. Abridged translation into Czech by Miroslav Balcar of several chapters from item **372**.

533 "Mapovanie národov bez štátu: východní Slovania v Karpatoch," *Človek a společnost'*, II, 2 (Košice, 1999), www.saske.sk/cas/ 99/ magocas.html, 7 maps. Translation of item **492** into Slovak by Daniela Slančová.

Reviewed:
Peter Šoltés in *Karpatskie rusiny v slavianskom mire* (Moscow and Bratislava, 2009), pp. 41-42.

534 "Nova slavianska natsionalnosts?," *Shvetlosts*, XXXVII, 1-4 (Novi Sad, 1999), pp. 53-67. Translation of item **529** into Vojvodinian Rusyn by Helena Medješi.

535 *Of the Making of Nationalities There is No End*, Vol. I: *Carpatho-Rusyns in Europe and North America.* Introduction by Christopher M. Hann. New York: Columbia University Press/East European Monographs, 1999, xxxviii and 482 p., 14 maps.

Reviewed:
Wiesław Witkowski in *Slavia Orientalis*, XLIX, 4 (Cracow, 2000), pp. 637-641.
Andrew Wilson in *Slavonic and East European Review*, LXXIX, 2 (London, 2001), pp. 340-342.
M.T. [Miroslav Tejchman] in *Slovanský přehled*, LXXXVII, 1 (Prague, 2001), p. 124.
Hugo Lane in *Nationalities Papers*, XXIX, 4 (Oxfordshire, England, 2001), pp. 689-696.

Stefan Troebst in *Zeitschrift für Ostmitteleuropa-Forschung*, L, 4 (Marburg, 2001), pp. 626-628.

Elaine Rusinko in *Slavic and East European Journal*, XLV, 3 (Berkeley, Calif., (2001), pp. 586-587.

Anna Veronica Wendland in *Jahrbücher für Geschichte Osteuropas*, L, 2 (Stuttgart, 2002), pp. 286-288.

Austin Jersild in *The Russian Review*, LXI, 4 (Columbus, Ohio, 2002), pp. 639- 641.

Tomasz Kamusella in *Canadian-American Slavic Studies*, XXXVI, 1-2 (Idyllwild, Calif., 2002), pp. 230-233.

Alla Kasianova in *Europe-Asia Studies*, LIV, 6 (Glasgow, 2002), pp. 1000-1003.

Stanislav J. Kirschbaum in *Österreichische Osthefte*, XLIV, 3-4 (Vienna, 2002), p. 750.

Vasyl Markus in *The Ukrainian Quarterly*, LVIII, 2-3 (New York, 2002), pp. 256-259; in Ukrainian: *Informatsiinyi lystok*, XIII [57-58] (Chicago, 2002), pp. 4-6.

Andriy Zayarnyuk in *Nations and Nationalism*, VIII, 3 (Oxford, 2002), pp. 412-414.

Liu [Lubomir Medjesi] in *Messenger/Hlasnïk*, IX [20] (Kitchener, Ont., 2004), pp. 10-11

536 *Of the Making of Nationalities There is No End*, Vol. II: *Speeches, Debates, Bibliographic Works*. Introduction by Tom Trier. New York: Columbia University Press/East European Monographs, 1999, xxiv and 536 p.

Reviewed:

Wiesław Witkowski in *Slavia Orientals*, L, 1 (Cracow, 2000), pp. 152-153.

M.T. [Miroslav Tejchman] in *Slovanský přehled*, LXXXVII, 1 (Prague, 2001), p. 124.

Roger E. Kanet and Nouray V. Ibryamova in *Osteuropa*, LI, 1 (Stuttgart, 2001), p. 105.

Hugo Lane in *Nationalities Papers*, XXIX, 4 (Oxfordshire, England, 2001), pp. 689-696.

Stefan Troebst in *Zeitschrift für Ostmitteleuropa-Forschung*, L, 4 (Marburg, 2001), pp. 626-628.

Elaine Rusinko in *Slavic and East European Journal*, XLV, 3 (Berkeley, Calif., (2001), pp. 586-587.

Anna Veronica Wendland in *Jahrbücher für Geschichte Osteuropas*, L, 2 (Stuttgart, 2002), pp. 286-288.

Austin Jersild in *The Russian Review*, LXI, 4 (Columbus, Ohio, 2002), pp. 639- 641.

Tomasz Kamusella in *Canadian-American Slavic Studies*, XXXVI, 1-2 (Idyllwild, Calif., 2002), pp. 230-233.

Alla Kasianova in *Europe-Asia Studies*, LIV, 6 (Glasgow, 2002), pp. 1000-1003.

Stanislav J. Kirschbaum in *Österreichische Osthefte*, XLIV, 3-4 (Vienna, 2002), p. 750.

Vasyl Markus in *The Ukrainian Quarterly*, LVIII, 2-3 (New York, 2002), pp. 256-259.

Andriy Zayarnyuk in *Nations and Nationalism*, VIII, 3 (Oxford, 2002), pp. 412-414.

Liu [Lubomir Medješi] in *Messenger/Hlasnïk*, IX [20] (Kitchener, Ont., 2004), pp. 10-11

537 "Nacionalne država: val budućnosti ili ostatak prošlosti?"/"Nation-States: The Wave of the Future, or a Remnant of the Past?" In Aleksander Ravlić, ed. *Međunarodni znanstveni skup "Jugoistočna Europa 1918.-1995./"Southeastern Europe 1918-1995": An International Symposium.* Zagreb: Hrvatska matica iseljenika i Hrvatski informativni center, 1999, pp. 155-159 and 358-362. Shortened version and translation into Croatian of item **354**.

538 "Okrugli stol: Problemtika od 1918. do danas/Round Table: Historical Issues from 1918 Until Today"—Commentary. In ibid., pp. 201-202 and 407-409.

2000

539 "Hail Diversity!" [a response to Timothy Garton Ash's "Hail Ruthenia!"], *Trembita*, XII, 1 (Minneapolis, 2000), pp. 4-5. Reprinted in *The New Rusyn Times*, VII, 3 (Pittsburgh, 2000), pp. 11-13.

540 "Kinets' natsional'nykh derzhav," *Krytyka*, IV, 4 (Kyiv, 2000), pp. 11-13. Translation of item **354** into Ukrainian by Bohdan Tkachenko.

Reviewed:
Vitalii Ponomar'ov in *Krytyka*, IV, 5 (Kyiv, 2000), p. 31.

541 *Karpato-Russinen*. Munich: Deutsch-Ruthenische Freundschaft, 2000, 36 p. Revised translation of item **388** into German by Amalija Kučmaš-Klemens.

542 Series editor: Juraj Vaňko, *The Language of Slovakia's Rusyns/ Jazyk slovenských Rusínov*. Classics of Carpatho-Rusyn Scholarship, Vol. XI. New York: Columbia University Press/East European Monographs, 2000, xx, 114 p. and xix, 121 p.

Reviewed:
H. Leeming in *Slavonic and East European Review*, LXXIX, 3 (London, 2001), pp. 498-499
Reinhard Ibler in *Zeitschrift für Ostmitteleuropa-Forschung*, L, 3 (Marburg, 2001), pp. 473-474.
George Cummins in *Canadian Slavonic Papers*, XLIII, 4 (Edmonton, 2001), pp. 573-575.
Robert A. Rothstein in *Harvard Ukrainian Studies*, XXIII, 3-4 (Cambridge, Mass., 1999 [2002]), pp. 185-187.
Štefan Švagrovský in *Slovenská reč*, LXVII, 2 (Bratislava, 2002), pp. 100-102.
David Short in *Slavonic and East European Review,* LXXXII, 3 (London, 2004), pp. 707-708.
Jiří Rejzak in *Slovo a slovesnost*, LXV, 4 (Prague, 2004), pp. 297-299.
Wiesław Witkowski in *Slavia Orientalis*, L, 2 (Cracow, 2001), pp. 345-346.

543 "The Catholic Church in the United States and the Rusyns." In *Kalendár—Almanac of the National Slovak Society of the USA for the Year 2000*. Canonsburg, Pa., 2000, pp. 63-65.

544 "Prežívame proces národného obrodenia," *Podvihorlatské noviny* (Humenné, Slovakia), February 2000. Interview on the Rusyn national revival conducted by Jana Otriová.

545 "Rusynŷ i ïkh domovyna," *Rusyn*, X, 1-2 (Prešov, 2000), pp. 30-31. Reprinted in *Kalendar'-Al'manakh na 2001 hod*. Edited by Antonii Liavynets. Budapest: Rusynskoe menshynovoe samoupravlenie Iozhefvarosha, 2001, pp. 52-55.

546 "Karpats'ka Rus'/Ruthènes des Carpathes/Carpathian Rusyns" and "Slovenskŷ Rusynŷ/Ruthènes de Slovaquie/Slovakia's Ruthenes." In Marcel Meaufront, ed. *Le guide multilingue des communautés* *d'Europe/The European Communities Multilingual Guide*. Le Cannet, France: Fédération Européenne des Maisons de Pays, 2000, pp. 237- 253.

547 Series editor: Robert A. Karlowich, *Guide to the Amerikansky Russky Viestnik*, Vol. II. *1915-1929*. Preface by Edward Kasinec. New York: Columbia University Press/East European Monographs, 2000, xviii, 469 p.

548 Series editor: Mary Halász, *From America With Love: Memoirs of an American Immigrant in the Soviet Union*. Introduction by István Deák. New York: Columbia University Press/East European Monographs, 2000, xiv, 182 p.

549 "Zakarpattia i ioho narody," *Romani iag* (Uzhhorod), February 29, 2000, p. 7.

550 "Vidomyi i nevidomyi Magocsi," *Universum*, No. 7-10 [81-84] (L'viv, 2000), pp. 70-72. Interview conducted by Vitalii Zhuhai. Also published in *Staryi zamok* (Mukachevo, Ukraine), March 23, 2000, p. 13; and in Vitalii Zhuhai, *Postati: interv"iu z ukraïntsiamy svitu*. Uzhhorod: Vyd-vo "Mystets'ka liniia," 2001, pp. 83-90.

551 "Paul Robert Magocsi: Kanada ani Amerika nie sú v starostlivosti o menšiny štandardom," *Sme* (Bratislava), November 28, 2000, p. 5. Interview conducted bt Táňa Rundesová.

552 *Východní Slovania v Karpatoch*. Bratislava: Združenie inteligencie Rusínov Slovenska, 2000, 23 p., 12 maps, 7 illustrations. Translation of item **492** into Slovak by Daniela Slančová.

553 "Konec národního státu?: Revoluce roku 1989 a budoucnost Evropy," *Střední Evropa*, No. 104-105 (Prague, 2000), pp. 58-69. Translation of item **354** into Czech by Viktor Faktor.

554 "Transcarpathia." In Peter Jordan, Andreas Kappeler, Walter Lukan, and Josef Vogl, eds. *Ukraine*. Special volume of *Österreichische Osthefte*, XLII, 3-4. Vienna: Peter Lang, 2000, pp. 423-436.

555 "Carpatho-Rusyns." In Richard Frucht, ed. *Encyclopedia of Eastern Europe: From the Congress of Vienna to the Fall of Communism.* New York and London: Garland Publishing, 2000, pp. 121-123.

556 "Subcarpathian Rus." In *ibid.*, pp. 771-772.

557 *Karpat'skŷ Rusynŷ.* Prešov: Karpatorusyn'skŷi nauchnŷi tsenter, 2000, 24 p. Translation of second edition of item **388** into Rusyn by Anna Kuzmiakova. Second revised and expanded edition, 2006, 32 p.

Reviewed:
Iudita Kishshova in *Országos Ruszin Hírlap/Vsederzhavnŷi rusynskŷi visnyk*, III, 6 (Budapest, 2001), p. 13.

558 Review of John-Paul Himka, *Religion and Nationality in Western Ukraine*, in *Journal of Ukrainian Studies*, XXV, 1-2 (Toronto, 2000), pp. 232-235.

559 "Mapovanie narodokh bez derzhavi," *Studia Ruthenica,* VII [20] (Novi Sad, 1999-2000), pp. 89-91. Excerpts from item **492** translated into Vojvodinian Rusyn by Mikhailo Feisa.

2001

560 *The Carpatho-Rusyn Americans.* The Immigrant Experience Series. Introduction by Daniel Patrick Moynihan. 2nd revised edition. Philadelphia: Chelsea House Publishers, 2001, 112 p., 2 maps, 60 illustrations.

Reviewed:
Imre Kardashinets' in *Narodna volia* (Scranton, Pa.), June 21, 2001.

561 "Stalo sia chudo" [remarks at the 10th anniversary of the Organization of Rusyns in Hungary], *Országos Ruszin Hírlap/ Vsederzhavnŷi rusynskŷi visnyk*, III, 7 (Budapest, 2001), p. 5.

562 "Tut naihirshyi stan rusyns'kykh sprav, ale ia bachu ïkhniu perspektyvu," *Rio* (Uzhhorod, Ukraine), September 22, 2001, p. B6. Interview on Rusyns in Ukraine conducted by Mykhailo

Fedynyshynets'.

563 "Warhol, Andy (né Andrew Warhola, 1928-1987)." In Elliott Robert Barkan, ed. *Making It in America: A Sourcebook on Eminent Ethnic Americans.* Santa Barbara, Calif., Denver, Colo., and Oxford, England: ABC Clio, 2001, p. 406.

564 Review of Vincent Shandor, *Carpatho-Ukraine in the Twentieth Century*, in *Canadian-American Slavic Studies*, XXV, 2-3 (Idyllwild, Calif., 2001), pp. 359-361.

565 "Try hlavní priorití v nastupnim desiat'richu: výstup na 6. Svitovim kongresi Rusyniv u Prazi," *Narodný novynký*, No. 44-46 (Prešov, Slovakia), November 14, 2001, p. 3. Translated into Rusyn by Anna Plishkova. Reprinted in *Rusyn*, XII, 2 (Prešov, 2002), pp. 18-20.

566 "Vstup/Úvod/Introduction." In Fedor Vico. *Il'ko Sova z Baiusova/ Il'ko Sova from Bajusovo.* Prešov: Róbert Vico, pp. 5-19. Rusyn and English texts republished as "Istoriia Rusyniv u karikaturakh Fedora Vitsa/History of the Rusins in the Caricatures by Fedor Vico." In *Rusyn'skýi narodnýi kalendar' na rik 2002.* Prešov: Rusyn'ska obroda, 2001, pp. 78-88.

567 Translation into English from Rusyn and Slovak, Fedor Vico, *Il'ko Sova z Baiusova/Il'ko Sova from Bajusovo.* Prešov: Róbert Vico, 2001, 125 p.

568 "Rusyn Literature: Its Present Status." In Franz Görner, ed. *Internationale Zusammenarbeit im neuen Jahrtausend: 30. ABDOS—Tagung, Thorn, 4-7. Juni 2001.* Berlin: Staatsbibliothek zu Berlin, 2001, pp. 77-83.

569 "Evidence." In *Proceedings of the Standing Senate Committee on Foreign Affairs*, Issue No. 16: *Examination of emerging political, social, economic, and security developments in Russia and Ukraine.* Ottawa: Public Works and Government Services Canada, 2001, pp. 4-18.

570 Review of Ronald Grigor Suny and Michael D. Kennedy, eds., *Intellectuals and the Articulation of the Nation*, in *Slavic Review*, LX, 4 (Champaign, III., 2001), pp. 825-827.

571 "Transcarpathia." In Bernard A. Cook, ed. *Europe since 1945: An Encyclopedia*. Vol. II. New York and London: Garland Publishers, 2001, pp. 1257-1258

2002

572 *Karpats'ki Rusynŷ*. Uzhhorod: Karpatorusyns'kyi nauchnii tsentr, 2002, 24 p. Translation of revised second edition of item **388** into Rusyn by Dymytrii Pop.

573 "Poznamkí: vŷstup na 6. Svitovim kongresi Rusyniv u Prazi," *Besida*, XIV, 1 [64] and 2-3 [65-66] (Krynica and Legnica, 2002), pp. 17-19 and 20-21; *Vsederzhavnŷi rusynskŷi vistnyk*, III, 11 (Budapest, 2001), pp. 5-7; *Kalendar'-al'manakh/Ruszin nyelvű naptár-almanach 2002*. Budapest: Józsefvárosi Ruszin Kisebbségi Önkormányzat, 2002, pp. 75-82; *Rusnats'kyi svit*. Vol. III. Uzhhorod: Vyd-vo V. Padiaka, 2003, pp. 56-61.

574 "Liud'skŷ prava i medzhigrupnŷ odnosynŷ na Sloven'sku: poznamkŷ k vŷstupiniu pidpredsedŷ vladŷ Pala Chakiia," *Rusyn*, XII, 3-4 (Prešov, 2002), pp. 29-30. Translation of item **600** into Rusyn by Anna Plishkova.

575 "Chiia zhe to molodezh?," *Narodnŷ novynkŷ*, No. 43-44 (Prešov), October 30, 2002, p. 1.

576 "Ne treba balamutyty chitatelia," *Narodnŷ novynkŷ*, No. 43-44 (Prešov), October 30, 2002, p. 3.

577 "Narodne obrodzhinia i rik 1848: kapitola z istorichnoho perehliadu *Rusynŷ na Sloven'sku*." In Miron Sysak. *Rusyn'ska literatura pro 1. klasu serednikh shkol iz navchaněm rusyn'skoho iazŷka*. Prešov: Rusyn'ska obroda, 2002, pp. 5-9.

578 "Galicia: A European Land." In Sabrina P. Ramet, James R. Felak, and Herbert J. Ellison. *Nations and Nationalisms in East-Central Europe, 1806-1948: A Festschrift for Peter F. Sugar.* Bloomington, Ind.: Slavica, 2002, pp. 35-50.

Reviewed:
Elizabeth Bakke in *Nordisk Østforum,* No. 2 (Oslo, 2003), pp. 279-282.

579 *The Roots of Ukrainian Nationalism: Galicia as Ukraine's Piedmont.* Toronto, London, and Buffalo: University of Toronto Press, 2002, xviii and 214 p., 5 maps, 11 tables.

Reviewed:
Constantin Simon in *Orientalia Christiana Periodica,* LXIX (Rome, 2003), pp. 546-548.
Bohdan Klid in *Canadian Slavonic Papers,* XLV, 3-4 (Edmonton, 2003), pp. 507-508.
Leonard R. N. Ashley in *Geolinguistics,* Vol. XXIX. New York: Cummings and Hathaway, 2003, pp. 104-105.
George O. Liber in *The International History Review,* XXV, 4 (Burnaby, B.C., 2003), pp. 913-914.
Philip Longworth in *University of Toronto Quarterly,* LXXIII, 1 (Toronto, 2003-04), pp. 124-126.
Myroslav Shkandrij in *Canadian Book Review Annual 2002* (Toronto, 2003), p. 282.
Taras Kuzio in *Europe-Asia Studies,* LV, 4 (Oxfordshire, England, 2003), pp. 653-655.
Andrew Wilson in *Slavonic and East Europen Review,* LXXXII, 2 (London, 2004), pp. 383-384.
Kerstin S. Jobst in *Österreische Osthefte,* XLVI, 4 (Vienna, 2004), pp. 621-624.
Frank Golczewski in *Zeitschrift für Ostmitteleuropa-Forschung,* LIII, 3 (Marburg, 2004), pp. 468-469.
Przemysław Żurawski vel Grajewski in *Kwartalnik Historyczny,* CXI, 1 (Warsaw, 2004), pp. 167-173.
Jaro Bilocerkowycz in *Canadian Review of Studies in Nationalism,* XXXII, (Charlottetown, Prince Edward Is., 2005), pp. 171-173.
Victor Hugo Lane in *Austrian History Yearbook,* XXXVI (Minnepolis, 2005), pp. 232-233.
Danuta Sosnowska in *Harvard Ukrainian Studies,* XXVII, 1-4 (Cambridge, Mass., 2004-05), pp. 370-375.

Tomoko Shimada in *Shisen*, No. 103, Kansai University Institutional
Repository (Tokyo?, 2006), pp. A52-A57.

580 *Aboriginal Peoples of Canada: A Short Introduction*, editor.
Toronto, Buffalo, and London: University of Toronto Press, 2002,
viii and 308 p.

Reviewed:
Edmund J. Danziger, Jr. in *American Review of Canadian Studies*, XXX, 3
(Washington, D.C., 2003), pp. 440-441.
Barbara Ann Hocking in *Australian Canadian Studies*, XXI, 2 (Syndey,
Australia, 2003), pp. 155-158.
Geoff Hamilton in *Canadian Book Review Annual 2002* (Toronto, 2003), pp.
344-345.
Jan Grabowski in *Histoire sociale/ Social History*, XXXVII [No. 73] (Ottawa,
Ont., 2004), pp. 136-138.
Keith Thor Carlson in *Canadian Historical Review*, LXXXV, 1 (Toronto,
2004), pp. 143-145.
Olive Patricia Dickason in *Revue d'histoire de l'Amérique française*, LVIII, 2
(Montreal, 2004), pp. 268-271.
Gundula Wilke in *Canadian Literature*, No. 186 (Vancouver, 2005), pp. 156-
158.

581 *Historical Atlas of Central Europe*. Second revised and expanded
edition. Seattle: University of Washington Press; Toronto:
University of Toronto Press; London: Thames and Hudson, 2002,
xiv and 274 p., 109 maps, 47 tables. Third revised and expanded
edition, see item **848**.

Reviewed:
Edward Cone in *Library Journal*, No. 127 [November 15] (N. Hollywood, Ca.,
2002), p. 62.
Reference and Research Book News, XVIII, 2 (Portland, Ore., 2003), p. 69.
Raibo Electronic Reviews, wysingg://31//http://www.rainboreviews.com/
nonfict.htm
[Richard Custer], *The New Rusyn Times*, X, 1 (Pittsburgh, 2003), p. 11.
T. Miller in *Choice*, XL, 6 (Middletown, Conn., 2003) p. 967.
Christine Kulke in *Center for Slavic and East European Studies Newsletter,
University of California*, XX, 1 (Berkeley, Ca., 2003), pp. 17-18.
Peg Glisson in *School Library Journal*, XLIX, 2 (No. Hollywood, Ca., 2003),
p. 99.

Jaroslaw Zurowsky in *Canadian Book Review Annual 2002* (Toronto, 2003), p. 22.

John B. Romeiser in *American Reference Books Annual 2003*. Westport, Conn and London, 2003, pp. 205-206.

Roger E. Kanet et al. in *Osteuropa, LIII*, 12 (Berlin, 2003), p. 1854.

Paul Rolfe in *Library Review*, LII, 5 (Bradford, Eng., 2003), p. 238.

Ivan T. Berendt in *Central European History,* XXXVII, 3 (Boston and Leiden, 2004), pp. 492-494.

Bertalan Pusztai in *Magyar egyháztörténeti vázlatok/Essays in Church History in Hungary* [1989], XVI, 3-4 (Budapest, 2004), pp. 242-243.

Ömer Turan in *H-Net Reviews* (March, 2005), http.//www.h-net.org/reviews/ showrev.php?id=10339

Jerzy Borzęcki in *The Polish Review,* LI, 1 (New York, 2006), pp. 75-79.

Bertalan Pusztai in *Kisebbségkutatás*, XIV, 2 (Budapest, 2005), pp. 304-305.

582 *Encyclopedia of Rusyn History and Culture*, co-editor with Ivan Pop and author of 471 entries. Toronto, Buffalo, and London: University of Toronto Press, 2002, xiv and 520 p., 13 maps, 11 illustrations. Second revised and expanded edition, see item **617** (with analytics of entries by the author).

Reviewed:

Volodymyr Fedynyshynets' in *Novyny Zakarpattia* (Uzhhorod, Ukraine), February 4, 2003, pp. 6-7.

Oksana Zakydalsky in *The Ukrainian Weekly* (Parsippany, N.J.), February 23, 2003, pp. 10 and 16.

Liubomir Medieshi in *Hlasnïk/The Messenger,* VIII [18] (Kitchener, Ont, 2003), p. 3.

Ianko Ramach in *Ruske slovo* (Novi Sad), February 7, 2003, p. 9.

PT [Petro Trokhanovskii] in *Besida,* XV, 3 (Krynica, 2003), pp. 24-25.

René Kočík in *Podkarpatská Rus,* XIII, 4 (Prague, 2003), p. 2. Abridged English translation in *Outpost Dispatch*, II, 7 (Pittsburg, 2004), p. 14.

Sławomir Michalik in *Magury '03* (Warsaw, 2003), pp. 132-133.

T. Miller in *Choice*, XL, 6 (Middletown, Conn., 2003), p. 1728.

Laura Gardner in *Reference Reviews,* XVII, 5 (Harlow, 2003), pp. 59-60.

Piotr Wróbel in *University of Toronto Quarterly,* LXXI, 1 (Toronto, 2003-04), pp. 123-124.

Klaus Schreiber in *Informationsmittel (IFB),* XI, 1 (Konstanz, Gemany, 2003), 03-1-300.

Harm Ramkema in *Ablak: tijdschrift voor Centraal Europa,* VIII, 3 (Amsterdam, 2003), pp. 28-29.

Myroslav Shkandrij in *Canadian Book Review Annual 2002* (Toronto, 2003), pp. 11-12.

D. Barton Johnson in *American Reference Book Annual 2003*, Vol. XXXIV. Westport, Conn. and London, 2003, p. 209.

Vasyl' Markus in *Informatsiinyi lystok KOZI*, XIV [61-62] (Chicago, 2003), pp. 6-9.

Patricia A. Krafcik in *Canadian Slavonic Papers*, XLVI, 1-2 (Edmonton, 2004), pp. 253-254.

Vilém Kodýtek in *Literární noviny*, No. 42 (Prague), October 11, 2004, p. 4.

Vasyl' Khoma in *Rusyn'skŷi literaturnŷi almanakh na rik 2004*. Prešov: Spolok rusyn'skŷkh pysateliv Sloven'ska, 2004, pp. 110-112. Reprinted in Vasyl' Khoma and Maria Khomova, *Obrodzhinia Rusyniv*. Prešov: Spolok rusyn'skŷkh pysateliv Sloven'ska, 2005, pp. 96-98.

Kerstin S. Jobst in *Österreichische Osthefte*, XLVI, 4 (Vienna, 2004), pp. 621-624.

C. Simon in *Orientalia Christiana Periodica*, LXX (Rome, 2004), pp. 521-516.

Stephane Mund in *Journal of European Studies*, XXXV, 3 (Chalfont St. Giles, Eng., 2005), pp. 387-389.

Patrice M. Dabrowski in *Harvard Ukrainian Studies*, XXV, 3-4 (Cambridge, Mass., 2001 [2005]), pp. 304-305.

Bertalan Pusztai in *Magyar egyháztörténeti vázlatok/ Essays in Church History in Hungary*, XVII, 1-2 (Budapest, 2005), pp. 236-237.

Juraj Vaňko in *Jahrbücher für Geschichte Osteuropas*, LII, 4 (Wiesbaden, 2005), pp. 573-574.

Teresa Polowy in *Slavic and East European Journal*, L, 2 (Berkeley, Ca., 2006), pp. 366-367.

583 "Ruteni din Europa centrală şi de est." *Rus'ka vira/Credinţa Rusină*, I, 4 ([Deva], 2002), pp. 21-26. Published separately in *Revista de Studii slave: Extras I*. [Deva, Romania]: Uniunea Culturală a Rutenilor din România, [2003], 30 p. Translation of item **474** into Romanian by Maria Basarab.

2003

584 "Naibil'shym postupom ie te, shcho svit dovidavsia pro rusyns'kyi etnos," *Staryi zamok* (Uzhhorod, Ukraine), January 16, 2003, p. 12. Interview on minority cultures and stateless peoples conducted by Mykhailo Fedynyshynets'.

585 "Češi přišli na Podkarpatskou Rus s dobrou vůli," *Dějiny a současnost,* XXV, 3 (Prague, 2003), pp. 50-53. Interview conducted by Miroslav Balcar.

586 "Naşteria unei noi limbi slave." In *Revista de Studii slave: Extras II.* [Deva, Romania]: Uniunea Culturală a Rutenilor din România, [2003], 14 p. Translation of item **393** into Romanian by Ioan Leviţchi.

587 "The Old and the New: Address to the World Congress of Rusyns, Prešov, Slovakia—June 7, 2003," *Trembita,* XV, 2 (Minneapolis, 2003), pp. 1-4.

588 "Stare i nove: výstup chlena SRR za Severnu Ameryku na 7. Svitovim kongresi Rusyniv, Priashiv, Slovensko, 7. iuna 2003, *Rusyn,* XIII, 3-4 (Prešov, 2003), pp. 16-17 and *Vsederzhavnŷi rusynskŷi visnyk,* V, 7 (Budapest, 2003), pp. 3 and 5. Translation of item **587** into Rusyn by Anna Plishkova. Also in *Besida,* XV, 4 (Legnica nad Krynica, 2003), pp. 17-19. Translation into Lemko Rusyn by Petro Trokhanovskii.

589 "Mŷ Rusynŷ, a ne Rusy," *Narodnŷ novynkŷ,* No. 37-38 (Prešov), September 17, 2003, p. 2.

590 "Opysŷ abo predpysŷ v nautsi: Entsiklopediia istoriï i kul'turŷ Rusyniv," *Rusyn,* XIII, 5-6 (Prešov, 2003), pp. 20-22. Translation of item **645** into Rusyn by Anna Plishkova.

591 *Rutenii.* Deva: Uniunea Culturală a Rutenilor din România, 2003, 24 p. Translation of revised text of item **388** into Romanian by Ivan Moisiuc.

592 "Rozmowa z Paulem Robertom Magocsim." In *Magury '03.* Warsaw: Studenckie koło przewodników Beskidzkich, 2003, pp. 102-113. Interview conducted by Miroslav Balcar; translated from Czech by Jakub Wojtaszczyk.

593 "Priashivs'ka hreko-katolyts'ka ieparkhiia: rusyns'ka chy slovats'ka tserkva," *Kovcheh,* IV (L'viv, 2003), pp. 170-173.

594 "Ukraine." In Joel Mokyr, ed. *The Oxford Encyclopedia of Economic History,* Vol. V. Oxford, Eng.: Oxford University Press, 2003, pp. 141-142.

2004

595 "Karpat'skŷ Rusynŷ: etno-geografichnŷi a istorichnŷi perehlad." In *Kalendar'-almanakh na 2004 hod/Ruszin nyelvű naptár-almanach 2004.* Edited by Marianna Liavynets. Budapest: Rusyns'koe menshynovoe samoupravleniie, 2004, pp. 67-89.

596 "Chekhy pryishly na Podkarpats'ku Rus' iak dobrozhelateli," *Podkarpats'ka Rus'* (Uzhhorod), February 2004, p. 3. Translation of item **585** into Rusyn.

597 "Rusyns'ke pytannia v Ukraïni," *Trembita* (Svaliava, Ukraine), No. 11(30), March 23, 2004, p. 4. Translation of item **614** into Ukrainian.

598 "Rusyns'kŷi vopros—na Ukraïni," *Narodnŷ novynkŷ* (Prešov), No. 13-15, April 7, 2004, p. 2. Translation of item **614** into Rusyn.

599 "Carpatho-Rusyns." In James R. Millar, ed. *Encyclopedia of Russian History.* New York: Thomson Gale/Macmillan Reference USA, 2004, pp. 198-200.

600 "Comments by Pál Csáky: Human Rights and Inter-Group Relations in Slovakia." In M. Mark Stolarik, ed. *The Slovak Republic: A Decade of Independence, 1993-2002.* Wauconda, Ill.: Bolchazy-Carducci Publishers, 2004, pp. 105-108.

601 "Political History [of Transcarpathia]." In Peter Jordan and Mladen Klemenčić, eds. *Transcarpathia—Bridgehead or Periphery?: Geopolitical and Economic Aspects and Perspectives of a Ukrainian Region.* Wiener Osteuropa Studien, Vol. XVI. Frankfurt am Main: Peter Lang, 2004, pp. 23-38.

602 "A Short History [of the Carpatho-Rusyn Research Center]." In Patricia Krafcik and Elaine Rusinko, eds. *Carpatho-Rusyn Research Center, Inc.: The First Quarter Century.* Ocala, Flo.: Carpatho-Rusyn Research Center, 2004, pp. 1-14.

603 "Narodnomu samousvidomliniu sia cholovik musyt' uchity." Excerpts from item **584** translated into Rusyn, in Vasyl' Iabur and Anna Plishkova, *Rusyn'skŷi iazŷk pro 3. klasu serednikh shkol.* Prešov: Rusyn i Narodnŷ novynkŷ, 2004, pp. 61-63.

604 "Carpatho-Rusyns: Their Ethno-Geographic and Historical Setting." In *Kalendár-Almanac of the National Slovak Society of the USA 2004.* Pittsburgh, Pa.: National Slovak Society, 2004, pp. 130-142.

605 "On the Writing of the History of Peoples and States," *Canadian Slavonic Papers,* XLVI, 1-2 (Edmonton, 2004), pp. 121-140.

606 "Geography and Borders." In Marcel Cornis-Pope and John Neubauer, eds. *History of the Literary Cultures of East-Central Europe: Junctures and Disjunctures in the 19th and 20th Centuries,* Vol. I. Amsterdam and Philadelphia: John Benjamins Publishing, 2004, pp. 17-30.

607 "Istoriia Rusyniv u karikaturakh Fedora Vitsa," *Narodnŷ novynkŷ.* (Prešov), No. 46-47, November 17, 2004, pp. 1 and 3. Publication of Rusyn-language introduction from item **566**.

608 *Rusyn'skŷi iazŷk,* editor. Najnowsze dzieje języków słowiańskich, Vol. XIV. Opole: Uniwersytet Opolski, Instytut Filologii Polskiej, 2004, 474 p., 4 maps. Reprinted with corrections, 2007.

Reviewed:
Anna Plishkova in *Narodnŷ novynkŷ.* (Prešov), January 31, 2005, pp. 1-2; reprinted in *Besida,* XVII, 2 (Krynica and Legnica, 2005), pp. 6-7.
M. T. [Miroslav Tejchman] in *Slovanský přehled,* XCI, 2 (Prague, 2005), p. 232.
Iurii Pan'ko in *Rusyn'skŷi literaturnŷi almanakh na 2005 rik.* Prešov: Spolok rusyn'skŷkh pysateliv Sloven'ska, 2005, pp. 117-119.
Iurii Pan'ko in *Info-Rusyn,* II, 9 (Prešov, 2005), p. 8.

Gary H. Toops in *Slavic and East European Journal*, XLIX, 4 (Berkeley, Calif, 2005), pp. 722-723.
Tomasz Kwoka in *Slavia Orientalis*, LIV, 3 (Cracow, 2005), pp. 482-486.
Tomasz Kwoka in *Zbornik Matice Srpske za filologiju i lingvistika*, XLVIII, 1-2 (Novi Sad, 2005), pp. 405-411. Reprinted in Vojvodinian Rusyn translation in *Shvetlosts*, XLVI, 4 (Novi Sad, 2008), pp. 591-597.
Michael Moser in *Harvard Ukrainian Studies*, XXIX, 1-4 [2007] (Cambridge, Mass., 2011), pp. 440-446.
Liubomyr and Les' Belei in *Naukovyi zbirnyk Muzeiu ukraïns'koï kul'tury*, Vol. XXVIII. Svidník: Hromads'ke ob'iednannia 'Rus'ko-ukraïns'ka initsiatyva/ Muzei ukraïns'koï kul'tury, 2016, pp. 44-55.

609 "[Karpat'skŷ Rusynŷ]: etno-geografichnŷi i istorichnŷi perehliad." In *ibid.*, pp. 15-38.

610 "Iazŷkovŷi vopros." In *ibid.*, pp. 85-112.

611 "Sotsiolingvistichnŷi aspect [rusyn'skoho iazŷka]: Ameryka." In *ibid.*, pp. 383-390.

612 "Bibliografiia rusyn'skoho iazŷka." In *ibid.*, pp. 427-462.

613 Translation from Ukrainian into English of "Declaration of the Assembly of Rusyn Intelligentsia," *The Ukrainian Weekly*, December 5, 2004, pp. 6 and 32.

614 "The Rusyn Question in Ukraine," *Trembita*, XVI, 1-2 (Blaine, Minnesota, 2004), pp. 12-13.

615 "O sposobach pisania historii narodów i pánstw narodowych." In Antoni Podraza, Andrzej Zięmba, and Helena Duć-Fajfer, eds. *Prace Komisji wschodnio-europejskiej*, Vol. IX. Cracow: Polska Akademia Umiętności, 2004, pp. 41-49.

2005

616 "Mapping Central Europe in the 20th Century," *Ideas: University of Toronto Arts and Science Review*, II, 1 (Toronto, 2005), pp. 34-35.

617 *Encyclopedia of Rusyn History and Culture,* co-editor with Ivan Pop and author of 524 entries and 13 maps. Revised and expanded edition. Toronto, Buffalo, and London: University of Toronto Press, 2005, xxvi and 569 p., 13 maps, 11 illustrations.

"Almashii, Mykhailo," with Ivan Pop, p. 2.

"American Carpatho-Russian Central Conference," p. 3.

"American Carpatho-Russian Orthodox Greek Catholic Diocese," p. 3.

"American National Council of Uhro-Rusyns," with Ivan Pop, pp. 3-4.

"Amerikansky russky viestnik/Amerykanskii russkii vîstnyk," p. 4.

"Anthems, Rusyn National," pp. 5-6.

"Anthologies," pp. 6-7.

"Archimandrite," with Gorazd A. Timkovič, pp. 10-11.

"Autonomous Agricultural Union," with Ivan Pop, pp. 21-22.

"Autonomy," with Ivan Pop, pp. 22-23.

"Babota, Liubytsia/Babotová, L'ubica," p. 24.

"Bacha, Iurii/Bača, Juraj," p. 24.

"Baitsura, Ivan/Bajcura, Ivan," p. 26.

"Baitsura/Bajcurová Tamara," pp. 26-27.

"Bakov, Iakim/Iasha," p. 27.

"Baludians'kyi, Andrii/Baludjánszky, András," p. 29.

"Banat," p. 30.

"Barabolia, Marko," pp. 30-31.

"Baran, Alexander," p. 31.

"Barbareum," with Bogdan Horbal, p. 31.

"Basilian Order," pp. 32-33.

"Bereg county," pp. 35-36.

"Beskyd, Antonii/Beskid, Anton/Beszkid, Antal," with Ivan Pop, p. 37.

"Beskyd, Konstantyn/Beskid, Konstantin M.," p. 38.

"Beskyd, Nykolai/Beskid, Mikuláš/Beszkid, Miklós," with Ivan Pop, p. 38.

"Best, Paul," pp. 38-39.

"Bihar," p. 39.

"Bindas, Diura/Dura," p. 40.

"Blahovîstnyk," with Ivan Pop, p. 41-42.

"Blazhovs'kyi, Havriïl Georgii /Blazsovszky, Gabriel Georgius," p. 42.

"Boikos," with Ivan Pop, p. 43-44.

"Bolyki, Lajos," p. 46.

"Bonkalo, Aleksander/Bonkáló, Sándor," with Ivan Pop, pp. 46-47.
"Borshod/Borsod county," with Ivan Pop, p. 48.
"Botlik, József," p. 48.
"Bradach, Ioann," with Mykhailo Almashii, p. 49.
"Breshko-Breshkovskaia, Ekaterina," with Ivan Pop, pp. 50-51.
"Broch, Olaf," p. 51.
"Brovdi, Ivan," p. 52.
"Bukova Horka/Bukov Monastery," with Jozafát A. Timkovič, pp. 52-53.
"Bulgarians," p. 53.
"Bunganych, Shtefan/Bunganič, Štefan," pp. 53-54.
"Bytsko, Mykhal/Bycko, Michal," p. 54.
"Byzantine Catholic World," p. 54.
"Calvi, Luca," p. 55.
"Cantors/Kantorŷ," p. 55.
"Carpathian Plainchant/Prostopiniie," with Jerry Jumba, pp. 56-57.
"Carpathian Rus'/Karpats'ka Rus'," p. 57.
"Carpatho-Russian Autonomous Council for National Liberation," p. 58.
"Carpatho-Russian Congress," p. 58-59.
"Carpatho-Rusyn American," p. 60.
"Carpatho-Rusyn Research Center," p. 60.
"Carpatho-Rusyn Society," p. 60.
"Carpatica," p. 63.
"Cathedral chapter/Kapitula," pp. 63-64.
"Chepa, Steven," p. 65.
"Chernetskii, Vasylii," with Bogdan Horbal, p. 66.
"Chopei, Laslov/Csopey, László," p. 67.
"Chornock, Orestes," p. 67.
"Church Messenger/Cerkovnyj vistnik," p. 68.
"Church Slavonic," pp. 68-69.
"Churchich, Mariia/Čurčić, Marija," p. 69.
"Cinema," pp. 69-71.
"Communism," with Bogdan Horbal, Ivan Pop, and Boris Varga,
    pp. 72-75.
"Communist party," with Bogdan Horbal and Ivan Pop, pp. 75-77.
"Compossessoratus," p. 77.
"Consistory/Konsystoriia," pp. 77-78.
"Council of Free Sub-Carpathian Ruthenia in Exile," p. 78.
"Cultural Society of Rusyns in Romania," pp. 79-80.

"Cultural Union of Ukrainian Workers," p. 80.
"Cum Data Fuerit," p. 80.
"Curia/Kuriia," pp. 80-81.
"Cyrillic Alphabet," with Ivan Pop, p. 81.
"Czajkowski, Jerzy," pp. 81-82.
"Czechoslovak Army Corps," p. 82.
"Czechs," with Ivan Pop, pp. 83-87.
"Dami, Aldo," p. 88.
"Danyliuk, Dmytro," pp. 88-89. *"Den'/Deň,"* p. 90.
"Dezső, László," p. 91.
"Diadia Rusyn National Theater," p. 91.
"Dobosh, Shtefan/Doboš, Štefan," pp. 92-93.
"Dobrians'kyi Carpatho-Russian Student Society," p. 94.
"Dolynai, Mykola," with Ivan Pop, p. 95.
"Dominium, Latifundium," with Bogdan Horbal, pp. 96-97.
"Dovhanych, Omelian," pp. 96-97.
"Dubai, Mykhaïl/Dubaj, Michal," p. 99.
"Dudick, Michael J.," pp. 100-101.
"Dukhnovich Society of Carpatho-Russian Canadians," p. 101.
"Dukhnovych, Aleksander," with Ivan Pop, pp. 101-103.
"Dukhnovych Society," with Ivan Pop, pp. 103-104.
"Dukhnovych Theater," p. 104.
"Duklia," pp. 105-106.
"Dulichenko, Aleksandr Dmitrievich," p. 106.
"Dumen," with Ivan Pop, pp. 106-107.
"Dushpastyr'," pp. 107-108.
"Duts'-Faifer, Olena/Duć-Fajfer, Helena," p. 108.
"Dzendzelivs'kyi, Iosyp Oleksiiovych," with Ivan Pop, p. 108.
"Dzubay, Alexander," p. 109.
"Ea Semper," p. 110.
"Eger," p. 111.
"Fedelesh, Vira," p. 119.
"Fedor, Pavel," with Ivan Pop, p. 119.
"Fedynets', Atanas/Fedinecz, Atanáz," p. 120.
"Feisa, Mikhailo/Fejsa, Mihajlo," p. 121.
"Filevich, Ivan Porfir'evich," pp. 123-124.
"Fincicky, Mihály," with Mykhailo Almashii, p. 124.
"Fontański, Henryk," p. 125.

"Gabriel, František," with Ivan Pop, p. 127.
"Gajdoš, Marián," p. 128.
"Geography and Economy," with Ivan Pop, pp. 131-135.
"German-Rusyn Friendship Society," p. 135.
"Germans," with Ivan Pop, p. 135-136.
"Gerovskii, Georgii Iulianovich," p. 137-138.
"Glagolitic alphabet/Glagolitsa," with Ivan Pop, pp. 138-139.
"Goch, Fedor/Gocz, Teodor," with Bogdan Horbal, pp. 139-140.
"Goga, Lawrence A.," p. 140.
"Goidych, Shtefan/Gojdič, Štefan," p. 141.
"*Görög katolikus szemle,*" p. 142.
"Gorzo, Valentine," p. 142.
"Greater Moravian Empire," p. 143.
"Greek (Byzantine Ruthenian) Catholic Church in the USA," pp. 143-144.
"Greek Catholic Central Seminary," p. 144.
"Greek Catholic Eparchy of Hajdúdorog," pp. 144-146.
"Greek Catholic Eparchy of Križevci," pp. 146-147.
"Greek Catholic Eparchy of Mukachevo," with Ivan Pop, pp. 147-148.
"Greek Catholic Eparchy of Prešov," pp. 149-150.
"Greek Catholic Eparchy of Premyzśl," with Bogdan Horbal, pp. 150-152.
"Greek Catholic Union of Rusyn Brotherhoods," p. 152.
"Greshlyk, Vladyslav," pp. 153-154.
"Gubash, Emilian/Gubaš, Emiljan," p. 154.
"Gubash/Gubaš, Milutin," p. 154.
"Gustavsson, Sven," p. 154.
"*Gymnasium* ," with Bogdan Horbal and Ivan Pop, pp. 154-156.
"Gypsies/Roma," with Ivan Pop, pp. 156-158.
"Habsburg family," pp. 159-160.
"Hadzhega, Iulii/Hadzsega, Gyula," with Ivan Pop, pp. 160-161.
"Halchak, Anna/Halčáková, Anna," p. 162.
"Hanchin, Michael J.," pp. 162-163.
"Hanudel', Zuzana/Hanudel'ová, Zuzana," p. 163.
"Hanulya, Joseph/Hanulia, Iosyf," pp. 163-164.
"Hapak, Shtefan/Hapák, Štefan," with Ivan Pop, p. 164.
"Haraksim, L'udovít," p. 165.
"Hardy, Peter S.," with Bogdan Horbal, pp. 165-166.
"Hattinger-Klebashko, Gabriel/Gabor," p. 167.

"Hegumen, Protohegumen," with Gorazd A. Timkovič, p. 167.
"Historiography: Vojvodina; United States," pp. 183-185.
"History," pp. 185-191.
"Hnatiuk, Volodymyr Mykhailovych," with Ivan Pop, pp. 192-193.
"Holovats'kyi, Iakiv Fedorovych/Golovatskii, Iakov F. ," p. 195.
"Hopko, Vasyl'," pp. 196-197.
"Horbal, Bogdan," p. 197.
"Horoshchak, Iaroslav," with Bogdan Horbal, pp. 198-199.
"Horozhans'ka shkola," with Mykhailo Almashii, p. 199.
"Horthy, Miklós/Nicholas," pp. 199-200.
"Hrabar, Aleksander," p. 201.
"Hryb, Ian," p. 205.
"Humetskii, Modest," p. 206.
"Húsek, Jan," p. 206.
"Hyriak, Mykhailo," p. 207.
"Iablochyn Monastery of St. Onufrius," p. 208.
"Iabur, Vasyl'/Jabur, Vasil'," p. 208.
"Iavorskii, Iulian Andreevich," with Ivan Pop, p. 209.
"*Iazŷchiie*," p. 210.
"Illés, Béla," p. 211.
"Irredentism," with Ivan Pop, p. 215.
"Iuhasevych-Skliars'kyi, Ivan," with Ivan Pop, p. 215.
"*Iunoshestvo*," p. 216.
"Jews: Subcarpathian and the Prešov Region," pp. 217-221.
"Jumba, Jerry," p. 222.
"Kabaliuk, Aleksei," with Ivan Pop, p. 222.
"Kachkovs'kyi Society," with Bogdan Horbal, pp. 223-224.
"Kaigl, Ladislav," p. 225.
"*Kalendar/Mîsiatsoslov*," pp. 225-226.
"Kamins'kyi, Viktor/Kaminszky, Géza," p. 227.
"Kapral', Mykhailo/Káprály, Mihály," p. 227.
"Karaman, Vasyl'," p. 228.
"Karpatorusskii golos," p. 229.
"Karpatorusskii viestnik ," p. 230.
"*Karpato-russkoe slovo/Carpatho-Russian Word* ," p. 230.
"*Karpatska Rus'/Carpatho-Rus'*," with Bogdan Horbal, p. 230.
"*Karpatskaia/Karpats'ka pravda*," pp. 230-231.
"*Karpatskii krai*," p. 231.

"*Karpatskii sviet*," p. 231.
"*Karpats'kyi krai* ," p. 231.
"*Karpats'kyi proletar* ," p. 232.
"Kasinec, Edward," p. 232.
"*Kelet* ," pp. 232-233.
"Kemyn', Mykhailo," p. 233.
"Kercha, Igor," p. 233.
"Kholoshniaï, Ioakim/Hološnjaj, Joakim," p. 234.
"Khoma, Vasyl'/Choma, Vasil'," pp. 234-235.
"*Khrystyians'ka rodyna*," p. 235.
"Kinakh, Hlib Hryhorovych," with Ivan Pop, pp. 236-237.
"Kishshova, Iudita/Kiss, Judit," p. 237.
"Klochurak/Kločurak, Stepan," pp. 237-238.
"Klympush, Dmytro," p. 238.
"Kobal', Iosyp/Kobály József," p. 239.
"Kochish, Evgen/Kočiš, Jovgen," p. 239.
"Kochish, Evgenii/Kočiš, Jevgenij," p. 239.
"Kocisko, Stephen J.," pp. 240-241.
"Kohut/Kohutov, Petro," with Bogdan Horbal, p. 241.
"Kokhannyi-Goral'chuk, Kirill Vasil'evich/Kochannyj-Goralčuk, Cyril," pp. 241-242.
"Koliadkŷ," pp. 242-243.
"Koliesar, Dragen/Kolesar, Dragutin," p. 243.
"Koliesar, Iuliian/Kolesar, Julijan," p. 243.
"Konečný, Stanislav," p. 245.
"Kontingent/Zdacha," p. 246.
"Kontratovych/Kondratovych, Irynei/Kontratovics, Irén," with Ivan Pop, p. 246.
"Kostelnik, Vlado," pp. 249-250.
"Kostiuk, Iurii/Kost'uk, Juraj," p. 250.
"Kotigoroshko, Viacheslav," p. 250.
"Kovach, Fedir/Kováč, Fedor," p. 252.
"Kožmínová, Amalie," p. 254.
"Krafcik, Patricia A.," p. 254.
"Krainiak, Frantishek/Krajňak, František," p. 254.
"Kralyts'kyi, Anatolii," with Ivan Pop, p. 255.
"Krasnŷi Brid Monastery," with Ivan Pop, pp. 255-256.
"Krofta, Kamil," p. 257.

"Kroh, Antoni," with Bogdan Horbal, p. 257.
"Krushko, Shtefan/Kruško, Štefan," pp. 257-258.
"Kseniak, Mikulai/Kseňák, Mikuláš," p. 258.
"Kubek, Emilij A.," p. 258.
"Kukhar/Kuchar, Silvester," with Ivan Pop, p. 259.
"Kustodiev, Konstantin Lukich," p. 261.
"Kuzmiak, Petro," p. 262.
"Kyzak, Ioann, Ivan/Kizák Joann," pp. 263-264.
"Kyzak, Iosyf/Kizák, Jozef," p. 264.
"Labosh/Laboš, Fedor," p. 265.
"Lacko, Michael," p. 265.
"Ladyzhin'skíi, Shtefan/Ladižinský, Štefan," pp. 265-266.
"Ladižinsky, Ivan A.," p. 266.
"Ladomirová Monastery," pp. 266-267.
"Language question," with Aleksandr D. Dulichenko, pp. 276-281.
"Latiak, Diura/Latjak, Dura," p. 281.
"Latta, Vasyl'," pp. 281-282.
"Lazho, Iurii/Lažo, Juraj," p. 282.
"Lehoczky Provincial Muzeum," p. 284.
"*Lemko* (1934-39)," p. 286.
"Lemko Region," pp. 288-289.
"Lemko Region Society in Ukraine," pp. 288-289.
"Liberty Association/Svoboda," p. 295.
"Lintur, Petro," with Ivan Pop, p. 296.
"Literature: United States," pp. 305-306.
"Liubimov, Aleksandr Andreevich," pp. 308-309.
"Liubymov, Volodymyr," p. 309.
"Luchkai, Mykhaïl/Lutskay, Michael," with Ivan Pop, pp. 309-310.
"Lyzanets', Petro/Lizanec, Péter," p. 311.
"Machik, Konstantyn/Mačik, Konstantin," p. 312.
"Machoshko, Mariia/Mačošková, Marka," p. 312.
"Maczkov, Peter J.," p. 312.
"Magyars/Hungarians," with Ivan Pop, pp. 314-316.
"Makaï, Silvester," with Aleksandr D. Dulichenko, pp. 316-317.
"Makara, Mykola," with Mykhailo Almashii, p. 317.
"Makovytsia," pp. 317-318.
"Mal'tsovs'ka, Mariia/Mal'covská, Mária," p. 318.
"Malyniak, Mykolai," p. 318.

"Maramorosh/Máramaros, county," with Ivan Pop, p. 320.
"Maramureş Region," p. 321.
"Markovych, Pavlo/Markovič, Pavol," pp. 322-323.
"Markus, Vasyl'," p. 323.
"Martel, René," pp. 323-324.
"Marton, István/Stepan," p. 324.
"Maryna, Iulii/Marina, Gyula," pp. 324-325.
"Matezonskii, Konstantin," with Mykhailo Almashii, p. 326.
"Matsyns'kyi, Ivan/Macinský, Ivan," p. 327.
"Mayer, Mária," p. 327.
"Medieshi, Helena/Međeši, Helena," pp. 327-328.
"Medieshi, Liubomir/Međeši, Ljubomir," p. 328.
"Melika, Georg," p. 328.
"Mid-European Democratic Union," pp. 329-330.
"Miz, Roman," p. 331.
"Moklak, Jarosław/Mokliak, Iaroslav," p. 331.
"Mol'nar, Mykhailo," with Ivan Pop, p. 332.
"Mondok, Ivan," p. 332.
"Mount St. Macrina," p. 333.
"Mudri, Mikhailo," p. 333.
"Museum of Ukrainian-Rus' Culture in Svidník," pp. 337-338.
"Mushynka, Mykola/Mušinka, Mikuláš," p. 339.
"Myhovych, Ivan," p. 339.
"*Narodna shkola*," p. 344.
"*Narodnaia gazeta*," pp. 344-345.
"*Narodný novynkŷ*," p. 345.
"*Nashi stremleniia*," p. 346.
"Nationalism," pp. 346-347.
"*Naukovi zapysky Uzhhorods'koho derzhavnoho universytetu*," pp. 347-348.
"*Naukovyi zbirnyk Muzeiu ukrains'koi kul'tury v Svydnyku*," p. 348.
"*Naukovŷi zbornyk Tovarystva 'Prosvîta'*," with Ivan Pop, p. 348.
"*Nedîlia* (1898-1919)," with Ivan Pop, p. 349.
"Nedzel'skii, Evgenii Leopol'dovich," with Ivan Pop, p. 350.
"Neumann, Stanislav Kostka," p. 351.
"*New Rusyn Times*," p. 352.
"Niaradii, Dionisii," with Ivan Pop, p. 353.
"Nod', Nikolai/Nagy, Nikolaj," with Mykhailo Almashii, pp. 353-354.

"Notary public/Notar," p. 354.
"*Nova dumka*," p. 354.
"*Nova svoboda*," p. 354.
"*Nove zhyttia*," pp. 354-355.
"*Novoe vremia*," p. 355.
"*Novoje vremja*," p. 355.
"Ofitsyns'kyi, Roman Andriiovych," p. 358.
"Old Ruthenianism," p. 359.
"Oleiar, Nikola D./Oleiarov, Nikolai D.," p. 359.
"Olszański, Tadeusz," p. 360.
"Organization of Rusyns in Hungary," p. 364.
"Orosvygovs'kyi-Andrella, Mykhaïl," with Ivan Pop, p. 365.
"Orthodox Eparchy of Mukachevo-Uzhhorod," pp. 365-366.
"Ortynsky, Soter," pp. 367-368.
"*Ouchytel'*," p. 368.
"Padiak, Valerii," p. 369.
"Pahyria, Vasyl'," pp. 369-370.
"Pan'ko, Iurii/Paňko, Juraj," pp. 371-372.
"Pan-Slavism," with Ivan Pop, pp. 372-373.
"Pap, Stepan/Papp, Štefan," with Ivan Pop, pp. 373-374.
"Papuga, Irina," p. 375.
"Parkanii/Párkányi, Ivan," with Ivan Pop, pp. 375-376.
"Pekar, Athansius B./Atanasii V.," pp. 379-380.
"Peniak, Stepan," p. 380.
"Perényi, Jószef," p. 380.
"Pešek, Josef," p. 381.
"Petrov, Aleksei Leonidovich," p. 382.
"Petrovai, Vasyl' Ben'ko/Petrovaj, Vasil Beňko," pp. 382-383.
"Petrovtsii, Ivan," p. 383.
"Petrushchak/Petruščak, Ivan," p. 383.
"Plishkova/Plišková, Anna," p. 385.
"*Podkarpatská Rus* (1991-)," pp. 385-386.
"*Podkarpatska Rus'* (1923-36)," p. 386.
"*Podkarpats'ka Rus'* (1992-)," p. 386.
"*Podkarpatské hlasy*," p. 386.
"Podolák, Ján," pp. 386-387.
"Polianskii, Petro," p. 390.
"Political Rusynism," pp. 390-391.

"Polivka, Ivan," p. 391.
"Polivka, Mikhailo," pp. 391-392.
"Pop, Dymytrii," p. 392.
"Pop, Ivan," p. 392.
"Popov, Aleksandr Vasil'evich," pp. 392-393.
"Popovič, Michal," p. 393.
"Popovych, Tibor Miklosh/Popovics, Tibor Miklós," p. 394.
"Popovych, Vasylii/Popovics, Bazil," with Ivan Pop, p. 394.
"*Pravoslavnaia Karpatskaia Rus'/Pravoslavnaia Rus'*," p. 396.
"Prešov Greek Catholic Teachers' College," p. 397.
"Prešov Region," p. 398.
"*Priashevshchina*," p. 398.
"*Priashevskaia Rus'*," p. 398.
"Printing and Publishing," pp. 399-403.
"*Prosvita/The Enlightenment*," pp. 403-404.
"Prosvita Society/Tovarystvo "Prosvita," with Bogdan Horbal and Ivan Pop, pp. 404-405.
"Prykhod'ko, Oleksii Kindratovych," with Ivan Pop, p. 405.
"PULS," p. 406.
"*Radians'ke Zakarpattia/Karpaty*," p. 408.
"Radio and Television," pp. 408-409.
"Rákóczy, Ferenc II," with Ivan Pop, p. 410.
"Ramach, Ianko/Ramač, Janko," p. 412.
"Renaissance Carpatho-Russian Student Society," p. 413.
"Reunification," with Ivan Pop, pp. 413-414.
"Rieger, Janusz," p. 415.
"Righetti, John Senich," pp. 415-416.
"Riznich-Diadia, Petro," p. 416.
"Roccasalvo, Joan," pp. 416-417.
"Roman, Michael," pp. 417-418.
"Roman, Mykhailo," p. 418.
"Romanians," with Ivan Pop, pp. 418-419.
"Rudlovchak, Olena/Rudlovčáková, Helena," pp. 421-422.
"*Rusin/The Ruthenian* (1910-16)," p. 423.
"Rusin Association of Minnesota," p. 423.
"Rusinko, Elaine," p. 423.
"*Rus'ka molodezh'*," p. 425.
"*Rus'ka nyva*," p. 426.

"*Ruske slovo*," p. 426.
"Ruske Slovo Publishing House," p. 426.
"*Ruski novini*," p. 426.
"Russian National Autonomist party," p. 427.
"Russian National party," p. 428.
"Russian Orthodox Church in North America," pp. 428-429.
"Russians," with Bogdan Horbal and Ivan Pop, pp. 429-431.
"*Russka zaria*," p. 431.
"*Russkaia zemlia*," p. 431.
"*Russkii narodnyi golos*," with Ivan Pop, pp. 431-432.
"*Russkii vîstnyk*," p. 432.
"*Russkii zemledielets*," p. 432.
"*Russkoe slovo* (1924-38)," p. 432.
"*Russkoe slovo* (1940-44)," p. 432.
"Russophiles," p. 433.
"Rusyn," p. 434.
"*Rusyn* (1920-21)," p. 434.
"*Rusyn* (1990-)," p. 435.
"*Rusyn/Rusin/Ruthenian* (1952-60)," p. 435.
"Rusyn Association of North America," p. 435.
"Rusyn Cultural Foundation/Ruska matka," pp. 435-436.
"Rusyn Minority Self-government," pp. 436-437.
"Rusyn National Enlightenment Society," p. 437.
"Rusyn National Union," with Bogdan Horbal, pp. 437-438
"Rusyn Renaissance Society/Rusyn'ska obroda," p. 438.
"Rusyn-Ukrainian," pp. 439-440.
"Rusynophiles," p. 440.
"*Rusynskŷi zhŷvot/Ruszin élet*," p. 440.
"Ruthenian," p. 440.
"Rychalka, Mykhailo/Ričalka, Michal," pp. 440-441.
"Sabados, Julian/Sabadosh, Iulian," p. 442.
"Sabol, Sevastiian," p. 442.
"St. Basil the Great Society," with Ivan Pop, pp. 444-445.
"Sak, Iurii," p. 446.
"Salamon, Silvester," pp. 446-448.
"Sas, Andor/Šaš, Ondrej," pp. 447-448.
"Schönborn family," with Ivan Pop, pp. 448-449.
"Segedi, Ioakim," p. 449.

"Servyts'ka, Anna/Servická, Hanka," pp. 450-451.
"Shandor, Vikentii/Vincent," p. 451.
"Sharysh/Sáros/Šariš, county," pp. 451-452.
"Shchavnyts'kíi, Mykhaïl," p. 452.
"Shelepets', Iosyf/Šelepec, Jozef ," pp. 452-453.
"Shereghy, Basil/Sheregii, Vasylii," p. 453.
"Sheregii, Iurii-Avhustyn/Šeregij, Juraj," p. 453.
"Shkol'naia pomoshch'," p. 454.
"Shlepets'kyi, Andrii/Šlepecký, Andrej," p. 454.
"Shlepets'kyi, Ivan/Šlepecký, Ivan," pp. 454-455.
"Shtets', Mykola/Štec, Mikuláš," pp. 457-458.
"Shuhai, Nikolai/Šuhaj, Nikola," with Ivan Pop, p. 458.
"*Shvetlosts*," p. 459.
"Sichyns'kyi, Volodymyr Iukhymovych," p. 459.
"Sil'vai, Sion," with Mykhailo Almashii, p. 460.
"Simon, Constantine," p. 460.
"Sivch/Sivč, Helena," p. 461.
"Sivch, Iakim/Sivč, Jakim," p. 461.
"Slavjane," p. 462.
"Slivka, John," p. 464.
"Slovaks," pp. 464-467.
"Social-Democratic party," p. 468.
"Society for Rusyn Language, Literature, and Culture," p. 468.
"Society of Carpatho-Rusyns," pp. 468-469.
"Society of Friends of Subcarpathian Rus'," with Ivan Pop, p. 469.
"Society of Rusyn Intelligentsia in Slovakia," p. 469.
"Sokols," p. 470.
"Solynko, Dmytro," with Bogdan Horbal, p. 471.
"Sopolyha, Myroslav/Sopoliga, Miroslav," p. 472.
"Špála, František," with Ivan Pop, p. 473.
"Spish/Szepes/Spiš, county," p. 473.
"Stadtkonvikt," p. 474.
"Stalin, Iosif Vissarionovich," pp. 474-475.
"Stara vira," p. 475.
"Starosta," pp. 475-476.
"Stavrovs'kyi, Emilian/Stavrovský, Emilián," p. 476.
"Stefanovskii, Pavel/Stefanowski, Paweł," with Bogdan Horbal, p. 477.
"Stercho, Peter G./Petro," pp. 477-478.

"Strumins'kyi, Bohdan/Strumiński, Bogdan," with Bogdan Horbal, p. 479.
"Subcarpathian Rusyn National Theater," p. 482.
"Sukhíi, Shtefan/Suchý, Štefan," pp. 483-484.
"Svidník Folk Festival," p. 484.
"Švorc, Peter," p. 486.
"Sydor, Dymytrii," p. 486.
"Sysak, Iaroslav/Sisák, Jaroslav," p. 487.
"Szémán/Szántay-Szémán, István," p. 487.
"Takach, Basil/Vasylii," p. 488.
"Tamash, Iuliian/Tamaš, Julijan," with Aleksandr D. Dulichenko, p. 489.
"Timko, Onufrii," pp. 492-493.
"Tomeček, Jaromír," pp. 493-494.
"Toth, Alexis/Tovt, Aleksii," p. 494.
"Transcarpathian Oblast," p. 495.
"Transcarpathian Regional Museum," pp. 495-496.
"Treaty of St. Germain," pp. 497-498.
"Treaty of Trianon," p. 498.
"Trier, Tom," p. 498.
"Trnava Adalbertine College," pp. 498-499.
"Trokhanovskii, Iaroslav/Trochanowski, Jarosław," with Bogdan Horbal, p. 499.
"Tsymbora, Iurii/Cimbora, Juraj," p. 502.
"Turianytsia, Ivan M.," p. 503.
"Turok-Hetesh, Vasyl'/Turok-Heteš, Vasil'," pp. 503-504.
"Tvorchosts/Studia Ruthenica," p. 504.
"Tymkovych, Iosafat/Timkovič, Jozafát," p. 505.
"Uchytel'," p. 506.
"Uchytel s'kyi holos," p. 506.
"Udvari, István," p. 506.
"Uhlia Monastery," with Jozafát A. Timkovič, p. 507.
"Uhors'ka Rus'/Hungarian Rus'," pp. 507-508.
"Uhro-Rusyn party," p. 508.
"Ukrainian Insurgent Army," with Bogdan Horbal, pp. 508-510.
"Ukrainian National Council of the Prešov Region," pp. 510-511.
"Ukrainians," with Bogdan Horbal and Ivan Pop, pp. 511-514.
"Ukrainophiles," p. 514.
"Ukraïns'ke slovo," p. 514.

"Unia/Church Union," with Ivan Pop, pp. 515-517.
"Unio Publishing Company," p. 517.
"Union of Rusyn-Ukrainians in Slovakia," p. 518.
"Union of Rusyns and Ukrainians in Croatia," p. 519.
"Union of Rusyns and Ukrainians in Serbia and Montenegro," p. 519.
"Union of Subcarpathian Rusyn Students," p. 519.
"United Russian Orthodox Brotherhood of America," with John
    Righetti, p. 520.
"United Societies of Greek Catholic Religion of the USA," p. 520.
"University departments/katedry," pp. 520-521.
"Val'kovs'kyi, Andrii," with Mykhailo Almashii, p. 524.
"Vanat, Ivan," p. 524.
"Vaňko, Juraj," p. 525.
"Varga, Mikhailo," p. 525.
"Varzaly, Stefan," pp. 525-526.
"Vegesh, Mykola," with Ivan Pop, pp. 528-529.
"Verets'kyi/Vorits'kyi pass," p. 529.
"Verkhovyna/Highlands," p. 531.
"*Visnyk narodnoï rady Zakarpats'koï Ukraïny*," p. 531.
"*Vîstnyk rusynov*," p. 531.
"Vitso, Fedor/Vico, Fedor," p. 532.
"Voitkovskii, Vasilii Mironovich," p. 533.
"Vojvodina," pp. 533-534.
"*Vostok/The East*," p. 537.
"*Vpered*," p. 537.
"Warhol, Andy," p. 539.
"Weller, Catherine Roberts," p. 539.
"World Congress of Rusyns," p. 541.
"Yurcisin, John," p. 543.
"*Zahoroda*," p. 544.
"Zaria Cultural and Enlightenment (National) Union of Yugoslav
    Rusyns," p. 546.
"Zeedick, Peter I.," pp. 546-547.
"*Zemlia i volia*," pp. 547-548.
"Žganec, Vinko," p. 548.
"Zhatkovych/Žatkovič/Zsatkovich, Gregory I.," pp. 548-549.
"Zhatkovych, Pavel/Zhatkovich, Paul J.," pp. 549-550.
"Zheguts', Ivan/Žeguc, Ivan," p. 550.

"Zhirosh/Žiroš, Miron," p. 550.
"Zhupan, Ishpan," with Ivan Pop, pp. 550-551.
"Zięba, Andrzej," p. 552.
"Zilyns'kyi, Ivan," pp. 552-553.
"Zilyns'kyi, Orest/Zilynskyj, Orest," p. 553.
"Zoria," pp. 553-554.
"Zoria/Hajnal," p. 554.
"Zozuliak, Aleksander/Zozul'ák, Alexander," p. 554.
"Zubryts'kyi, Dionizii/Zubrický, Dionýz," with Ivan Pop, pp. 555-556.
"Zvolinskii, Iaroslav/Zwolinski, Jaroslaw," with Bogdan Horbal, p. 556.

Reviewed:
Natalya Lazar in *Euromonitor*, April 8, 2006, http://www.ssve.sk/index.php/page=clanok+ide=40
Natalya Lazar in *Bukovyns'kyi zhurnal*, XV, 2-3 (Chernivtsi, 2005), pp. 277-280.
Natalya Lazar in *Slovenský národopis*, LIV, 2 (Bratislava, 2006), pp. 258-260.
Ernest Gyidel in *Ukraïna moderna*, No. 12 (Kyiv and L'viv, 2007), pp. 191-216. Translation into Rusyn by Mariia Mal'tsovska in *Rusyn*, XVII, 6 (Prešov, 2007) and XVIII, 4 and 6 (2008), pp. 12-13, 2-3, and 2-3.
Andriy Chirovsky in *Logos*, XL, 1-2 (Ottawa, 2008), pp. 169-176.
Yeshayahu A. Jelínek in *Journal of Jewish Studies*, LX, 2 (Oxford, 2009), p. 363.

618 "Národ nie musi mieć państwa." In *Indeks: Pismo Uniwersytetu opolskiego*, No. 3-4 [59-60]. Opole: Uniwersytet Opolski, 2005, pp. 45-47. Interview conducted by Barbara Stankiewicz.

619 "In Step or Out of Step with the Times?: Central Europe's Diasporas and Their Homelands in 1918 and 1989." *Austrian History Yearbook*, XXXVI (Minneapolis, Minn., 2005), pp. 169-189. Forum essay with commentaries by Mark Biondich, M. Mark Stolarik, and Steven Beller.

620 "Eastern, East-Central, or Central Europe: Where is It and What is It?" In *Kalendár-Almanac National Slovak Society of the USA*, Vol. CXIII. Pittsburgh, Pa.: National Slovak Society, 2005, pp. 128-140.

621 *Nasha ottsiuznyna: istoryia karpatskŷkh rusynüv.* Uzhhorod: Vŷd-vo V. Padiaka, 2005, 52 p., 5 maps, 44 illustrations.

Reviewed:
Kevin Hannan in *Slavic and East European Journal,* LI, 2 (Berkley, Calif., 2007), pp. 426-428.
Sviatoslav Semeniuk in *Aktual'ni napriamy doslidzhennia Lemkivshchyny: istoria, postati, hovir.* L'viv: Svitova fedratsiia ukraïns'kykh lemkivs'kekh ob'iednan', 2008, pp. 15-53.

622 *"Ia rusyn bŷl, iesm'y budu…":* vŷstupŷ na Svitovŷkh kongresakh *rusynüv.* Uzhhorod: Vŷd-vo V. Padiaka, 2005, 68 p.

623 *Our People: Carpatho-Rusyns and Their Descendants in North America.* 4th revised edition. Wauconda, Ill.: Bolchazy-Carducci Publishers, 2005, xvi and 232 p., 4 maps, 102 illustrations.

624 "Who and Where are the Carpatho-Rusyns: Their Ethno-Geographic Setting." In Richard D. Custer, ed. *Rusyn-American Almanac of the Carpatho-Rusyn Society.* Pittsburgh, Pa.: Carpatho-Rusyn Society, 2005, pp. 49-52. English version of item **609**.

625 "The Rusyn Language in North America: The Sociolinguistic Aspect." In *ibid.,* pp. 129-133. English version of item **611**.

626 "Chmielnicki, Bogdan." In *Encyclopedia of Genocide and Crimes against Humanity.* Edited by Dinah L. Shelton. Detroit: Thomson Gale/Macmillan Reference USA, 2005, pp. 176-177.

627 "Iak naukovets' ia ne maiu zhodnoï oriientatsiï," *Staryi zamok Palanok* (Mukachevo, Ukraine), August 18-24, 2005, p. 13. Reprinted in *Besida,* XVII, 6 (Krynica and Legnica, 2005), pp. 6-7. Interview conducted by Oleksandr Timkov.

628 "Osmi kongres naiuspishneishi po teraz," *Ruske slovo* (Novi Sad, Serbia), October 7, 2005, p. 2. Reprinted in *Rusnak,* I, 3 (Ruski Kerestur, 2005), p. 8. Interview conducted by M. Zazuliak.

629 "Carpatho-Rusyns." In *The Encyclopedia of New York State.* Edited by Peter Eisenstadt. Syracuse: Syracuse University Press, 2005, p. 267.

630 "Buduchnost' rusyniv zalezhyt' od roboty z molodezhov: výstup na 8. Svitovim kongresi rusyniv 24. iuna 2005 v Krynytsi," *Rusyn,* XV, 4 (Prešov, 2005), pp. 10-11.

631 *Galicia: A Multicultured Land,* co-editor with Christopher Hann. Toronto, Buffalo, and London: University of Toronto Press, 2005, x and 259 p., map, 5 illustrations.

Reviewed:
Kelly Stauter-Halsted in *Canadian Slavonic Papers,* XLVIII, 3-4 (Edmonton, 2006), pp. 398-399.
Peter Galadza in *Logos,* XLVIII, 1-2 (Ottawa, 2007), pp. 146-156.
Harold Binder in *Austrian History Yearbook,* XXXVIII (Minneapolis, 2007), pp. 236-237.
Alison Frank in *Slavic Review,* LXVI, 1 (Cambridge, Mass., 2007), pp. 115-117.
Hugo Lane in *Canadian Journal of History,* XLII, 1 (Saskatoon, Sask., 2007), pp. 104-106.
Rudolf A. Mark in *Jahrbücher für Geschichte Osteuropas,* LV, 3 (Wiesbaden, 2007), pp. 435-436.
Michael Moser in *Journal of Ukrainian Studies,* XXXII, 2 (Toronto, 2007), pp. 116-119.
Rayk Einax in *Historische Zeitschrift,* CCLXXXV, 1 (Oldenbourg, 2007), pp. 410-411.
Serhy Yekelchyk in *University of Toronto Quarterly,* LXXVI, 1 (Toronto, 2007), pp. 362-363.
Taras Hunczak in *Nationalities Papers,* XXXV, 2 (Charlotte, N. C., 2007), pp. 383-394.
Tomasz Gąsowski in *Kwartalnik Historyczny,* CXV, 1 (Warszaw, 2008), pp. 94-98.
Julia Verkholantsev in *Slavic and East European Journal,* LIII, 1 (Beloit, Wisc., 2009), pp. 144-146.
G. Hausmann in *Slavonic and East European Review,* LXXXVII, 2 (London, 2009), pp. 365-366.

632 "Galicia: A European Land." In *ibid.,* pp. 3-21.

633 "Paru slov na poslïdniu put' Vasylëvy Turkovy-Heteshovy," *Rusyn,* XV, 6 (Prešov, 2005), p. 3.

634 "Iak naukovets' ne mam nyiaku or'ientatsiiu," *ibid.,* pp. 18-19. Translation into Rusyn of item **627** by Anna Plishkova.

635 *Ievreï na Zakarpatti: korotkyi istorychnyi narys/Jews in Transcarpathia: A Brief Historical Outline.* Uzhhorod: V. Padyak Publishers, 2005, 28 p., map, 17 illustrations.

Reviewed:
V. Padiak in *UA.Reporter.com* (http://ua-reporter.com/new/14866); *Staryi Zamok Palanok* (Mukachevo, Ukraine), December 22-28, 2005, p.15; and *Evreivskii obozrevatel'* 24/115 December 2005 (www.jewukr.org) Aleksandr Mashkevich in *Ukraina i mir segodnia,* No. 51 (350), December 29, 2005; *Ukraïna i svit s'ohodni,* No. 50, December 23-29, 2005, p. 15; and *Trud* (Donets'k), December 28-30, 2005, p. 4.
Vek: ezhenedel'nik Vseukrainskogo evreiskogo kongressa (Kyiv), No. 51 (362), December 30, 2005, p. 3.
Bogdan Cherepania in *Pravda Ukrainy* (Kyiv), December 22-28, 2005, p. 15.

2006

636 *Carpatho-Rusyn Studies: An Annotated Bibliography,* Vol. III: *1995-1999.* New York: Columbia University Press/East European Monographs, 2006, xii and 260 p., 2 maps.

637 "Rusyns'kŷi iazŷk: doteper' dosiahnytŷ vŷslïdkŷ i zadachi do buduchnosty," *Rusyn,* XVI, 1-2 (Prešov, 2006), pp. 24-27. Translation into Rusyn of item **638** by Anna Plishkova.

638 "The Rusyn Language: Recent Achievements and Present Challenges," *Rusyn,* XVI, 3-4 (Prešov, 2006), pp. 18-21.

639 "Ruthenische kulturpolitische Organisationen." In Helmut Rumpler and Peter Urbanitsch, eds. *Die Habsburgermonarchie 1848-1918,* Vol. VII: *Politische Öffentlichkeit und Zivilgesellschaft,* Pt 1. Vienna: Verlag der Österreichischen Akademie der Wissenschaften, 2006, pp. 1349-1357.

640 *Narod nizvidky: Iliustrovana istoriia karpatorusyniv.* Uzhhorod:
Vyd-vo V. Padiaka, 2006, 119 p., 6 maps, 183 illustrations.
Translation of item **641** into Ukrainian by Serhii Bilen'kyi and
Nadiia Kushko.

Reviewed:
Igor Kercha in *Pudkarpats'kyi Rusyn* (Uzhhorod), No 12 [15], December
2006, p. 1. Reprinted in *Rusyns'kŷi svit/Ruszin világ*, V [49] (Budapest,
2007), p. 11.
Liubomyr Belei in *Dzerkalo tyzhnia* (Kyiv), No. 36 [665], September
29-October 5, 2007. Reprinted in *Ekzyl'*, No. 8 (Uzhhorod, 2007), pp. 14-
15; *Duklia,* LV, 5 (Prešov, 2007), pp. 40-43; and *Ridne slovo* (Novi Sad),
November 30, 2007, p. 10.
Liubomyr Belei in *Uriadovyi kur'ier* (Kyiv), No. 187, October 11, 2007, p. 20.
Oleksandr Havrosh in *Fest* (Uzhhorod), April 12, 2007; reprinted in *Nove
zhyttia* (Prešov), No. 17-18, April 25, 2008, pp. 4 and 6.
Natalia Iusova in *Krytyka,* XII, 1-2 [123-124] (Kyiv, 2008), p. 39.

641 *The People from Nowhere: An Illustrated History of Carpatho-
Rusyns.* Uzhhorod: V. Padiak Publishers, 2006, 120 p., 6 maps, 183
illustrations. Second revised edition. New York: Carpatho-Rusyn
Research Center, 2018, vi, 114 p., 6 maps, 183 illustrations.

Reviewed:
Natalia Laas in *Krytyka,* XII, 1-2 [123-124] (Kyiv, 2008), pp. 38-39.
Mark Morozowich in *Catholic Historical Review*, XCIV, I (Washington, D. C.,
2008), p. 191.
Katarína Panová in *Slovenský národopis,* LVI, 1 (Bratislava, 2008), pp. 109-
110.
Stjepan G. Mestrovic in *Kosmas: Czechoslovak and Central European
Journal,* XXI, 2 (Bethesda, Md., 2008), pp. 115-116.
Rachel Stauffer in *Slavic and East European Journal,* LII, 3 (Beloit, Wisc.,
2008), pp. 486-487.
William Jay Risch in *The Russian Review*, LXVIII, 3 (Columbus, Ohio, 2009)
pp. 553-554.
S. Senyk in *Orientalia Christiana Periodica,* LXXV, 2 (Rome, 2009), p. 523.

642 "Chetverta Rus': nova realnost' v novii Evropi." *Rusyn,* XVI, 5
(Prešov, 2006), pp. 15-19. Translation of item **706** into Rusyn by
Kvetoslava Koporova.

643 *"Novaia latyn'* kak sposob podniatiia prestizha maloupotrebitel'nykh iazykov." In A. Kiunnap, V. Lefel'dt, and S. N. Kuznetsov, eds., *Mikroiazyki, iazyki, interiazyki: sbornik v chest' ordinarnogo professora Aleksandra Dmitrievicha Dulichenko.* Tartu: Tartuskii universitet, Kafedra slavianskoi filologii, 2006, pp. 30-33. Translation of item **792** into Russian by Nadezhda Kushko.

644 *Karpatští Rusíni.* Prague: Společnost přátel Podkarpatské Rusi, 2006, 38 p. Translation of item **390** into Czech by Miroslav Kopecký.

645 "Opysy chy prypysy u nautsi: 'Entsyklopediia istoriï ta kul'tury rusyniv'." In *Eidos: al'manakh teoriï ta istoriï istorychnoï nauky,* Vol. II, pt. 1. Kyiv: Natsional'na akademiia nauk Ukraïny, Instytut istoriï Ukraïny, 2006, pp. 330-343. Translation of item **692** into Ukrainian by Nadiya Kushko.

646 "Rusinskii iazyk: dostizheniia poslednego vremeni i predstoiashchiie zadachi." In Aleksandr D. Dulichenko and Sven Gustavsson, eds., *Slavianskie literaturnye mikroiazyki i iazykovye kontakty.* Slavica Tartuentsia, Vol. VII. Tartu: Tartu Ülikooli Kirjastus, 2006, pp. 207-222. Translation of item **638** into Russian by Nadiya Kushko.

647 643 "A Comparison: The Rusin Identity in the United States and the Homeland." *Trembita,* XVIII, 1-2 (Blaine, Minn., 2006), pp. 4-6.

2007

648 "First Doctoral Dissertation in the Rusyn Language Defended." *Trembita,* XVIII (Minneapolis, Minn., 2007), p. 10. Translated into Rusyn: "Obhaiena persha doktor'ska robota u svitï napysana rusyn'skŷm spysovnŷm iazŷkom," *Narodnŷ novynkŷ* (Prešov), January 24, 2007, p. 1.

649 *Ievreï na Zakarpatti: korotkyi istorychnyi narys/Evreii în Transcarpatia: scurtă prezentare istorică.* Deva: Kulturne tovarystvo Rusyniv Romaniï/Uniunea Culturală a Rutenilor din

România, [2007], 27 p. Translation of item **635** into Romanian by Ioan Leviţchi.

650 "Letter to the Ambassador [Ivan Vujačić] of the Republic of Serbia to the United States." *Ruske slovo* (Novi Sad, Serbia), January 2, 2007, p. 11 and *Rusyn,* XVII, 1 (Prešov, 2007), p. 16.

651 "Uznania Rusyniv na Ukraïni—pershoriadna zadacha." *Rusyn,* XVII, 1 (Prešov, 2007), p. 8.

652 *Narod nyvŷdkŷ: iliustrovana istoriia karpatorusynôv.* Uzhhorod: Vŷd-vo V. Padiaka, 2007, 120 p., 6 maps, 183 illustrations. Translation of item **641** into Rusyn by Valerii Padiak.

Reviewed:
Stanislav Koniechni [Konečný] in *Rusyn,* XVII, 1 (Prešov, 2007), p. 3. Reprinted in *Rusyns'kŷi svit/Ruszin világ,* V [49] (Budapest, 2007), p. 12-13.
A. Z. [Aleksander Zozuliak] in *Narodnŷ novynkŷ* (Prešov), April 18, 2007, p. 1.
Tetiana Khorunzha in *Forum natsii* (Kyiv), No. 6 [61], 2007, p. 2.
Dmytrii Pop in *Rusyns'kŷi svit,* V [47] (Budapest, 2007), pp. 3-5.
Ivan Manailo in *Trybuna* (Uzhhorod), August 21, 2007; and *Podkarpats'kyi rusyn* (Uzhhorod), September 27-October 11, 2007, pp. 4-5.
Dmytro Pop in *Trybuna* (Uzhhorod), September 14, 2007, pp. 1 and 13.
Sergei Suliak in *Rusin,* III, 4 [10] (Chişinǎu, 2007), p. 177-178.
Natalia Iusova in *Krytyka,* XII, 1-2 [123-124] (Kyiv, 2008), p. 39.
Liubomyr Belei in *Ukraïns'kyi tyzhden'* (Kyiv), No. 49 [110], December 4, 2009.

653 *Poporul de niciunde: Istorie in imagini a rutenilor carpatici.* Uzhhorod: Editura lui V. Padeac, 2007, 120 p., 6 maps, 183 illustrations. Translation of item **641** into Romanian by Elvira Chilaru.

654 *Istoriia Ukraïny.* Kyiv: Krytyka, 2007, 640 p., 46 maps, 19 tables. Translation of item **452** into Ukrainian by Ernest Gyidel and Sofiia Hrachova. Second revised and expanded edition, see item **733**.

Reviewed:
Valerii Smolii, Hryhorii Hrabovych, Stanislav Kul'chyts'kyi, Oleksandr

Halenko, Serhii Bilen'kyi, Marta Bohachevs'ka-Khomiak, and Oleksandr Kresin in *Trembita* (Svaliava), August 25, 2007, p. 13.
Krytyka, XI, 9 [119] (Kyiv, 2007), p. 1.
[Petro Trochanovskii] in *Besida,* XX, 6 [105] (Krynica and Leginca, 2008), p. 24
Oleksandr Havrosh in *Dzerkalo tyzhnia* (Kyiv), No. 26 [705], July 12-18, 2008. Reprinted in *Duklia,* LVI, 4 (Prešov, 2008), p. 92.
Łukasz Adamski in *Polish Quarterly of International Affairs,* XVII, 4 (Warsaw, 2008), pp. 99-109, and in *Sprawy Międzynarodowe,* XVII, 4 (Warsaw, 2008), pp. 90-99.
Miroslav Tejchman in *Slovanský prehled,* XCV, 2 (Prague, 2009), pp. 251-252.
Tomasz Stryjek in *Kwartalnyk Historyczny,* CXXIV, 4 (Warsaw, 2017), pp. 773-804.

655 "Speredslovo/Preface." In Larysa Il'chenko, comp. *Bibliografiia rusyns'koiazýchnýkh výdan': 1989-2004/ A Bibliography of Rusyn-Language Publications.* Uzhhorod: Výd-vo V. Padiaka, 2007, pp. 3-6.

656 "Report of the Delegation from North America to the Ninth World Congress of Rusyns, Sighet, Romania, June 22, 2007," *Trembita,* XIX, 1-2 (Blaine, Minnesota, 2007), pp. 5-6.

657 "Sprava delegatsiï Rusyniv Severnoi Amerykŷ na plenarnim zasidaniu 9. Svitovoho kongresu Rusyniv, Maramorosh-Siget, 22. iuna 2007," *Rusyn,* XVII, 3 (Prešov, 2007), pp. 23-24. Translation of item **652** into Rusyn by Anna Plishkova.

658 "Dvi naihlavnïshŷ zadachi—shkolŷ i spysovania liudei: hlavnŷi výstup na 9. Svitovim kongresï Rusyniv, Maramorosh-Siget, 22. iuna 2007," *Rusyn,* XVII, 2 (Prešov, 2007), pp. 8-10. Reprinted in *Rusyns'kŷi svit,* V [46] (Budapest, 2007), pp. 5-8; in slightly abridged form in Lemko Rusyn in *Besida,* XIX, 4 (Krynica and Legnica, 2007), pp. 13-15; and in item **751**.

659 "Zakarpats'ki rusyny na vidminu vid rusyniv Ievropy, obdileni u pravovomu poli," *Novynka* (Uzhhorod, Ukraine), July 14, 2007, p. 3. Interview conducted by Tetiana Hrytsyshchuk.

660 "Zadachi III. mizhnarodnoho kongresu rusyn'skoho iazŷka," *Narodnŷ novynkŷ* (Prešov), No. 33-36, September 5, 2007, pp. 1-2.

661 *Ukraine: An Illustrated History.* Toronto and London: University of Toronto Press; Seattle: University of Washington Press, 2007, x, 336 p., 46 maps, 16 tables, 310 illustrations. Reprinted 2014, 2015, 2016 (with updates).

Reviewed:
Davis Daycock in *Winnipeg Free Press* (Winnipeg, Man.), February 25, 2008.
University of Toronto Bulletin (Toronto), February 26, 2008, p. 14.
The Ukrainian Weekly (Parsippany, N. J.), March 30, 2008, p. 10.
Henry S. Cohn in *The Federal Lawyer,* LV, 2 (Arlington, Va., 2008), pp. 69-70.
P. E. Heineman in *Choice,* XLV, 11 (Middleton, Conn., 2008).
Taras Hunczak in *The Russian Review,* LXVII, 3 (Lawrence, Kans., 2008, pp. 516-517.
Andrew Gregorovich in *Forum,* No. 115 (Scranton, Pa., 2008), pp. 26-27.
S. Senyk in *Orientalia Christiana Periodica,* LXXIV, 2 (Rome, 2008), p. 576.
Book News (Portland, Ore.), www.booknews.com, February 2008.
Kerstin Jobst in *H-Net Book Review,* http.//www.h-net.org/reviews/showrev. php?=14704, July 2008.
Kerstin Zimmer in *Europe-Asia Studies,* LXI, 5 (Glasgow, 2009), pp. 895-896.
John-Paul Himka in *Canadian Slavonic Papers,* LI, 1 (Edmonton, 2009), pp. 141-142.
Serhy Yekelchyk in *University of Toronto Quarterly*, LXXVIII, 1 (Toronto, 2009), pp. 188-189.
Thomas M. Prymak in *Journal of Ukrainian Studies,* XXXIII-XXXIV [2008-2009] (Edmonton, 2011), pp. 503-505.
Serhii Bilenky in *Harvard Ukrainian Studies,* XXIX, 1-4 [2007] (Cambridge, Mass., 2011), pp. 524-529.

662 *Židé na Podkarpatsku: stručný historický přehled.* Užhorod: Nakladatelství V. Padjaka, 2005, 22 p., map, 16 illustrations. Translation of item **635** into Czech by Hana Jiřičková.

663 "Subcarpathian Rus' and the New Slovak Historiography: Peter Mosný, *Podkarpatská Rus: nerealizovaná autonómia* and Peter Švorc, *Krajinská hranica medzi Slovenskom a Podkarpatskou Rusou,*" in *Slovakia,* XXXIX [Nos. 72-73] (Passaic, N. J., 2007), pp. 119-123.

664 Review of Alison Fleig Frank, *Oil Empire: Visions of Prosperity in Austrian Galicia,* in *Slavic Review,* LXVI, 4 (Cambridge, Mass., 2007), pp. 736-737.

665 Series editor: Yeshayahu A. Jelinek, *The Carpathian Diaspora: The Jews of Subcarpathian Rus' and Mukachevo, 1848-1948.* Photographic essay and maps by Paul Robert Magocsi. Classics of Carpatho-Rusyn Scholarship, Vol. XIII. New York: Columbia University Press/East European Monographs, 2007, xii, 412, and 32 p., 3 maps, 61 illustrations.

Reviewed:
Miloslav Szabó in *Bohemia,* XLIX, 1 (Munich 2009), pp. 247-249.
Henry Abramson in *American Historical Review,* CXIV, 3 (Chicago and Washington, D.C., 2009), pp. 860-861.
Jean-Pierre Osier in *Revue des études juives,* CLXIX, 1-2 (Paris, 2010), pp. 266-268.
Michael L. Miller in *East European Jewish Affairs,* XL, 2 (London, 2010), pp. 192-195.
Rafal Żebrowski in *Kwartalnik Historii Żydów,* No. 1 (Warsaw, 2010), pp. 115-119.
Steven Beller in *Slavonic and East European Review,* LXXXIX, 1 (London, 2011), pp. 153-155.
Rebekah Klein-Pejšová in *Journal of Ukrainian Studies,* XXXIII-XXXIV [2998-2009] (Toronto, 2009), pp. 520-522.

666 *Národ znikadial': ilustrovaná história karpatských Rusínov.* Prešov: Rusín a L'udové noviny, 2007, 120 p., 6 maps, 183 illustrations. Translation of item **641** into Slovak by Anna Plišková.

Reviewed:
Ján Botík in *Český lid,* XCV, 3 (Prague, 2008), pp. 332-334.

667 "Foreword." In Taras Kuzio. *Theoretical and Comparative Perspectives on Nationalism.* Stuttgart: Ibidem Verlag, 2007, pp. 7-8.

668 "Rusini i Podkarpatje." *Hrvatska Revija: časopis Matice Hrvatske,* VII, 4 (Zagreb, 2007), pp. 55-61.

669 "Kodifikatsiia rusyn'skoho iazŷka ochamy istoryka." In Anna
Plišková, ed. *Jazyková kultúra a jazyková norma v rusínskom
jazyku/ Iazŷkova kultura i iazŷkova norma v rusyn'skim iazŷku.*
Prešov: Prešovska univerzita, Ústav regionálnych a národostných
študií, 2007, p 24-30. Reprinted in item **709**.

670 *Rozmawiajmy po łemkowsku/Besiduime po lemkivskŷ/Let's Speak
Lemko-Rusyn,* with Helena Duć-Fajfer and Tomasz Kwoka.
Warsaw: Fundacja Rutenika, 2007, 344 p., 27 illustrations by Fedor
Vico.

2008

671 "Pozitsiia Svitovoi radŷ Rusyniv," *Narodnŷ novynkŷ* (Prešov), No.
5-8, February 22, 2008, pp. 2-3. Reprinted in *Rusnakovo klaski,* V
[8] (Petrovci, Croatia, 2008), p. 14; in *Besida,* XX, 2 [101] (Krynica
and Legnica, Poland, 2008), p. 14; in *Rusnak,* IV, 8 (Ruski Kerestur,
Serbia, 2008), p. 10; and in *Ruteanul/Rusyn,* No. 1-3 (Deva,
Romania, 2008), p. 8—together with translation in Romanian,
"Poziţia Consiliului Mondial al Rutenilor," p. 9.

672 "Zvolikaiuchy, Ukraïna provokuie ekstremizm," *Krytyka,* XII, 7-8
[129-130] (Kyiv, 2008), p. 21—excerpted in *Besida,* XX, 6 [105]
(Krynica and Legnica, Poland, 2008), p. 7. Reprinted under the title
"Nerishuchist' Ukraïny pryzvodyt' do esktremizmu," *Ukraïns'ka
pravda* (Kyiv), November 12, 2008.

673 "Vahania Ukraïnŷ vede do ekstremizmu," *Rusyn,* XVII, 3 (Prešov,
2008), p. 5. Translation of item **672** into Rusyn. Reprinted in
Rusyns'kŷi svit, IV [59] (Budapest, 2008), p. 15.

674 "Vidkrytyi lyst-zaiava pro vidmezhuvannia vid ekstremizmu v
karpatorusyns'komu rusi," with Steven Chepa. *Krytyka,* XII, 7-8
[129-130] (Kyiv, 2008), p. 21. Translated into Rusyn: "Otvorene
pysmo-vŷholoshinia o dishtantsovaniu sia od ekstremizmu v
karapatorusyn'skim rusï," *Rusyn,* XVIII, 2 (Prešov, 2008), p. 12.

675 "Vŷstup avtora knyzhky *Narod znikadial'* na iei prezentatsiï v

Slovens'kim narodnim muzeiu u Bratislavi," *Narodný novynký* (Prešov), No. 21-24, June 18, 2008, p. 5.

676 "Mukacheve." In Gershon David Hundert, ed. *The YIVO Encyclopedia of Jews in Eastern Europe,* Vol. II. New Haven and London: Yale University Press, 2008, pp. 1209-1210.

677 "Na slovichko z akademikom, prof. dr. Pavlom Robertom Magochiiom," *Info-Rusyn,* V, 11 (Prešov, 2008), p. 10. Interview conducted by Silviia Lysinova.

678 "The Scholar as Nation-Builder, or as Advisor and Advocate: Remarks Delivered ... at the Special Panel 'Paul Robert Magocsi on the Scholar as Nation-Builder' at the ASN 2007 World Convention, Columbia University," *Nationalities Papers,* XXXVI, 5 (Basingstoke, Eng., 2008), pp. 881-892.

679 "Valerii Ivanovych Padiak: 50-richchia vid dnia narodzhennia filoloha, vydavtsia (nar. 1959)." In *Kalendar kraieznavchykh pam'iatnykh dat na 2009 rik.* Uzhhorod: Vyd-vo V. Padiaka, 2008, pp. 130-136.

680 "Zadachi III. Medzhinarodneho kongresu rusyn'skoho iazýka." In Anna Plïshkova, ed. *Rusyn'skýi iazýk medzhi dvoma kongresamy.* Prešov: Svitovýi kongres Rusyniv/Inshtitut rusyn'skoho iazýka i kulturý Priashivskoi univerzitý, 2008, p. 8-14.

681 "Choosing Life Over Death: On Remembering Ukraine's Genocidal Famine." In Lubomyr Y. Luciuk, ed. *Reflections on the Great Famine of 1932-1933 in Soviet Ukraine.* Kingston, Ont.: Kashtan Press, 2008, pp. 221-224.

682 "Pro napysannia istoriï narodiv i derzhav." In *Eidos: al'manakh teoriï ta istoriï istorychoï nauky,* Vol. III, pt. 1. Kyiv: Natsional'na akademiia nauk Ukraïny, Instytut istoriï Ukraïny, 2008, pp. 58-76. Translation of item **605** into Ukrainian by Serhii Bilenky.

683 "Greek Catholics: Historical Background." In Stéphanie Mahieu and

Vlad Naumescu, eds. *Churches In-between: Greek Catholic Churches in Postsocialist Europe.* Halle Studies in the Anthropology of Eurasia, Vol. XVI. Berlin: Lit Verlag, 2008, pp. 35-64.

684 "Greetings on the Occasion of the 150th Anniversary of the Birth of Father Emil Kubek/Pozdravný telegram," in *Zborník dokumentov z oslav 150. Výročia narodenia Emila Kubeka.* Prešov: Petra, 2008, pp. 36-37.

2009

685 "Karpat'ska Rus' i karpat'skŷ rusynŷ: etno-geografichnŷi i istorychnŷi perehlad." In Mikhailo Feisa, ed. *Rusini/Rusnaci/ Ruthenians, 1745-2005,* Vol. II. Novi Sad: Prometej, 2008, pp. 7-22.

686 "World Academy of Rusyn Culture Fellows." In *ibid.,* pp. 168-190.

687 "Profesor Toront'skoi univerzitŷ P. R. Magochii odshtartovav pershyi nauchnŷi seminar z karpatorusynistikŷ," *Narodnŷ novynkŷ* (Prešov), No. 5-8, February 18, 2009, p. 2. Interview conducted by Kvetoslava Koporova.

688 "Foreword." In Sonya Jason. *Maria Gulovich, OSS Heroine of World War II: The Schoolteacher Who Saved American Lives in Slovakia.* Jefferson, N.C. and London, Eng: McFarland Publishers, 2009, pp. 1-2.

689 "The Carpatho-Rusyns of East Central Europe: A New Slavic Nationality." In Elaine Rusinko, ed. *Committing Communities: Carpatho-Rusyn Studies as an Emerging Scholarly Discipline.* New York: Columbia University Press/East European Monographs, 2009, pp. 5-19.

690 "Textbooks and National Identity: the Rusyn Question in East-Central Europe." In ibid., pp. 121-127.

691 "Comments [on the presentation by Christopher Hann]." In ibid., pp. 189-191.

692 "Descriptive or Prescriptive Scholarship: The Making of the *Encyclopedia of Rusyn History and Culture.*" In ibid., pp. 195-209.

693 "Comments [on the presentation by Nadiya Kushko, Bogdan Horbal, and Elaine Rusinko]." In ibid., pp. 292-296.

694 "Carpatho-Rusyns in the Twenty-First Century." In ibid., pp. 347-361.

695 "Skusenŷi vŷdavatel', naukovets', pedagog: k 50 narodenynam Valeriia Padiaka, k. n.," *Rusyn,* XIX, 1 (Prešov, 2009), pp. 18-19. Translation of item **679** into Rusyn by Mariia Mal'tsovs'ka.

696 "Carpathian Rus': Interethnic Co-existence without Violence." In Gerhard Besier and Katarzyna Stokłosa, eds. *Geschichtsbilder in den postdiktatorischen Ländern Europas.* Berlin: Lit Verlag, 2009, pp. 137-154.

697 *Narod nïodkadz: ilustrovana istoriia Karpatskikh Rusinokh.* Uzhhorod and Novi Sad: Vyd-vo V. Padiaka/NVU Ruske slovo, 2009, 120 p., 6 maps, 183 illustrations. Translation of item **641** into Vojvodinian Rusyn by Anita Govlia, Liubomir Medieshi, and Mikhailo Feisa.

Reviewed:
Mikhailo Feisa in *Rusin,* V, 4 [18] (Chişinău/Kishinev, 2009), pp. 107-108.

698 *Narod niotkuda: ilustrirana povijest Karpatorusina.* Uzhhorod: Naklada V. Pađaka, 2009, 120 p., 6 maps, 183 illustrations. Translation of item **641** into Croatian by Eugenija Vrabec.

Reviewed:
Tomislav Mashir in *Rusyn,* XIX, 2 (Prešov, 2009), pp. 22-23.
Evgeniia Vrabec in *Rusyn,* XIX, 2 (Prešov, 2009), p. 21.
Mladen Klemenchich in *Rusyn,* XIX, 3 (Prešov, 2009), p. 19.

699 "Dosiahnutia, problemŷ i zadachi Svitovoho kongresu Rusyniv." *Rusyn,* XIX, 2 (Prešov, 2009), pp. 4-8. Reprinted in *Rusyns'kŷi svit,* VII [69] (Budapest, 2009), pp. 6-10.

700 "Előszó/Preface/Speredslovo/Hakdomah." In Milada Nagy, ed. *Nagyszőlős, a világ közepe/ Nagyszőlős, the Centre of the World/ Sevlush, tsenter svita/Selish, Merkaz Haolam.* Budapest: Aposztróf Kiadó, 2009, pp. 5-8.

701 "Rusyns'kyi atlant." *Staryi zamok Palanok* (Mukachevo), June 2009, p. 20. Interview conducted by Mykhailo Fedynyshynets'.

702 Series editor: Anna Plishkova, *Language and National Identity: Rusyns South of Carpathians.* Translated by Patricia A. Krafcik. Classics of Carpatho-Rusyn Scholarship, Vol. XIV. New York: Columbia University Press/East European Monographs, 2009, xx, 230 p., 2 maps, 66 illustrations.

Reviewed:
Andriii Danylenko in *Canadian Slavonic Papers,* LII, 3-4 (Edmonton, 2010), pp. 471-473.

703 "Biography of Anna Plishkova." In ibid., pp. v-xiii.

704 "Works by Anna Plishkova on Carpatho-Rusyns." In ibid., pp. xiv-xvii.

705 "Karpatska Rus'—region spoluzhŷtia narodiv a narodnostei bez nasylstva." In Kvetoslava Koporova, ed. *Studium Carpato-Ruthenorum 2009: shtudiï z karpatorusynistykŷ.* Prešov: Priashovska univerzita, Inshtitut rusyn'skoho iazŷka i kulturŷ, 2009, pp. 6-24. Translation of item **696** into Rusyn by Kvetoslava Koporova.

706 "The Fourth Rus': A New Reality in a New Europe." In Paul Best and Stanisław Stępień, eds. *Does a Fourth Rus' Exist? Concerning Cultural Identity in the Carpathian Region.* Przemyśl and Higganum, Conn.: South-Eastern Research Institute/Carpathian Institute, 2009, pp. 11-25.

707 "Hanulia Iosyf (Joseph Hanulya)"; "Dzhumba Dzheri (Jerry Dzhumba)"; "Kokhanyk Petro (Peter Kohanik)"; in Vasyl' Markus' and Dariia Markus', eds. *Entsyklopediia ukraïns'koï diiaspory,* Vol.

I: *Spolucheni Shtaty Ameryky*. New York and Chicago: Naukove tovarystvo im. Shevchenka v Amerytsi, 2009, pp. 149, 237, and 405.

2010

708 "Statistics Canada: Classification of Ethnic Identity and Cultural Ancestry/Kanadska statistika: etnïchna klasifikatsiia i kultyurne pokhodzenie," *Saskatchewan Ruthenian Messenger/Saskachevanski ruski hlasnïk,* IV [7] (North Battleford, Saskatchewan, 2010), pp. 8-10. Translated into Vojvodinian Rusyn by Ljubomir Medješi.

709 "Kodifikatsiia rusyn'skoho iazŷka ochamy istorika," *Rusyn,* XX, 1 (Prešov, 2010), pp. 1-4. Reprinted in *Narodnŷ novynkŷ* (Prešov), No. 2. February 28, 2013, pp. 2-3.

710 "Traditsiia avtonomiï na Pidkarpat'skii Rusy (Zakarpatiu)," *Rusyn,* XX, 2 (Prešov, 2010), pp. 1-7.

711 Series editor: Bogdan Horbal, *Lemko Studies: A Handbook.* Reference Works in Carpatho-Rusyn Studies, No. 6. New York: Columbia University Press/East European Monographs, 2010, xii, 706 p.

Reviewed:
Jiří Friedl in *Slovansky přehled,* XCVII, 1-2 (Prague, 2011), p. 116.
Andriy Zayarnyuk in *Canadian Slavonic Papers*, LIII, 1 (Edmonton, 2011), pp. 147-148.
Besida, XXIII, 1 (Krynica, 2011), p. 25. Reprinted in *Rusyn,* XXI, 2 (Prešov, 2011), p. 10.
Mikhail Dronov in *Slavianskii al'manakh 2010.* Moscow: Indrik/Institut Slavianovedeniia RAN, 2011, pp. 528-553.
Stefan M. Pugh in *Slavic and East European Journal*, LVI, 1 (Clinton, N.Y., 2012), pp. 131-133.

712 "Traditsiï avtonomiï na Pidkarpat'skui Rusy (Zakarpatiu)," *Rusyns'kŷi svit,* VIII [82 and 83] (Budapest, 2010), pp. 8-10 and 3-6. Revised translation into Rusyn by Marianna Liavynets [-Uhryn].

713 "Carpathian Rus': Interethnic Coexistence Without Violence." In Olga A. Andriewsky, Zenon E. Kohut, Serhii Plokhy, and Larry Wolff, eds. *Tentorium Honorum: Essays Presented to Frank E. Sysyn on His Sixtieth Birthday*. Edmonton and Toronto: Canadian Institute of Ukrainian Studies Press, 2010, pp. 317-335. Also in a special issue of the *Journal of Ukrainian Studies,* XXXIII-XXXIV (Toronto, 2008-09), pp. 317-335. Revised version of item **696**.

714 *Entsyklopediia istoriï ta kul'tury karpats'kykh rusyniv,* general editor. Uzhhorod: Vyd-vo V. Padiaka, 2010, xxii and 856 p., 13 maps, 1150 illustrations. Translation of item **617** into Ukrainian by Nadiya Kushko.

Reviewed:
Ihor Burkut in *Bukovyns'kyi zhurnal*, XXII, 3 [85] (Chernivtsi, 2012), pp. 233-237.
Serhii Hirik in *Krytyka*, XVI, 11-12 [181-182] (Kyiv, 2012), p. 27.
Sergei M. Sloistov in *Slavianskii al'manakh 2015*, No. 1-2. Moscow: Indrik/ Institut Slavianovedeniia RAN, 2015, pp. 443-450.

715 "Traditsiia avtonomiï na Karpat'skii Rusy (vrakhovano suchasnoho Zakarpatia)." In Kvetoslava Koporova, ed. *Studium Carpato-Ruthenorum 2010: shtudiï z karapatorusynistikŷ*. Prešov: Priashivska univerzita, Inshtitut rusyn'skoho iazŷka i kulturŷ, 2010, pp. 19-38.Translation of item **778** into Rusyn by Kveta Koporova.

716 "Opysŷ abo predpysŷ v nautsï: entsiklopediia istoriï i kulturŷ rusyniv." In ibid., pp. 103-114. Translation of item **692** into Rusyn. Reprinted in *Rusyn*, XXI, 1 (Prešov, 2011), pp. 1-4; http://historians. in.ua/index.php/doslidzhennya/674 (April 25, 2013).

717 "Natsionalizm i natsional'na bibliohrafiia: Ivan Omelianovych Levyts'kyi i dev'iatnadtsiatyvichna Halychyna." In Luiza I. Il'nyts'ka, ed. *Bibliohrafichna komisiia Naukovoho tovarystva imeni Shevchenka u L'vovi (1909-1939): napriamy diial'nosti ta postati*. L'viv: NAN Ukraïny, L'vivs'ka natsional'na biblioteka Ukraïny im. V. Stefanyka, 2010, pp. 72-100. Translation of item **65** into Ukrainian.

718 *A History of Ukraine: The Land and Its Peoples.* Second, revised and expanded edition. Toronto, Buffalo, and London: University of Toronto Press, 2010, xxviii, 894 p., 46 maps, 23 tables.

Reviewed:
Novyi shliakh (Toronto), September 23, 2010, p. 6.
P.E. Heineman in *Choice*, XLVIII, 10 (Middletown, Conn., 2011), p. 509.
Marton Gellért Ernő in *Klio*, XXI, 4 (Budapest, 2012), pp. 7-12.
Thomas M. Prymak in *Journal of Ukrainian History*, XXXV-XXXVI [2010-2011] (Toronto, 2012), pp. 303-304.
Jeannick Vangansbeke in *Tijdingen uit Leuven*, No. 1 (Louvain, 2012), pp. 60-61.

2011

719 "Concluding Observations." In Special Section: The Scholar, Historian, and Public Advocate. The Academic Contributions of Paul Robert Magocsi, *Nationalities Papers*, XXXIX, 1 (Basingstoke, Eng., 2011), pp. 129-134.

720 "Eine rusynische Nation?" In Andreas Kappeler, ed. *Die Ukraine: Prozesse der Nationsbildung.* Köln, Vienna, and Weimar: Böhlau Vlg., 2011, pp. 269-278.

721 *Carpatho-Rusyn Studies: An Annotated Bibliography*, Vol. IV: *2000-2004.* Reference Works in Carpatho-Rusyn Studies, No. 7. New York: Columbia University Press/East European Monographs, 2011, xiv, 229 p., 2 maps, 4 tables.

722 "Tradytsiia avtonomiï na Karpats'kii Rusi (vkliuchaiuchy Zakarpattia)." In András Zoltán, ed. *In memoriam István Udvari (1950-2005): a 2010. május 25-26-i nyíregyházi emlékkonferencia anyaga/Materialy konferentsiï pamiati Ishtvana Udvari.* Nyíregyháza: Nyíregyházi Főiskola, Ukrán és Ruszin Filológiai Tanszéke, 2011, pp. 217-245, and in Olena Duts'-Faifer, ed., *Richnyk Ruskoi Bursŷ 2013.* Gorlice: Ruska Bursa, 2013, pp. 77-92. Reprinted in *Rusin*, VII, 2 [24] (Chişinău, Moldova, 2011), pp. 104-124, and in item **786**, pp. 47-73. Translation of item **778** into Ukrainian by Serhii Bilen'kyi and Nadiya Kushko.

723 "Rusyns'ka natsiia?" in Andreas Kappeler, ed. *Ukraïna: protysesy natsiotvorennia*. Kyiv: Vyd-vo K.I.S., 2011, pp. 258-267. Reprinted in item 786, pp. 95-106. Translation of item 720 into Ukrainian by Iurii Durkot.

724 "Chy potriben Konhres rusynam?" *Nedilia* (Uzhhorod), No. 28 [396], 15-21 July 2011, p. 4. Interview conducted by Liliia Zalevs'ka.

725 "Tsi treba Kongres Rusynam?," *Rusyn*, XXI, 3 (Prešov, 2011), pp. 4-5. XXI, Translation of item 724 into Rusyn by Aleksander Zozuliak.

726 "Tsïna nepererŷvnoho uspikhu: vŷstup . . . na 11 zasïdaniu Svitovoho kongresu Rusyniv u Madiar'sku 18. iuna 2011." *Narodnŷ novynkŷ* (Prešov), No. 7, July 14, 2011, pp. 2-3. Reprinted in *Rusyns'kŷi svit/Ruszin Világ*, IX [91] (Budapest, 2011), pp. 8-9.

727 "Terytoriia istorykiv," *Krytyka*, XV, 9-10 [167-168] (Kyiv, 2011), pp. 30-32. Translation of item 719 into Ukrainian by Oleksii Sydorchuk.

728 "Aleks Rovt (Oleksandr Semenovych Rovt): 60-ricchia vid dnia narodzhennia vidomoho pidpryiemtsia, metsenata, pochesnoho hromadianyna m. Mukacheva." *In Kalendar kraieznavchykh pam'iatnykh dat na 2012 rik*. Uzhhorod: Vyd-vo V. Padiaka, 2011, pp. 207-210. Translation from English into Ukrainian by Nadiya Kushko.

2012

729 "Probudzhenŷi Rusynŷ z hlubokoho sna—viryme, zhe navse," *Rusyn*, XXII, 1 (Prešov, 2012), pp. 1-2. Reprinted in *Rusyns'kŷi svit/Ruszin Világ*, XI [100] (Budapest, 2013), pp. 7-8. Translation of item 730 into Rusyn.

730 "Awakened from Deep Slumber—Permanently," *Trembita*, XXIV (Minneapolis, Minn., 2012), p. 18-19.

731 "Mŷ—ieden narod," *Narodnŷ novynkŷ* (Prešov), No. 4, April 30, 2012, pp. 1-2.

732 "Metropolitan Andrei Sheptyts'kyi/Mytropolyt Andrei Sheptyts'kyi." In *Honouring Metropolitan Andrei Sheptytsky and His Legacy/Vshanuvannia mytropolyta Andreia Sheptyts'koho ta ioho spadku.* Mississauga, Ont.: Ukrainian Jewish Encounter, 2012, pp. 4-5 and 4-5. Reprinted in Peter Galadza, ed. *Archibishop Andrei Sheptytsky and the Ukrainian Jewish Bond.* Ottawa: Metropolitan Andrey Sheptytsky Institute/Ukrainian Jewish Encounter, 2014, pp. 5-6.

733 *Ukraïna: istoriia ïï zemel' ta narodiv.* Uzhhorod: Vyd-vo V. Padiaka, 2012, xxii and 794 p., 46 maps, 23 tables. Translation of item **718** into Ukrainian by Ernest Hyidel', Sofiia Hrachova, Nadiya Kushko, and Oleksii Sydorchuk. Second edition, with additions, 2017, xxii and 812 p., 46 maps, 23 tables.

Reviewed:
Serhii Shebelist in *Ridnyi krai: almanakh Poltavs'koho derzhavnoho pedahohichnoho instytutu,* No. 1 [26] (Poltava, 2012), pp. 273-274.
Valerii Trofimov in http://www.historians.in.ua/index.php/avtorska-kolonka/289
Valerii Padiak in *Rusyn,* XXII, 2 (Prešov, 2012), pp. 17-18.
[Oleh Romanyshyn] in *Homin Ukraïny* (Toronto), March 12, 2013, p. 9.
Volodymyr Sklokin in *Drynov's'kyi zbirnyk,* Vol. VI. Kharkiv and Sofia: Kharkivs'kyi natsional'nyi universytet/Instytut za balkanistika, Bulgarska akademiia na naukita, 2013, pp. 430-431.
O.V. Ias' in *Ukraïns'kyi istorychnyi zhurnal,* LVII, 5 (Kyiv, 2013), pp. 212-215.
Elena Iu. Borisenok and Svetlana S. Lukashova in *Belorussiia i Ukraina: istoriia i kul'tura,* Vol. 5. Moscow: Institut slavianovedeniia RAN, 2015, pp. 521-534.
L.V. Bazhenov in "Pavlo-Robert Magochii i rehional'na istoriia Ukraïny," *Visnyk Kam'ianets'-Podil's'koho natsional'noho universytetu im. Ivana Ohiienka: Istorychni nauky,* No. 10 (Kam'ianets'-Podil's'kyi, 2017), pp. 8-12.

734 "Zakluchni notatky z pryvodu sympoziumu." In Hryhorii Hrabovych, Taras Kuz'o, Serhii Plokhii, Oleksandr Motyl', and Dominik Arel'. *Vnesok Pavla-Roberta Magochiia v nashe rozuminnia Ukraïny ta tsentral'noï Ievropy*. Uzhhorod: Vyd-vo V. Padiaka, 2012, pp. 71-81. Reprinted, 2013. Translation of item **719** into Ukrainian by Oleksii Sydorchuk.

735 *Iliustrovana istoriia Ukraïny*. Kyiv: Krytyka, 2012, 448 and xlviii, p. 46 maps, 16 tables, 417 illustrations. Translation of item **661** into Ukrainian by Serhii Bilenkyi.

Reviewed:
Elena Iu. Borisenok and Svetlana S. Lukashova in *Belorussiia i Ukraina: istoriia i kul'tura*, Vol. 5. Moscow: Institut slavianovedeniia RAN, 2015, pp.521-534.

736 "Na Zakarpatti my robymo te, shcho rukh hromadivtsiv robyv v Ukraïni v XIX stolitti." Interview conducted by Volodymyr Sklokin. http://historians.in.ua/index.php/intervyu/291 (June 7, 2012).

737 "Chetverta Rus': nova real'nist' v novii Ievropi." In Julian Tamaš, ed. *Veličina malih jezičkih, književnih, kulturnih i istorijskih tradicijah: zbornik radova*. Novi Sad: Filozofski fakultet, Odsek za rusinistiku, 2012, p. 65-76. Also published in Olena Duts'-Faifer, ed. *Richnyk Ruskoi Bursŷ 2012*. Gorlice: Ruska Bursa, 2012, pp. 83-93, and in item 786, pp. 29-45. Translation of item **706** into Ukrainian by Nadiya Kushko.

738 *Carpatho-Rusyn Studies: An Annotated Bibliography*, Vol. V: *2005-2009*. New York: Columbia University Press/East European Monographs, 2012, xvi and 256 p., 2 maps, 4 tables.

Reviewed:
S. Caprio in *Orientalia Christiana Periodica*, LXXI, 2 (Rome, 2014), pp. 536-537.

739 "Karpats'ka Rus': mizhetnichne spivisnuvannia bez nasyllia." http://www.historians.in.ua/index.php/doslidzhennya/580 (February 12, 2012). Also published in Olena Duts'-Faifer, ed. *Richnyk Ruskoi Bursŷ 2014*. Gorlice: Ruska Bursa, 2014, pp. 117-132, and reprinted in item **781**, pp. 7-27. Translation of item **713** into Ukrainian by Nadiya Kushko.

740 "The Fourth Rus': A New Reality in a New Europe." In *Confronting the Past: Ukraine and Its History—A Festschrift in Honour of John-Paul Himka/Journal of Ukrainian Studies*, XXXV-XXXVI [2010-2011] (Toronto, 2012), pp.167-177.

2013

741 Review of Michal Šmigel and Štefan Kruško, *Opcia a presídlenie Rusínov do ZSSR 1945-947, in Slovakia,* XLI [76-77] (Passaic, N. J., 2013), pp. 203-206.

742 "Slavic Immigrant Cultures in North America: The Language Factor." In Michael Moser and Maria Polinsky, eds., *Slavic Languages in Migration*, Zürich and Munich: Lit Verlag, 2013, pp. 11-23.

743 "Zhŷva legenda—Aleksander Zozuliak," *Rusyn,* XXII, 1 (Prešov, 2013), pp. 2-4. Reprinted in *Lemkivskii richnyk 2013.* Ed. Petro Trokhanovskii. Krynica and Legnica: Stovaryshŷnia Lemkiv, 2013, pp. 162-167.

744 "Memorandum [on Ukraine's Law No. 5029-VI: The Principles of the State's Language Policy]," *The New Rusyn Times,* XX, 3 (Pittsburgh, 2013), p. 4. [unsigned]

745 "Memorandum amerykans'kykh rusyniv, 8.III. 2013" [Ukraine's Law No. 5029-VI: "The Principles of the State's Language Policy"], *Rusyn,* XXIII, 1 (Prešov, 2013), pp. 12-13. Reprinted in *Besida,* XXV, 4 [133] (Krynica and Legnica, 2003), p. 19. Translation of item **744** into Ukrainian by Nadiya Kushko. [unsigned]

746 "Carpathian Rus': Interethnic Coexistence Without Violence." In Omer Bartov and Eric D. Weitz, eds. *Shatterzone of Empires: Coexistence and Violence in the German, Russian, and Ottoman Borderlands.* Bloomington and Indianapolis: Indiana University Press, 2013, pp. 449-462.

747 "The 'Other' Peoples of Subcarpathian Rus': 1919-1939." In Wolf

Moskovich, Roman Mnich, and Renata Tarasiuk, eds. *Jews and Slavs*, Vol. 23: *Galicia, Bukovina and Other Borderlands in Eastern and Central Europe*. Jerusalem/Siedlce University of Natural Sciences and Humanities, 2013, pp. 266-278.

748 "Východní krest'ania v Habsburskej monarchii v rokoch 1526-1918." In Jaroslav Coranič, ed. *Gréckokatolícka cirkev na Slovensku v svetle výročí*, Vol. III. Prešov: Vyd-vo Prešovskej univerzity, 2013, pp. 215-234. Translation of item **810** into Slovak by Eva Eddy.

749 "Glosa," *InfoRusyn*, X, 8-9 (Prešov, 2013), p. 1.

750 "Nasha pozitsiia k Svitovomu kongresu rusyniv," *Rusyn*, XXIII, 4 (Prešov, 2013), pp. 6-8. Reprinted in *Podkarpats'kyi rusyn* (Uzhhorod), No. 57 [70], October 2013, pp. 1 and 4. [signed Carpatho-Rusyn Research Center as member of the Carpatho-Rusyn Consortium of North America, 17.VI.2013]

751 "Dvi naihlavnïshŷ zadachi—shkolŷ i spysovania liudei: hlavnŷi vŷstup na 9. Svitovim kongresï, Maramuresh-Siget, Rumuniia." In Iulius Firczak et al. *Svitovoi radŷ Rusyniv/ Consiliul mondial al Rutenilor—2007*. Deva: Cetate Deva, 2013, pp. 57-62.

752 "Două cele mai importante sarcini—şcoala şi recensământul populaţiei: cuvântul rostit la cel de-al IX-lea Congres Mondial de la Sighetu Marmaţiei, Rômania." In *ibid.*, pp. 63-67. Translation of item **751** into Romanian.

753 "Konstruiuvannia chy dekonstruktsiia: iak povynna vyhliadaty 'maibutnia istoriia Ukraïny'?," *Ukraïns'kyi istorychnyi zhurnal*, LVII, 4 (Kyiv, 2013), pp. 4-7. Translation into Ukrainian by Nadiya Kushko.

754 "Felébredtek a mély álomból—bizunk benne, hogy végleg," *Rusyns'kŷi svit/Ruszin Világ*, XI [100] (Budapest, 2013), pp. 16-17. Translation of item **729** into Hungarian by Ferencné Tudlik.

755 "Rozhovory s akademikmi," *Mladá veda*, No. 2. Prešov: Universum, 2013, pp. 6-8. Interview conducted by Branislav A. Švorc.

756 "Doctor honoris causa Address." In Anna Plišková, ed. *Profesor Dr. Paul Robert Magocsi—Doctor honoris causa Prešovskej univerzity v Prešove*. Prešov: Vyd-vo Prešovskej univerzity, 2013—Slovak text, pp. 19-24; Rusyn text, pp. 40-46; English text, pp. 61-67.

2014

757 "Na pamiatku Stefana Piu," *Rusyn*, XXIV, I (Prešov, 2014), pp. 14-15.

758 "Malorosiia abo Ukraïna: evroaziis'kŷi vŷkhod, abo evropskŷi zapad?," *Rusyn*, XXIV, 1 (Prešov, 2014), pp. 8-10. Excerpt in *Narodnŷ novynkŷ* (Prešov), No. 5, May 14, 2014, p. 1.

759 *This Blessed Land: Crimea and the Crimean Tatars*. Toronto: University of Toronto Press/Chair of Ukrainian Studies, 2014, vi and 154 p., 9 maps, 1 table, 140 illustrations.

Reviewed:
Bülent Tanatar in *Emel*, LXXXIV, 246/249 (Istanbul, 2014), pp. 137-140.
Bartosz Marcinkowski in *New Eastern Europe*, No. 3-4 (XVII) (Cracow, 2015), pp. 176-178.
Greta Uehling in *Canadian Slavonic Papers*, LVII, 1-2 (Edmonton, 2015), pp. 152-153.
Kristen Kletke in *The Ukrainian Quarterly*, LXXI, 1-3 (New York, 2015), pp. 123-127.
Ekin Günaysu in Center for Eurasian Studies (AVIM) website: https://www.avim.org.tr/en/Yorum/BOOK-REVIEW-THIS-BLESSED-LAND-CRIMEA-AND-CRIMEAN-TATARS
Yuliya Biletska in *International Crimes and History/Uluslararasi Suçlar ve Tarih*, No. 16 (Ankara, 2015), pp. 155-160.
Dan Shapira in *Karaite Archives*, No. 3 (Poznań, 2015), pp. 199-208.
Gunter Schaarschmidt in *East/West: Journal of Ukrainian Studies*, VI, I (Edmonton, 2019), pp. 169-171.
Michael Geistlinger in *Europa Ethnica*, LXXIV, 1-2 (Vienna, 2017), pp. 48-51.

760 *Krym: nasha blahoslovenna zemlia.* Uzhhorod: Vyd-vo V. Padiaka, 2014, 160 p., 9 maps, 1 table, 140 illustrations. Translation of item **759** into Ukrainian by Oleksii Sydorchuk and Nadiya Kushko.

Reviewed:
Oleksandr Halenko in *Ukraïns'kyi istorychnyi zhurnal*, LVIII, 3 (Kyiv, 2014), pp. 219-226.
Valentyn Krysachenko and Oleh Chyrkov in *Ukraïnoznavstvo*, 1 [54] (Kyiv, 2015), pp. 241-246.

761 *Krym: nasha blagoslovennaia zemlia.* Uzhhorod: Vyd-vo V. Padiaka, 2014, 160 p., 9 maps, 1 table, 140 illustrations. Translation of item **759** into Russian by Nadiya Kushko.

762 "Little Russia or Ukraine: The Eurasian East Versus the European West," *Homin Ukraïny/Ukrainian Echo* (Toronto), May 6, 2014, p. 2. Reprinted as the "Afterword" in Lubomyr Luciuk, ed. *Jews, Ukrainians, and the Euromaidan.* Kingston, Ont. and Toronto: Kashtan Press/Chair of Ukrainian Studies, University of Toronto, 2014, pp. 233-238.

763 "Malorosiia chy Ukraïna: Ievraziis'kyi Skhid chy Ievropeis'kyi Zakhid?," *Homin Ukraïny* (Toronto), July 29, 2014, p. 9. Reprinted in *Rusyn*, XXIV, 3 (Prešov, 2014), pp. 11-13. Translation of item **762** into Ukrainian by Nadiia Kushko.

764 "Iubiluiucha rusynistka" (dots. PhDr. Anna Plïshkova, PhD.), *Rusyn*, XXIV, 3 (Prešov, 2014), pp. 1-3. Reprinted with some additions, „Vŷznachna rusynistka, znama doma i za hranitsiamy," in Aleksander Zozuliak, ed., *100 vŷznamnŷkh Rusyniv ochamy suchasnykiv*, Vol. III. Prešov: Akademiia rusyn'skoi kulturŷ v SR, 2020, pp. 68-78.

765 "Wpływ rządów komunistycznych w Czechosłowacji na sytuację miejscowych Rusinów-Ukraińców." In Magdalena Semczyszyn and Jarosław Syrnyk, eds. *Między ideologią a socjotechniką: kwestia mniejszości narodowych w działalności władz komunistycznych.* Warsaw, Szczecin, and Wrocław: Instytut Pamięci Narodowej, 2014, pp. 86-100. Translation of item **776** into Polish.

766 *Naród odnikud: ilustrované dějiny karpatských Rusínů.* Uzhhorod: Vydavatelství V. Pad'aka, 2014, 120 p., 6 maps, 2 tables, 183 illustrations. Translation of item **641** into Czech by Miloslav Kopecký.

Reviewed:
Ivo Pospišil in *Proudy: středoevropský časopis pro vědu a literature,* No. 2 (Brno, 2014), 3 p., www.phil.muni.cz/journal/proudy/filologie/recenze/2014/2/pospisil_magocsi_rusini.php

767 *A nép, amelyik sehonnan sem jött: a kárpáti ruszinok képes története.* Uzhhorod: V. Pagyak Kiadója, 2014, 120 p., 6 maps, 2 tables, 183 illustrations. Translation of item **641** into Hungarian by Béla Varga.

768 "I Fear the Day that Technology Will Surpass Human Interaction," *Canada-Ukraine Parliamentary Program Newsletter,* No. 1 (Toronto, 2014), pp. 45-47. Reprinted in *Homin Ukraïny/Ukrainian Echo* (Toronto), February 7, 2017, p.1; and *Slovak Studies Association Newsletter* (Urbana, Ill., 2016-17), pp. 15-18.

769 "Carpatho-Rusyn Americans." In Thomas Riggs, ed. *Gale Encyclopedia of Multicultural America,* Vol. I. Farmington Hills, Mich.: Gale Cengage Learning, 2014, pp. 419-432.

770 "Russian Americans." In ibid. Vol. IV, pp. 31-45.

771 "Mifŷ i stereotipŷ v istoriï karpat'skŷkh Rusyniv," *Rusyn,* XXIV, 6 (Prešov, 2014), pp. 3-7. Translation of an abridged version of item **783** into Rusyn.

772 "Istoriia ukraïns'kykh ievreïv: shcho my pamiataiemo, choho ne pamiataiemo?" Interview conducted by Iryna Slavinska. https://hromadskeradio.org/2014/10/31/istoriya-ukrayinskih-yevreyiv-shho-mi-pam-yatayemo:robrt-pol-magochiy

773 "Hromadske Radio: The History of Ukrainian Jews: What Do We Remember and What Do We Not Remember?," December 5, 2014. Translation of item **772** into English by Olesya Kravchuk. http://

ukrainianjewishencounter.org/en/hromadske-radio-the-history-of-ukrainian-jews

774 *Naród znikąd: ilustrowana historia Rusinów Karpackich.* Uzhhorod: Wydawnictwo W. Padiaka, 2014, 120 p., 6 maps, 2 tables, 183 illustrations. Translation of item **641** into Polish by Edyta Tkacz.

Reviewed:
[Petro Trokhanovskii] in *Besida*, XXVII, 1 (Legnica, 2015), pp. 22.

775 Review of M. Mark Stolarik, *Where is My Home?: Slovak Immigration to North America*, in *Histoire sociale/Social History*, XLVII [95] (Ottawa, 2014), pp. 835-837.

776 "The Impact of Communist Rule on the Rusyns-Ukrainians of Czechoslovakia." In Jaroslav Coranič, ed. *Cirkev v dejinách krest'anstva na Slovensku*. Prešov: Vyd-vo Prešovskej univerzity, 2014, pp. 195-210.

2015

777 "Evropeis'ka Ukraïna chy evraziis'ka Malorosiia?" *Krytyka*, XVIII, 9-10 [203-204] (Kyiv, 2015), pp. 19-22. Translation of item **779** into Ukrainian by Myroslava Luzina. Reprinted in *Besida*, XXVII, 3 and 4 (Krynica, 2015), pp. 21 and 18-20.

778 "The Heritage of Autonomy in Carpathian Rus' and Ukraine's Transcarpathian Region," *Nationalities Papers*, XLIII, 4 (Abingdon, Eng., 2015), pp. 577-594.

779 "European Ukraine or Eurasian Little Russia?," *New Eastern Europe* (Cracow, 2015), http://neweasterneurope.eu/articles-and-commentary/1520-european-ukraine-or-eurasian-little-russia Print version in *Karpatska Rus'/Carpathian Rus'*, LXXXV, 2: Series IV (Higganum, Conn., 2015), pp. 14-18. Shorter version in *The New Rusyn Times*, XXII, 2 (Pittsburgh, 2015), pp. 1, 9-10.

780 "Evropska Ukraïna, tsi evraziiska Malorosiia?," *Rusyn*, XXV, 1

(Prešov, 2015), pp. 8-10. Translation of item **779** into Rusyn by Aleksander Zozuliak. Reprinted in *InfoRusyn*, XII, 14 (Prešov, 2015), pp. 6-7.

781 *Let's Speak Rusyn/Bisïduime po rusyn'skŷ: Prešov Region Edition.* New York and Prešov: Carpatho-Rusyn Research Center/Academy of Rusyn Culture in the Slovak Republic, 2015, xii, 115 p., 2 maps, 23 illustrations by Fedor Vico.

Reviewed:
Andrii Danylenko in *Slavonic and East European Review*, XCVII, 3 (London, 2019), pp. 529-531.
Gleb P. Pilipenko in *Slavianskii almanakh 2019*. Moscow: Indrik/Institut Slavianovedeniia, 2019, pp. 536-540.

782 "'Counting Sheep' Leaves Professor Speechless," *St. Vladimir Institute Visty/News*, Winter-Spring (Toronto, 2015), p. 8.

783 "Myths and Stereotypes in Carpatho-Rusyn History." In Francisc Gal and Liviu Lazăr, eds. *Studii de istorie, sociologie, etnografie și retrologie agrară: volum dedicat istoricului Gheorghe Firczak la 60 de ani.* Deva: Editura Cetate Deva, 2015, pp. 445-474.

784 "Protestantism and the Carpatho-Rusyns." *Karpatska Rus'/ Carpathian Rus'*, LXXXV, 2 (Series IV) (Higganum, CT, 2015), pp. 8-11.

785 "Speredslovo/Preface." In Larysa Il'chenko and Valerii Padiak, eds. *Bibliografiia rusyns'koiazŷchnŷkh vŷdan'/A Bibliography of Rusyn Language Publications: 2005-2014.* Uzhhorod: Vŷd-vo V. Padiaka, 2015, pp. 4-7

786 *Kozhen karpatorusyn ie rusynom. . . ale ne kozhen rusyn ie karpatorusynom: statti.* Uzhhorod: Vyd-vo V. Padiaka, 2015, 132 p., 2 maps. Translations of items **713**, **720**, **740**, **776**, **778**, and **783** into Ukrainian by Nadiya Kushko, Serhii Bilenky, and Iurii Durkot.

Reviewed:
Andrei Blanutsa in *Krytyka*, XX, 5-6 (Kyiv, 2016), pp. 17.

787 "Vplyv komunistychnoho pravlinnia na rusyniv-ukraïntsiv Chekhoslovachchyny." In Pavlo-Robert Magochii. *Kozhen karpatorusyn ie rusynom . . . ale ne kozhen rusyn ie karpatorusynom.* Vyd-vo V. Padiaka, 2015, pp. 75-93. Translation of item **776** into Ukrainian by Nadiya Kushko.

788 "Mifi ta stereotypy v istoriï Karpats'koï Rusi." In ibid., pp. 109-127. Translation of item **783** into Ukrainian by Nadiya Kushko. Reprinted in *Studium Carpatho-Ruthenorum 2016.* Prešov: Priashivska univerzita, Inshtitut rusyn'skoho iazŷka i kul'tury, 2016, pp. 84-100.

789 "Tsi nam treba chetvertŷi kongres rusyn'skoho iazŷka?," *Rusyn*, XXV, 5 (Prešov, 2015), pp. 2-4.

790 *With Their Backs to the Mountains: A History of Carpathian Rus' and Carpatho-Rusyns.* Budapest and New York: Central European University Press, 2015, xx, 544 p., 34 maps, 6 tables, 102 illustrations. Reprinted 2016 (with corrections) and 2017 (with additions).

Reviewed:
P. W. Knoll in *Choice*, LIV, 1 (Middletown, Conn., 2016), p. 100.
Stanislav Holubec in *Hungarian Historical Review*, V, 3 (Budapest, 2016), pp. 713-716.
Paul Best in *The Polish Review*, LXII, 4 (New York, 2017), pp. 85-87; reprinted in *Karpatska Rus'/Carpathian Rus'*, LXXXVI, 4 (Higganum, Conn., 2016), pp. 24-26.
Sergei I. Zhuk in *Russian Review*, LXXVI, 1 (New York, 2017), p. 158.
Keith P. Dyrud in *Slovakia*, XLIII [80-81] (Passaic, N. J., 2017), pp. 156-158.
Sebastian Paul in *Zeitschrift für Ostmitteleuropa-Forschung*, LXVI, 3 (Marburg, 2017), pp. 413-414. Reprinted in *Sehepunkte*, XVII, 11 (2017), www.sehepunkte.de/2017/11/31023.html
Peter Švorc in *Slovanský přehled*, CIII, 1 (Prague, 2017), pp. 147-156.
Curtis Murphy in *Slavic and East European Journal*, LXI, 2 (Clinton, N.Y., 2017), pp. 375-377.
Piotr J. Wróbel in *Przegląd Historyczny*, CIV, 4 (Warsaw, 2017), pp. 775-778.
Agnieszka Halemba in *Ab Imperio*, No. 4 (River Forest, Ill., 2017), pp. 321-326.

Tomasz Stryjek in *Kwartalnyk Historyczny*, CXXIV, 4 (Warsaw, 2017), pp. 773-804.

Kirill V. Shevchenko in *Slavianskii al'manakh 2018*. Moscow: Indrik/Institut Slavianovedeniia RAN, 2018, pp. 379-393.

Ernest Gyidel in *Austrian History Yearbook*, XLIX (Minneapolis, 2018), pp. 281-282.

Nicholas K. Kupensky, Harvey Goldblatt, John-Paul Himka, Peter Galadza, Valerii Padiak, and Chris Hann in *Nationalities Papers*, XLVII, 3 (New York and Cambridge, Eng. 2019), pp. 506-536.

Sophia Wilson in *Harvard Ukrainian Studies*, XXXVI, 1-2 (Cambridge, Mass. 2019), pp. 200-203.

Christophe von Werdt in *Jahrbücher für Geschichte Osteuropas*, LXVII, 4 (Stuttgart, 2019), pp. 635-637.

André Liebich in *Nationalism and Ethnic Politics*, XXVI, 2 (Belfast, 2020), pp. 202-208.

Serhii Hirik in *Krytyka*, XXIV, 5-6 (Kyiv, 2020), p. 21.

791 "Rusyn." In *Encyclopaedia Britannica Online*. Accessed on 17 December 2015. http://www.britannica.com/topic/Rusyn-people

792 "The New Latin as an Enhancement to Lesser-Used Languages," *Harvard Ukrainian Studies*, XXXII – XXXIII: *Zhnyva: Essays Presented in Honor of George G. Grabowicz on His Seventieth Birthday*, Part 2 (Cambridge, Mass., 2015), pp. 509-512.

793 *Dějiny Ukrajiny*, co-author with Jan Rychlík and Bohdan Zilynskyj. Prague: Nakladatelství Lidové noviny, 2015, 524 p., 45 maps, illustrations.

794 "Kul'tury slov'ians'kykh immihrantiv v Pivnichnii Amerytsi: movnyi faktor." In *Naukovi zapysky Natsional'noho universytetu "Ostroz'ka akademiia,"* Seriia: "Istorychni nauky," No 23. Ostroh, 2015, pp. 274-279. Translation of item **742** into Ukrainian by Nadiya Kushko.

2016

795 "A Borderland of Borders: The Search for a Literary Language in Carpathian Rus'." In Tomasz Kamusella, Motoki Nomachi, and Catherine Gibson, eds. *The Palgrave Handbook of Slavic Languages, Identities, and Borders*. Basingstoke, England and New York: Palgrave Macmillan, 2016, pp. 101-123.

796 "Iak u Kyievi vidznachat' 75-ti rokovyny trahediï v Babynomu Iaru?" Interview conducted by Iryna Slavinska. http://hromadskeradio.org/programs/zustrichi/yak-u-kyyevi-vidznachat-75-ti-rokovyny-tragediyi-v-babynomu-yaru

797 "Kul'tury slov'ians'kykh immihrantiv v Pivnichnii Amerytsi: movni faktor." In Vilmos Gazdag, Zoltán Karmacsi, and Enikő Tóth, eds. Értékek és kihivások. Ungvár/Uzhhorod, 2016, pp. 137-144. Translation of item **742** into Ukrainian by Nadiya Kushko.

798 "Pisliamova." In Nadiia Kushko, *Nadiia i demon samotnosti: vybrani poeziï*. Chernivtsi: Meridian Czernowitz, 2016, pp. 77-91.

799 *Jews and Ukrainians: A Millennium of Co-Existence*, co-author with Yohanan Petrovsky-Shtern. Toronto: University of Toronto/Chair of Ukrainian Studies, 2016, xii, 320 p., 29 maps, 335 illustrations. Second revised edition, 2018.

Reviewed:
Simon Geissbühler in *Israel Journal of Foreign Affairs*, XI, 1 (Basingstoke, Eng., 2017), pp. 139-140.
Admin in *Texas Jewish Post*, April 20, 2017.
Aaron Leibel in *Washington Jewish Week* (Washington, D.C.), July 27, 2017.
World Literature Today, May 2017.
Philip K. Jason in *Jewish Book Council* (where?), May 9, 2017.
Amos Lassen Reviews, June, 2017
[Vlad Davidzon] in *Odessa Review*, No. II (Kyiv, 2017), pp. 74-75.
Marina Batsman in *Ab Imperio*, No. 2 (River Forest, Ill., 2017), pp. 328-335.
Alexander Sydorenko in *Russian Review*, LXXVI, 3 (New York, 2017), pp. 555-556.
Alla Marchenko in *Journal of Soviet and Post-Soviet Politics and Society*, III, 2 (Stuttgart, 2017), pp. 301-304.
Iryna Zakharchuk in *The Ukrainian Weekly* (Parsippany, N.J.), October 14, 2018, p. 9; *The New Pathway-Ukrainian News* (Toronto), October 4, 2018, p. 12; *Kyïv Post* (Kyiv, Ukraine), October 12, 2018, p. 21; *Homin Ukraïny* (Toronto), November 27, 2018, p. 10.

Matthew D. Pauly in *Reading Religion: American Academy of Religion.* http://readingreligion.org/books/jews-and-ukrainians
Alois Woldan in *Zeitschrift für Slavische Philologie*, LXXVI, 1 (Heidelberg, 2020), pp. 203-212.

800 *Ievrei ta ukraïntsi: tysiacholittia spivisnuvannia*, co-author with Yohanan Petrovsky-Shtern. Uzhhorod: Vyd-vo Valeriia Padiaka, 2016, xii, 314 p., 29 maps, 335 illustrations. Second revised edition with index, 2018, xii, 340 p. Translation of item **799** into Ukrainian by Oksana Forostyna.

Reviewed:
Serhii Hirik in *Krytyka*, XX, 11-12 [241-242] (Kyïv, 2017), p. 23.
Volodymyr Fenych in https:goloskarpat.info/analytics/
historyzakarpattya/?utm_content=031 (28.06.2017)

801 *Babyn Yar: History and Memory*, co-editor with Vladyslav Hrynevych. Kyïv: Dukh i litera, 2016, 328 p. and lxiv p., 144 illustrations. Translation of item **802** into English by Marta Olynyk.

Reviewed:
Vladyslav Hrynevych in *Odessa Review*, No. II (Kyiv, 2017), pp. 76-77.
David M. Crowe in *Russian Review*, LXXVI, 4 (New York, 2017), pp. 772-773.
Kai Struve in *Problemy istoriï Holokostu: ukraïns'kyi vymir*, No. 10 (Dnipropetrovs'k, 2018), pp. 256-262.
Per A. Rudling in *Slavic Review*, LXXVIII, 4 (New York, 2019), pp. 1061-1063.

802 *Babyn Iar: istoriia i pamiat'*, co-editor with Vladyslav Hrynevych. Kyïv: Dukh i litera, 2016, 352 p. and lxiv p., 144 illustrations.

Reviewed:
Iana Prymachenko in *Krytyka*, XXI, 1-2 (Kyiv, 2017), p. 39.

803 "Zhertovnost' i smilost': Vasyl' Iabur i rusyn'skŷi iazŷk," *Rusyn*, XXVI, 5 (Prešov, 2016), pp. 1-2.

804 "Teaching the History of Ukraine in North America." In Serhii Plokhy, ed. *The Future of the Past: New Perspectives on Ukrainian History*. Cambridge, Mass.: Harvard University Press/Ukrainian

Research Institute Harvard University, 2016, pp. 483-488. Reprinted in *Harvard Ukrainian Studies*, XXXIV, 1-4 (Cambridge, Mass., 2015-16), pp. 493-498.

805 "Zhertovnost' i odvaha: Vasyl' Iabur i rusyn'skŷi iazyk." In *Dynamické procesy v súčasnej slavistike: zborník príspevkov z medzinárodnej vedeckej konferencie 3.-4. novembra 2016.* Prešov: Vyd-vo Prešovskej univerzity, 2016, pp. 12-15.

806 *Chrbtom k horám: dejiny Karpatskej Rusi a karpatských Rusínov.* Prešov: Universum, 2016, 596 p., 34 maps, 6 tables, 144 illustrations. Translation of item **790** into Slovak by Eva Eddy.

Reviewed:
Peter Švorc in *Rusyn*, XXVII, 1 (Prešov, 2017), pp. 1-4.
Petro Medvid' in *Rodnyi krai, dodatok do Podkarpatská Rus*, XXVII, 1 (Prague, 2017), p. 13.
AP [Agátá Pilatová] in *ibid.*, p. 6.
Petro Krainak in *Narodnŷ novynkŷ—InfoRusyn*, XIV, 1-2 (Prešov, 2017), p. 16.
Petro Medvid' in *Narodnŷ novynkŷ—InfoRusyn*, XIV, 5 (Prešov, 2017), p. 11.
Agátá Pilátová in *Podkarpatská Rus'*, XXVII, 2 (Prague, 2017), p. 8.
Magdalena Lavrintsova in *Rusyn*, XXVII, 4 (Prešov, 2017), pp. 11-12 and 21-23.
Petro Trokhanovskii in *Besida*, XXIX, 4 (Krynica and Legnica, 2017), pp. 28-29.
Andrej Sulitka in *Český lid*, CIV, 2 (Prague, 2017), pp. 275-277.
Peter Koval in *Dejiny: internetový časopis*, No. 2 (Prešov, 2017), p. 160. http://dejiny.unipo.sk/PDF/2017/15_2_2017.pdf
Magdaléna Lavrincová in *Historický časopis*, LXV, 4 (Bratislava, 2017), pp. 744-747.
Valerii Padiak in *Rusyn*, XXX, 1 (Prešov, 2020), pp. 30-32.

807 "Setting the Context: Terminology, Regional Diversity, and the Ukrainian-Jewish Encounter." In Wolf Moskovich and Alti Rodal, eds. *The Ukrainian-Jewish Encounter: Cultural Dimensions. Jews and Slavs*, Vol. 25. Jerusalem: Philobiblion/Hebrew University of Jerusalem, Center for Slavic Languages and Literatures, 2016, pp. 19-28. Also under the title "Regionalism and Jewish Ukraine," https.//ukrainianjewishencounter-org/en/lecture-by-paul-robert-magocsi-regionalism-and-jewish-ukraine

808 "Carpatho-Rusyns: Myths and Stereotypes," *The New Rusyn Times*, XXIII, 4 (Pittsburgh, 2016), pp. 13-14, 18.

809 "Hidnist' liudyny narodzhuiet'sia z trahediï/De la tragédie à la dignité humaine/From Tragedy to Human Dignity." In Gaby and Youry Bilak, eds. *Maïdan—Donbas: une histoire d'avenir*. Paris: p.a., 2016, pp. 21-41. Translation into Ukrainian by Nadiya Kushko and into French by Youry Bilak.

810 "Eastern Christians in the Habsburg Monarchy, 1526-1918." In *Naukovi zapysky Uzhhorods'koho universytetu. Seriia: istorychno-relihiini studiï*, Vol. 5. Uzhhorod: Uzhhorods'kyi natsional'nyi universytet/Tsentr 'Lohos', 2016, pp. 106-124.

811 Review of Jaroslav Coranič, *Z dejín Grékokatolickej cirkvi na Slovensku*, in *Logos: A Journal of Eastern Christian Studies*, LVII, 1-4 (Ottawa, 2016), pp. 332-334.

812 "Zhertvennist i smilist: Vasyl' Iabur i rusyn'skii iazŷk." In *Lemkivskii richnyk 2016*. Edited by Petro Trokhanovskii. Krynica and Legnica: Stovaryshŷnia Lemkiv, 2016, pp. 143-147.

812a "Ukraine Remembers Babyn Yar," *The Ukrainian Weekly* (Parsippany, N.J.), October 9, 2016, pp. 1 and 3. Interview conducted by Mark Rackiewycz.

2017

813 "Tradícia autonómie na Karpatskej Rusi," *Historický časopis*, LXV, 1 (Bratislava, 2017), pp. 79-97. Translation of item **778** into Slovak by Timea Verešová.

Reviewed:
Éva Császári in *Kisebbségkutatás*, XXVI, 2 (Budapest, 2017), pp. 171-174.

814 "Pravoslaviie: problem iurisdiktsiï," *Narodnŷ novynkŷ—InfoRusyn*, XIV, 1-2 (Prešov, 2017), pp. 10-11. Translation into Rusyn by Petro Medvid'.

815 *Let's Speak Rusyn/Hovor'me po rusyns'kŷ: Transcarpathian Region Edition.* New York: Carpatho-Rusyn Research Center, 2017, xii, 115 p. 2 maps, 23 illustrations by Fedor Vico.

Reviewed:
Andrii Danylenko in *Slavonic and East European Review*, XCVII, 3 (London, 2019), pp. 529-531.
Gleb P. Pilipenko in *Slavianskii almanakh 2019.* Moscow: Indrik/Institut Slavianovedeniia, 2019, pp. 536-540.

816 *Carpathian Rus': A Historical Atlas.* Toronto: University of Toronto Press/Chair of Ukrainian Studies, 2017, vi, 80 p., 34 maps, index.

Reviewed:
Petro Trokhanovskii in *Besida*, XXIX, 4 (Krynica and Legnica, 2017), p. 29.
Paul J. Best in *Karpatska Rus'*, LXXXVII, 4 (Higgunum, Conn., 2017), pp. 19-20.
Franz A.J. Szabo in *Canadian Slavonic Papers*, LX, 1-2 (Abington, Eng., 2018), pp. 347-348.
Ernest Gyidel in *Russian Review*, LXXVII, 2 (New York, 2018), pp. 314-315.
Jiří Martínek in *Journal of Historical Geography*, LXV (London, 2019), p. 106.
Anton Kotenko in *Harvard Ukrainian Studies*, XXXVI, 1-2 (Cambridge, Mass., 2020), pp. 225-228.

817 "Choho i iak s'me pryshly o Pidkarpatia: choho sia Chekhoslovakiia zrekla Pidkarpats'koi Rusy?," *Narodnŷ novynkŷ—InfoRusyn*, XIV, 1-2 (Prešov, 2017), pp. 6-7. Translation into Rusyn by Petro Medvid'.

818 "Iak Karpat'skŷkh rusyniv vŷholosyly za ukraïntsiv," *Narodnŷ novynkŷ—InfoRusyn*, XIV, 7 (Prešov, 2017), p. 12. Translation into Rusyn by Petro Medvid'.

819 "Zhŷly zhŷteli Karpat'skoi Rusy pered 1. Svitovov voinov u velykii bidi?," *Narodnŷ novynkŷ—InfoRusyn*, XIV, 10 (Prešov, 2017), pp. 10-11. Translation into Rusyn by Petro Medvid'.

820 "No Friends but the Mountains." Interview conducted by Boris Varga. *Trembita*, XXV (Blaine, Minn., 2017), pp. 2-7.

821 "Okrem horokh, nie maiu pryiatel'okh," *Ruske slovo u shvetse*, XI,

39 [141] in *Ruske slovo*, LXXIII, 37 (Novi Sad, 2017), pp. 18-19. Excerpts from item **820** translated into Vojvodinian Rusyn by Boris Varga.

822 "Liubov do Vostoka," *Narodnŷ novynkŷ—InfoRusyn*, XIV, 12 (Prešov, 2017), p. 11. Translation into Rusyn by Petro Medvid'.

823 "Nainovsha voina Ukraïnŷ," Lem. fm, 31.10.2017, pp. 1-4; and in *Narodnŷ novynkŷ—InfoRusyn*, XIV, 20 (Prešov, 2017), pp. 6-7 [Sanford White]. Translation of item **824** into Rusyn by Petro Medvid'.

824 "Ukraine's Newest War," *Lem. fm*, 31.10.2017, pp. 1-4. [Sanford White].

825 "Serednĕvichnŷi karpatorusyn'skŷi shtat: fakt tsi vŷdumka?," *Narodnŷ novynkŷ—InfoRusyn*, XIV, 15 (Prešov, 2017), p. 9; and in *Rusyn*, XXVII, 5 (Prešov, 2017), p. 27. Translation into Rusyn by Petro Medvid'.

826 "Iazykovŷi vopros," *Narodnŷ novynkŷ—InfoRusyn*, XIV, 17 (Prešov, 2017), pp. 10-11. Translation into Rusyn by Petro Medvid'.

827 "Odnosynŷ midzhi Zhŷdamy i karpat'skŷma Rusynamy," *ibid.*, XIV, 18, p. 11. Translation into Rusyn by Petro Medvid'.

828 "Protestantizm i karpat'skŷ Rusynŷ," *Narodnŷ novynkŷ—InfoRusyn*, XIV, 21 (Prešov, 2017), pp. 10-11. Translation into Rusyn by Petro Medvid'.

829 "Shtatistichnŷ problem," *ibid.*, XIV, 22, p. 11. Translation into Rusyn by Petro Medvid'.

830 "Khocheme znaty, khto mŷ," *ibid.*, XIV, 23-24, p. 15. Translation into Rusyn by Petro Medvid'.

831 *Şu Mübarek Topraklar: Kirim ve Kirim Tatarlari.* Istanbul: Yapi Kredi Yayinlari, 2017, 171 p., 9 maps, 1 table. Translation of item

759 into Turkish by Ferit Burak Aydar.

Reviewed:
Emel, LXXXVII, 258/261 (Istanbul, 2017), pp. 142-143.
Cumhuriyet Kitap (Istanbul), January 11, 2018, p. 28.

832 *Historia Ukrainy: ziemia i ludzie.* Preface by Adam Świątek. Afterword by Andrzej Zięba. Cracow: Księgarnia Akademicka, 2017, 1062 and 32 p., 46 maps, 23 tables, 81 illustrations. Translation of item **718** into Polish by Marek Król and Alicja Waligóra-Zblewska.

833 "Okresliuiuchy kontekst: terminolohiia, rehional'ne rozmaïttia ta ukraïns'ko-ievreis'ka zustrich." In Vol'f Moskovych and Alti Rodal, eds. *Ukraïns'ko-ievreis'ka zustrich: kul'turni vymiry/Ievrei ta slov'iany*, Vol. 25. Kyiv: Dukh i litera, 2017, pp. 19-28. Translation of item **807** into Ukrainian.

2018

834 "Karpatorusyn'kyŷ narodnŷ himnŷ," *Narodnŷ novynkŷ—InfoRusyn*, XV, 4 (Prešov, 2018), p. 10. Translation into Rusyn by Petro Medvid'.

835 "Istorychna pamiat' i politichna realnost'," *Narodnŷ novynkŷ— InfoRusyn*, XV, 5 (Prešov, 2018), p.10. Translation into Rusyn by Petro Medvid'.

836 "Turkey and Ukraine," *Ukrainian Echo/Homin Ukraïny* (Toronto), January 23, 2018, p. 7, and *Novyi shliakh/New Pathway* (Toronto), January 25, 2018, p. 7.

837 *Let's Speak Rusyn/Besiduime po lemkivskŷ: Lemko Region Edition.* New York: Carpatho-Rusyn Research Center, 2018, xii, 115 p., 2 maps, 23 illustrations by Fedor Vico.

Reviewed:
Andrii Danylenko in *Slavonic and East European Review*, XCVII, 3 (London, 2019), pp. 529-531.
Gleb P. Pilipenko in *Slavianskii almanakh 2019*. Moscow: Indrik/Institut Slavianovedeniia, 2019, pp. 536-540.

838 "The Rusyn Decision to Unite with Czechoslovakia," *The New Rusyn Times*, XXV, 1 (Pittsburgh, Pa., 1918), pp. 9-12.

839 *On Becoming a Ukrainianist*. Toronto: Chair of Ukrainian Studies, University of Toronto, 2018, iv, 103 p.

Reviewed:
Paul J. Best in *Karpatska Rus'/Carpathian Rus'*, XCI, 1 (Higganum, Conn., 2020), pp. 25-26.

840 *Iak ia stav ukraïnoznavtsem*. Uzhhorod: Vyd-vo V. Padiaka, 2018, 144 p., 22 illustrations. Translation of item **839** into Ukrainian by Serhii Bilenky.

Reviewed:
Inna Bulkina in *Krytyka*, XXIII, 11-12 (Kyiv), 2019), p. 37.
Volodymyr Kravchenko in *Krytyka*, XXIV, 1-2 (Kyiv, 2020), pp. 20-23.

841 "Ukrainian Studies in the West: Challenges of the Present, Views of the Future" and discussion. In Volodymyr Kravchenko, ed. *Ukrainian Studies in Canada: Texts and Contexts—Proceedings of the CIUS 40th Anniversary Conference, 14-15 October 2016*. Edmonton and Toronto: Canadian Institute of Ukrainian Studies Press, 2018, pp. 22-25, 36-37, 41, 74, 100, and 124.

842 Letter to Mårten Ehnberg, Council of Europe Office in Ukraine, *Narodnŷ novynkŷ-InfoRusyn*, XV, 13 (Prešov, 2018), p. 13.

843 "The Rusyn Language: Recent Achievements and Challenges." In Aleksander D. Dulichenko and Motoki Nomachi, eds. *Slavianskaia mikrofilologiia*. Slavica Tartuensia XI/Slavic Eurasian Studies, No. 34. Sapporo, Japan and Tartu, Estonia: Slavic-Eurasian Research Center, Hokkaido University/Vene ja slaavi filoloogia osakond, Tartu Ülikool, 2018, pp. 83-101.

Reviewed:
Marinela Marinova in *Balkanistichen forum*, No. 3 (Blagoevgrad, Bulgaria, 2018), pp. 261-267.

844 "The Political Activity of Rusyn-American Immigrants in 1918," *The New Rusyn Times*, XXV, 2 (Pittsburgh, 2018), pp. 1, 9-14, 19.

845 "Khto iz vostochnŷkh Slavianiv iak pershŷi pryiav khristianstvo?," *Narodnŷ novynkŷ—InfoRusyn*, XV, 17 (Prešov, 2018), p. 10. Translation into Rusyn by Petro Medvid'.

846 "Manzheltsvo i maietok: dvi problematichnŷ oblasty," *Narodnŷ novynkŷ—InfoRusyn*, XV, 19 (Prešov, 2018), p. 8-9. Translation into Rusyn by Petro Medvid'.

847 "Recenzi [do eventuatné vydania knihy Ministerstva školstve Slovenskej republike] Narodnostné menšiny—zoznámme sa," *Rusyn*, XXVIII, 5 (Prešov, 2018), p. 10.

848 *Historical Atlas of Central Europe.* Third revised and expanded edition. Toronto, Buffalo, and London: University of Toronto Press, 2018, xiv and 275 p., 110 maps, 48 tables. Reprinted with corrections, 2019.

Reviewed:

L.I. Zelens'ka in *Ukraïns'kyi heohrafichnyi zhurnal*, XXVII, 2 [106] (Kyïv, 2019), pp. 65-67.

Nikolaus Schobesberger in *Austrian History Yearbook*, LI (Cambridge, Eng., 2020), pp. 324-325.

Serhii Hirik in *Krytyka*, XXIV, 1-2 (Kyiv, 2020), p. 21.

Francis King in *European History Quarterly*, XLIX, 4 (Norwich, Eng., 2019), pp. 701-702.

D.S. Azzolina in *Choice*, LVI, 8 (Middletown, Conn., 2019), p. 1048.

Anna Medvedovs'ka in *Ukraïna moderna*, No. 26 (L'viv, 2019), pp. 240-243.

Anton Kotenko in *Harvard Ukrainian Studies*, XXXVI, 1-2 (Cambridge, Mass., 2020), pp. 225-228.

849 "Kodifikachnŷi protses rusyn'skoho iazŷka: dosianutia i novŷ zadachi." In Kveta Koporova, ed. *20 rokiv vŷsokoshkol'skoi rusynistikŷ na Slovakiï/20 rokov vysokoškolskej rusinistiky na Slovensku.* Prešov: Prešovská univerzita, Ústav rusínskeho jazyka a kultúry, 2018, pp. 43-66. Reprinted without bibliography in *Rusyn*, XXVIII, 6 (Prešov, 2018], pp. 21-32.

850 "Uvodne slovo" [Greetings on the 20ᵗʰ Anniversary of the Institute of Rusyn Language and Cutlure at Prešov Univsersity]. In ibid, p. 8.

851 "Istorychne interv'iu" [on interwar Poland]. In Igor Shchupak, *Vsesvitnia istoriia: pidruchnyk dlia 10 klasu. Zahal'noï seredn'oï osvity*. Kyïv: Orion, 2018, p. 148.

852 "Mifŷ y stereotipŷ v ystoriï Karpats'koï Rusy." In *Rusyns'kŷi almanakh 2017*. Budapest: Vsederzhavnoe obshchestvo rusyns'koï yntelygentsiï ym. A. Hodynkŷ, 2018, pp. 31-47. Translation of item **788** into Rusyn by Marianna Liavynets'-Uhryn.

853 "The End of the Old and the Birth of a New Order, 1918-1919." In *Richnyk Ruskoi Bursŷ*, Vol. XIV. Edited by Olena Duts'-Faifer. Cracow: Księgarnia Akademicka, 2018, pp. 125-140.

854 *Istoriski atlas na Centralna Evropa*. Skopje: Nampres, 2018, xiv, 290 p. Translation of item **848** into Macedonian by Maja Ristovska.

2019

855 "Ia vidchuv, shcho robliu shchos' take, shcho liudy tsinuiut' i potrebuiut'." Interview conducted and translated into Ukrainian by Oksana Kis'. http://uamoderna.com/jittepis-istory/robert-magocsi

856 "Neotsïnenŷ uchastnyk karpatorusyn'skoho narodnoho vozrodzhinia Rusyniv: z nahodŷ 60-rocha od dnia narodzhinia Valeriia Padiaka," *Rusyn*, XXIX, 3 (Prešov, 2019), pp. 1-2.

857 "Remarks at the Dinner Celebrating the 25th Anniversary of the Carpatho-Rusyn Society, May 17, 2019," *The New Rusyn Times*, XXVI, 2 (Pittsburgh, 2019), pp. 6-7.

858 "Mav iem toto pryvilegiie spoznaty krasnoho cholovika/I have been privileged to know a beautiful person: Patricia Krafcik: On the Occasion of her 70th Birthday," *Rusyn*, XXIX, 4 (Prešov, 2019), pp. 1-3. Translation from English into Slovak by Eva Eddy and from Slovak into Rusyn by Aleksander Zozuliak. Reprinted in Aleksander Zozuliak, ed. *100 vŷznamnŷkh Rusyniv ochamy suchasnykiv*.

Prešov: Akademiia rusyn'skoi kultury v SR, 2020, pp. 47-50.

859 "Anti-Semitism in Ukraine?," *Novyi shliakh/The New Pathway* (Toronto), September 12, 2019, p. 7; *The Ukrainian Weekly* (Parsipany, N.J.), October 6, 2019, p. 9: *Kyiv Post* (Kyïv, Ukraine), October 25, 2019, p. 29; *The Jerusalem Post* (Jerusalem, Israel), November 7, 2019; Ukrainian Jewish Encounter, https.// ukrainianjewishencounter.org/en/news/magocsi-anti-semitism-in-ukraine, November 4, 2019.

860 "Myths and Stereotypes in Carpatho-Rusyn History." In Helena Duć-Fajfer and Józef Kuffel, eds. *Słowianie Wschodni a europejskie tradycje kulturowe*. Cracow: Księgarnia Akademiczna, 2019, pp. 241-259.

861 "Umenia i pokhodzhinia Endi Varhola: odborna diskusiia, Ukraïn'skŷi muzei, Niu Iork, 15. februara 2019," *Rusyn*, XXIX, 6 (Prešov, 2019), pp. 26-28.

862 "The Author's Observations." In Book Symposium: With Their Backs to the Mountains: A History of Carpathian Rus' and the Carpatho-Rusyns, *Nationalities Papers*, XLVII, 3 (New York and Cambridge, Eng., 2019), pp. 530-536.

2020

863 "120 rokiv od smerty Petra Kuzmiaka," *Rusyn*, XXX, 1 (Prešov, 2020), p. 23. Translation of item **714** into Rusyn by Aleksander Zozuliak.

864 "Krasnŷi iubilei nashoho dirigenta, kompozitora i kulturno-spolochens'koho dïiatelia na Slovakiï [Shtefan Ladizhyn'skyi]," *Rusyn*, XXX, 2 (Prešov, 2020), pp. 2-3. Translation of item **714** into Rusyn by Aleksander Zozuliak.

865 "20 rokiv Kul'turnoho obshchestva Rusyniv Rumuniï, *Rusyn*, XXX, 2 (Prešov, 2020), p. 12. Translation of item **714** into Rusyn by Aleksander Zozuliak.

866 "155 rokiv od smerty vŷznachnoho budytelia Rusyniv—Aleksandra Dukhnovicha," with Ivan Pop, *Rusyn*, XXX, 3 (Prešov, 2020), pp. 1-3. Translation of item **714** into Rusyn by Alesander Zozuliak.

867 "Prof. PhDr. Iurii Van'ko, k.n., slavyt' 75 rokiv od narodzhinia," *Rusyn*, XXX, 3 (Prešov, 2020), p. 23. Translation of item **714** into Rusyn by Aleksander Zozuliak.

868 "125 rokiv od zalozhinia Priashivskoi grekokatolyts'koi seminariï," *Rusyn*, XXX, 3 (Prešov, 2020), p. 32. Translation of item **714** into Rusyn by Aleksander Zozuliak.

869 "Chlovek, shto ostal prezydentom ievropskoi respublykŷ: Hryhoryi Yhnatyi Zhatkovych." In *Richnyk Ruskoi Bursŷ*, Vol. XV. Edited by Olena Duts'-Faifer. Cracow: Księgarnia Akademicka, 2020, pp. 207-240. Translation of item **877** into Rusyn by Marta Watral.

870 "České národní hnutí a Karpatští Rusíni." In Antonie Doležalová and Miroslav Hroch, eds. *Pohledem druhých: Praha jako inspirace a vzor pro emancipační zápas malých národů*. Prague: Karolinum, 2020, pp. 81-102. Translation into Czech by Antonie Doležalová.

871 "Okruhlŷi zhŷvot iubilei vŷsokoshkol'skoi uchitel'kŷ, poetkŷ i kulturnoi dïiatel'kŷ—Olenŷ Duts'-Faifer," *Rusyn*, XXX, 5 (Prešov, 2020), p. 1. Translation of item **714** into Rusyn by Aleksander Zozuliak.

872 "100-rocha od zasnovania Obshchestva rusyn'skŷkh shtudentiv u Prazï—Vozrodzhinia," *Rusyn*, XXX, 5 (Prešov, 2020), p. 21. Translation of item **714** into Rusyn by Aleksander Zozuliak.

873 "55 rokiv od smerty naukovtsia-lingvistŷ Vasylia Lattŷ," *Rusyn*, XXX, 5 (Prešov, 2020), p. 22. Translation of item **714** into Rusyn by Aleksander Zozuliak.

874 "30 rokiv od zasnovania Obshchestva karpat'skŷkh rusyniv," *Rusyn*, XXX, 5 (Prešov, 2020), p. 26. Translation of item **714** into Rusyn by Aleksander Zozuliak.

875 "80 rokiv od smerty pershoho rusyn'skoho romanopysatelia Emiliia Kubeka," *Rusyn*, XXX, 5 (Prešov, 2020), p. 32. Translation of item **714** into Rusyn by Aleksander Zozuliak.

876 "Peredmova/Introduction." In *Volodymyr Fenych: bibliohrafiia prats' ta naukovo-pedahohichna i hromads'ka diial'nist'*. Uzhhorod: Vyd-vo Valeriia Padiaka, 2020, pp. ix-xiv.

2021

877 "The Fellow Who Made Himself President of a European Republic: Gregory Ignatius Zhatkovych," *Nationalities Papers*, XLIX, 6 (New York and Cambridge, Eng., 2021).

878 *Pidkarpatska Rus': formuvannia natsional'noï samosvidomosti, 1848-1948*. Second edition, revised and expanded. Introduction by Volodymyr Fenych. Uzhhorod: Vyd-vo. Valeriia Padiaka, 2021, xlviii, 746 p., 6 maps, 6 tables. Revised translation of item **372**.

Writings about Paul Robert Magocsi

A *The First Five Years.* Toronto: University of Toronto Chair of Ukrainian Studies, 1985, 16 p.

B Budurowycz, Bohdan. "Introduction." In Luba Pendzey, ed. *Paul Robert Magocsi: A Bibliography, 1964-1985.* Toronto: University of Toronto Chair of Ukrainian Studies, 1985, pp.v-ix. Reprinted in item **ZZ**, pp. xi-xvi.

C Marunchak, Mykhailo H. "Magochi, Pavlo Robert." In *Biohrafichnyi dovidnyk do istoriï ukraïntsiv Kanady.* Winnipeg, 1986, p. 401.

D Medieshi, Liubomir. "Rusinistika na Katedri za Ukraïnski Studiï Universiteta u Toronto, Kanadu," *Tvorchosts*, XII (Novi Sad, Yugoslavia, 1986), pp. 62-69. Reprinted in Liubomir Medieshi, *Ruska traditsiia.* Novi Sad: Druzhtvo za ruski iazik, literaturu i kulturu, 2007, pp. 415-426.

E "Piat' rokiv zasnuvannia katedry ukraïns'kykh studiï pry Universyteti v Torontu, u Kanady," *Nova dumka*, XVI [62] (Vukovar, Yugoslavia, 1987), pp. 33-36.

F Zozuliak, Oleksandr. "I ukraïns'ka istoriia tut vyvchaiet'sia," *Nove zhyttia* (Prešov, Czechoslovakia), February 17, 1989, p. 7.

G "The Chair of Ukrainian Studies at the University of Toronto." In *Information Bulletin of the International Association for the Study and Dissimination of the Slavonic Cultures*—UNESCO, No. 20 (Moscow, 1989), pp. 34-44.

H [Lupul, Manoly]. "Magocsi, Paul." In *Encyclopedia of Ukraine*, Vol. III. Toronto: University of Toronto Press, 1993, p. 268.

I Myshanych, Oleksa V. "Magochi, Pol Robert." In *Ukraïns'ka literaturna entsyklopediia*, Vol. III. Kyiv: Ukraïns'ka entsyklopediia, 1995, pp. 251-252.

J   Hann, Chris. "Intellectuals, Ethnic Groups and Nations: Two Late-Twentieth-Century Cases." In Sukmar Periwal, ed. *Notions of Nationalism*. Budapest, London, and New York: Central European University Press, 1995, pp. 106-128.

K   Fedynyshynets', Volodymyr. *Istorychna metafora profesora Magochiia*. Uzhhorod, Ukraine, 1995, 272 p.

L   Plishkova, Anna. "Ëho dolia: Rusynŷ," *Narodnŷ novynkŷ* (Prešov, Slovakia), January 25, 1995, p. 3.

M   Medieshi, Liubomir. "Treba ho budze pametats'," *Ruske slovo* (Novi Sad, Yugoslavia), September 29, 1995, p. 10.

N   *Canadian Who's Who*. Toronto: University of Toronto Press, 1996-

O   *Contemporary Authors*, Vol. CXLVIII. Detroit: Gale Research, 1996, pp. 273-274.

P   Medve, Zoltan and Anna Ujj, "Ruszinok és ukránok," *Klio*, V, 1 (Budapest, 1996), pp. 1-4.

Q   Black, Jeremy. *Maps and History: Constructing Images of the Past*. New Haven and London: Yale University Press, 1997, pp. 163-172, 209, and 220.

R   Panchuk, Mai. "Politychne rusynstvo." In Serhii Makeiev, ed. *Demony myru ta bohy viiny*. Kyïv: Politychna dumka, 1997, pp. 319-333. English translation: "Political Rusynism." In *The Demons of Peace and the Gods of War: Social Conflicts of the Postcommunist Epoch*. Kyïv: Poltical Thought, 1997, pp. 292-306.

S   Hann, Christopher M. "On Nation(alitie)s in General, and One Potential Nation(ality) in Particular." In Paul Robert Magocsi. *Of the Making of Nationalities There is No End*, Vol. I. New York: Columbia University Press/East European Monographs, 1999, pp. xiii-xxxvii.

T Trier, Tom. "Introduction." In Paul Robert Magocsi. *Of the Making of Nationalities There is No End*, Vol. II. New York: Columbia University Press/East European Monographs, 1999, pp. ix-xxiii.

U Nowak, Jacek. *Zaginiony świat?: nazywają ich Łemkami*. Cracow: Universitas, 2000, pp. 175-196.

V Himka, John-Paul. "Introduction." In Gabriele Scardellato, ed. *Paul Robert Magocsi: A Bibliography 1964-2000*. Toronto: University of Toronto Chair of Ukrainian Studies, 2000, pp. v-ix. Reprinted in item **ZZ**, pp. xvii-xxii.

W Choma, Vasil'. "Renesancia rusínstva a Paul Robert Magocsi." In *Slovo: almanach vedeckých úvah a umeleckých aktivít*, No. 1. Bratislava: Nadácia Ladislava Novomeského, 2001, pp. 117-123. Translation into Russian: "Renessans rusinstva i Pol' Robert Magocsi," *Khrystyians 'ka rodyna*, No. 5 [90] (Uzhhorod, 2001), pp. 12-13. Translation into Rusyn: "Kanadskŷi akademik Pavel Robert Magochi i rusyn'ski rukh na Sloven'sku i v sviti," *Rusyn*, XI, 1-2 (Prešov, 2001), pp. 29-31, and *Vsederzhavnŷi rusynskŷi visnyk,* V, 12 (Budapest, 2003), pp. 10-12.

X Horbal, Bogdan. "Magocsi, Paul Robert." In Paul Robert Magocsi and Ivan Pop, eds. *Encyclopedia of Rusyn History and Culture.* Toronto: University of Toronto Press, 2002, pp. 300-301. Second revised and expanded edition, 2005, pp. 313-314.

Y Ziac, Martin Fedor. "Professors and Politics: The Role of Paul Robert Magocsi in the Modern Carpatho-Rusyn Revival," *East European Quarterly*, XXXV, 2 (Boulder, Colo., 2001), pp. 213-232. Translated into Rusyn by Anna Plishkova: "Zadacha Pavla Roberta Magochiia v modernim karpatorusyn'skim vozrodzhiniu," *Rusyn*, XII, 5-6 (Prešov, 2002), pp. 13-15.

Z *The Writers Directory*, 17th ed. Detroit: St. James Press/Gale Group, 2002, pp. 972-973.

AA *Contemporary Authors: New Revision Series,* Vol. CII. Detroit: Gale Group, Thomson Learning, 2002, pp. 320-321.

BB Tokar, Marian Ia. "Vidomi doslidnyky Karpats'koï Ukraïny: Mahochii, Pavlo Robert." In Mykola M. Vegesh, ed. *Vony boronyly Karpats'ku Ukraïnu.* Uzhhorod: Vyd-vo Karpaty, 2002, pp. 555-557.

CC Vidnians'kyi, Stepan. "Magochii Pavlo Robert." In V. A. Smolii, ed. *Ukraïns'ki istoryky XX stolittia: bibliohrafichnyi dovidnyk,* Vol. II, pt. 1. Kyiv and L'viv: Natsional'na akademiia nauk Ukraïny, Instytut istoriï Ukraïny, 2003, pp. 201-202

DD Baleha, Iurii. "Vidpovid' profesoru Mahochi." In idem. *Politychne rusynstvo i budivnytstvo ukraïns'koï derzhavy.* Uzhhorod: Vyd-vo Grazhda, 2003, pp. 75-103. Reprinted in Iurii Baleha. *Politychne rusynstvo, abo Fentsyko-Brodiïvs'ki pryvydy na Zakarpatti.* Uzhhorod: Vyd-vo Grazhda, 2010, pp. 162-185.

EE Wilczyński, Włodzimierz. "Magocsi, Paul Robert." In *Leksykon kultury ukraińskej.* Zielona Góra; Wyższa szkoła pedagogiczna im. Tadeuza Kotarbińskiego, 2000, p. 100; 2nd edition: Cracow: Universitas, 2004, p. 139; 3rd revised edition: *Ukraina leksykon: historiia, gospodarka, kultura.* Warsaw: Książka i Wiedza, 2010, 144-145.

FF Padiak, Valerii. "Pavel Robert Magochii: 60-richcha z dnia narodzhenia vyznachnoho rusynista suchasnosti, karpatoznavtsia." In Tamara I. Vasyl'ieva, ed. *Kalendar kraieznavchykh pam'iatnykh dat na 2005 rik.* Uzhhorod: Vyd-vo V. Padiaka, 2004, pp. 55-59. Reprinted in *Trembita* (Svaliava, Ukraine), January 22, 2005, p. 3. Rusyn translation: "Iubiluiuchii vŷznamnŷi rusynista," *Narodnŷ novynkŷ* (Prešov), No. 1-4, January 31, 2005, pp. 1 and 3, *Rusnakovo klaski,* II, 3 (Petrovci, Croatia, 2005), p. 13; and "Rusŷns'kŷi spadok akademika P. R. Magochiia: do 60-rücha yz dnia narodzhenia uchenoho," *Rusyns'kŷi svit/Ruszin világ,* III [16] (Budapest, 2005), 14-15. Russian translation: "Pavel Robert Magochii: k 60-letiiu so dnia rozhdeniia vydaiushchegosia rusinista sovremennosti," *Rusin*, I, 1 (Chişinaŭ, Moldova, 2005), pp. 106-110.

GG "Magocsi Paul Robert, Prof. PhD." In Jaroslav Pánek, Svatava Raková, and Václava Horčaková. *Scholars of Bohemian, Czech and Czechoslovak History Studies*, Vol. II. Prague: Institute of History, 2005, pp. 211-215.

HH Medieshi, Liubomir."Akademik Magochi, popravdze," *Ruske slovo* (Novi Sad, Serbia), August 18 and September 8, 2006, pp. 11 and 11.

II Horbal, Bogdan; Krafcik, Patricia; and Rusinko, Elaine. "Introduction." In idem, eds. *Carpatho-Rusyns and Their Neighbors: Essays in Honor of Paul Robert Magocsi*. Fairfax, Va.: Eastern Christian Publications, 2006, pp. 1-9.

JJ Vidnians'kyi, Stepan V. and Bohdan Horbal', "Pavel Robert Magochii: osnovatel' modernoho rusynstva." In Mariia Mal'tsovska, ed. *100 vŷznamnŷkh Rusyniv ochamy suchasnykiv*. Prešov: Svitovŷi kongres Rusyniv, 2007, pp. 94-96.

KK Stryjek, Tomasz. *Jakiej przeszłości potrzebuje przeszłość?: Interpretacje dziejów narodowych w historiografii i debacie publicznej na Ukrainie, 1991-2004*. Warsaw: Instytut Studiów Politycznych PAN/Oficyna Wydawnycza RYTM, 2007, pp. 562-603, 674-685, and 698-700.

LL Bahan, Oleh. "Iakyi narod zhyve za Karpatamy?: teoriï rusynstva v suchasnosti." *Universum*, No. 9-10 (L'viv, 2008), pp. 28-34.

MM Zaremba, O. and Rafal's'kyi, O. "Etnopolitychnyi vymir Zakarpattia: istoriohrafichnyi ohliad." In Mai Panchuk, ed., *Zakarpattia v etnopolitychnomu vymiri*. Kyiv: Natsional'na akademiia nauk Ukraïny, Instytut politychnykh i etnonatsional'nykh doslidzhen' im. I. F. Kurasa, 2008, pp. 63-67.

NN Burkut, Ihor. *Rusynstvo: mynule i suchasnist'*. Chernivtsi: Vyd-vo Prut, 2009, pp. 304-308, and 362-364.

OO   "Profesor Dr. Pavel Robert Magochii, PhD." In Kvetoslava
Koporova, ed. *Studium Carpato-Ruthenorum 2009: studii z
karpatorusynistykŷ.* Prešov: Priashovska univerzita, Inshtitut
rusyn'skoho iazŷka i kulturŷ, 2009, pp. 114-116.

PP   Panchuk, Ihor. "Magocsi Pol Robert." In *Istoriia Ukraïny ochyma
inozemtsiv: dovidnyk-khrestomatiia.* Ternopil': Mandrivets', 2009,
p. 78.

QQ   Fenych, Volodymyr I. "Poserednyk chy prystosuvanets':
tserkva pered vyklykom natsionalizmu." In *Naukovyi visnyk
Uzhhorods'koho universytetu, Seriia: Istoriia,* Vol. XXIII.
Uzhhorod: Vyd-vo Uzhhorods'koho natsional'noho universytetu
"Hoverla", 2009, pp. 149-161. Reprinted in *Naukovyi zbirnyk
Muzeiu ukraïns'koï kul'tury,* XXV (Svidník, 2010), pp. 61-77.

RR   Plïshkova, Anna. "Iubilei uchenoho svitovoho mena i
karpatorusynistŷ," *Narodnŷ novynkŷ* (Prešov), No. 5-8, February
24, 2010, p. 1.

SS   Vidnians'kyi, Stepan V. "Mahochii Pavlo-Robert." In
Entsyklopediia istoriï Ukraïny, Vol. VI. Kyiv: Naukova dumka,
2009, pp. 417-418.

TT   Burkut, Ihor. "Pavlo Robert Mahochi—doslidnyk istoriï Ukraïny,
zasnovnyk suchasnoho rusynoznavstva,*"* Bukovyns'kyi zhurnal,*
XX, 3-4 (Chernivtsi, 2010), pp. 145-154.

TTa Adamovych, Serhii. "Pavlo Robert Magochii—ideoloh
politychnoho rusynstva," *Visnyk Prykarpats'koho universytetu:
Istoriia,* No. 18 (Ivano-Frankivs'k, 2010), pp. 78-84.

UU   Kuzio, Taras. "A Multi-Vectored Scholar for a Multi-Vectored
Era: Paul Robert Magocsi," *Nationalities Papers,* XXXIX,
1 (Basingstoke, Eng., 2011), pp. 95-104. Rusyn translation:
"Mnohostrannŷi uchenŷi na mnohostrannu epokhu," *Rusyn,* XXII,
1 (Prešov, 2012), pp. 3-8. Ukrainian translation: "Bahatohrannyi
naukovets' dlia bahatohrannoï epokhy," *Besida,* XXIV, 3, 4, 5, and
6 (Krynica, 2012), pp. 18-19, 18-19, 16-17, and 20-26, and in item
AAA, pp. 19-37.

VV Motyl, Alexander J. "The Paradoxes of Paul Robert Magocsi: The Case for Rusyns and the Logical Necessity of Ukrainians," *Nationalities Papers*, XXXIX, 1 (Basingstoke, Eng., 2011), pp. 105-109. Ukrainian translation: "Paradoksy Pavla-Roberta Magochiia: dokazy na koryst' rusyniv i lohichna neobkhidnist' ukraïntsiv," in item **AAA**, pp. 55-64. Rusyn translation: "Paradoksŷ P. R. Magochiia: dokazŷ na khosen Rusyniv i logichna potreba Ukraïntsiv," *Rusyn*, XXI, 5-6 (Prešov, 2011), pp. 12-16.

WW Grabowicz, George G. "'The Magocsi Problem' (Problema Magochoho): A Preliminary Deconstruction and Contextualization," *Nationalities Papers,* XXXIX, 1 (Basingstoke, Eng., 2011), pp. 111-116. Ukrainian translation: "'Problema Magochiia': poperednia dekonstruktsiia ta kontekstualizatsiia," in item **AAA**, pp. 7-18, and in item 57, pp. 281-289.

XX Plokhy, Serhii. "Between History and Nation: Paul Robert Magocsi and the Rewriting of Ukrainian History," *Nationalities Papers,* XXIX, 1 (Basingstoke, Eng., 2011), pp. 117-124. Ukrainian translation: "Mizh istorieiu ta natsiieiu: P. R. Magochii i pereosmyslennia ukraïns'koï istoriï," item **AAA**, pp. 39-53 and in *Krytyka*, XV, 9-10 (Kyiv, 2010), pp. 27-29—reprinted in *Ukraïns'kyi istorychnyi zhurnal*, XVII, 3 (Kyiv, 2013), pp. 4-12, and in item **III**, pp. 475-487.

YY Arel, Dominique. "The Scholar, Historian, and Public Advocate: The Contributions of Paul Robert Magocsi to Our Understanding of Ukraine and Central Europe," *Nationalities Papers,* XXIX, 1 (Basingstoke, Eng., 2011), pp. 125-127. Rusyn translation: "Vklad P. R. Magochiia do nashoho rozuminia Tsentralnoi Evropŷ i Ukraïnŷ," *Rusyn*, XXI, 5-6 (Prešov, 2011), pp. 22-24. Ukrainian translation: "Naukovets', istoryk i hromads'kyi diiach: vnesok Pavla-Robert Magochiia v nashe rozuminnia tsentral'noï Ievropy ta Ukraïny," in item **AAA**, pp. 65-70.

ZZ Kiebuzinski, Ksenya. "Preface." In *Paul Robert Magocsi: A Bibliography, 1964-2011.* 3rd revised ed. Toronto: University of Toronto, Chair of Ukrainian Studies, 2011, pp. v-x.

AAA   *Naukovets', istoryk i hromads'kyi diiach: vnesok Pavla- Robert Magochiia v nashe rozuminnia Ukraïny ta tsentral'noï Ievropy.* Uzhhorod: Vyd-vo V. Padiaka, 2012, 84 p. Reprinted 2013. Translation of items **UU,VV, WW, XX, YY** into Ukrainian by Oleksii Sydorchuk.

BBB   Plishkova, Anna. "Promotsiï prof. Dr. Pavla Roberta Magochiia," *Narodnŷ novynkŷ* (Prešov), No. 6, June 19, 2013, p. 2.

CCC   Zozuliak, Aleksander. "Prof. Dr. Pavel Robert Magochii— Doctor honoris causa," *Rusyn*, XXIII, 3 (Prešov, 2013), pp. 1-6.

DDD   "Magochii, Pavlo-Robert." In Ivan Krasovs'kyi and Ivan Chelak. *Entsyklopedychnyi slovnyk Lemkivshchyny.* L'viv: Kyïvs'ke tovarystvo "Lemkivshchyna"/Fundatsiia doslidzhennia Lemkivshchyny u L'vovi, 2013, pp. 380-381.

EEE   Babotová, L'ubica. "Pocta kanadskému historikovi," *Dejiny: internetový časopis Inštitútu historie FF Prešovskej univerzity,* VIII, 2 (Prešov, 2013), pp. 123-130.

FFF   Plišková, Anna. "Prof. Dr. Paul Robert Magocsi, Doctor honoris causa Prešovskej univerzity v Prešove," *Na Pulze:* časopis Prešovskej univerzity, VI, 3 (Prešov, 2013), pp. 10-11.

GGG   Plišková, Anna, ed. *Professor Dr. Paul Robert Magocsi—Doctor honoris causa Prešovskej univerzity v Prešove.* Prešov: Vyd-vo Prešovskej univerzity, 2013, 84 p.

HHH   Padiak, Valerii. "Naukovŷ magistralŷ profesora Pavla Roberta Magochiia," *Rusyn*, XXV, 1 (Prešov, 2015), pp. 5-7. Reprinted in item 61, pp. 109-115.

III   Padiak, Valerii and Krafcik, Patricia. "Khto takyi profesor P.-R. Magocsi?/Who is Professor Magocsi?" In *Iubileinyi zbirnyk na chest' profesora Pavla-Roberta Magochiia/A Jubilee Collection: Essays in Honor of Professor Paul Robert Magocsi.* Uzhhorod, Prešov, and New York: Vyd-vo V. Padiaka, 2015, pp. 9-12. Rusyn translation: "Khto ie profesor P. R. Magochii?," *Rusyn*, XXV, 6 (Prešov, 2015), p. 24. Lemko-Rusyn translation by Petro Trokhanovskii in *Lemkivskii richnyk 2015.* Krynica and Legnica:

Stovaryshŷnia Lemkiv, 2015, pp. 145-151.

JJJ   Recollections by Henry Abramson, Ihor Bardyn, Peter Galadza, Lubomyr Luciuk, Michael R. Marrus, René Matlovič, Derek J. Penslar, Anna Plishkova, John Righetti, Andrew Stirling, M. Mark Stolarik, and Jolanta Tambor. In *ibid.*, pp. 27-57.

KKK   Duts'-Faifer, Olena. "Paul'o Robert Magochii a Karpatska Rus'—konstruktsyia, rekonstruktsyia tsy doslidnycha pasyia." In *ibid.*, pp. 71-80.

LLL   Kuzio, Taras. "Andy Warhol and Paul Robert Magocsi: from Pennsylvania and New Jersey to Toronto." In *ibid.*, pp. 81-93.

MMM Kushko, Nadiia. "Svii sered chuzhykh, chuzhyi sered svoïkh." In *ibid.*, pp. 95-107.

NNN   Timkovič, Gorazd Andrej. "Nákazlivo sebavedomý Rusín Prof. Dr. Paul Robert Magocsi: spomienka na prvé stretnutie s výnimočnou osobnost'ou . . . v talianskom Rime v roku 1989." In *ibid.*, pp. 117-121.

OOO   Karas', Hanna. "Muzychne kraieznavstvo u naukovykh doslidzenniakh profesora Pavla Roberta Magochiia." In *ibid.*, pp. 309-316.

PPP   Kolesnyk, Iryna. "Istoriia Ukraïny mizh intelektual'nymy dohmamy ta novatsiiamy." In *ibid.*, pp. 341-349.

QQQ   Krainiak, Frantishek. "Pershŷ krochkŷ na krestnii rusyn'skii dorozi viedno z profesorom Pavlom Robertom Magochim." In ibid., pp. 373-380. Reprinted in *Grekokatolîc'kyj rusîňskyj kalendar' 2016.* Svetlice, Slovakia: Obščestvo svjatoho Joana Krestîtel'a, [2015], pp. 48-53.

RRR   "Pavel Robert Magochi." In *Rusyns'kŷi al'manakh 2015.* Edited by Antonii Liavynets. Budapest: Vsederzhavnoe obshchestvo rusyns'koi yntelihentsyi, 2015, pp. 110-111.

SSS   Dronov, Mikhail. "K 70-letiiu Pola-Roberta Magochi." In
        Slavianskii al'manakh 2015, No. 1-2. Moscow: INDRIK/Institut
        slavianovedeniia RAN, 2015, pp. 466-467.

TTT   Koporova, Kvetoslava. "Prof. Dr. Pavel Robert Magocsi." In
        Studium Carpato-Ruthenorum 2016. Prešov: Priashivska univerzita,
        Inshtitut rusyn'skoho iazŷka i kultury, 2016, pp. 116-119.

TTTa   Filiniuk, Anatolii M. "Pavlo-Robert Magochii: pochesnyi
        profesor Kam'ianets'-Podil's'koho natsional'noho universytetu
        im. Ivana Ohiienka." In *Osvita, nauka, kul'tura na Podilli*, Vol.
        XXIII. Kamianets'-Podil's'kyi, 2016, pp. 426-438.

UUU   Lavrincová, Magdaléna. "Najvýznamnejši vedec histórie
        Rusínov." In Magdaléna Lavrincová. *Rub a líce doby: rusínske
        eseje*. Bratislava: ML, 2017, pp. 161-163.

VVV   Zięba, Andrzej A. "O Paulu Robercie Magocsi i jego *Historii
        Ukrainy*." In Paul Robert Magocsi. *Historia Ukrainy: ziemia i
        ludzie*. Cracow: Księgarnia akademiczna, 2017, pp. 975-988.

WWW Stryjek, Tomasz. "First Nation Europy Środkowej?: Historia
        i współczesność Rusi Karpackiej w ujęciu Paula Roberta
        Magocsiego," *Kwartalnyk Historyczny*, CXXIV, 4 (Warsaw,
        2017), pp. 773-804.

XXX   Sen'kus', Roman. "Magochii Pavlo-Robert." In *Entsyklopediia
        suchasnoï Ukraïny*, Vol. 18. Kyïv: Natsional'na akademiia nauk
        Ukraïny, Instytut entsyklopedychnykh doslidzhen', 2017, p. 468.

YYY   Kupensky, Nicholas K., Harvey Goldblatt, John-Paul Himka,
        Peter Galadza, Valerii Padiak, and Chris Hann. "The Tensions
        and Triumphs of the First History of Carpathian Rus' and
        Carpatho-Rusyns," *Nationalties Papers*, XLVII, 3 (New York
        and Cambridge, Eng., 2019), pp. 506-529.

ZZZ   Padiak, Valerii. "Naukovŷi zdobŷtia profesora Pavla Roberta
        Magochiia: ku 75-rochu od dnia narodzhinia," *Rusyn*, XXX, 1
        (Prešov, 2020), pp. 7-9.

Commentaries in Periodicals and the Media

"In my letter of thanks a few days ago, I mentioned sending a copy of your Cultural Seminar program on Carpatho-Ruthenia to my friend Peter Mihalik of Minneapolis. . . . Mr. Mihalik and I strongly object to the term Carpatho-Ruthenia. We . . . would certainly substitute Carpatho-Russia if we had anything to do with it. From my earliest childhood I have heard our people from the Carpathians call themselves Rusnaks; that is to say, Russians." Peter V. Masica, Peter Mihalik
    "Editorial comment: Dr. Magocsi, for reasons known only to himself, is performing a cheap political trick tried on many occasions in the past by Austro-Hungarian and Polish oppressors against our people with the intention to destroy us."

—Editor
Karpatska Rus' (Yonkers, N.Y.)
10. IX. 1976, p. 2

"As is clear, Ukrainian Harvard has acquired a 'valuable' associate, who has prepared a textbook [*Hovorim po-rus'kŷ*] for the Ukrainians of Carpatho-Ukraine in order to teach them the 'Rusyn language'. This is an age-old policy of imperialist occupiers designed to divide the Ukrainian people and, under the guise of language, to keep them more easily in bondage. It is both strange and incomprehensible that now Ukrainian Harvard is contributing to this by engaging Paul Magocsi."

—*Shliakh peremohy* (Paris)
No. 11, 13. III. 1977

"Dr. Magocsi has been responsible for several scholarly monographs on the political, cultural and social history of the Rusyns at home and in the diaspora. . . . He clearly knows the uses of history, not as the science of a dead past, but as the genetic illuminator of the present through the study of its origins and evolution. From the beginning the Ruthenians were a subject people both politically and ecclesiastically (it is sobering to note the ironies of history: peoples that spent so much of their past pushing the Ruthenians around are now themselves tasting the boot). This subject status naturally retarded the growth of national consciousness. Dr. Magocsi's analysis of this vexing question is penetrating."

—Reverend Robert Taft, SJ
Diakonia (New York)
Vol. XIII, No. 2 (1978), pp. 169 and 172

"Dr. Magocsi's monograph [*The Shaping of a National Identity*] is the first comprehensive treatment of modern Subcarpathian history in English, and, as a matter of fact, in any language. The work is based on meticulous research . . . and deals with these materials in a well-balanced and judicious manner."

—Ivan L. Rudnytsky
Svoboda (Jersey City, N.J.)
8. VI. 1978

"On 8 June 1978, there appeared on the pages of the newspaper *Svoboda* an article about the book by Dr. Magocsi [*The Shaping of a National Identity*], in which he promotes the idea of some kind of separate Rusyn people, who are spiritually connected to the Hungarian crown. This is not terribly surprising, since he is simply acting as a loyal son of his [Magyar] people. It is particularly sad, however, that his concept about a separate Rusyn people is being adopted as the position of our Ukrainian Harvard. Completely beyond our understanding is the fact that the former [Czechoslovak] advisor for schools in Subcarpathian Rus' and the former prime minister of Carpatho-Ukraine, Mr. Julian Revay, is also in agreement with Dr. Magocsi's views and speaks with praise about his book. . . .

"But most insulting for all us countrymen [from Carpatho-Ukraine] is that Mr. Julian Revay has brought into the ranks behind Magocsi our entire organization, the Carpathian Alliance, . . . which has been primed to sing the praises of Magocsi's book. . . ."

—Vasyl' Kachurovs'kyi and Ivan Savardii, June 1978
in Stanislav Arzhevitin, *Karpats'ka Ukraïna: epokha v dobi*, Vol. VI
(Kyiv, 2013), pp. 740-741

"The appearance of Dr. Magocsi's book [*The Shaping of a National Identity*] is terribly harmful for the Transcarpathian branch of the Ukrainian people. Its harmfulness lies in the fact that it is, in essence, pro-Hungarian, since it is based on the view that the dominant element in Transcarpathia is not the Ukrainian people, but rather some kind of Rusnak, Carpatho-Russian, or Uhro-Rusyn people, which someday may decide its own political destiny."

—Volodymyr Komaryns'kyi
Homin Ukraïny (Toronto)
4. X. 1978, p. 7

"Our members [of the Carpathian Alliance] are distraught that a Ukrainian scholarly institution [at Harvard University] has provided a platform to a person who is unfriendly and non-objective towards Ukrainian matters in order to promote his 'pro-Rusyn' writings."

—Mykhailo Shpontak
Homin Ukraïny (Toronto)
4. X. 1978

"This book [*The Shaping of a National Identity*] is not only the most extensive but also the most significant and, one might say, the best book about Subcarpathian Rusyns."

—Reverend Michal Lacko
Slovenské hlasy z Rima (Rome)
Vol. XIX, No. 8-9 (1979), p. 31

"Paul R. Magocsi's book, *The Shaping of a National Identity: Subcarpathian Rus', 1848-1949* (Harvard University Press, 1978, 640 pp.), has already gained signal importance for having occasioned a lively and impassioned debate. Some reactions have appeared in print as more or less professional reviews; others are making the rounds in oral samizdat in various circles. Most of these critical voices sound an alarm, as if a national and political scandal had occurred; that is to say, how could such a book have appeared under the aegis of the Harvard Ukrainian Research Institute?! . . . .

"The book under review is truly a rare and significant event in the field of Ukrainian scholarship. It is many years since our modern historiography has seen a monograph so solid in breadth, scholarly apparatus, and methodology."

—Vasyl' Markus'
"An Attempt at a Modern History of Transcarpathia"
Suchasnist' (Munich)
Vol. XX, No. 6 (1980), p. 105

"With each new public lecture for the Ukrainian community Dr. Magocsi garners more and more sympathy and respect, especially for his continually improving Ukrainian language; his precise knowledge of the subject matter has totally ended the controversies that earlier surrounded his person."

—"Three Evenings in Toronto"
Novyi shliakh (Toronto)
11. IV. 1981, p. 12

"The 26th Congress of the Communist party of the Soviet Union, taking into consideration the important current tasks facing the social sciences, took note of the need to intensify its on-going struggle against bourgeois ideology. . . .

". . . the book by the Canadian 'Soviet specialist' P. R. Magocsi, *The Shaping of a National Identity: Subcarpathian Rus', 1848-1949,* is an example of a work motivated by anti-Soviet and anti-Communist . . . false methodologies. . . .

"It is precisely such nefarious goals that led the author to the following conclusion: that the Soviet Union declared Transcarpathians were of the Ukrainian nationality in order 'to justify their new territorial acquisition [in 1945]'. Based as it is on such a deceitful thesis, the book by Magocsi is clearly a filthy falsification of historical truth."

—I. S. Khmil'
"Against the Bourgeois Falsification of History"
Ukraïns'kyi istorychnyi zhurnal (Kyiv)
Vol. XXV, No. 2 (1982), pp. 39 and 43

"I was totally fascinated reading a copy of *The Shaping of a National Identity*. Since then I've developed a great interest in the Rusyn people. Part of this interest has been fueled by similarities which exist between the situation of the Rusyn people and the people of southeastern Silesia, from where my ancestors come. Many of these similarities are only superficial. But I understand very well the problem that the Rusyns have gone through in developing a national identity, because the people of southeastern Silesia have experienced the same thing."

—Kevin Hannan
Carpatho-Rusyn American (North Madison, Ohio)
Vol. V, No. 1 (1982), p. 5

"Ukrainians in America *en masse* are taught (as part of the Ukrainian ideology) that Carpatho-Rusyns are merely backward Western Ukrainians who need to be enlightened about their origins. . . . The violent attacks the Ukrainian academic community has periodically made on Paul R. Magocsi are testimony to that."

—Reverend Evan Lowig
Carpatho-Rusyn American (North Madison, Ohio)
Vol. V, No. 2 (1982), p. 5

"Our forefathers here in America, while struggling with nomenclature, nonetheless preserved the identity of their people perhaps even better than in the old country. It was with the appearance of Dr. Magocsi on the American scene, however, that our people were finally able to read in English the involved historical evolution of our people in the Carpathians and to begin to understand it from an unbiased scholar and historian.

"I agree with Dr. Markus that Dr. Magocsi is the 'intellectual mentor' of our people. By a stroke of luck he is unaffiliated with either the Byzantine or Orthodox faiths and their establishments, and thus [he] can be objective in his approach and conclusions. A century later he becomes another 'Dukhnovych' of our people, whether he denies it or not."

—Orestes J. Mihaly
Carpatho-Rusyn American (North Madison, Ohio)
Vol. V, No. 2 (1982), p. 5

"I consider the work of Paul R. Magocsi, *The Shaping of a National Identity*, the best one ever written on the question of Rusin national development in the century 1848-1948. . . . [The] book certainly will have a strong impact on the 'Rusyn renaissance in America'."

—Reverend Michael Lacko
Carpatho-Rusyn American (North Madison, Ohio)
Vol. V, No. 3 (1982), p. 5

"After the first explosion, when Ukrainian students at the University of Toronto boycotted the Chair held by Professor Magocsi and the community tried to remove him, things have quieted down. Now hardly anyone speaks or writes about the matter. Someone has even proposed a wise 'Solomonic' approach: if we cannot get rid of Magocsi, then we have to ukrainianize him. . . .

"Now we realize that not only has Magocsi not been ukrainianized, but instead he is spreading his Rusynism even further."

—Pomudrilyi Rusyn
"A Tale of Three Whales, a Turtle, and Professor Magocsi"
Anabazys (Toronto)
Vol. III, No. 5 [8] (1982), p. 32

"Professor Paul Magocsi, former associate at the Chair [Institute] of Ukrainian Studies in Harvard University and at the same time the founder of the [Carpatho-] Rusyn Research Center, can become an outstanding example for a possible rapprochement between Carpatho-Rusyns and Ukrainians. Based on my experience with him up to now, I have complete confidence in and respect for him. He is not only an exceptionally dynamic and highly educated person, but also a great supporter of Carpatho-Rusyn and Ukrainian rapprochement. Ukrainians should be pleased that people like him are part of our scholarly institutions."

—Ivan Ia. Hamuliak
Svoboda (Jersey City, N.J.)
XII. 1982

"Professor Magocsi has irrefutably established that the history of national development in Subcarpathian Rus' before 1945 cannot be viewed simply as Ukrainian history. His work is not the first to do so, but it does constitute the greatest scholarly authority on the subject and represents a great victory for truth."

—Julianna Dranichak
Carpatho-Rusyn American (North Madison, Ohio)
Vol. VI, No. 2 (1983), p. 6

"I do not consider myself a 'super-patriot', but today I feel obligated to perform 'the dog's task, to bark' (in the words of Ivan Franko—to raise alarm and give warning before it is too late).

"I have learned—and this information has been confirmed by several sources—that preparations are underway for a large-scale profanation of the Ukrainian Millennium of Christianity. On more than one occasion, the head of the Vatican's Secretariat of Christian Unity, Cardinal Jan Willebrands, has demonstrated that for him Ukrainians of all religious persuasions are the principal obstacle to 'Christian unity' in his peculiar understanding of term. . . .

"Perhaps the capstone of Cardinal Willebrands' Ukrainophobia is a new, most clever, and Machiavellian design to celebrate the Millennium of Kievan Christianity together with the Moscow Patriarchate and representatives of the Soviet regime. . . . As his tool, Cardinal Willebrands has chosen Prof. Magocsi, who occupies the Chair of Ukrainian Studies at the University of Toronto. . . . Prof. Magocsi is distinguished for his remarkable organizational skills. These he demonstrated while still an associate of the Harvard Ukrainian Research Institute. They were in evidence again last year, when he performed brilliantly in organizing the conference commemorating the Servant of God, Metropolitan Andrei Sheptytskyi.

"It was the great success of this conference that brought him to the attention of a representative of the Secretariat of Christian Unity. . . .

"I do not doubt for a moment that Professor Magocsi has become involved in this nefarious affair unwittingly, and not to do harm to the Ukrainian community. He simply is unaware of the meaning of national dignity, blinded by the prospect of organizing something 'grand'."

—Omeljan Pritsak
"The Millennium of Christianity in Rus'-
Ukraine and Ukrainian National Dignity"
America (Philadelphia)
13. V. 1985, pp. 2 and 4

"Last week there appeared in the Ukrainian press [in North America] my article under the title, 'The Ukrainian Millennium and Ukrainian National Dignity', in which I presented information about a conference on the occasion of the Millennium [of Christianity] planned by Professor Paul Magocsi at the University of Toronto.

"It has now come to light that I based my article on incomplete and, in part, erroneous information. Therefore, I retract what I wrote in my article and request that all Ukrainian newspapers and journals do not publish or re-publish any material written and sent by me about this matter. I also request all bodies that I called upon to act, not to do so, because now any such actions are unnecessary."

—Omeljan Pritsak
"A Declaration"
Svoboda (Jersey City, N.J.)
15. V. 1985

"I believe that not only me in particular, but that all readers of the Ukrainian press in Canada are astonished by the article of Professor Pritsak entitled, 'An Analysis of the Circular of Professsor Magocsi'. . . .

"The normal procedure for someone who receives a project proposal is to provide comments or reservations. Instead, Professor Pritsak sounded 'an alarm' to the press and began, as he himself said, 'to bark like a dog' and slander not only Professor Magocsi but other church dignitaries associated with the project. . . .

"Professor Magocsi, whose previous activity has proven to be an example of exceptional success [the Sheptyts'kyi conference], deserves more trust from the Ukrainian community. . . .

"Now, as a result of plain professional jealously on the part of an older colleague toward a younger one, Ukrainians have once again lost an opportunity to inform the world about us at a truly high academic level. . . .

"Professor Pritsak has shown that he is incapable of objectively evaluating the merits of a younger colleague and his courageous, bold, and unconventional project that would truly defend the dignity of the Ukrainian people."

—Petro Jacyk
"An Analysis of Professor Pritsak's 'Analysis'"
Novyi shliakh (Toronto)
12. X. 1985, p. 12

"The Chair of Ukrainian Studies created five years ago at the University of Toronto and headed by Professor Paul Magocsi has prepared for publication *Ukraine: A Historical Atlas*. . . . There is no question that this publication (already praised by the nationalist newspaper *Homin*

Ukraïny), which was prepared by P.R. Magocsi from a position of 'neutrality', will become part of [diaspora] nationalist propaganda with its all encompassing anti-Soviet goals."

"Information from the Soviet Embassy in Canada for the
Central Committee of the Communist Party of Ukraine"
November 1985
Facts of History: Archival Documents
(Kyiv, 2003), p.711

"Once again Dr. Paul R. Magocsi . . . has shown to the world his ability to inform, entertain, and stimulate via the medium of learned monographs. [As for] his latest publication. . . . I can only recommend that *Our People* be read, savoured, and read again."

—Reverend Evan Lowig
St. Vladimir's Theological Quarterly (Tuckahoe, N.Y.)
Vol. XXX, No. 2 (1986) pp. 182, 184

"Professor Magocsi . . . is the major voice in the study of that variously named Slavic ethnic group whose homeland . . . covers the Carpathian Mountain regions of Subcarpathian Rus' . . . and the area on both sides of the present border between Poland and northeastern Slovakia. . . .

"Through this highly charged field Magocsi weaves his way with exemplary objectivity. . . .

"Any ethnic group would be grateful to have such a thorough, knowledgeable, and at the same time objective chronicler as Magocsi."

—Reverend Robert Taft, SJ
Orientalia Christiana Periodica (Rome)
Vol. LII, No. 2 (1986) pp. 485-487

"We should note that Professor Magocsi is in the broadest sense one of the most influential contemporary Rusynists. Through his scholarly work . . . he has helped enormously to bring Yugoslav Rusyns to the attention of people in all the continents of the world."

—G. Koljesar
"A Guest from Canada"
Ruske slovo (Novi Sad, Yugoslavia)
18. IX. 1987

"Professor Magocsi, together with the help of a few young, mixed-up Transcarpathian Ukrainian intellectuals (Edward Kasinec, Patricia Krafcik, Richard Renoff, and others) is trying to separate that branch of the Ukrainian people which lives on the southern slopes of the Carpathian Mountains and to create some kind of distinct 'Rusyn people'."

—Stepan Zhenets'kyi
Anabazys (Toronto)
Vol. VIII, No. 3-4 (1987), p. 13

"You asked me why I chose to study Rusyns. . . . No one [in Hungary] recommended that I look at this subject. However, when I was a student in Debrecen, Paul Magocsi, [today] head of the Chair of Ukrainian Studies at the University of Toronto in Canada, came to the [1974] summer session at our university (the program in Hungarian language). As a student I showed him around and I received from him a book about Dukhnovych. This book was published in Prešov—it was the first volume of his collected works—and it made a great impression on me."

—István Udvari
Shvetlosts (Novi Sad, Yugoslavia)
Vol. XXVI, No. 2 (1988), p. 229

"Among the participants and guests of the first International Congress of Ukrainianists . . . whom I sought out was the professor from Canada, Paul Robert Magocsi. . . . Having met a lively person of athletic build who is far from fifty years old, I could not conceal my surprise, since I expected to meet a greying professor bent over from work in an office."

—Ivan Petrovtsii
Nove zhyttia (Irshava, Ukraine)
27. IX. 90

"Just as at one time before World War I Rusynism stubbornly pushed its way into the Ukrainian environment, so now it has unexpectedly become aggressive again.

"In the very center of this development there stands one word: Magocsi. . . ."

—Valentyn Moroz
Anabazys (Toronto)
No. 1 (1990), p. 7

"The son of a Hungarian immigrant, the American scholar Paul Robert Magocsi, has come several times to Transcarpathia in order to revive Rusynism."

—Iurii Balega
Anabazys (Toronto)
No. 1 (1990), p. 7

"Professor Paul Magocsi has become known as a recognized specialist on the 'Rusyn question'. He is a frequent presence in scholarly circles both in the West and East.

"Thanks to the scholarly research and writings of Professor Magocsi, today in the western world more people know about the 'Rusyn question'. America itself has begun to become more interested in its 'Carpatho-Rusyns'. This is evident from the introduction of the category *Carpatho-Rusyn* in U.S. census data.

"The basic position of Professor Paul R. Magocsi is that there is good reason to conclude that historical conditions made possible the formation of Carpatho-Rusyns as a distinct ethnic group, and that such a development cannot be dismissed by administrative policies of the Warsaw Bloc nations that classify Rusyns as Ukrainians."

—Liubomir Medieshi
"America Returns to Its Ethnic Roots"
Shvetlosts (Novi Sad, Yugoslavia)
Vol. XXVIII, No. 5 (1990), pp. 630-631

"And so how can one be a Rusyn of Ukrainian origin? Perhaps in the old country, but now we're in America. Back then we did not have such outstanding historians like Magocsi."

"'To read Magocsi is to laugh or to cry,' said one serious activist who wasn't ashamed of being a Ukrainian.

"'The way Magocsi writes', I thought, 'he could become a millionaire writing best-sellers instead of just being an ordinary Rusyn historian'."

—Val'ter Caps
Novyi shliakh (Toronto)
8. XII. 90

"In conversations with younger activists, it is clear that the views of Professor Paul Magocsi from Canada regarding a 'Carpatho-Rusyn people' have gained a certain popularity.

"If this were occurring a century ago I would support it with both hands. But today, on what basis can one create such a people? From these few thousand Lemkos who live in the western part of Poland and who don't want to call themselves Ukrainians? The northern corner, the Lemko Region, is depopulated, while Transcarpathia and the Prešov Region are Ukrainian. I really doubt whether one can create a people today. And what would it lead to? Only to polonization.

"I don't believe the theories of Professor Magocsi will find real support in the Lemko Region. In any case, I met the professor when I was in Canada. He is an outstanding scholar and is interested in publishing as well as political activity. . . .

"In Poland the ideas of Magocsi are of interest to a certain number of young scholars or students from Cracow. . . . I know, moreover, that there are even more supporters of his ideas, although only a few in the Lemko Region. I believe that in the future his ideas will survive only among a few small groups."

—Michal Donski
Zustrichi (Warsaw, Poland)
No. 1 (1990), pp. 38-39

"Recently in our press and in public discussions the name Paul Magocsi is appearing more and more frequently. . . . In the words of some of his American and Canadian countrymen who met him last August-September in Kyiv at the International Congress of Ukrainianists, Paul Magocsi has collected among his countrymen abroad millions of dollars which he is using to spread among the Rusyn-Ukrainians of Transcarpathia, Poland, and Czecho-Slovakia an old magyarone intrigue—political Rusynism. . . . Those who think like him call Paul Magocsi a specialist in 'creating new nations'. According to him, one of those new nations among the Slavic peoples of Europe is the 'Rusyn nation'. It is not without irony that his countrymen on the American continent call him the 'Rusyn tsar', the 'Rusyn emperor', and yet some other kind of 'leader'. At the Kyiv Congress mentioned above my colleagues from the United States and Canada openly said that among our Rusyns there are indeed some people who have been taken in by P. Magocsi's Rusyn hook."

—Fedir Kovach
Duklia (Prešov, Czechoslovakia)
No. 2 (1991), p. 27.

"I believe that for Subcarpathia particularly dangerous is Professor Magocsi. He was raised and educated in the United States and it is quite possible that he belongs to some Masonic lodge and is in the service of other dark forces. . . . As a professor at the Ukrainian Chair in Toronto he is certainly very well informed about national and political developments in Ukraine . . . and cannot but know that the Rusyns of Subcarpathia are part of the very same people who live in Galicia, Bukovina, and Dnieper Ukraine. Our scholars have already had enough time and opportunity to expose the true essence of Magocsi's 'scholarship' that reigns in academic circles. . . . Why does not someone [among us] defend Ukrainian matters and truth in American society?"

—Ivan Savardii
"Letter to Reverend Sevastiian Sabol", 16. III. 1991
in Stanislav Arzhevitin, *Karpats'ka Ukraïna: epokha v dobi*, Vol. VI
(Kyiv, 2013), p. 752

"In fact, dear readers, do you know who has the greatest reputation as a historian or philosopher in Subcarpathian Rus'?—Paul Robert Magocsi. His name figures directly or indirectly in every Rusyn and anti-Rusyn public statement. . . . I would say that Professor Magocsi is our Rusyn Hrushevs'kyi.

"I will end a poem in free verse which I am now writing with the lines:
Professor Magocsi is among the Rusyns.
The Rusyns are learning from Professor Magocsi
The Rusyns are enchanted with Professor Magocsi
Ave Magocsi!
Ave Rusyns!!

"Professor Paul Robert Magocsi is without question a person of the widest scholarly breadth. . . . Perhaps he has been sent by God to give rebirth to an unjustly treated people?! Surely his profound ideas and his energy . . . reflect a rare gift of nature. Whatever the case, one thing is clear: the work of Professor Magocsi is honest activity on behalf of the renaissance of the Rusyn people and Rusyn culture. . . . The rebirth of a people that had been on its knees and dispersed throughout the world is of concern to all humanity. Sooner or later such work will be recognized. "Professor Magocsi is a distinguished son of the Rusyn people. He is valued highly in Rusyn circles throughout the world and in Subcarpathian Rus'. He is our intellectual center. The more he is criticized in Uzhhorod the more his authority increases. This is because we Soviet people are accustomed to the way things were done in the old days, when we knew that whoever was publicly criticized had, therefore, to be an honest person.

"I was transformed by [the First World] Congress of Rusyns and by conversations with Professor Magocsi. It is as if this architect of the Rusyns has programmed me to undertake some major work. It is rare to meet such people in life."

—Volodymyr Fedynyshynets'
"To Be a Rusyn You Have to be Loyal to Rusyns"
Molod' Zakarpattia (Uzhhorod)
25. V. 91

"It was with great anticipation that they waited [at the First World Congress of Rusyns] for the speech of Professor Magocsi. And he didn't disappoint them. His lecture had an academic tone, and in a comprehensible manner he traced the historical development of the Rusyn people from earliest times to the present and throughout the whole central European region."

—Peter Juščak
Literárny týdenník (Bratislava, Czechoslovakia)
21. VI. 91

"At the [First World] Congress we felt that we are a people, that we are a force, and that we must unite our strengths with all Rusyns throughout the world. Professor Magocsi gave us special help in that he explained in a scholarly fashion that we are Rusyns, that we are a people."

—Vasyl Sochka
Ruske slovo (Novi Sad, Yugoslavia)
26. VI. 91

"Among the most distinguished guests [at the opening of the Medzilaborce Museum of Modern Art] was Paul Robert Magocsi

180

from Canada, director of the Carpatho-Rusyn Research Center, whose assistance in negotiations with the Andy Warhol Foundation was invaluable."

—Jarmila Andrejčáková
Literárny týždenník (Bratislava)
26. VII. 91

"In Canada, Magocsi has made for himself a positive image. Not too long ago, at a meeting of some of our scholars, someone suggested to make public just who he is and for whom he is working.

"I believe that through our [Ukrainian] ambassador [in Ottawa] we should bring to the attention of the Canadian government how a Canadian scholar, through his Ukrainophobic activity—whose origins are to be found in the work of the Bolshevik KGB—is bringing disrepute to Canada.

"The time has come to 'bury' Magocsi."

—Iuliian Khymynets' [24.08.1991]
Epistolariï Iuriia Balehy
(Uzhhorod, 2018), p. 125

"In order to judge the civic and scholarly activity of P. Magocsi we must take into consideration the following contradiction: on the one hand, Professor Magocsi is full of creative energy, but on the other he is a person who is confused regarding the ethnic identity of 'Carpatho-Rusyns' in general and the Lemkos in particular. . . . The ideologists of neo-Rusynism spread rumours that the birth and development of the idea of Rusyn separatism is positively accepted by a group of young intellectuals in Transcarpathia, scholars at Uzhhorod State University, Lemkos in Poland, Hungary, and elsewhere. . . . This anti-scholarly conception of P. Magocsi is a myth which is uncritically repeated by several dilettantes and even professional historians in Transcarpathia, Poland, Yugoslavia, Hungary, the United States, and Canada.

"The Society of Carpatho-Rusyns is under the influence of Americans of Rusyn origin, in particular their chief ideologist, Professor P. Magocsi, who has promised generous financial and other assistance to all who work to revive Rusynism in the Carpathian homeland."

—Vasyl' Mel'nyk
Zakarpats'ka pravda (Uzhhorod)
21-22. VIII. 91

"Volodymyr Fedynyshynets' [the Transcarpathian writer] wants . . . to convince us of his filial devotion to the Soviet president Gorbachev and of his platonic love for University of Toronto Professor P. R. Magocsi . . . He is still singing the old refrain about the Canadian professor ('the excellent advisor', 'the creator of Rusyns', 'the outstanding son of the Rusyn people', 'our intellectual center'). Even more, Paul Robert Magocsi is now the new Messiah, that is, 'the person sent by God to revive an oppressed people'. The Rusyn V. Fedynyshynets' is entranced. 'Ave Magocsi! Ave Rusyns', he sings out in a full voice his Rusyn partisan greetings. . . . If the article by Magocsi, 'A New or Revived People?', had not been published, one could get the impression from Fedynyshnets's description that indeed a new Stalin, a Rusyn one, had arisen."

—Mrs. Ïvha and R. Ofitsyns'kyi
Molod' Zakarpattia (Uzhhorod)
31. VIII. 91

"I should mention the appearance of Professor P. R. Magocsi in the [Transcarpathian] region. In the United States he is an outstanding scholar of the history of Ukraine and of the regional cultures in the Carpathians. He has a sharp and critical mind. He is a realist with the skills of a businessman. He is both a Ukrainian and local Carpathian patriot. This professor has indicated that he is interested in the phenomenon of the revival of Rusynism. It is inevitable that he, this specialist, studies to what degree political Rusynism can increase friction in the Slavic world, since its activity extends to four countries. This professor of American background does not provide us with an answer to the question of just whose orders he is fulfilling."

—Fedir Myshanych
Karpats'ka Ukraïna (Uzhhorod)
7. IX. 91

"Rusyns as a separate nation? Only a historically illiterate person would make such an assertion. . . . My opinion of his [Magocsi's] pseudotheory— if one could call it a 'theory' at all—is completely negative. I cannot understand how a person with an advanced education, a person who considers himself a historian, is capable of such nonsense. It is quite likely that the reasons are not academic, but commercial. A person who creates myths must be called a mythologist, one who falsifies facts a falsifier, and one who does it and makes a profit from it, a businessman. Beyond the borders of Ukraine, the 'theory' of Magocsi is not treated seriously. It would be a waste of time to be concerned with it."

—Ivan Fizer
Zakarpats'ka pravda (Uzhhorod)
12. IX. 91

"You [Professor Magocsi] and your supporters, with your hatred toward everything Ukrainian, are not only calling for the de-Ukrainianization of the Prešov Region, but are describing Ukrainianism as a product of Communism. . . . I am concerned about the fate of my homeland, because you want to set it back over a hundred years to the beginning of the century, in order to carry out an experiment to see if it is possible to make from Rusyns a new nation?!. . . . We know who we are, whose children we are, and what are our roots! I suggest that you carry out your experiments with creating new nations somewhere in Africa or in the jungles of the Amazon. Leave my Rusyn-Ukrainian people alone, because without you they know who they are!"

—Iosyf Sirka
"We Know Whose Children We Are and What Are Our Origins"
Nove zhyttia (Prešov)
3. IX. 91

"The idea of the rebirth of Rusyns and the declaration of them as a distinct East Slavic people was brought to us from beyond the ocean by P. Magocsi and M. Zarechnak."

—Fedir Kovach
Nove zhyttia (Prešov)
20. IX. 91

"The Society of Carpatho-Rusyns, having as their chief ideologue the American professor Magocsi. . . . believe in him with all their heart, not seeing that we are at the end of the twentieth century and not at its beginning, and that our people are not at all what they were then."

—Kh. Petryshche
Zakarpats'ka pravda (Uzhhorod)
15. X. 91

"I know quite well Paul Magocsi, who is the 'spiritual father' of this [Rusyn] orientation. And I also know that the roots of political Rusynism are really in America."

—Interview with Iurii [George] Shevelov
Lisova industriia (Uzhhorod, Ukraine)
25. X. 91

"We know that just upon hearing his name the blood of the Ukrainophiles and Ukrainianizers begins to boil, simply because they don't control him and don't know how to debate him, but only to besmirch him and depict him as the greatest enemy of our people. . . . I know Magocsi well. . . . He is not for the creation of a Rusyn state . . . since he knows quite well that this is not realistic. . . . He is simply working to have Rusyns recognized in the world with all the rights that are due to them."

—Aleksander Zozuliak
Narodný novynký (Prešov)
30. X. 91

"On the streets of Uzhhorod, Columbia University Professor George Shevelov meets Professor Paul Robert Magocsi from Toronto. . .
"Shevelov: So what are you doing in Uzhhorod?
"Magocsi: I've come to build a Subcarpathian state. And you?
"Shevelov: And I've come to demolish it."

Karpats'ka Ukraïna (Uzhhorod, Ukraine)
30. X. 91

"The views of the Ukrainian specialist Professor Paul Magocsi have during the past two years enjoyed remarkable popularity not only in western countries, but especially in the Czech and Slovak press. . . . He has the reputation of being one of the leading experts on the question of 'Rusynism' in the contemporary world.

"At the [Bratislava] symposium, 'National Minorities in Central and Southeastern Europe', the majority of participants were sympathetic to his views. This does not mean, however, that truth was on his side."

—Mykola Mushynka
Political Rusynism in Practice:
The Speech of Professor Paul Robert Magocsi at the Bratislava Symposium
(Prešov, 1991), pp. 4 and 12

"The most outstanding figure among present-day researchers of the
Rusyn immigration is Paul Robert Magocsi from Toronto, Canada."
—Vasyl' Lemak
Novyny Zakarpattia (Uzhhorod, Ukraine)
7. XII. 91

"Just who is this Mr. Magocsi? It's worth reflecting on this question.
For example, it's enough for the professor to cross our country's borders
and, enamoured with his appearance on the horizons, [Transcarpathia's]
Regional Assembly newspaper is suddenly overwhelmed with a
hysterical-like ecstasy. . . . On July 2, the assembly's newspaper [*Novyny
Zakarpattia*] broke all previous records: aside from a large front-page
photograph of Magocsi, the adoring admirers of 'this creator of new
nationalities' got four more photos of their idol on the inside of this same
issue. Not even an earlier expert on the creation of new peoples, the
greying party bureaucrat M. Suslov, was ever so honored. . . .

"The Ukrainian Theater in Prešov has been transformed into the
anational Aleksander Dukhnovych Theater and the Museum of Ukrainian
Culture in Svidník is . . . no longer Ukrainian. All this comes from the
efforts undertaken by the Rusyn Renaissance Society. Professor Magocsi
cannot help but be pleased that besides the Rusyn Renaissance Society
his activity has also led to the revival of the Russophile Dukhnovych
Society in the Prešov Region and the Society of Friends of Subcarpathian
Rus' in Prague, which is working for the return of Transcarpathia to
Czechoslovakia.

"This newly-arisen apostle of Rusynism considers as an 'achievement'
the fact that the 'Rusyns are officially recognized as a distinct national
minority in Czechoslovakia'. There is nothing new in this, however,
because as has already been said the 'concept' of Magocsi coincides with
the 'conceptions' of Rusynism coming out of Moscow."
—Iurii Balega
Who Are We and Whose Children Are We?: A Polemic With Professor P.R. Magocsi
(Kyiv, Ukraine, 1991), pp. 5, 15-16

"During the past few years quite active work in Lemko circles in Canada has been undertaken by the Toronto University professor, Paul Magocsi. . . . One must stress, however, that his idea about the existence of an artificial 'Carpatho-Rusyn' people—and to the degree that this includes Lemkos as well—is particularly destructive for Lemko unity."
—Ivan Krasovs'kyi and Dmytro Solynko
Khto my lemky . . . populiarnyi narys
(L'viv, Ukraine, 1991), p. 39

"I mention [the interwar Hungarian publicist Albert] Bereghy and Magocsi because their common interest is not to strengthen Rusyn identity in relation to its mother nation but rather to use a Rusyn identity as a means for other non-Rusyn and non-Ukrainian state interests.
—Iuliian Tamash
Narodni kalendar 1992
(Novi Sad, Yugoslavia, 1991), p. 261

"The attempt to weaken the Ukrainian national minority [in Czecho-Slovakia] imported here by the Magocsis, the Zarechnaks, the Hořeces, and others has been successful."
Nove zhyttia (Prešov)
3. I. 92

"In Transcarpathia, where Rusynism has been supported by certain conservative circles, hatred of Ukrainianism began at the same time as the Ukrainian national revival. This is not happenstance. Even the well-known Canadian specialist on the 'Rusyn question' who has such an 'odious' fame—P. Magocsi—himself points out that Rusynism in Transcarpathia came into being as an alternative to the Ukrainian national movement, although there is no doubt that former [Communist] party functionaries have also given it their support."
—Anatolii Ivchenko
Nove zhyttia (Prešov)
3. 1. 92

"I was able to hear Professor Magocsi, who consciously ignores scholarly data and whose lectures focus on the destabilization of the situation in the [Carpathian] region at a time when the Ukrainian people have achieved independence."

—Iurii Hoshko
Nove zhyttia (Prešov)
17. I. 92

"One does not have to have much foresight to understand where the ideology of political Rusynism imported from Canada by Professor Magocsi is headed. Nor is it strange that this 'creator' of new nationalities has received wide support from government circles in the [Czecho-Slovak] republic. From this fact it is obvious how the idea of political Rusynism in the present political constellation is in the interest of certain representatives of our republic."

—Ivan Iatskanyn
Nove zhyttia (Prešov)
10. II. 92

"Magocsi is interested in the anachronistic and yet undispersed remnants of 'Rusyn consciousness'. From the standpoint of scholarship, such an interest reminds one of those people who still believe that the sun revolves around the earth and not the reverse."

—Borys Halas
Karpats'kyi krai (Uzhhorod, Ukraine)
18. II. 92

"Since the time of [the interwar leaders] Andrei Brodii and Stepan Fentsyk, the most important political agitation or, to use the terminology of the KGB, 'the most outstanding theoretician of Rusynism', is a professor from Toronto, Paul Robert Magocsi. With the blessings of his alma mater, that is the KGB (and not only that organization), he has played in Transcarpathia the rotten 'Rusyn' card, dividing among little known and naive 'leaders' of 'Rusynism' the cabinet portfolios of premier, vice-premier, and other 'ministers' in the cherished KGB empire of 'Rusinia', and he has tried to attract to his ephemeral domain leaders from among the democratic forces in Transcarpathia. Magocsi's local group of supporters, together with the help of the all-powerful Communist party mafia, has through means of wide-spread disinformation exploited for purposes of anti-Ukrainian propaganda the difficult economic situation in Transcarpathia. In a round about way he debases people with ideas of self-rule and 'Rusyn' separatism, and he struggles for the right of [Transcarpathia's] Ukrainians to identify themselves as an age-old nationality—Rusyn—while at the same time frightening them with the KGB-Magocsi created spectre of aggression from Galicia."

—Vasyl' Dovhei
"Neo-Rusynism? No, Shady Revanchism"
Karpats'ka Ukraïna (Uzhhorod, Ukraine)
1. IV. 92

"Messrs. Hranchak, Boldyzhar, Kryvs'kyi and a few others want to push out Magocsi himself from his dominant ideological position in Transcarpathia."

—Emil Vushko
Karpats'kyi krai (Uzhhorod)
1. IV. 92

"Particularly important for us is the Rusyn theory successfully worked out by the distinguished son of our people, the American professor, Paul Robert Magocsi."

—Vladymyr Fedynyshynets'
Podkarpats'ka Rus' (Uzhhorod, Ukraine)
8. V. 92

"Professor Paul Robert Magocsi . . . is known as the author of numerous works . . . which today remain the most extensive publications about the history of the Rusyn ethnos. . . . This world-renowned scholar is doing everything to help the rebirth of Rusyns and their recognition in the world. . . . Our true friend and advisor . . . argues that the only way to achieve our goals is to conduct our struggle by civilized methods and legal means."

Respublika (Khust, Ukraine)
4. VI. 92

"I read your brochure, *Khto my ie i chyï my dity?* [Who Are We and Whose Children Are We? by Iurii Baleha and Iosyf Sirka]. You've really hit Magocsi precisely in a way that hurts him the most."

—Iuliian Khymynets' [09.VI.1992]
Epistolariï Iuriia Balehy
(Uzhhorod, 2018), pp. 127-128

"Readers of *Podkarpats'ka Rus'* write and telephone us with requests that we inform them more about Professor Magocsi on the pages of our newspaper—who he is and what does he do. . . .

"I believe our readers are convinced now that Professor Magocsi is an exceptional figure among Carpatho-Rusyns. He is indeed the powerful Magocsi [*mohuchyi Mahochyi*]! . . . In general, Carpatho-Rusyns can feel satisfied that we are not without any influence in this world when we have such a true friend and such an outstanding scholar as Professor Magocsi from Canada. He writes for us, for the scholarly world, and he is with us. We should thank him and praise him for that."

—Volodymyr Fedynyshynets'
Podkarpats'ka Rus' (Uzhhorod)
30. VI. 92, p. 2

"Oleksa Myshanych had to be a good Communist and cooperate with Magocsi. Magocsi was working with the secret services. . . .

"I spoke with the now deceased prime-minister [of Carpatho-Ukraine] Julian Revay, who invited us Transcarpathians to the [Ukrainian Institute] in New York City to hear a lecture by Magocsi. . . . In his lecture, he referred to us Transcarpathians as Rusnaks. I spoke out against Magocsi, saying that 'Rusnak' is a demeaning term which is insulting to us Ukrainians. . . .

"Before we left, I had a long conversation with prime-minister Revay and told him in no uncertain terms that the Communists have sent Magocsi among us Ukrainians as a kind of 'Trojan Horse.' Revay looked at me and said in a soothingly disarming manner: 'Mykola, you really shouldn't be so suspicious of people'. . . .

"It's because of Magocsi that I argued with Revay. I also must tell you I am cerain that Oleksa Myshanych is part of the Magocsi mafia. We in the immigration are very trustworthy people, who various secret agents and faithful Communists try to deceive. Let them all perish in our independent Ukraine."

—Mykola Teslevych [18. IX.1992]
Epistolariï Iuriia Balehy
(Uzhhorod, 2018), p. 121-123

189

"How far have you gotten along in writing your book about Magocsi? I have heard that Magocsi has a two-year leave of absence from the Ukrainian Chair in Toronto. Now he is actively engaged with the University of Budapest which is dear to him. Perhaps he is preparing to become another [pro-Hungarian] Andrii Brodii."

Iuliian Khymynets' [8.X.1992]
Epistolariï Iuriia Balehy
(Uzhhorod, 2018), p. 129

"As for Professor Paul Magocsi at the University of Toronto, he only deals with Lemkos to the extent that he includes them in his mythical Rusyn nation. . . . For Lemkos he is a negative factor. He acts negatively on their behalf, not for their welfare. Using people like Magocsi, Polish and other chauvinists have created a division in the ranks of Lemkos and have divided them for their own interests, and now they continue further in this destructive work."

—Mykola Duplak
Lemkivshchyny (Clifton, N.J.)
No. 3 (1992), p. 9

"Thanks to him [Professor Paul Magocsi], 'Rusynism' has created deeper and deeper roots that are in opposition to the interests of the Ukrainian people."

—Pavlo Lopata
Lemkivshchyny (Clifton, N.J.)
No. 3 (1992), p. 19

"Professor Paul Magocsi, educated at Harvard's Ukrainian [Institute] and with the help of its activists, in particular Professor Omeljan Pritsak, has had an outstanding career. . . .

"In the beginning he masked his views, concluding, for instance, his inaugural lecture at University of Toronto with a paraphrase of the national anthem: 'Ukrainian civilization will live on'.

"Soon, however, this energetic professor began to undermine profoundly Ukrainian civilization, which found expression in his political and 'scholarly' activity on behalf of forming in southwestern Ukraine's ethnic territory a new Rusyn nation."

—Zynovii Bliakhars'kyi

"Something about Mago, the Spiritual Leader of Carpatho-Russians"
Literaturna Ukraïna (Kyiv)
No. 41, 15. X. 1992, p. 1

"The uncensored Czech newspaper, *Rudé krávo*, has . . . begun this year to publish the names of former agents and collaborators of the Czechoslovak Secret Services. . . .
"Surprisingly, among the names mentioned in the 14th issue of *Rudé krávo* (1992) is that of the renowned Professor Dr. Paul Robert Magocsi, holder of the Chair of Ukrainian Studies at the University of Toronto. . . .
"The truth cannot be concealed, and while for many not only in Czechoslovakia this is regrettable, their eyes are now open."
"The Shameful Dethronement of the Ideologue of Rusynism
—the Canadian Professor P. Magocsi"
Ukraïns'ke slovo (Paris)
5. VII. 1992

"In the past few years [1980s], activity among Rusyns in the United States and Canada has developed because of the work of the University of Toronto professor, Paul Robert Magocsi. . . . an enterprising scholar and the author of a wide range of articles and scholarly works on the Rusyn problem. Too bad that all his energy is directed toward the thankless task of creating from Rusyns a separate 'Carpatho-Rusyn' people. Caught up in the labyrinth of various theories about Rusyns in the Carpathians, P. Magocsi has through his ideas wrought significant damage to the unity of the Ukrainian population in the Carpathians."
—Ivan Krasovs'kyi
*Til'ky z ridnom narodom . . . pro sytuatsiiu
v seredovyshchi karpats'kykh rusyniv*
(L'viv, 1992), p. 29

"Perhaps students at the Department of History at the University of Toronto can also learn something from [Subtelny's] history [of Ukraine]. But it is also true that first they must all go through the difficult process of being 'de-Magocsi-ized'."
—Katsaveiko [Vasyl' Sirs'kyi
Vsesmikh (Toronto)
No. 18 (1993), p. 3

191

"Having organized his anti-Ukrainian fifth column in Slovakia, the agent of the Czechoslovak Security Services (ŠtB) and Canadian professor P. R. Magocsi has turned his attention first and foremost toward certain mercenary, demoralized, and crude extremists from among the ranks of the Rusyn-Ukrainian nationality. Such people are easy to buy and, having bought them, they are easy to direct. . . . It is from such filth that the fierce enemy of our people, P. R. Magocsi, has put together the so-called Rusyn Renaissance Society (Rusyn'ska Obroda), an organization with a foreign name that works against the people. . . . The Rusyn Renaissance Society, like analogous Magocsi-created fifth columns in Transcarpathia, Poland, Yugoslavia, and Hungary, was created to struggle against Ukraine and the Ukrainian people. . . . Inspired by Magocsi's foreign agency and the anti-Ukrainian policy of Czecho-Slovak governmental circles, the Rusyn Renaissance Society has betrayed the interests of its own people and followed the path of shameful service on behalf of foreign interests. . . .

—Stepan Hostyniak, Myroslav Sopolyga, Mykola Rusynko
Nove zhyttia (Prešov)
13. II. 1993, p. 3

"It's been for quite some time already that in the Ukrainian press in Prešov . . . one reads how Professor Paul R. Magocsi of the University of Toronto is an agent of the KGB. Such 'news' is like a thunderbolt from heaven!

"But what is an ordinary person to make of such news ? . . . .

"When I read such lines in the newspapers, in which editors are trying to scare us with all kinds of agents and spies, I thought to myself: Maybe it is true that Magocsi is what they say, especially if they curse and hate him so. Yet where have these editors gotten such 'information from so-called first-hand sources'? . . .

"I first saw this so-called 'agent of the KGB'—P. R. Magocsi—in Medzilaborce two years ago at the First World Congress of Rusyns. When this so-called 'agent' went up to the podium and began to read a lecture on Rusyn history I thought to myself: 'this person cannot be bad'. Self-control, broad erudition, a profound knowledge of the subject, clarity of argument, reflection, and expression—that was the Magocsi I saw. Then I thought to myself: May God give us Rusyns more 'agents' with such intelligence."

—Nykolai Shkurla
Narodnŷ novynkŷ (Prešov)
17. III. 93

"From the very beginning Magocsi has used the 'Ukrainian Chair' for his own 'scholarly' and pseudo-political ambitions. Since the days of his doctoral studies his clear goal has been to create a separate Carpatho-Rusyn people. . . . Toward these ends he has attracted the wealthy Greek Catholic Church of the Pittsburgh Metropolia which long ago lost its own 'Rusyn' character, but whose leaders he has convinced to turn toward the old country and to weaken Ukrainianism there. It is from that source that financial support comes for Magocsi's 'extracurricular' activities."

—Vasyl' Markus'
"How Does Magocsi Create a Distinct People and New Language?"
Novyi shliakh (Toronto)
20. III. 93

"The Ukrainian Students' Club [at the University of Toronto] has been criticized by various people for its lack of concern over the Magocsi issue. The answer to this is that there really is no issue. The article publicized by the Czechoslovakian newspaper *Rudé kravo* about Paul Robert Magocsi's supposed career as a KGB agent is about as valid as a *National Enquirer* story. There are no valid reasons for the Students' Club to protest Professor Magocsi's position as the Chair of Ukrainian Studies. . . . For all that matters there could be an Indian from Poland in his position."

—Paul Grod
President, Ukrainian Students' Club
Studynets' (Toronto)
March 1993, p. 5

"The questionable period of de-Ukrainianization began in Czecho-Slovakia. . . . when President Václav Havel himself, on the eve of the [1991] census, referred to more than 60,000 Ukrainians in the country only as Rusyns. . . .

"As for who formulated the policy of de-Ukrainianization, who brought to the world's attention 'the problem of Subcarpathian Rus'", and who dreamed up the idea of a 'separate Rusyn people', one need only cite that professional provocateur of nationality issues, that agent of several security forces, that most important advisor to official Prague and Bratislava on the question of 'Rusynism'—P. R. Magocsi."

—Stepan Hostyniak
"At the End of Former States and the Beginning of New Ones"
Nove zhyttia (Prešov)
16. I. 1993, p.7

"The Rusyn 'leaders' Turok and Magocsi once again have proclaimed that for their 'Rusyns', that is, for their anti-Ukrainian experiments, the most favorable conditions are in Slovakia. . . . The new Slovak state has set out along a path of active anti-Ukrainianism. . . . In its relationship with Ukraine, Slovakia really does not have a choice: either it continues to follow the path of Magocsi's comedians and primitive provocations, or for its own good it must begin to undertake a serious political policy toward its eastern neighbor."

—Stepan Hostyniak
Nove zhyttia (Prešov, Slovakia)
29. V. 93

"In the beginning of the period of *perestroika*, the Communist party apparatus led the Rusyn movement along the well-trodden path of Russophilism, which favored the Soviet Union instead of Ukrainian independence. . . . After the [anti-Gorbachev] putsch, it was necessary to change tactics. As elsewhere the trend toward separatism increased. They found a theoretician in the person of Professor Magocsi from the University of Toronto. The same ideologists who before proclaimed, 'We are Russians', now began to work toward creating a distinct Carpatho-Rus' or Rusyn nation."

—Leonid Pliouchtch
Ukraine: à nous l'Europe
(Paris, 1993), p. 172

"We look upon Rusyns as our own brothers. . . . You can distinguish Rusyns from Ukrainians [in Yugoslavia], and they can differentiate themselves however they wish. That's their business, but we will treat them as the same nonetheless.

"For that reason, we find unacceptable the idea of Rusynism, which has been provoked especially by Professor Magocsi, who unfortunately is a professor of Ukrainian language, history, and Ukrainian studies in general at the University of Toronto, and who has put into the heads of our Rusyn brothers that they have nothing in common with Ukrainians, that they are without question a separate Slavic nationality which should have the right to self- determination. . . . It is quite obvious that such a provocation will have a tragic end for [Rusyn separatists in Transcarpathia], because they will forfeit good relations with the Ukrainian people and with the Ukrainian state, which will bring them no good."

—Dmytro Pavlychko
Chairman of Ukraine's parliamentary committee for international relations
Interview with Radio Novi Sad
Ruske slovo (Novi Sad, Yugoslavia)
27. VIII. 93, p. 2

"The malicious attacks by Galician and Galicianized voices have not stopped. . . . This applies as well to the outstanding University of Toronto professor, Paul Robert Magocsi, whose mother—a native of the Irshava district—was able even in the far away diaspora to instill in him a love for his people. As for the invented accusations of cooperation with the Czechoslovak secret police, this has provoked laughter among Czechs and Slovaks as well as among agents of the secret service themselves, who know how to distinguish fact from fiction."

—Hanna Kuz'ma
"Personal Reflections on the Serious Problem of [Galician-Ukrainian] Immigrants to Our Land and Their Inexcusable Attacks on Its Inhabitants"
Novyny Zakarpattia (Uzhhorod)
28. VIII. 93, p. 5

"The major theoretician and practioner of political Rusynism in Canada and the United States is the University of Toronto Professor Paul Robert Magocsi, the well-known historian and Carpathian studies specialist. Much has already been written about his activity in creating a new fourth East Slavic Carpatho-Rusyn people. We would only add that much more than necessary is attributed to him. In fact, Professor Magocsi himself did not expect that the rather tempered ideas put forth by him in the beginning would, in the favorable environment for the creation of a new

Rusyn people, be so blown out of proportion and carried beyond the borders of Ukraine. The Rusyn movement was not even diminished by the 'discovery' of Professor Magocsi as an agent of the Czechoslovak secret service and the accusations in the press of his close relations with the Soviet KGB. All of this reveals without any doubt the role of 'big-time politics' directed against Ukraine and its status as a state."

—Oleksa Myshanych
"What's Behind Political Rusynism?"
Literaturna Ukraïna (Kyiv)
28. X. 1993. p. 3

"One of the experts in creating separate zones for state and national entities is Professor Magocsi from the United States. Although Communist party propaganda had all the time criticized the scholarship of scholars from abroad, the Communist leaders in Transcarpathia are now using that scholarship to defend its own positions."

—Myroslav Levyts'kyi
Nashe slovo (Warsaw)
5. XII. 93, p.1

"Paul R. Magocsi (formerly of Harvard's Ukrainian Institute and currently of the University of Toronto, Chair of Ukrainian Studies, and the Multicultural History Society of Ontario) is the major researcher of Rusyn language, literature, history, and culture."

—Joshua A. Fishman
International Journal of the Sociology of Language
(Berlin and New York)
No. 104 (1993), p. 119

"Professor Magocsi, the main theoretician of contemporary political Rusynism, openly states that he is a 'one-hundred percent American'; therefore, it is not appropriate to connect him with the political concept of a Rusyn nationalist."

—Oleksa V. Myshanych
"Political Rusynism Has No Future"
Nove zhyttia (Prešov)
3. 1. 94

"The younger generation among the Rusyn intelligentsia took part in the changes that began with the fall of Communism in Europe, while the older [Ukrainian] intelligentsia is still holding on to the old ways and national views.

"It is useful to note that P.R. Magocsi gives particular attention to the younger Rusyn intelligentsia. He has provided them with encouragement and self-confidence."

—Liubomir Medieshi
Rusyn (Prešov)
Vol. V, No. 2 (1994), p. 23

"Look what's happening all around us. Separatists are on the rise in the Crimea under [that regime's] newly-elected president, Iurii Meshkov. Transcarpathia has also been affected, where the ambituous professor from the diaspora, P. Magocsi, is trying in every way possible to confirm the existence of a so-called 'Rusyn' nationality. That idea, which has attracted as well the local ruling bureaucracy, will surely lead to a situation in which Ukraine's [central] government will no longer have control over the region."

—Raiïsa Ivanchenko
Literaturna Ukraïna (Kyiv)
9. VI. 94, p. 2

"Ukrainians are not against the idea of 'the formation of a national identity' among American Rusyns; they are not against the Rusyn revival in America carried out during the past fifteen years by the Carpatho-Rusyn Research Center headed by Professor Magocsi. We believe Magocsi deserves full credit for such activity. . . . We wish the professor can repeat the success of the Englishman Reichlin, who in the nineteenth century revived modern Hebrew.

"On the other hand, with regard to ruining the otherwise unstable national consciousness of Ukrainians in the Carpathian region and the attempt to re-orient them into some kind of Rusyns, and promising them a separate phantom-like state, we must openly reply that the inhabitants of the Transcarpathian oblast condemn such a political affair. Political Rusynism is not only without any perspective, it is also destructive."

—Pavlo Chuchka

"Ukrainians and Rusynism in Transcarpathia"
"Karpatorusynstvo": istoriia i suchasnist'
(Kyiv, 1994), p. 60

"It is obvious that the appearance of political Rusynism is based on the anti-Ukrainian and Muscovite activity that occurs worldwide under the direction of a professor from Toronto, Paul Robert Magocsi. The goal of this Muscovite activity is to divide the Ukrainian people and to detach from Ukrainians the Lemkos, the inhabitants of Transcarpathia, and the Rusyns of Slovakia, Yugoslavia, Romania, and Hungary. . . . We have our own historical and scholarly potential and individuals capable of defending our cultural values and our Lemko origins so as not to permit people like Magocsi to deceive himself and the entire Lemko people."
—Vasyl' Kolodiichyk
Nashe slovo (Warsaw)
17. VII. 1994

"Many months ago I received my copy of *Our People*. . . . When the book first arrived, I flipped through and was quickly moved to tears when I saw my mom and dad looking back at me from the picture of the mock wedding at St. John's in Perth Amboy. I took the book to show to my mom, who is eighty-seven and an invalid. She rarely shows strong emotions anymore, but when I opened the book to her picture, she gasped and cried and showed more feeling than I've seen in a decade."
—Elizabeth Chechur Short
Our People: Carpatho-Rusyns and Their Descendants in North America,
3rd rev. ed. (Toronto, 1994), end papers

"I believe every international news reporter and diplomat should be locked in a room with Magocsi's *Historical Atlas of East Central Europe* and not allowed out until he/she has fully assimilated its content. We may then see some accuracy in the news coverage by the former and wisdom in the decisions of the latter."
—Mehrdad Izady
International Journal of Kurdish Studies
Vol. VIII, No. 2 (1995), pp. 127-128

"The idea of a Carpatho-Rusyn people was first promoted by a professor of Slavistics at the University of Toronto, Paul Robert Magocsi. In Transcarpathia, it is said half-jokingly that the real source of Rusyn separatism was the result of a dispute between academic circles in the diaspora.

"As long as the dispute was academic in nature and revolved around dissertations and lectures, it was not dangerous. Academic arguments were not enough for Professor Magocsi, however, and he set out on the road of political activism. In 1991, he appeared in Transcarpathia and before long became the leading ideologist of Rusyn separatism. It was under his influence that the Society of Carpatho-Rusyns [in Uzhhorod] was established.

—Grzegorz Górny
Rzeczpospolita (Warsaw)
No. 111 [4064] 15. V. 1995, p. 26

"Just what is the phenomenon of Professor Magocsi. . . . or the 'All-powerful Magocsi', as I have referred to him in one my poems? . . .

"His humane and scholarly power lies in the fact that at the very end of this century and millennium, he, like a messiah, has brought attention to an unjustly treated people in central Europe called Rusyns, Ruthenes, or Rusnaks. And this people, like a sleeping or dead volcano, is living, has gotten back its breath, and perhaps will revive itself."

—Volodymyr Fedynyshynets'
Istorychna metafora profesora Mahochiia
(Uzhhorod, 1995), p. 12

"P.R. Magocsi . . . is completely driven by and tied to the idea of separating the Carpathian Rusyns-Ukrainians from Ukraine. . . . The professor proclaims that all of Transcarpathia's ills began in June 1945, when 'the policy of Ukrainianization began'.

"Magocsi is like a scholar-experimenter who, with his potions, carries out experiments on live people. He's doing this in Transcarpathia, where at the end of the twentieth century he has set out to create a nation unknown to anyone in the world. . . . His efforts go beyond all ethical norms . . . not unlike the scholar described by H.G. Wells in the novel, *The Island of Dr. Moreau* [who ended badly]. . . . Meanwhile, Professor

P. R. Magocsi's experiments on us continue. Aside from the questionable morality of this activity, there is also the question of legal responsibility: why should this person who hates our state be allowed to visit here systematically and even be greeted officially by [Ukraine's] central government representatives in Uzhhorod? After all, civilized countries, including Canada where P. R. Magocsi lives and works, would quite naturally react in a civilized manner: declare someone like him *persona non grata* and bar him from the country [Ukraine] toward which he is doing so much damage."

—M. Rusnak
"The So-Called All-Powerful Magocsi"
Karpats'ka Ukraïna (Uzhhorod)
No. 10 [150], 20.VI. 1995, p. 1

"On January 27, 1995, a scholarly conference devoted to the 'codification of the Rusyn language' took place in Bratislava. . . . The natural father of this illegitimate child is Paul Magocsi.

"How long is Kyiv and Uzhhorod going to tolerate interference in such an essential Ukrainian matter as our national being? . . . How long is the Ukrainian community going to tolerate such a 'professor of Ukrainian history', who is an inspiration to all those forces (Hungarians, Poles, Slovaks, Czechs and other chauvinists from Moscow and St. Petersburg) who are opposed to the independence of Ukraine?

"Has not the time come to say openly to those who have supported and still support his university chair that it does not promote Ukrainian historical scholarship but ruins it?! . . .

"I believe that with this 'achievement in Slovakia' Magocsi's escapade will end. . . . This illegitimately born child [the Rusyn language] of a Slovak mother (and several fathers) will perhaps soon expire. It will not have a long life, because it began in an unnatural fashion. . . ."

—Vasyl' Markus'
"Magochiïv manifest pro 'rusyns'ku' movu»
Novyi shliakh (Toronto)
24. VI. 95, pp. 8-9

"Professor Paul Magocsi from Toronto has about as much a relationship to Rusyns as Karl Marx, who did not stand beside the proletariat on the barricades of revolution for a single second. . . . The most Magocsi has achieved is in gaining the support of the Slovak government in the elimination of everything that is Ukrainian in the Prešov Region, and in the future that will lead to the complete assimilation of everything there that is East Slavic."

—Ivan Antalyk
Nasha respublyka (Kyiv)
28. VII. 95, p. 11

"Every one of the present-day leading Rusyn activists has an epithet given to him by his opponents. Professor Magocsi, for example, is often referred to on the pages of the [Transcarpathian] press as 'the father of a new nation', a modern-day [Nikolai] Mikhlukho-Maklai [the 19th-century Russian ethnographer who uncovered new peoples in Polynesia]."

—Volodymyr Fedynyshynets'
Istorychna metafora profesora Mahochiia
(Uzhhorod, 1995), p. 194

"Paul Robert Magocsi, the American grandson of an East Slav immigrant and now Professor of Ukrainian Studies in Toronto, has been leading what he calls the 'Lemko national revival' in present-day Poland, where this subdivision of Ruthenes, themselves a subdivision of the East Slavs, have been plumped by history.... Professor Magocsi's own surname happens to be Hungarian; the Ukrainians in Toronto who sponsor his chair are not best pleased at this effort to subdivide the East Slavs....
    "Magocsi is at least a sort of Slav."

Ferdinand Mount
"How to Invent your Own Nation"
Times Literary Supplement (London)
17. XI. 1995, p. 34

"One can view this [multi-authored] collection from the perspective provided. . . . by Professor Paul Magocsi. . . . that there are two kinds of Ukrainian Canadians: (1) Canadians of Ukrainian background; and (2) Ukrainians who live in Canada.
    "Magocsi's lens provides a useful tool with which to view the motivations of the many local minorities that now collectively may comprise the majority of the voting Canadian population."

—Stephen Carey
Canadian Review of Studies in Nationalism
Vol.XXII, No. 1-2, (1995), pp. 191-192

"The most recent political developments, namely the collapse of Communist power throughout the region, have brought about a situation in which the old issues of national identity can once again be freely aired. This is the stage on which Paul Robert Magocsi, Professor of Ukrainian Studies at the University of Toronto and prolific author on the history and culture of all these people, now makes his appearance. . . .

"In Magocsi's case we are certainly facing much more than a private quest for roots. He has been extremely active for many years in promoting a particular view of 'Carpatho-Rusyn identity' among the large North American diaspora communities. . . .

"Magocsi found himself, like his nineteenth-century predecessors, becoming embroiled in controversies that had repercussions well beyond the seminar rooms. . . . [He] has not argued explicitly for the creation of a new state; but he clearly does believe that, through forging a unified Rusyn culture, a new nation can be brought into existence.

"'Outsiders' have often been among the founders of national movements in the past, and yet the gulf between Toronto and the Lemko homeland is considerable. . . . But Paul Robert Magocsi, in spite of his family links with the region, is basically a secular man who espouses the cosmopolitan or 'multi-cultural' values of North American society. This renders him well equipped to promote Lemko and Rusyn causes through a range of scholarly activities, but less well suited to a more active personal engagement. . . .

"These intellectuals are liberal humanists. . . . I have formed very much the same impression with correspondence and in a (much briefer) meeting with Professor Magocsi. Their deep conviction that the collective rights of ethno-national groups should be observed is a conviction that demands respect."

—Chris Hann
"Intellectuals, Ethnic Groups, and Nations"
Notions of Nationalism
(Oxford, 1995), pp. 110-111, 124-125

"[The Ukrainian National Theater in Prešov] did not make it to its 50th anniversary. This is because in 1991 a group of irresponsible self-declared leaders and Janissaries changed at will the name and the national character of the Ukrainian National Theater, thereby literally burying this seat of culture. Fulfilling the desires of our enemies, . . . these people . . . brought into the theater the antinational clique of [Vasyl'] Turok and [Paul Robert] Magocsi."

—Stepan Hostyniak
"The Anti-National Play on the National Stage"
Druzhno vpered (Prešov)
No. 9-10 (1995), p. 9

"The activity of the Rusyn Renaissance Society (Rusyn'ska obroda) in Slovakia is complemented by the activity of similar organizations in states bordering on Ukraine. . . . "All of this clearly anti-Ukrainian activity is in the interests of Moscow (which favors everything that weakens Ukraine), and most especially it is favorable to Budapest (which supports everything in favor of a greater Hungarian state). But such activity is also favored by Prague (in its efforts to create a federal state comprised of three lands together with Transcarpathia), and in part by Bratislava (which is content to let Rusyns fight with Ukrainians just as Greek Catholics already fight with the Orthodox), not to mention the Vatican and the United States which also has interests in the region.

"The initiator and the head of the entire [Rusyn] separatist and anti-Ukrainian effort is the Canadian of Hungarian origin, P. R. Magocsi."

—Juraj Bača
"Present Nationality Policy in Slovakia"
Slovenský sever (Bratislava)
Vol. VI, No. 2 (1996), p. 9

"It is more than obvious that in the case of the *Encyclopedia of National Cultures in Slovakia* [Bratislava: Slovak Academy of Sciences, 1995] the "problem" surrounding Rusyn-Ukrainians has been politicized, and specifically by following a "plan" from the laboratory of 'P. R. Magocsi and company'. The attempt to create a new European people and the realization of the so-called program of de-Ukrainianization of Rusyns has caused so many problems in Slovakia that it will without question remain a topic of continual debate and not only among ethnographers."

—Myroslav Sopolyga
Duklia (Prešov)
Vol. XLIV, No. 2, 1996, p. 95

"Dividing Ukraine into small territorial blocks is among the goals of political Rusynism. In his study, 'Carpatho-Rusyns', the creator of a new Slavic nationality, Paul Robert Magocsi, writes that . . . 'it is necessary that Ukraine become a decentralized state in which each regional component will have a high degree of autonomy in economic and cultural mattters'. It is obvious from this that P. R. Magocsi is from afar already dividing Ukraine."

—Ivan Iatskanyn
Nove zhyttia (Prešov)
7. VI. 1996, p. 1

"The Ukrainian minority has only recently begun to organize since it is dispersed throughout various parts of Hungary. There are only two or three villages, in particular Múcsony in Borsod county and Komlóska in Abaúj county. It is on the basis of these two villages that P. Magocsi has initiated the creation of an organization for the country's 'Rusyn' minority, called the Organization of Rusyns in Hungary and headed by Gabriel Hattinger.

"From its creation, Hungary's Rusyn organization has taken part in the 'world' congresses of Rusyns which are organized by Magocsi."

—[Vasyl' Markus']
Nove zhyttia (Prešov)
27. IX. 96, p. 5

"The initiator, founder, and ideologist of political Rusynism, which more or less simultaneously arose in Transcarpathia, Czecho-Slovakia, Poland, and Yugoslavia and that has as well strong support in Romania and Hungary. . . . is Paul Robert Magocsi. At a time when it was difficult even for birds and mice to cross the borders of Communist countries, in particular the Soviet Union, he freely flew in everywhere several times a year and had access to places and archives that were not even accessible to local Communists."

—Iurii Bacha
"'Political Rusynism' is a Political Provocation"*Vsesvit* (Kyiv)
No. 4 (1996), p. 153

"It is especially known that the infamous source of political Rusynism, Professor Magocsi, was financed by the British capitalist [Robert] Maxwell, a Jew born in Transcarpathia. Magocsi has used these funds, appropriately manipulating people as he spreads his anti-Ukrainian theories."

—Vasyl' Markus'
Rozbudova derzhavy (Kyiv)
No. 9, 1996, p.

"Yes, there are really such 'wise' people who, not knowing us [Rusyn-Ukrainians], still like to talk about us. Even more they would like to write and teach us about ourselves, . . . such types may become professors, even academicians, and eventually get into the *Guiness Book of World Records*.

"Without any exaggeration, we must admit there are such people, among whom is the pseudo-scholar and creator of peoples, Paul Robert Magocsi. . . . Magocsi will go down in history as the creator of the 'Carpatho-Rusyn people'."

"Will he get into the Guiness Book of Records?"
Nove zhyttia (Prešov)
29. IX. 96, p.3

"Among those who have joined P. R. Magocsi in the propagation of his separatist ideas are: outspoken nationalists in Slovakia and Poland; people with academic titles who in effect are professional chauvinists working at universities in Slovakia and Poland (in particular at Jagiellonian, Wrocław, and Poznań universities); and serious journals such as *International Affairs*, published by the Polish Institute for the Study of National Minorities."

—Lev Gal'
Vatra (Gorlice, Poland)
No. 4 [15], 1996, p. 13

"Who is it that so generously finances the [Rusyn] separatists? . . . It is the Mukachevo district and city governmental apparatus and the gas industry and bread factories in Svaliava and Mukachevo . . . . It is from these sources that the horns of political Rusynism in Transcarpathia have grown. But its head is in America. There lives the person who provides the ideological inspiration for Rusynism, the University of Toronto professor, P. R. Magocsi, who was recently named an academician."

—Iaroslav Karychak
Vyzvolnyi shliakh (London and Kyiv)
No. 9 (1996), pp. 1078-1079

"Hungarians have established in Nyíregyháza a Department of Ukrainian and Rusyn Studies. The creation of this department is considered by the ideologue of Rusynism, P. R. Magocsi, as an example of scholarly recognition for his theories about a distinct Rusyn nation. This is an obvious anti-Ukrainian move behind which is Mr. Magocsi and his friend Professor István Udvari . . . .

"The last, or perhaps next to last, act of this Rusyn tragic comedy has just occurred. At a press conference in Bratislava the formation of a 'provisional government' was announced, which some are referring to as a 'shadow' government for Subcarpathian Rus'. . . . The shadow 'cabinet' is not yet filled. . . . It is rumoured that Ivan Turianytsia the [government's] main inspirer, is preparing to take on the post of premier or even president. . . . The only unknown is what post is being reserved for Magocsi. Perhaps, that of governor who will arrive from Toronto in Uzhhorod riding a white horse? Or perhaps he'll be the 'republic's' representative at the United Nations?"

—Vasyl' Markus'
"Pudkarpats'ka rypublyka"
Mala entsyklopediia etnoderzhavoznavstva
(Kyiv, 1996), p. 783

"Paul Magocsi's stimulating paper on the limitations of nationalism . . . caused some controversy. Some of the Croatian speakers felt, understandably enough, that having just won their national freedom at great cost, they were not about to hear its importance minimized; Magocsi, on the other hand, was speaking from the unique perspective of an expert on Subcarpathian Rus', and argued equally persuasively that a group might live within another state and yet preserve its 'national' identity."

—Brendan Simms
Croatian Times (London)
No. 11 (1996), p. 3

"They are saying that in Ukraine everyone is cursing Bob Magocsi. He has truly lost his mind over the Rusyn matter. He is a good scholar and perhaps his history of Ukraine will indeed give us something new. But why is he becoming politically engaged? That he is directing Rusyns [in Europe] from the diaspora makes him no better than our Banderites who also want to influence developments in the home country....To preach political Rusynism from the Chair of Ukrainian Studies is simply vile. But in Canada academic freedom allows anything, while the Ukrainian community which provided funding for his academic chair says nothing."

—Iurii (George S.N.) Luts'kyi
The Years of Expectations and Loss: Notes from My Diary [1996]
(L'viv, 2004), pp. 359-360

"It would be interesting to know why that twisted [Professor Danylo] Struk replaced the reliable article by Orest Zilyns'kyi about the Prešov Region for the *Encyclopedia of Ukraine* with one written by Magocsi? Why was that done? At the same time one cannot help but recall the death under suspicious circumstances of Orest. It seems that Magocsi was the last person to see him alive. But then this must be my Ukrainian paranoia taking over."

—Iurii (George S.N.) Luts'kyi
The Years of Expectations and Loss: Notes from My Diary [1996]
(L'viv, 2004), p. 360

"The dedication and skill [Professor Magocsi has] displayed throughout [his] distinguished career has yielded important contributions to Canadian society."

—Jean Chrétien
Prime Minister of Canada
The Ukrainian Weekly (Jersey City, N.J.)
2. I. 1997, p. 9

"In the summer of 1996 there was a new outburst of the 'Rusyn syndrome'. It came as a result of another regular visit to Ukraine, the Czech Republic, Slovakia, and Poland by the main theorist and supporter of political Rusynism, the master of political intrigue from Canada, Professor Paul Robert Magocsi. . . . Arriving in these countries at his own initiative, he openly molds the 'Rusyn people' according to the model of a 'single Soviet people' and provokes misunderstanding between Ukraine and those neighboring states where Ukrainians and Rusyns live. He is deligently assisted by local toadies, so-called writers, and political speculators whom he generously finances. In return, they falsely praise him, bless him with incense, and carry out political intrigues and pseudo-scholarly activity. The dear professor simply cannot understand that in the present world such anti-Ukrainian efforts will produce in return only deadening results."

—Oleksa Myshanych
Literaturna Ukraïna (Kyiv)
6. II. 97

"It is Paul Robert Magocsi of the Carpatho-Rusyn Research Center, who has provided us [Rusyns] with exceptional, one might say, the most outstanding assistance. That assistance has been primarily of a scholarly nature, including the organization of international scholarly conferences, providing copies of material documenting our past history, and information about our situation in a whole host of forums worldwide which recognize the Rusyn identity. It is through him that thinking people throughout the world know about us, about our difficult situation, and about the fact that there are still in this world forces that would wish to destroy Rusyns and not allow their further national development. To him we give our thanks."

—Vasyl' Turok
Statement of Chairman of the World Council of Rusyns
Zbornik robotokh zoz Tretsoho Shvetovoho Kongresa Rusinokh
(Ruski Kerestur, 1997), pp. 49-50

"Let us work hard and hope that the words spoken [at the IV World Congress of Rusyns] by P. R. Magocsi—'Rusyns exist and will continue to do so'—will be heard by God and reach the hearts of every Rusyn."

—Mykhailo Zavadiak
Visti Svaliavshchyny (Svaliava)
8. VII. 97

208

"Many people know that the biggest Rusyn in the world is the well-known scholar and special services agent, Professor Paul R. Magocsi."

—A. Makovyts'kyi
Nove zhyttia (Prešov)
25. VII. 97, p. 4

"In the course of my work abroad, I have met frequently with Rusyns. They have numerous organizations which hold divergent political views. We must remain clear that there is a Ukrainian nation (*natsiia*) and that Rusyns are a part of that nation. If this principle continues to guide us, then we will be able to find a common path. But this will be a gradual process. For this reason I have often said that we must act with tolerance. We cannot simply declare, 'Professor Magocsi is an enemy of Ukrainians', or other such phrases. We must engage in a dialogue with Professor Magocsi. I realize that we are not going to change his views, but we must nevertheless adopt a tolerant approach in order to resolve these problems."

—Hennadii Udovenko
Minister of Foreign Affairs of Ukraine
President of the United Nations General Assembly
Nove zhyttia (Prešov)
5. VIII. 97, p. 3

"Unlike many of our present-day scholars . . . the historian from Canada, P. R. Magocsi, is the first to publish a history of Ukraine at a world-class level and has promised to translate it into Ukrainian for 'scholars' in Ukraine.

"It is probably because of scholarly envy that our insecure (yet politically engaged) scholars still continue to criticize Magocsi."

—Mykhailo Kemin'
"Who is Destroying Materials in Archives?"
Khrystyians 'ka rodyna (Uzhhorod)
II. IX. 97

"Paul Robert Magocsi's *History of Ukraine* . . . is a far more monumental work than the typical product in that genre. Indeed, it is reminiscent of some of the great works of Russian and Ukrainian history of the nineteenth century, such as Kluchevsky's *A Course on Russian History.*

. . . . .

"The book is characterized by wide and deep learning, remarkable objectivity, rational organization, clarity of presentation, and profound awareness of a variety of national sensitivities."
—Dennis R. Papazian
History: Reviews of New Books (Washington, D.C.)
Vol. XXVI, No. 3 (1997), p. 30

"Paul Robert Magocsi has already received a high measure of recognition and reward from the intellectual and political leaderships his career has done most to serve. In the long run, one devoutly hopes that whatever scientific authority he may hold among broader segments of historical researchers will fade away along with the artificial reality of the 'Rusyn nation' [that] his writings and voyages did so much to promote amongst tiny but noisy elements of the East European and North American Ukrainian and Ukrainian-origin populations."
—George Knysh
The Ukrainian Quarterly (New York)
Vol. LIII, No. 3 (1997), p. 268

"The theoretical basis for the anti-Ukrainian movement in Transcarpathia began to be formulated in the late 1960s and early 1970s by the American scholar of Magyar origins, Paul Magocsi, who, on instructions from the secret services of neighboring states, has for more than two decades worked toward creating a new Rusyn nation and state."
—O. Malets'
Sotsial'no-ekonomichni ta etnopolitychni zminy v kraïnakh
tsentral'noï i pivdenno-skhidnoï Ievropy
(Uzhhorod, 1997), p. 185

"Academic elites often were seen as crossing over the line between being 'dispassionate' scholars and active political activists. Within North American scholarly circles, some regard Magocsi as having become as much the 'father of his country' as a detached social scientist. . . . It seems clear that the work of the diaspora elites was more actively nationalist than humanitarian or specifically 'cultural' in emphasis."

—Raymond A. Smith
Harvard Ukrainian Studies (Cambridge, Mass.)
Vol. XXI, No. 1-2 (1997), p. 152

"The executive board of the [pro-Ukrainian] Union of Lemkos in Gorlice [Poland] . . . expresses its deepest dissatisfaction with a so-called scholarly conference . . . being held in November 1994. . . . It includes the same people brought together at the scandalous symposium organized by the Cracow branch of the Polish Academy of Sciences in March 1991 to promote the destructive theories of Paul Robert Magocsi from the University of Toronto, who is 'being blessed' in Poland by this country's scholarly circles for dealing with 'a new people in the Carpathians, the Carpatho-Rusyns'. . . . A part of this new 'Carpatho-Rusyn people' is, according to Magocsi, the Lemko population of Poland. The supporters of his theory in Poland at the II World Congress of Rusyns in Krynica (1993) have tried in Poland to restore usage of the old historical name 'Rusyn'."

—Wacław Szlanta
Protest to the Polish Academy of Sciences and Rector of Jagiellonian University,
December 5, 1994
Problemy Ukraińców w Polsce po wysiedleńczej akcji 'Wisła'
(Cracow, 1997), p. 308

"Paul Robert Magocsi needs no introduction to students of Eastern Europe. He has distinguished himself with a series of first-rate publications. . . . [and] has given Ukrainian history the breadth it has always deserved and without which it is usually unintelligible. The breadth is also conceptual. Magocsi is a master at describing Ukrainian realities within the larger cultural and historical contexts that have driven—and usually determined—Ukraine's fate. Few Ukrainianists alive today share Magocsi's talent at 'painting the big picture'."

—Reverend Peter Galadza
Logos (Ottawa)
Vol. XXXIX, 1 (1998), p. 133

"In the field of Ukrainian studies Magocsi has gained some notoriety for his preoccupation with Transcarpathian Rus' (a mountainous region along the western border of Ukraine) and its inhabitants who Magocsi calls 'Rusyns'. Magocsi has even been derided by some Ukrainianists, including [Orest] Subtelny, for his apparent desire to become the father of the 'Rusyn nation'. Nonetheless, given this reputation as a Carpathian separatist, Magocsi's treatment of the Carpatho-Rusyns appears balanced and is far less radical than one would expect. . . .

"In short, Magocsi's *History of Ukraine* is a major achievement and the new standard history of this vitally important yet little understood European country."

—Paul S. Pirie
Slavic and East European Journal (Tucson, Ariz.)
Vol. XLII, No. 2 (1998), pp. 339-340

"Hann looks at two living national awakeners and the questions of political and ethical responsibility that their activities raise. One of these living national awakeners is Professor Paul Robert Magocsi, the awakener of the Rusyns. . . . But the ultimate fate of the Rusyn idea is not really what interests Hann here: it's the late twentieth-century awakener, who cannot be presented as the unwitting agent of the Gellnerian modernizing process. He [Magocsi] knows exactly what he is constructing."

—John-Paul Himka
Journal of Ukrainian Studies (Toronto)
Vol. XXIII, No. 2 (1998), p. 133

"The Greek Catholic Union [in the United States] is well informed about us, the Rusyns of Yugoslavia, because they have information from Professor Magocsi whom they esteem very highly."

—Iuliian Kameniïtski
Ruske slovo (Novi Sad)
28. VIII. 98, p. 11

"In such a situation it is understandable that a portion of the younger Lemko intelligentsia, grouped around the Lemko Association founded in 1989 in Legnica—and considering themselves members of a distinct people linked to the concept of a Rusyn/Carpatho-Rusyn people as elaborated by Professor P. R. Magocsi of Toronto—began to undertake efforts in the late 1980s to create their own linguistic community at the same time that they were aware of their differences from Ukrainian-oriented Lemkos and from Ukrainians."

—Janina Fras
Acta Universitatis Wratislaviensis (Wrocław, Poland)
No. 2049 (1998), pp. 160-161

"Now we would like to expose how the theory of Rusynism, in the sense of a distinct nationality, was thought up by the KGB and how it supposedly exists in Transcarpathia . . . .

"As you know this idea was put forth by the last ruling Communist-party organization in Transcarpathia at a time when its activists felt it was necessary to stir up disturbances in Ukraine. The originator of the idea was Magocsi, the agent of the KGB listed in the archives of the Czech security services.

—V'iacheslav Chornovil
Rio-inform (Uzhhorod)
31. X. 98, p. 4

"The noted American Rusyn Paul Robert Magocsi is not only one of the best historians of Transcarpathia but in general of the entire Ukraine."

—Luca Calvi
Aino (Uzhhorod)
No. 2-5 (1998), p. 48

"Present-day independent Ukraine is faced with a complex problem: how to fuse and integrate the three historic Ukraines about which Magocsi writes into one national state? In order to resolve successfully this problem it would be useful for both Ukrainian and Russian leaders to familiarize themselves with the work [*History of Ukraine*] of Magocsi. At the very least his history would teach both sides the value of mutual tolerance. Today this is an essential precondition in order to overcome the prejudices that have burdened relations between the two related Slavic peoples."

—Marc Raeff
Novyi zhurnal (New York)
No. 211 (1999), p. 286

"In his previous work Magocsi has demonstrated considerable interest in Jewish history. It is therefore not surprising that Ukrainian Jewry receives wide coverage. . . . [and that his] description of Ukrainian history in modern times suggests many parallels with Jewish history. Both peoples faced difficult and divisive questions of identity, both developed national secular movements at around the same time, in both cases the national church was ambivalent with regard to nationalism, and, most obviously, both were the victims of severe national and religious oppression. Of special interest to the modern historian of Jewish Eastern Europe is Magocsi's discussion of Ukrainian history in interwar Poland. Those accustomed to thinking of the Jews as the only persecuted minority in that state will have much to learn from the author's description of . . . Eastern Galicia."

—Ezra Mendelsohn
Studies in Contemporary Jewry (New York)
Vol. XIV (1998), pp. 295-296

"Magocsi, don't stir up waters!
We are the native sons of Taras!
Don't anger the Lord with lies.
You're destined for the dust-bin of history.

From the depths of the Dnieper River
The Great Bard has stepped across the Carpathians.
This apostle of truth and goodness
Will stand here for ages to come."

—Iaroslav Rus'kyi
"On the Occasion of the Erection of a Statue of Taras Shevchenko in Uzhhorod"
Karpats'kyi holos (Uzhhorod)
6-12. III. 1999, p. 1

"It is such political principles—the interests of pro-imperialist forces to transform the region's inhabitants into a distinct nation—that form the basic views of the newest creator of an independent 'Rusyn nationality', the University of Toronto professor, Paul Robert Magocsi. This pretender to the role of 'father of the Rusyn people', who confuses the concepts people, nation, and nationality, writes about a 'Subcarpathian Rusyn ethnic group' . . . and of how Subcarpathian Rusyns 'might become a completely distinct nationality', etc."

—Mykhailo Tyvodar
Carpatica-Karpatyka (Uzhhorod)
Vol. VI (1999), p. 17

"Professor Paul Magocsi, 'a sealed vessel that loses not a drop' (*Avot* 2:11), has done far more than supervise the doctoral dissertation. . . . He strove to inculcate in me a sense of responsibility to the discipline that would embrace all aspects of the historian's *Weltanschauung*. I recall with much fondness our contemplative strolls along the Khreshchatyk [in Kyiv] and through Queen's Park [in Toronto].

—Henry Abramson
A Prayer for the Government
(Cambridge, Mass., 1999), p. xi

"It is not the Rusyn and Ukrainian elites (who were decimated by Soviet domination in the Soviet Ukraine) but rather overseas immigrant intellectuals in Canada and the United States who have worked out a national program and who have, through 'scholarly argumentation', undertaken a no less important task: to propagate their ideas among international organizations, non-government organizations, and the international public at large. A good example of this phenomenon is the Carpatho-Rusyn Research Center in the United States, which since 1978 has been headed by the already mentioned Paul Robert Magocsi. The center has produced on an on-going basis high-quality volumes filled with a national history attractive to Rusyns."

—Stefan Troebst
Osteuropa (Berlin)
No. 6 (1999), p. 613

"Paul Robert Magocsi, though ostensibly working as a historian and political scientist, comes curiously closer to the usual specifications of anthropology. . . . For [Ernest] Gellner, a national identity is the *sine qua non* of life in a developed industrial society; he pays little attention either to the historical roots of the new high culture or to the subjective satisfaction that such an identity brings to group members. Professor Magocsi, in contrast, has devoted enormous energy to documenting the precise details of the culture, both in his scholarly work and in other publications aimed more at non-academic 'roots-seekers'. The nationality is not there to serve macrosociological functions, it is there to meet psychological needs.

. . . . .

"The work of Professor Magocsi on the Rusyns demands the attention and engagement not only of anthropologists but of anyone with serious interests in the issues of collective identity in the modern world. His combination of emancipatory humanitarian motivation and high-level scholarship can be an inspiration, even to those who wish to proceed in somewhat different directions. It is no mean feat to be able to reconcile the academic demonstration of the *contingency* of the Carpatho-Rusyn nationality with the program of multicultural advocacy which asserts the *authenticity* of this identity for all those who wish to embrace it."

—Chris Hann
"On Nation(alitie)s in General, and One Potential Nation(ality) in Particular"
in Paul Robert Magocsi, *Of the Making of Nationalities There Is No End*,
Vol. I (New York, 1999), pp. xxxii and xxxvi

"I do not think anyone would dispute that Professor Magocsi has played the leading role in shaping and clarifying a Carpatho-Rusyn identity since the 1970s. In short, in North America the cause of the Carpatho-Rusyns has clearly succeeded and professor Magocsi's contribution is an achievement that few social scientists can hope to emulate. He has shown himself in this work to have a humane commitment to enabling ordinary people to answer questions that matter to them very dearly, by helping them to understand to which group they belong in some ultimate sense. While many academic theorists have argued that the future of democracies throughout the world lies in collective mutual recognition of identity differences, Professor Magocsi's work with and for Rusyns goes farther by putting these ideas into practice.

. . . . .

"The collapse of Communist rule, beginning in 1989 in east-central Europe and extending within two years to the Soviet Union itself, created a quite new situation, one that came as a surprise to Professor Magocsi as it did to virtually everyone else. To put it very simply, the new circumstances gave him an opportunity to become, for the first time, practically involved in the affairs of the homeland. Perhaps he felt that he had no choice in the matter. . . .

"There have been frequent tensions with post-Communist governments, notably with officials of the new government who have rejected notions of a separate Rusyn nation(ality) with much the same dogmatism as their predecessors.

"Elsewhere in eastern Europe, such sources of tension have boiled over into open hostilities and violence. The Carpathian region has been mercifully free of such excesses, and perhaps Professor Magocsi should be given some of the credit for this."

—Chris Hann
"On Nation(alitie)s in General, and One Potential Nation(ality) in Particular"
in Paul Robert Magocsi, *Of the Making of Nationalities There Is No End*,
Vol. I (New York, 1999), pp. xxi and xxvi-xxvii

"My first 'encounter' with Professor Magocsi . . . took place in a rather different, and somewhat unorthodox, context.

"While an undergraduate student of social anthropology at the University of Copenhagen, I decided in January 1989 to visit the Carpathian mountain region in southeastern Poland in order to conduct fieldwork on the peasant economy of the ostensibly Ukrainian villagers living there.

"I had come to what I was told was a Lemko village . . . [where] I learned about the Lemkos and noted with surprise that the villagers certainly did not consider themselves to be Ukrainians, contrary to what I read before setting off for the Carpathians. A young Lemko, who had returned from a stay as a migrant-worker in the United States, gave me a spirited lecture on Professor Magocsi and his achievements in North America in 'putting the forgotten Lemkos back on the map' and in stressing the distinctive character of the Lemkos. I was puzzled. What impact could an American history professor possibly have on villagers in this remote corner of the Peoples Republic of Poland?

. . . . .

"Without detracting from Professor Magocsi's immense impact on the current nation-building process among Carpatho-Rusyns, one must reiterate that he merely contributed to a process that was already taking place. That said, however, it must also be noted that a Carpatho-Rusyn movement without the engagement of Paul Robert Magocsi would have been much less efficient, or might have taken other directions."

217

—Tom Trier
"Introduction"
in Paul Robert Magocsi, *Of the Making of Nationalities There Is No End*,
Vol. II (New York, 1999), pp. ix-x and xx

"Paul Robert Magocsi's scholarly achievements have had an enormous impact on Carpatho-Rusyn identity in North America as well as in the European homeland. Professor Magocsi is not a scholar studying history and contemporary social processes in the Carpathians from a comfortable distance across the Atlantic. On the contrary, he has played a decisive role in forming present-day socio-cultural realities at the same time that he has made crucially important contributions to reshaping our perception of the Carpathian region.

. . . . .

"It is in his speeches [at the World Congress of Rusyns] that Professor Magocsi's influence on the recent Carpatho-Rusyn national movement is particularly evident. Read together, they not only provide an outstanding introduction to the issues of Rusyn nation-building, but also function as a kind of 'recipe book' on how to build or revive a nation. In Professor Magocsi, we encounter a scholar, who apart from being a distinguished specialist on the past and present of the group in question, is also practically involved in the shaping of its national identity. In essence, he epitomizes the east-European tradition of the scholar-activist."

—Tom Trier
"Introduction"
in Paul Robert Magocsi, *Of the Making of Nationalities There Is No End*,
Vol. II (New York, 1999), pp. xiii and xvi-xvii

"Magocsi concludes the volume with [an essay], 'The End of the Nation-State', a masterly synthesis that, after five years, still provides a clear, unerring vision into the future of a new pan-European order; he confidently projects a truly diverse megasociety where the problems created by the nation-state have been resolved by sandwiching them between the greater, multinational European Union and more sensitive regional entities that will accommodate both the heretofore troublesome minorities of Europe's eastern half and the quaint linguistic vestiges that have barely survived centuries of assimilation in the west."

—Charles Ingrao

218

Austrian History Yearbook (Minneapolis, Minn.)
Vol. XXX (1999), p. 309

"In 1989, the Communist regimes collapsed in Poland and
Czechoslovakia. Professor Magocsi was quick to realize the implications
for the Lemkos/Rusyns/Ukrainians of these countries and pleased to
discover that there was considerable interest among these populations
in defining for themselves a non-Ukrainian Rusyn national identity.
Professor Magocsi plunged into the nation-building process with them,
writing numerous articles in the press of North America and Central
Europe about Carpatho-Rusyns and their aspirations. . . .

"He is in short not just studying history, but taking part as an actor in
the historical process. In other words, he uses his knowledge of history to
influence history."

—John-Paul Himka
in *Paul Robert Magocsi: A Bibliography*
(Toronto, 2000), p. vii and ix

"Paul Magocsi has with decisive consequences introduced into the public
forum the term Carpatho-Rusyns and stresses that their homeland, called
Carpathian Rus', is situated along the borders of Ukraine, Slovakia, and
Poland. . . .

"There is no doubt that part of the Lemko population [in Poland]
welcomes the activity of Paul Robert Magocsi, who has done much to
convince the Lemkos that they are part of a distinct people . . .

"Only time will tell how the destiny of the Lemkos will work itself
out. At the moment they are a people in search of a national identity. And
what will happen if this people becomes more vigorous and begins to
seek its own state? Is the map published by Paul Robert Magocsi only
an illustration to help readers situate what was or what seems to be the
homeland of various Rusyn and Lemko groups, or does it represent an
attempt to outline the borders of a future state?

"Time will tell."

—Michał Jagiełło
Partnerstwo dla przyszłości
(Warsaw, 2000), pp. 327-328

"Despite repudiating any ideological strain in his various writings, Paul Robert Magocsi nevertheless provides a relatively clear presentation and interpretation of the historical past. This author is quite active and popular, is frequently invited to various forums, and is the best-known and unquestioned leader of the Rusyn movement. He has encountered much criticism, first and foremost from the Ukrainian camp. . . .

"The impact of Magocsi's work is today not only of interest to scholars but to political leaders of the highest rank. Such is the case that the Rusyn question has been dealt with in Uzhhorod by Ukraine's first president Leonid Kravchuk and that the prime minister of Slovakia has given support to the Rusyn efforts to introduce their language into the public sphere."

—Jacek Nowak
Zaginiony świat? Nazywają ich Lemkami
(Cracow, 2000), pp. 187, 195

"Today the main ideologist promoting the idea of a distinct Rusyn language and its codification, and one who is actively engaged in the creation of a separate 'Rusyn' nationality on the territories of Ukraine's Transcarpathia, eastern Slovakia, southeastern Poland, northern Serbia, northeastern Romania, and Hungary is the Canadian historian P. R. Magocsi."

— P. P. Chuchka
"The Rusyn Language"
Ukraïns'ka mova: entsyklopediia
(Kyiv, 2000), p. 527

"The Lemkos have recently begun to produce their own intellectuals, as every *Kulturvolk* must. . . . These efforts are being supported from afar by the Toronto-based historian Paul Robert Magocsi, who has helped make the Carpatho-Rusyns a well-established ethnic group in 'multicultural' North America. The collapse of socialism enabled him to expand his activities for the first time to the Carpathian homeland. . . .

"His recent attempts to consolidate this identity show many parallels with nineteenth-century nation-building, notably his encouragement of the standardization of a fourth East Slavic language (successfully achieved in Slovakia in 1995). In comparison with the [renowned Polish ethnographer Roman] Reinfuss, Magocsi attaches greater weight to subjective identifications and historical contingencies. . . . He is not a primordialist but a modern constructivist, fully conscious of the intellectual's role in the shaping of collective identities."

—Christopher M. Hann
"All Kulturvölker Now?:
Social Anthropological Reflections on the German American Tradition"
Anthropology Beyond Culture
(Oxford and New York, 2000), pp. 269-270

"I also appreciate the work of Professor Magocsi in the field of Rusyn studies, which is very important for the existence of Rusyns as a distinct ethnicity. Such a status was denied them in Soviet times, and it is still the case even after the fall of the Soviet Union. In Hungary, there exists an autonomous Rusyn minority receiving much intellectual inspiration from Professor Magocsi, so it is not an exaggeration to speak about a Rusyn renaissance in recent years."

—Emil Niederhauser, Hungarian Academy of Sciences
The Chair at Twenty
(Toronto, 2000), p. 24

"Professor Magocsi's impact on a conference characterized by heated debates between state officials from Kyiv and activists of the Rusyn movement was twofold. One the one hand, he argued that multiculturalism should not necessarily be looked upon by the authorities as a source of concern and potential conflict, but as a positive phenomenon and an enrichment. . . . On the other hand, he managed in private conversation to convince Ukrainian government and presidential officials to agree to hold the Fifth World Congress of Rusyns in Ukraine. This was a major breakthrough towards a solution to the Rusyn question in Ukraine. In the wake of the World Congress, which did take place in 1999, the so-called Provisional Government of Subcarpathian Rus', which Rusyn extremists had founded in 1992, dissolved itself. Paul Magocsi has been instrumental in bringing about this rapprochement."

—Stefan Troebst, University of Leipzig
The Chair at Twenty
(Toronto, 2000), p.34

"Many scholars and academics appear to rely mostly on the numerous writings of Professor Paul Robert Magocsi—the assertive promoter of a separate Rusyn ethnicity and Rusyn language, who is often referred to, somewhat ironically, as 'Father of the Rusyn Nation' . . ."

—Natalya Belitser
"Political and Ethno-Cultural Aspects of the Rusyn Problem: A Ukrainian Perspective"
Centre for European Security Studies, University of Groningen
(The Netherlands, ca. 2000), p. 4

"Subcarpathian Rusyns [in Ukraine] share the viewpoint of Rusyns in the Prešov Region. Professor Magocsi is indeed the prophet Moses of the Rusyns."

—o. Dymytrii Sydor
Khrystyians'ka rodyna (Uzhhorod)
No. 5 [90] (2001), p. 13

"The heart of the Carpatho-Rusyn movement beats in America where the government, as in Slovakia, recognizes Rusyns as separate from Ukrainians. The aorta is the Carpatho-Rusyn Research Center and its plasma is Paul Robert Magocsi, a professor at the University of Toronto and indefatigable organizer and eulogist of Rusynism who is genuinely hated by Ukrainians. His enemies do not even hesitate to accuse him publicly of having cooperated with Communist Czechoslovakia's security services. Magocsi is, indeed, the initiator of the implantation or rather renewal of the Rusyn movement in the homeland of the Carpatho-Rusyns. This is the case as well in Poland."

—Andrzej Talaga
"The Carpathians for the Rusyns"
Nowe Państwo (Warsaw)
No. 41 (2001)

"After the Revolution of 1989 the Rusyn Renaissance Society, inspired from abroad, began to function in eastern Slovakia. It has made every effort to prove that Rusyns are a distinct 'fourth' East Slavic people, which has nothing to do with Ukrainians, the Ukrainian language, and Ukrainian culture. . . . The main proponent of such views is, as he says of himself, 'a true American', P. R. Magocsi, about whom it is said that he is an agent of several secret services."

—Mikuláš Nevrlý
"Who Are the Rusyns"
Slovo (Bratislava)
No. 10 (2001)

"In his article Nevrlý makes no effort to define the concept of a people. Nor does he respond to the arguments and feelings of those who state that Rusyns are a distinct people. He blames the creation of the Rusyn Renaissance Society on the American professor, P. R. Magocsi, 'about whom it is said that he is an agent of several secret services'. Nevrlý provides no proof, however, of Magocsi's ties with such services, nor does he inform us for which services he was an agent, nor does he provide any reasons why such secret services would be interested in initiating a Rusyn national revival in the first place. Instead, and again without any proof, reasons, or explanation, Nevrlý states that the Rusyn Renaissance Society supports the restoration of a greater Hungarian state. I cannot see any relationship between these matters, and it seems to me that the only goal of such statements is to incite anti-Rusyn feelings among Slovaks."

—Matthew J. Reynolds
"Quotations are Not Arguments"
Slovo (Bratislava)
No. 14 (2001)

"The opponents of the Orthodox Russian national revival, themselves not stupid people, realized that Rusyns would never accept the Galician-Banderite-Mazeppan [Ukrainophile] ideology. Therefore, as an alternative they created the so-called local national orientation. . . . In the 1940s the Hungarian government financed in Subcarpathian Rus' a scholarly society whose publications . . . argued the critically indefensible position that Rusyns have nothing to do with Russians. Still in our time such views are supported by a professor at the University of Toronto in Canada, Paul Magocsi."

—Valerii Razgulov
F.F. Aristov i Karpatorossiia
(Uzhhorod, 2001), p. 7-8.

"Certainly not in the interest of the unity of Ukrainians is the decision of the Polish government to register officially in Legnica—the center of Ukrainianism in the southwestern part of the country—the so-called Lemko Association/Stovaryshŷia Lemkiv. The association's leaders deny that Lemkos are a part of the Ukrainian people or that they are even part of the Rusyns. Instead, they claim that Lemkos belong to a distinct 'Lemko' people. . . . They are supported by paid agents of anti-Ukrainianism such as the Canadian professor Magocsi, who already in 1992 called for the 'creation of four Rusyn languages for Slovakia, Poland, Transcarpathian Ukraine, and Yugoslavia'. He is supported by the Polish government, which in 1993 granted 10 million zlotys to make possible the Second World Congress of Rusyns, at which representatives of the government welcomed participants of the congress and thereby recognized the existence of a 'Rusyn' people to which Lemkos belong. . . . At a seminar in Cracow, [Olena] Duć-Fajfer together with Magocsi, actively supported the view that Lemkos are a distinct people, basing their theories on the separatist ideas of the prewar Russophiles."

—Stefaniia Iavornyts'ka
Ridna mova
Internet publication, 2001

"Paul Robert Magocsi, a citizen of the United States, a university professor, a doctor of historical science, an academician in the Royal Society of Canada—is a complex personality. Some see him as the inspiration behind the Rusyn separatist force, others see him as a scholar of world renown who has made a major contribution to the study of the history of Ukraine."

—Vitalii Zhuhai
Postati: interv'iu z ukraïntsamy svitu
(Uzhhorod, 2001), p. 83

"It is now ten years [at the First World Congress of Rusyns in March 1991] that Paul Robert Magocsi presented to the world his conception or view about the revival of Rusynism. Since that time much has changed. The Rusyns with their organizations and newly-established institutes have not been idle but have been intensely active. They have organized festivals for culture, the arts, and sport; the Aleksander Dukhnovych

Theatre has travelled and performed widely; there have been numerous art exhibits; and works of literature have been published for which an award for the best has been established. Over all of this hovers the spirit of Magocsi. While he has not directed, or ordered, or controlled, or instructed how these things be done, nonetheless all of this has been come about within the framework of his supervisory vision."

—Vasiľ Choma
"Renesancia rusínstva a Paul Robert Magocsi"
Slovo (Bratislava)
No. 1 (2001), pp. 117 and 123

"Paul Robert Magocsi has put Carpathian Rus' on the map, both literally, in his atlases and cartographic works, and figuratively, through his extensive scholarship. . . .

"Whereas most Ukrainian critics of the idea of a distinct Rusyn nationality have cited the futility and senselessness of creating 'something contrary to the processes and efforts of the last sixty years in Transcarpathia', the recent emergence and growth of a Rusyn movement in eastern Europe and Ukraine, long after Rusyns were supposed to have been totally assimilated, has demonstrated the limitations of positivism in regard to the subject of Rusyn national identity."

—Elaine Rusinko
Slavic and East European Journal (Berkeley, Calif.)
Vol. XLV, No. 3 (2001), pp. 586-587

"Sincere as Magocsi may be in his belief that the Rusyns' resurgence will not complicate the current balance in East Central Europe, it is easy to see why some regard him as disingenuous. Even he admits that it is difficult to separate his scholarly involvement and his engagement with Rusyn cultural organizations, and, having written about the role scholars and cultural research have played in the early phases of national movements, he understands the path such activities have taken in the past. As a result, one cannot help wondering how Magocsi might react were the Rusyn activities to turn towards the goal of political independence. Would he use his influence to keep the Rusyns focused on the notion of a Europe of regional cultures as the best way to maintain peace, or would he publicize such efforts as more evidence of the depth of Rusyn distinctiveness, which is beyond his control, destabilizing as it might be?"

—Hugo Lane
Nationalities Papers (Oxfordshire, Eng.)
Vol. XXIX, No. 4 (2001), pp. 691

"Professor Paul Robert Magocsi, Chair of Ukrainian Studies at the University of Toronto, is the person most responsible for the active promotion of the study of the Carpatho-Rusyn ethnic group in the world today. His scholarship, in its depth and breadth, towers over the scant attention paid to the Rusyns by other scholars, especially those in the West. Indeed, Profesor Magocsi is reffered to in East Central Europe both pejoratively and admiringly as '*mohuchyi* Magocsi'—'Mighty Magocsi.' Yet this appellation is not simply due to his thorough and prodigious record of publication. Since 1989, various organizations in East Central Europe have asserted the cultural and linguistic rights of Carpatho-Rusyns as a distinct people in several countries. Most of them credit Professor Magocsi with giving them the self-confidence to act by providing the necessary historical framework of their people."

—Martin Fedor Ziac
"The Role of Paul Robert Magocsi in the Modern Carpatho-Rusyn Revival"
East European Quarterly
Vol. XXV, No. 2 (2001), pp. 213-214

"The Carpatho-Rusyn Research Center in the United States and the prolific work of University of Toronto Professor Paul Robert Magocsi have been vitally important to keeping Rusyn traditions alive."

—Richard Wallace
Endangered Peoples of Europe
(Westport, Conn. and London, 2001), p. 130

"Everything began with the head of the Chair of Ukrainian Studies at the University of Toronto, Paul Robert Magocsi. . . .

"In 1979, Magocsi published a study, *The Shaping of a National Identity: Subcarpathian Rus', 1848-1948,* which became the Bible for the creators of Rusynism. The book was indeed interesting, arguing that in theory, on the basis of any ethnographic group, there might be created a people and, analogously from any dialect a literary language. But the theoretical concept presented in Magocsi's work had no possibility of

being realized in the days of the Soviet Union.
"All that changed, however, in the days of *perestroika* [transformation in Gorbachev's Soviet Union]. . . .
"The Magocsi experiment was carried out further in Slovakia, where the government quickly adapted to a situation which it felt would be beneficial. . . .
"But the Magocsi theory in which it is possible to create a new Slavic nationality has turned out to have catastrophic results for the Ukrainian population of the Prešov Region. It has proved to be an experiment that only hastened irreversible assimilation."

Nashe slovo (Warsaw)
No. 14, 4. VIII. 2001

"The organizer and the theoretical inspiration behind the phenomenon of political Rusynism in all its shapes and forms is the University of Toronto (Canada) professor, head of the chair in the history of Ukraine, and director of the Multicultural History Society of Ontario, Paul Robert Magocsi, who has made the 'Rusyn problem' his profession. . . .
"Professor Magocsi carries out the political orders of worldwide anti-Ukrainian forces and attracts around himself all those political hacks who are displeased with Ukraine and are dependent on Moscow and to an even greater extent on Budapest and Prague. . . .

· · · · ·

"Obviously, Professor Magocsi knows his own strengths just as he knows the weaknesses of Ukraine's non-Ukrainian government; otherwise, he would not act so self-confidently as someone who, as a guest, should know not to interfere in the internal affairs of an independent state."

—Oleksa Myshanych
"Carpatho-Rusynism: Its Past and Present"
In Vsevolod Naulko, ed., *Etnonatsional'ni protsesy v Ukraïni*
(Kyiv, 2001), pp. 387 and 395

"Interviewer: You [Mykhailo Tyvodar] often refer to the name Paul Magocsi. Why precisely is it him, who has become the driving force behind this old forgotten idea [of Rusynism]?
—"Magocsi is a typical ethnically marginal individual, who is difficult to identify in terms of national belonging. His father is a Hungarian, his

mother is a Ukrainian (a Rusyn). . . . [He] began his scholarly career as a Ukrainianist, then got involved in the idea of Uhro-Rusynism within the framework of the Hungarian Kingdom of St. Stephen. Having developed a theory based on the experience of American immigrants from Transcarpathia, Magocsi set as his goal to revive Rusynism in the historic [European] homeland."

—Mykhailo Tyvodar
"There is No Need to Prove that Transcarpathia is in Essence Ukrainian"
Dzerkalo tyzhnia (Kyiv)
6-12. VI. 2002

"In these two lengthy books [*Of the Making of Nationalities There Is No End*] Professor Magocsi appears in the double role of scholar and public activist without a clear demarcation of one from the other. He is careful not to compromise his scholarly air, yet he does not always succeed in this. . . .

"Without being nasty, the epithet which best fits his role and performance could be mid-wife of the Rusyn movement and of the new nationality. No one knows yet whether the newly born will survive."

—Vasyl Markus
The Ukrainian Quarterly (New York)
Vol. LVIII, No. 2-3 (2002), pp. 258-259

"With his organizational endeavors, wide-ranging research, and copious writings on matters Rusynian, Professor Magocsi 'excavated' the forgotten world of the Rusyns and brought it to the attention of the West. . . .

"Some assert that Magocsi's research and publications actually created the Rusyns and put them on the road to nationhood. Christopher M. Hann developed this thesis in an article published in Sukmar Periwal's *Notions of Nationalism* (1995). . . .

". . . Magocsi's passionate but consistently impartial *oeuvre* on the Rusyns is destined to remain an outstanding example of solid scholarship to be emulated in research on other neglected groups such as the Roma, the Kashubs, or the Szlonzaks in Europe. Apart from making them known to the wider public, such research would allow these peoples to find themselves more at home in the globalized world of today. Magocsi has already created such a niche for the Rusyns with his publications."

—Tomasz Kamusella
Canadian-American Slavic Studies (Idyllwild, Calif.)
Vol. XXXVI, No. 1-2 (2002), pp. 230-233

"The Lemko move to differentiate from the Ukrainian identity and present itself as a separate national group was supported by the work of Professor Magocsi from the University of Toronto. Magocsi's study, *The Shaping of a National Identity*, which maintained the possibility of making a nation out of an ethnographic group and transforming a dialect into a literary language, became the 'Bible' for promoters of Rusyn identity in different countries and has earned him the title of 'Godfather' of a separatist Lemko movement. . . . Magocsi's work stimulated discussions of 'what does it mean to be Rusyn' and the importance of recovering the Rusyn identity and the unification of all Rusyns in the world."

—Aleksandra Jawornicka (Zelena Góra, Poland)
"Lemko Separatism and Ethnic Politics in Poland"
ASN Annual Convention 2002 Presentation, pp. 5-6

"Professor P. R. Magocsi has gone through a significant evolution. His first works in Carpathian studies were quite objective and based on archival sources. As late as the 1980s he had no thoughts about a separate 'Rusyn people', and he believed that the Transcarpathian Rusyns, given favorable conditions, might have become Russians, Czechs, or Magyars. But circumstances developed in such a way that they became Ukrainians. This seemed not to bother him at all.

"His book, *The Shaping of a National Identity: Subcarpathian Rus', 1848-1948,* became at the time it was published in English (1978) and Ukrainian (1994) an important factor in the ideologically charged field of Carpathian studies. . . . This book still holds an important place in contemporary Carpathian studies, although today its weak points are clear, that is, the political engagement of the author and his hostility to Ukraine and Ukrainianism.

"At the outset of the 1990s, the local Transcarpathian 'leaders' of political Rusynism made Professor Magocsi their leader and chief ideologue. He himself never expected that such a role would become his fate, but glorious praise and sycophancy had an impact. He listened neither to advice nor to criticism, and became so enamored with his messianic role as the leader of the worldwide Rusyn movement that his research lost all its scholarly value. Instead, he adopted as a second profession: to struggle against Ukraine and to create a separate Rusyn Transcarpathia (Subcarpathian Rus').

"It is too bad that this talented and energetic Carpathian specialist has succumbed to the false idea of trying to turn back the wheel of history. While his own role in the leadership of political Rusynism is doubtful, in the background are much greater anti-Ukrainian 'fish' who have not accepted the idea of an independent Ukraine and who continue to work on behalf of its weakening and collapse."

—Oleksa Myshanych
Nove zhyttia (Prešov)
25. IV. 2003, p. 5

"Maps have forever captured the imagination of the intrepid explorer and armchair traveler. When well-designed maps are accompanied by cogent analysis that contextualizes and interprets the social, political, and historical dimensions they illustrate, the researcher or interested reader stands to gain immeasurably from the encounter. Paul Robert Magocsi's *Historical Atlas of Central Europe* provides precisely that kind of experience for the student or scholar. . . . This is a masterfully done book that will be a necessity for college and university libraries, geographers of the European continent, as well as those, like this reviewer, who have a passion for maps of any kind."

—John B. Romeiser
American Reference Books Annual
(Westport, Conn. and London, 2003), pp. 205-206

"Paul Robert Magocsi's maternal grandparents were Carpatho-Rusyn immigrants to the USA. He is Professor of Ukrainian Studies at the University of Toronto, works in a number of Western and Eastern (or Central) European languages, and has written extensively on identity formation and nationalism. . . . Running 'Magocsi' through a search-engine not only reveals the range of his scholarship, but also retrieves some sites which show that his ideas are of more than 'historical' interest."

—Raul Rolfe
Library Reviev (Bradford, Eng.)
Vol. LII, No. 5-6 (2003), p. 238

"For the longest time the Prešov Region's Ukrainians have been for Slovaks, and even more so for independent Slovakia, like salt in the eyes. Professor Magocsi's 'theory' (in which there are no Ukrainians but Rusyns on Slovakia's territory) is for Slovakia like a gift from heaven. Therefore, it is not surprising that in what is now democratic Slovakia, with its democratic secret services, an act of such state importance such as the codification of the Rusyn language was supervised by an agent of the secret services of a former totalitarian regime."

—Mykola Shatylov and Sviatoslav Karavans'kyi
Vyzvol'nyi shliakh (London)
No. 7 (2003) p. 79

"Three years ago, the Romanian parliament without any justification recognized the existence in our country of a Rusyn minority separate from the Ukrainian minority. . . . The Rusyns are not a separate national minority and have no other fatherland than Ukraine. . . .

"Does Romania need another minority and one, moreover, which is not recognized by any other country in the world?. . . . In Romania Georghe Firczak functions as the representative of the main ideologist [of Rusynism], the Canadian of Hungarian origin, Paul Robert Magocsi, who is trying to create a Rusyn/Ruthenian nation on territory which includes Transcarpathian Ukraine, eastern Slovakia, southeastern Poland, northern Serbia, northwestern Romania and northeastern Hungary, and to proclaim the existence of a Rusyn state and then have it annexed to greater Hungary."

—Ştefan Tcaçiuc
România Mare (Bucharest)
No. 691, October 10, 2003 p. 8a

"The editors [of the Ukrainian Catholic University journal *Kovcheh*] consider it most appropriate to publish a study by the authoritative specialist in nationality studies and ethnoconfessional relations. . . . Paul Robert Magocsi's study is what one might call a 'classic in that genre,' even though until now it is little known in Ukraine."

—Oleh Turii
Kovcheh: naukovyi zbirnyk iz Tserkovnoï istoriï (L'viv)
No. 4 (2003), p. xi

"The thesis put forth by P.R. Magocsi that the 'Greek Catholic Church and its seminary in Uzhhorod were the last bastion of the Rusyn [national] orientation is on the mark. One must also agree with the views of Magocsi that in order to create the new Soviet society in Transcarpathia and to integrate the local populace into the broader Ukrainian community the [Communist] government had to undermine several aspects of the region's traditional life, in particular the peasant's love for his land and also the very basis of all local traditions, the Greek Catholic Church."

—Volodymyr Fenych
Carpatica/Karpatyka (Uzhhorod)
Vol. 21 (2003), p. 245

"The idea of Central Europe has of late provoked much fervor and enthusiasm because it is a neutral analytical concept. I remember the American Association for Slavic Studies (AAASS) convention in St. Louis (November 1999), where Paul Robert Magocsi noted that in the newest edition of his historical atlas he changed its name to 'Central Europe' without any reference to 'the East'. The audience broke out into applause, which until then had followed the party line throughout eastern Europe. I was very moved. It was obvious that behind the change in terminology there was something else that I had not noticed until then. In any case, not only Professor Magocsi but also the members in the Slavic Association changed the manner in which they understood and designated that part of Europe."

—John-Paul Himka
"What Comprises a Region"
Krytyka (Kyïv)
Vol. VII, No. 4 [66] (2003), p. 19

"This study like that of [others] has been inspired, shaped, and has taken its direction from the extraordinary work of the East European historian in Canada, Paul Robert Magocsi, who since the mid-1970s has devoted a significant part of his scholarly output to two closely related themes: the Rusyns and Transcarpathia. His work has successfully attracted in

Canada, the United States, and Europe a judicious circle of what can be considered Carpatho-Rusyn national historians, linguists, and literary specialists.

"After the collapse of Communist rule in countries inhabited by Rusyns, Magocsi has been able to make his presence felt, with the result that he has had an extremely powerful impact. Looking at his entire corpus, which on Rusyn-related themes reached into the several hundreds, one senses that his scholarship and political engagement are interwoven in the style of a nineteenth-century national awakener and innovator."

—Meinorf Arens
"The Fourth East Slavic Nationality: The Rusyns"
Südosteuropa im 20. Jährhundert
(Iaşi and Konstanz, 2004), p. 244

"At that time [1988], I was studying history at the University of Warsaw (Poland) and . . . collecting material on my primary research subject—Lemko history.

"I received a package of books gratis from Professor Paul Robert Magocsi. Later he sent a telegram informing me about his visit to Warsaw and suggesting that we meet there.

"That meeting was a grand experience. . . . I devoured the books I had been presented with and determined to continue with my Lemko studies. This passion, which continues unabated to this day, was effectively supported and strengthened during its early days by contact with . . . Professor Paul Robert Magocsi."

—Bogdan Horbal
Carpatho-Rusyn Research Center: The First Quarter Century
(Ocala, Flo., 2004), p. 31

"As a college history teacher from 1949 to 1984 . . . I have greatly benefitted from the scholarly work of the eminent American Carpatho-Rusyn historian, Professor Paul R. Magocsi. . . . For historians [his work] has put the Carpatho-Rusyns on the map, as it were."

—Victor Mamatey
Carpatho-Rusyn Research Center: The First Quarter Century
(Ocala, Flo., 2004), p. 40

"His [Paul Robert Magocsi's] visit to the Vojvodina, sometime in the early 1970s, brought to our region the first ideas that Rusyns should undertake scholarly work about themselves as a distinct nationality. In large part, this represented the platform for what later came into being in 1990 as the Rusyn Cultural Foundation (Ruska Matka) with its seat in Ruski Kerstur.

"The beginnings of our collaboration with Dr. Magocsi were not at all straightforward [during] the totalitarian regime of Josip Broz (Tito) . . . in Yugoslavia. . . . Nevertheless, private contacts with Dr. Magocsi were maintained and the essence of his views was often used in publications or expressed by certain leaders of the Rusyn movement in the Vojvodina. . . . Magocsi's views had less of an impact on spreading the phenomenon of Rusynism in political activity. This approach continues for Vojvodinian life even today."

—Djura Papharhaji
Carpatho-Rusyn Research Center: The First Quarter Century
(Ocala, Flo., 2004), p. 45

"Professor Paul R. Magocsi is the coordinator and initiator of the Rusyn revival worldwide and has written prolifically about Rusyns. He is not a scholar of Rusyn studies for the sake of politics, but rather for the sake of culture—and he is truly a Rusyn scholar from his heart."

—Aleksander Zozuliak
Carpatho-Rusyn Research Center: The First Quarter Century
(Ocala, Flo., 2004), p. 56

"The majority of Lemkos of Ukrainian orientation [in Poland] argue that without the support of Paul Robert Magocsi the present-day Rusyn movement would not have come into being.

"All respondents who support the idea of a distinct [Lemko people] reject any suggestion that Magocsi played any fundamental role in the creation of the Rusyn movement. . . . They also reject the notion that the movement is directed by Magocsi, arguing that such a view is a typical propaganda ploy by their opponents in an attempt to compromise the Rusyn movement. While most [Lemko-oriented] respondents reject the view that Magocsi in any way directs the Rusyn movement, they do nonetheless value his work, in particular his promotion of the Rusyn problem in international and scholarly circles. It is in this sense that his activity is valuable for the Rusyn movement."

—Ewa Michna
Przegląd Polonijny (Cracow)
Vol. XXX, No 3 (2004), pp. 198-199

"It is evident that the 'problem' surrounding Ukrainians in the [Slovak Academy of Science's] *Encyclopedia of National Cultures in Slovakia* has been deliberately politicized and done so according to the product brand, 'P. R. Magocsi and Company'. Such 'scholarly conclusions' have also appeared in the works of other specialists."

—Myroslav Sopolyha
Narodna tvorchist' ta etnohrafiia (Kyiv)
No. 3 (2005), p. 36.

"Magocsi's call for a study of the impact that émigrés had upon the states of east central Europe after the fall of Communism, and the use— or abuse—of émigrés by the post-Communist governments is right on target. . . .

"Meanwhile, the Slovak government has also interfered . . . in the affairs of Slovaks abroad. In 1992, I published an article by Paul Robert Magocsi about the Carpatho-Rusyns in Europe in the journal *Slovakia*. Magocsi's article very much annoyed president Leonid Kuchma of Ukraine, so much so that he complained to prime minster Vladimír Mečiar of Slovakia, who in turn complained to . . . the secretary-treasurer of the Slovak League of America. . . . , and the latter complained to me. That the president of the fifty-million strong Ukraine should be so concerned about Paul Robert Magocsi speaks volumes about the current leadership of some east central Europe's newly independent states and the impact or influence of political émigrés upon them."

—M. Mark Stolarik
"In Step with the Times: A Slovak Perspective"
Austrian History Yearbook (Minneapolis)
Vol. XXXVI (2005), pp. 206-207

"At the moment a 'Rusyn' people came onto the scene, it had to have its own language. With the help of some linguists, mostly specialists in Russian, the dialect or dialects of Rusyn were proclaimed to be the 'Rusyn literary language'. To provide a kind of authoritative veneer for this language-codification farce, a few Slovak politicians and scholars were enticed to participate. . . . Behind this entire comical farce stood a professor who, at home in Canada, makes his living from Ukrainian studies and with impunity muddies the minds of people. A descendant of magyarone ancestors, he speaks out [in Slovakia] as a tenacious proponent of 'political Rusynism' and the initiator of a de-ukrainianization policy. One must remain surprised at the short-sightedness of politicians in Slovakia and neighboring countries who are unable to see a real future danger. Behind the façade of 'political Rusynism' stands a concrete goal: to create from parts of several countries in east-central where Rusyn-Ukrainians live a state called Rusinia."

—Fedir Kovach
Nove zhyttia (Prešov)
3. III. 2006, p. 5

"After the fall of Communist Czechoslovakia [in 1989] it seemed that everything would be possible. And so there appeared a map of a new republic, or rather of the kingdom of Rusinia. The spiritual father of that dream was the Canadian Paul Magocsi.

"I met Paul Magocsi in the 1960s in Prešov. Based on his serious commentary about the nationality question, we considered him at the time to be a nationalist. It is true that family connections drew him to Rusyn matters. I believe that already then he thought of becoming a king, even of a small country, but nevertheless a king. His efforts to divide us into two nationalities was useful for certain Slovak 'patriots', who saw in such a move our liquidation as a people. . . .

"Magocsi's idea about Rusinia caused a flurry of attention for awhile, but has had no great success. In Transcarpathia the Rusyn idea is bankrupt. In Slovakia the future king has attracted only a few people who have been unable to fit into political and cultural life.

"And so the kingdom of Rusinia has turned out to be an unpleasant much ado about nothing."

—Vasyl' Datsei
"The Kingdom of Rusinia"
Nove zhyttia (Prešov)
28. IV. 2006, p. 5

236

"During the post-[World War II] years it was for the most part the ex-Harvard professor P. Magocsi, himself of Rusyn origin, who through his systematic work at American and Canadian universities has endeavoured to create in academic circles the image of Rusyns as one of the fully recognized peoples living in the Carpathian region. Together with Magocsi, the prestige of Harvard as well as the careers of a significant number of individual Rusyns on both sides of the Atlantic whose work is well known to the international public have all contributed even more to the positive image of Rusyns."

—Jiří Marvan
Sven R. Gustavsson, *Jihoslovanští rusíni, jejich kultura a jazyk*
(Prague, 2006), p. 16.

"For our last example let us return to Subcarpathian Ruthenia, a territory which approximates as well as any other Ernest Gellner's fictitious Ruritania. The homeland of the 'Rusyns' (the most common of the local self-descriptions) is nowadays divided between four states. . . .

"Thanks to the collapse of the USSR, it turns out that other options for the Ruthenians can once again be freely explored under the exhilarating conditions of post-socialism. Magocsi himself has been an active participant in the World Congress of Rusyns, supporting a kind of cultural nationalism which calls for recognition of the Rusyn/Ruthenians as a distinct East Slavic people. No longer a distant scholar of Ruthenian history, Magocsi visits the homeland regularly and, for all practical purposes, plays a role of an 'awakener', even a 'mobilizer'."

—Chris Hann
The Sage Handbook of Nations and Nationalism
(London, 2006), p. 407.

"The recognition of the category 'Rusyn' as a nationality by the Transcarpathian Regional Assembly (Oblasna rada) is the result of the enormous disinformation campaign by Professor Paul Robert Magocsi, one of the Rusyn ideologists. He has even misinformed the local governing authorities ."

—Iosyp Kobal'
Zakhidna informatsiïna korporatsiia
13. III. 2007

"The phenomenon of political Rusynism is actually the Magocsi phenomenon. He is a talented person—intellectually inclined, hardworking, but very ambitious. He wants to become a kind of Hrushevs'kyi or Masaryk for Transcarpathians, somewhat metaphorically hoping to arrive on a white horse in Uzhhorod as had [in 1919] governor Zhatkovych. . . . Magocsi became the ideologist of the Rusyn movement, taking advantage of the period of the Velvet Revolution [in Czechoslovakia] and democratization in central Europe . . . .

"I do not see any future for political Rusynism. . . . One thing does seem strange to me, however: why up until now Magocsi has not been declared [by Ukraine] a *persona non grata*? After all he has done so much harm to the Ukrainian cause!"

—Vasyl' Markus'
Zakhidna informatsiïna korporatsiia
7. III. 2007

"The question of recognition of Transcarpathian Rusyns is not a problem which has arisen only in the last year. It is also not worth reacting against it too strongly, since that would draw too much positive attention to the issue . . . Let us say that the Canadian professor, Paul Magocsi, the person considered to be the main ideologist of the Rusyn movement, is at the very least sympathetic to the secret services of three states. I do not wish to descend to such a level of discourse, but nonetheless I would be concerned about allowing him to enter the territory of Ukraine. This is not because we are afraid of him, but rather because he is negatively disposed to our state and really could not care about who Rusyns or Ukrainians are. Why? Because he is a politically destructive person whose goal is to carry out the tasks assigned to him."

—Borys Oliïnyk
UKRINFORM
30. III. 2007

"Concretely, in 1995, P. R. Magocsi stated that 'state census reports should publish statistical information about the number of people who identify as Rusyns and not simply classify them as Ukrainians'. In 2002 the dream of the respected scholar and Ukrainianist from Toronto was completely realized. When dreams are fulfilled, however, other new ones appear."

—Vasyl' Lemak
"Ukraine Has Long Ago Recognized Rusyns"
RIO (Uzhhorod)
7. IV. 2007, p. 10

"One had the feeling that suddenly he would arrive, and that with pomp and circumstance the well planned anti-Ukrainian event [at the Kyivan Caves Monastery Ukrainian Book Museum] would begin. That the moment would come when, posed on a horse, the very Paul Robert Magocsi himself would appear. That same Magocsi who has worked for (and certainly still works for) the secret services of several states. And then it was him; grey-browed, red-cheeked, and with eyes flashing like O. Omel'chenko [the mayor of Kyiv]—dressed in a white shirt, a black bow-tie around his pink neck, in a white summer suit, and bare-footed in sandals. A dandy and the very image of a Hollywood star. Perhaps not [President] Reagan, but then half a Reagan would suffice. . . .

"Sir Paul, in the first years of Ukraine's independence would, whenever he came to Kyiv, stop off at the residence of [former Vice-Premier] Ivan Kuras, who at the time was a persistent opponent of 'Ukrainian bourgeois nationalism'.

"In short, P. R. Magocsi has—and continues to have—protectors in Kyiv. . . . at the highest levels of government [the Ombudsman of Ukraine Nina Karpachova] and Hennadii Udovenko, both of whom lobby on behalf of the 'Subcarpathian Rusyns'. This is the very same Udovenko, who is a prominent leader of the RUKH movement and former chairman of the General Assembly of the United Nations."

—Iaroslav Oros
"The Blunder of the Espionage Chief Magocsi"
Ukraïns'ka hazeta (L'viv)
5-11. VII. 2007, p. 4

"Thanks [to the *Narodnŷ novynkŷ* editors for sending] the beautifully published book, *The People from Nowhere*. In my view Paul Robert Magocsi is the unceasing motor that drives the entire Rusyn movement. We wish him much strength in his tireless work on behalf of the Rusyns."

—Vasyl' Tsitsak
Narodnŷ novynkŷ (Prešov)
8. VIII. 2007, p. 5

"At the First World Congress of Rusyns [in 1991] the world came to know that Rusyns are a distinct people which has its own culture traditions, beliefs, and language. The process of national awakening was aided by Professor Paul Robert Magocsi, who showed theoretically and with historical argumentation that Rusyns have the right to a distinct existence."
—Marianna Liavynets'
Rusyns 'kŷi svit (Budapest)
Vol. V [45] (2007), p. 14

"An important influence on the decision to recognize the Rusyn nationality in Subcarpathia was the support given by the chairman of the World Council of Rusyns, P. R. Magocsi. At a meeting with members of the Transcarpathian Regional Council on February 22, 2007, he pointed out, among other things, that the recognition of Rusyns in Ukraine is one of the primary goals of the World Congress of Rusyns, which represents Rusyns in nine countries in Europe and North America."
—Silvia Lysinova
Info Rusyn (Prešov)
Vol. IV, No. 5 (2007), p. 8

"I was invited to the World Congress of Rusyns [in Sighet, Romania] as the personal guest of the University of Toronto professor and member of the Academy of Sciences of Canada Paul Robert Magocsi. . . . He is an extraordinary individual, and it is thanks to his enthusiasm that the World Council of Rusyns is able to organize every two years world congresses."
—Sergei Suliak
Rusin (Chişinău, Moldova)
No. 2 [8] (2007), pp. 183-184

"'Ukraine is a unitary state', repeated Mykhailo Marton, the vice-chairman of the Transcarpathian Regional Assembly (Oblasna rada). . . . Marton is a government functionary and therefore he must think like a state bureaucrat. He has to protect his own career. In contrast to Ukraine's Security Service (SBU), and with regard to the special case of the recent 2008 Congress of European Rusyns, he does not see the hand of Moscow but rather of Canada. There resides Professor Paul Robert Magocsi, head of the World Congress of Rusyns, who also believes that Rusyns are not Ukrainians."

—Galina Sapozhnikova
"Ukraine is Fostering Its Own Abkhazia"
Komsomolskaia pravda (Moscow)
12. II. 2008

"It is impossible to believe that the Ukrainian Internal Security Services (SBU) do not know that the initiators of the Rusyn question coordinate their activity with foreign citizens. This is because local Rusyns do not hide but carry out their activity quite openly. Two weeks before the [March 7, 2007] session of the Transcarpathian Regional Assembly, the press agency of Transcarpathian State Administration reported on the meeting of the oblast's leadership (the head of the Regional Assembly and several representatives of the governor) with the head of the World Council of Rusyns Paul Robert Magocsi, at which the question of the necessity to recognize Rusyns as a nationality was discussed. In any other country in the world, whose authorities truly care about their own safety, the acts of a Canadian scholar [Magocsi] would be considered a gross interference in internal affairs and, at the very least, the regional authorities would bring this to the attention of the country's Internal Security Services. Yet in our country things went on quietly as if nothing happened. For example, when asked for commentary on the decision to recognize the Rusyn nationality adopted by the Transcarpathian Regional Assembly, the regional head of Ukraine's Internal Security Services simply responded that this matter does not fall within his jurisdiction."

—Volodymyr Martyn
Dzerkalo tyzhnia (Kyiv)
No. 6 [685], February 16-22, 2008, p. 3

"It is important to note that at the present time the World Congress of Rusyns is headed by a citizen of the United States, Paul Robert Magocsi. An authoritative scholar of international repute and today's most well known Rusyn activist (some Ukrainophiles even use his name to scare their children), the professor remains nonetheless an American patriot and quite naturally supports the idea of bringing Rusyns closer to their homeland. Magocsi and his supporters do indeed carry out extensive nationality-building work; for example, they finance Rusyn Sunday schools in Transcarpathia and assist in the publication of Rusyn-language books.

"American Rusyns regularly meet with representatives of the U.S. State Department, individual congressmen, and diplomats from central European countries to discuss the status of their brethren in Europe. Thanks to Magocsi's efforts, representatives of Rusyn organizations in Transcarpathia were able to meet in June 2007 with the extraordinary and full ambassador of the United States to Ukraine, William Taylor. The general thrust of all these activities is to bring Rusyns in the direction of the European Union and away not only from Ukraine but also from Russia. As Professor Magocsi has said, for the Rusyns of Ukraine the European Union can be considered their symbolic homeland. Maintaining good relations with Rusyns, who consider themselves the masters of Transcarpathia, will obviously not hurt should eventually an American Anti-Missile Defence System be set up in that region."

—Mikhail Chernigovtsev
"The Rusyns: A People not Visible from Kyiv"
Der Spiegel/Profil', No. 6 (Kyiv) and No. 8 (Moscow)
February 18, 2008, pp. 13-14, and March 8, 2008, p. 35

"The 'Rusyns' as an entity and ideology came on to the scene in 1989, when Soviet totalitarian censorship came to an end. . . . Their conceptual leader became the scholar and historian from Canada, Paul R. Magocsi, who prepared several truly solid, well-written, and propagandistically effective books."

—Oleh Bahan
"The Threat of Separatism in its Transcarpathian Variant"
Banderivets' (L'viv?)
December 2008

"The idea of Lemko separateness was created and is still being implemented by the Canadian scholar Paul Magocsi. This idea is a great historical mistake."

—Ivan Krasovs'kyi
"Lemkos in the Light of Past and Recent History"
Aktual'ni napriamy doslidzhennia Lemkivshchyny
(L'viv, 2008), p. 14

"The one thread that goes through all of Magocsi's writings is not so much a concern to protect the local Rusyns from assimilation by the state

nationalities [in countries where they live] —something which is indeed
the greatest threat to their existence—but rather first and foremost to
argue that Rusyns are not Ukrainians, that the tripartite Lemko-Boiko-
Hutsul classification scheme is inadequate, and that Carpathian Rus' was
always part of the political and cultural sphere of central Europe and was
never under the hegemony of [medieval] Kyivan Rus'. Such falsification
and hatred toward the Ukrainian people dominate all the work of this
American magyarone who cannot even write in the language of these
people whom he suddenly has tried 'to protect' from Ukrainians."

—Sviatoslav Semeniuk
"The Lemko Region as an Ethnic Phenomenon of Ukraine-Rus'"
Aktual'ni napriamy doslidzhennia Lemkivshchyny
(L'viv, 2008), p. 22

"The Rusyn movement is even open to manipulation from the forces
of present-day Ukrainian liberalism. We have already cited the articles
by P. R. Magocsi in the leading Kyivan liberal organ *Krytyka* (editor—
George Grabowicz), which in its own way is trying 'to give voice' to the
Rusyn problem. *Krytyka* also published Magocsi's *History of Ukraine*
(2007), which not only treats the history of Ukraine from the a liberal
cosmopolitan point of view, but also sends signals about the possibility
of the existence of Rusyns as part of the 'polyethnic' essence of the
'Ukraine' project. . . . Who and what is behind all of this? Where does
this interest in Rusyn ethnicity on the part of non-ethnic liberals come
from? First of all, it comes from the ideologically cosmopolitan principle
of pluralism according to which even Evil has a right to be heard; and
secondly without question, from those whose strategic task is to stop
Ukrainian nationalism at any cost . . . Here the Rusyn factor with its
ethnic particularism can be a useful element . . ."

—Oleh Bahan
"The Rusyn Theory and the Lemko Region"
Aktual'ni napriamy doslidzhennia Lemkivshchyny
(L'viv, 2008), p. 102

"Although there are several Carpatho-Rusyn organizations in
Transcarpathia, the majority in one way or another are oriented toward
the World Congress of Rusyns, headed by Professor Dr. Paul Robert

Magocsi, holder of the Chair of Ukrainian Studies at the University of Toronto and academician in Canada's Royal Society. . . . Magocsi in particular supports the idea of Carpatho-Rusynism as a civic movement concerned primarily with ethnocultural matters, a movement, moreover, which is not opposed to any state and especially not opposed to Ukraine and which does not have political goals, such as autonomy for Transcarpathia or the creation of some kind of independent Carpatho-Rusyn state."

—O. Timkov
"Carpatho-Rusynism in Ukraine: Loyalty in Return for Recognition"
http://imhov.com/index2.php?option=content&task=view&id...

"The reasons for the neo-Rusyn revival can be explained by the general European ethno-cultural and ethno-political context in this age of globalization. . . .

"The uniqueness of the Rusyn situation depends to a significant degree on the large number of political activists in North America, in central Europe (particularly in Slovakia and Hungary), and in Russia. After World War II, traditions were recognized and cultivated only in North American diasporan circles, and it is in this context that one must understand the Magocsi phenomenon."

—O. Zaremba and O. Rafal's'kyi
Zakarpattia v etnopolitychnomu vymiri
(Kyiv, 2008), pp. 63-64

"Among the external factors related to the appearance of political Rusynism in Transcarpathia it is essential to note the organizational and scholarly-popular work of certain forces, for which the main spokesman is the University of Toronto professor P. Magocsi. It is precisely through his publications in the new [political] environment that the theory of Rusyn distinctiveness has been revived and that a 'road map', a plan of action has been worked out so that radical elements in Rusyns organizations are able to formulate specific demands (and how they should be carried out), which are then directed to the government of Ukraine and to world organizations. And even if his 2007 *History of Ukraine* Magocsi introduces certain correctives to his interpretation of the Rusyn problem, this does not change the essence of the matter.

About him one might say: 'The monster has done the job'. Now the Provisional Government of Subcarpathian Rus', the Soim [parliament] of Subcarpathian Rusyns, and certain secular and religious leaders of neo-Rusynism are trying to continue the path laid out for them."

—Mai Panchuk
Zakarpattia v etnopolitychnomu vymiri
(Kyiv, 2008), pp. 640-641

"The idea of Rusynism brought me to the World Council of Rusyns. . . . I made every effort to influence the activists in that organization . . . but each time I came to realize that this organization would not be able to help us [Carpatho-Rusyns in Transcarpathia], because it was headed by foreigners: a Canadian [P. R. Magocsi] whose heart and soul did not feel the pain of the Rusyns from Subcarpathia and rather acted from the perspective of American global politics. . ."

—Mykhayl Almashii
Moï metamorfozŷ
(Uzhhorod, 2008), p. 200

"As for 'The Savior' of Rusyns, Dr. Magocsi, who has built his career [on the idea] of Rusyn independence, he reminds me by his activity (among other things) of [the popular nineteenth-century German adventure writer] Karl May. This is because since I consider Magocsi as much a Rusyn as May is an American Indian. Magocsi is himself a person 'from nowhere', although a known quantity. . . . Building his career in Ukrainian academic circles abroad, he writes about us Rusyns as May did about American Indians. Magocsi's writings are actually a good read as imaginary Romantic literature, whose facts, however, do confuse other historians."

—Mikhal Byts'ko
Ukraïns'kyi zhurnal (Prague)
No. 1 (2009), p. 30

"The main news to come out of the [X World Congress] meeting was not pleasant. The chief formulator of political Rusynism, Paul Magocsi, voluntarily gave up the post of chairman of the World Council [of Rusyns]. He gave up from fatigue. After all, to lead the 'people from nowhere' is not an easy thing."

—Oleksandr Havrosh
Nove zhyttia (Prešov)
3. VII. 2009, p. 8

"The idea to establish a Scholarly Seminar in Carpatho-Rusyn Studies [at Prešov University] came from the speaker at the very first seminar (12 February 2009), the historian and professor at the University of Toronto in Canada, Paul Robert Magocsi."

—Kvetoslava Koporova
Studium Carpato-Ruthenorum 2009
(Prešov, 2009), p. 3

"Professor Magocsi called four young people to the second floor of the [Czech] National Center in the Vinohrady district [in Prague]—the site of the Sixth World Congress of Rusyns [2001]—and in private conversation urged them to begin setting up a youth organization. Although this was a brief conversation during the course of the World Congress, it nonetheless provided the impetus for the organized existence [at an international level] of Rusyn youth which continues to this day."

—Peter Krainiak, Jr.
Studium Carpato-Ruthenorum 2009
(Prešov, 2009), p. 133

"The leading ideologist of political Rusynism is Professor Paul Robert Magocsi. . . . The authoritative scholar has conducted and continues to carry out successfully discussions with highly placed representatives of several countries (including Ukraine) regarding recognition of Rusyns as a distinct nationality, the creation of scholarly and civic organizations for them, and other matters."

—Mykola Mushynka
"Political Rusynism in Its Current Stage"
Duklia (Prešov)
Vol. LVII, No. 4 (2009), p. 42

"The well-known Canadian scholar of central and eastern Europe, Paul Magocsi, developed the idea that, given certain favorable conditions, one might create a 'fourth East Slavic nation' out of the Transcarpathia Ukrainians. . . .

"The head of the Chair of Ukrainian Studies at the University of Toronto is the author several studies. . . . Among the most influential of these is *The Shaping of National Identity: Subcarpathian Rus', 1848-1948,* published abroad in 1978 and in Ukrainian in Uzhhorod in the mid-1990s. This work contains considerable factual material about the history and culture of Transcarpathia, and today the book is widely used by a whole host of followers and disciples of the famous scholar. Aside from its undoubted scholarly value, this book also has great political importance.

"The true value of Magocsi's monograph only became clear much later. It has had a rather strong impact on certain ethno-political endeavours that began to unfold a decade after the book's appearance, when, in the wake of the collapse of the Soviet Union, Moscow encouraged the latent discontent connected with widespread ethno-national problems in various [former Soviet] republics in an attempt to prevent the break-up of the Soviet Union."

—Ihor Burkut
Rusynstvo: mynule i suchasnist'
(Chernivtsi, 2009), pp. 304-306

"There is good reason why the mass media continually refers to Paul Magocsi as the potential president of a hypothetical state, 'Rusinia'. However, his career and personal inclinations suggest that he is not at all comfortable being in the role of a political leader. This truly profound researcher has rightly given priority in his life to scholarship. And in the Rusyn movement there is no equivalent to him as the leading authoritative figure abroad."

—Ihor Burkut
Rusynstvo: mynule i suchasnist'
(Chernivtsi, 2009), p. 363

"Professor Pugh speaks about the Rusyn language with great enthusiasm. What was it then that so attracted him to our language that he wants to know more and more about it? . . . Among other things, in November 2006, at the annual convention of the American Association for the Advancement of Slavic Studies, he met with the most distinguished person within the American Rusyn world, the academician and historian Paul Robert Magocsi.

—'And so it's you Professor Pugh who has published a Ukrainian grammar?', asked Magocsi. Pugh nodded.
—'And what about the Rusyn language?'

—Shtefan Sukhŷi
Info-Rusyn (Prešov)
Vol. VII, No. 1-2 (2010), p. 12

"Who is Magocsi and other separatists and researchers of the 'Carpatho-Russian' problem, those creators of a new nation and history? They are trying to revive the Muscophile orientation, to halt the evolution of the people, and to transform Rusyns into *'kacapy'* [Muscovite Russians]."

—Lemko z Krenytsi
Nashe slovo (Warsaw)
No. 25, 20. VI. 2010

"P. R. Magocsi is interesting to me as a scholar. More than one of today's critics could learn a lot from him. If it wasn't for his interpretation of the history of Carpathian Rus', our understanding of the transformation of Rus'-Ukrainian culture and political thought in that region would still be at the level of Galicia's 'popular enlighteners' at the outset of the twentieth century. Magocsi the scholar has himself contributed to the development of Rusyn and Ukrainian studies more than dozens of Krynytskyis [present-day Ukrainian-oriented civic patriots in L'viv]. I would love to read a history of the Lemko Region that would be as beautifully written as Magocsi's *History of Ukraine* . . .

"The Paul Robert Magocsi World Federation of Ukrainian Lemko Organizations? . . . That is how this organization might well be renamed, since it devotes virtually all of its energies to struggle against the views of one person—Magocsi. This struggle is obvious from the very name of the organization [Ukrainian Lemko] as from its pseudo-scholarly activity, its ineffectual annual Vatra festivals, and other such gatherings. The Magocsi question is a classical example of how the activity of one person in the world has become the basis of political paranoia among leaders of several civic organizations."

—Bohdan Huk
"Magocsi's Branch of Ukrainian Lemkos?"
Nashe slovo (Warsaw)
No. 34, 22. VIII. 2010

"Let us take as an example the stubborn Ukrainophobe, P. R. Magocsi. This greying, average scholar and persistent politicizer who his entire life has only been interested in creating in far-away Transcarpathia a 'fourth East Slavic people', the Rusyns, has managed to occupy the Chair of Ukrainian History at the University of Toronto and even achieve for himself life-long immunity; that is, the status of [academic] tenure."

—Iurii Baleha
Politychne rusynstvo, abo Fentsyko-Brodiïvs'ki pryvody na Zakarpatti
(Uzhhorod, 2010), p. 240

"P. R. Magocsi has submitted similar appeals to diplomatic representatives, including those from Ukraine, as well as to influential international organizations. A descendent of an Uhro-Rusyn family which emigrated to the United States 'in the era of Carpathian Rus'", he has focussed in his scholarly work and political activity on Carpatho-Rusyns—and certainly not on Carpatho-Russians. . . .

"The [extremist political] demands of Subcarpathian Rusyns [in Ukraine's Transcarpathia] have been met with a cold shoulder by the World Congress of Rusyns. P. R. Magocsi has not failed to note logically that, at a time when Europe is integrating, to speak of Subcarpathian Rus' as a separate entity is absurd. But the professor has not told us who and when there are plans to accept Rusyns into the European Union."

—Aleksandr Gegal'chii
"Carpathian Rus': Myths and Reality from Aristov to Magocsi"
Russkoe edinstvo (http://rusedin.ru)
3. II. 2010

"As part of his scholarly activity over many years, Professor Paul Robert Magocsi has published a considerable number of works which have provoked heated debate among his professional colleagues as well as among the larger public. Complicated is the fate of anyone who takes a particular stand in the scholarly world. Such a stand usually does not coincide with accepted opinion and, therefore, it becomes the subject of heated debate and polemics that often go far beyond the bounds of common civility. This is even more so the case when the works of a given scholar are closely connected to politics and, in particular, ethnic politics. . . .

"As a scholar Paul Magocsi is very cautious in his assessments and tries to avoid categorical statements. But his views are often used by political activists, who simplify what he says and who quite often carry his views to extremist conclusions. Magocsi's opponents for the most part do not criticize his views as such but rather the activities of political figures who hide behind his name."

—Ihor Burkut
"Paul Robert Magocsi—a Scholar of Ukrainian History and Founder of Contemporary Rusyn Studies"
Bukovyns'kyi zhurnal (Chernivtsi)
No. 3-4 (2010), pp. 145 and 152

"Today one of the most influential of world-class leaders among Carpatho-Rusyns is the University of Toronto professor and permanent head of the Carpatho-Rusyn Research Center in Pennsylvania, Paul Robert Magocsi. . . .

"A descendant of a Uhro-Rusyn family that emigrated to the United States during the 'era of Carpathian Rus', Magocsi's scholarly and political program is oriented specifically toward Carpatho-Rusyns and not Carpatho-Russians [*karpatorossy*]. His understanding of the historical homeland inhabited by Rusyns differs in principle from the views of Russian and Russophile-oriented Rusyn scholars as well as from Ukrainian scholars and so-called Rusyn-Ukrainians. . . . Consequently, the attempts of several Ukrainian political analysts to accuse P. R. Magocsi of Russophile sympathies cannot provoke in a normal and serious person anything other than a [condescending] smile."

—A. V. Gegal'chii
"Carpathian Rus': Mythology and Reality"
Russkoe slovo v kul'turno-istoricheskom i sotsial'nom kontekste
(Kemerovo-Dalian', 2010), pp. 96-97

"From the perspective of scholarship Professor Magocsi's work has easily passed the test of time and quality; his presence and his importance in the field are not in question. There is certainly no problem here.

"Scholarly achievement and standing, however, is not only built on a record of research and publications. . . . And here, too, Professor Magocsi has an outstanding record. . . . Where, or more precisely what, then, is the problem?

"Specifically the 'Magocsi problem' infers a perception that there is an inherent conflict of interest between, on the one hand, his scholarly work in Ukrainian Studies and institutionally his activity as holder of the Chair of Ukrainian Studies at the University of Toronto, and, on the other, his engagement in various Rusyn or Carpatho-Rusyn issues.

"Professor Magocsi's scholarship is animated by transnational, comparative, and inclusive values and criteria. As has so often been noted in reference to his *History of Ukraine*, Magocsi's approach programmatically focuses on the ethnic diversity and multicultural fabric of Ukrainian history and in so doing makes it not only more complex and attractive, but also unfetters it from the teleology (or primordialism) that often obtains in the discipline. In effect, rather than constituting a "problem," the scholar problematizes and thereby revitalizes the discipline."

—George G. Grabowicz
"'The Magocsi Problem': A Preliminary Deconstruction and Contextualization"
Nationalities Papers (Basingstoke, Eng.)
Vol. XXXIX, No. 1 (2011), pp. 112-114

"Paul Robert Magocsi the multi-vector scholar is by far at one and the same time the leading Western historian of Ukraine *and* the leading Western scholar of Rusyns. As Alexander Motyl points out, . . . the Ukrainian aspect of his scholarship could act as the 'Other' for his Rusyn scholarship. Or, perhaps the answer is more straightforward; namely, that Magocsi is a member of a small group of uncommon academics who have a gift of project management in publishing, teaching, and public advocacy that spans two fields of scholarly interest, in this case Ukrainian and Rusyn Studies."

—Taras Kuzio
"A Multi-Vectored Scholar for a Multi-Vectored Era"
Nationalities Papers (Basingstoke, Eng.)
Vol. XXXIX, No. 1 (2011), p. 103

"My esteemed colleagues . . . are echoing what has become incontrovertible in the field: Magocsi is a towering figure in Ukrainian Studies. And we could add: even if he had not written a line about the Rusyns, he would nevertheless tower over us all. Such conclusions are born out by his magisterial *History of Ukraine*, the *Illustrated History of Ukraine*, the cartographic volumes, the collections on Galicia and Sheptytskyi and, most of all, the stunning quality of his work, with its depth, nuances, and sweep. This was not exactly what was projected in Toronto's Ukrainian circles nearly thirty years ago, but since then Magocsi has developed into a leading scholar of Ukraine, and yes, of Ukrainians. He is, certainly, the most prolific."

—Dominique Arel
"The Scholar, Historian, and Public Advocate"
Nationalities Papers (Basingstoke, Eng.)
Vol. XXXIX, No. 1 (2011), p. 125

"How is it possible for a Rusyn nation-builder to have contributed to the historiography of Ukraine to such a significant degree that one might suspect that Magocsi is really a Ukrainian nation-builder? . . .

"Magocsi is a Rusyn nation-builder. He has written extensively about Carpatho-Rusyns and he has also actively participated in the Carpatho-Rusyn national revival of the last three to four decades. It is at just this same time, however, that Magocsi has also produced a large body of authoritative publications on Ukraine and Ukrainians and thereby helped to establish both groups as conceptually and politically real entities in North America and Europe . . . Magocsi's Rusyn nation-building activities do not contradict his Ukrainian scholarship. Quite the contrary, he has effectively become a Ukrainian nation-builder (*malgré soi*, if you will), precisely because he needs a distinct Ukraine in order to make the case for a Rusyn nationality. . . .

"In sum, Ukrainians logically *must* exist for Magocsi. They are, as it were, a necessary condition of his Carpatho-Rusyn nation-building efforts. To make the case for a distinct Ukrainian nationality and a distinct Ukraine—with 'a distinct territory (possibly but not necessarily statehood), language, historical tradition, religion, social attitudes, and ethnographic features'—is to make the case for a distinct Carpatho-Rusyn nationality and a distinct Carpathian Rus' homeland. . . .

"The paradoxes of Paul Robert Magocsi therefore dissolve, only to reveal what may be a true paradox—that all nation-builders are always builders of at least two nations, their own and the other's."

—Alexander J. Motyl

"The Paradoxes of Paul Robert Magocsi: The Case for Rusyns and the Logical Necessity of Ukrainians"
Nationalities Papers (Basingstoke, Eng.)
Vol. XXXIX, No. 1 (2011), pp. 105, 107, 109

"With regard to the post-Soviet era, the undoubted leader, the most outstanding popularizer, and at the same time the contemporary founder (in every sense of that word) of the pseudo-scholarly discourse regarding the ethno-linguistic classification of the indigenous inhabitants of the Carpathian Region is Paul Robert Magocsi."

—Liubomyr Belei
"Pseudonuaukovyi dyskurs etno-movnoï identyfikatsiï naselennia prykordonnykh raioniv Karpat posttotalitarnoï doby."
Naukovyi zbirnyk Muzeiu ukraïns'koï kul'tury (Svidník)
Vol. XXVI (2011), p. 54

"There are very powerful foreign hands involved in the creation of a new people (present-day eastern Slovakia has witnessed the official division of its Ukrainians into 'Rusyns' and 'Ukrainians'). The leading proponent of the idea of a 'Rusyn people' is the Canadian professor, P. R. Magocsi, who recently was uncovered as a paid agent of the Czechoslovak security services during the era of Communist rule. Now he is engaged in creating a distinct Rusyn literary language."

—Iaroslav Dashkevych
... Uchy nelozhnymy ustamy skazaty pravdu
(Kyiv, 2011), p. 549

"Thanks to the work of American and Canadian Ukrainians, the history of Carpatho-Ruthenia is reasonably accessible in English. The principal scholar in the field is Paul Robert Magocsi."

—Norman Davies
Vanished Kingdoms: The History of Half Forgotten Europe
(London, 2011), p. 780

"Sugar and Treadgold's [multi-volume] book series [a History of East Central Europe] most decisively influenced the post-Cold War concept of Central Europe with the publication of its long-awaited first volume in 1993, the *Historical Atlas of East Central Europe*. It was the work of

Paul Robert Magocsi from the University of Toronto. . . . Other authors who have written copiously on various Central European issues during the two decades after the fall of Communism have time and again adopted his maps for their books and articles."

—Tomasz Kamusella
"Central Europe in the Distorting Mirror of Maps, Languages, and Ideas"
Polish Review (New York)
Vol. LVII, No. 1 (2012), pp. 43-44

"Chernivtsi University students were also able to interact with the renowned scholar, Paul Robert Magocsi. While signing his book [*A History of Ukraine*], he found a warm word to say to each student whose hand he shook. There was no superficiality, conceit, or cheap pseudo-friendliness. Rather, what we saw in him was the sense of democratic equality, the characteristic of a true scholar when interacting with future colleagues. He is clearly an example for some of our local 'geniuses'."

—Ihor Burkut
"The Renowned American Ukrainianist—P. R. Magocsi in Chernivtsi"
Versiï (Chernivtsi)
No. 22 (2012), pp. 2

"Is the birth of a new Cossack nation indeed in the offing? It is at least clear that the singers have their mythology right, and there are other nation-building movements that can serve them as inspiration. In the year 2000 Paul Robert Magocsi, a professor of Ukrainian studies at the University of Toronto and an intellectual leader of the Rusyn movement, which claims that the people of Ukrainian Transcarpathia and neighbouring regions of Poland and Slovakia are not part of the Ukrainian nation but constitute a separate Rusyn nationality, published a collection of essays entitled, *Of the Making of Nationalities There Is No End*. It would appear that there is indeed no end in sight to imagining new nationalities, be they Rus', Rusyn, or Cossack."

—Serhii Plokhy
The Cossack Myth
(Cambridge, 2012), p. 368

"After the fall of the Communist order there occurred a peculiarly explosive rise of Carpatho-Rusynism, which in a somewhat modified form is defined as neo-Rusynism. This movement was given a scientific basis by the Canadian historian and political scientist Paul Robert Magocsi. He is inclined to include all the Ukrainian inhabitants in the Carpathians (Lemkos, Carpatho-Rusyns, Boikos, Hutsuls) as belonging to a distinct people of Carpathian Rus'."

—Bohdan Halczak
"The Lemkos' Place in the Universe"
Łemkowie, Bojkowie, Rusini, Vol. IV, pt.1
(Słupsk and Zielona Góra, 2012), p. 127

"More than once I thought of the possibility of getting to know and exchanging views with this person [Professor Paul Robert Magocsi], who holds a prominent place in historical scholarship. . . . My wish was fulfilled in September 1991, when I was on a visit to Toronto in Canada. We met at the university. Professor Magocsi greeted me with great politeness, which I did not expect. His friendliness, his show of deep respect toward whom he is speaking, and his general humane character and tactfulness completely disarmed any possibility of conflict with him.

"While on the one hand our three-hour conversation was at first glance very friendly, from the very outset it was nonetheless clear that we had diametrically opposed views regarding the historical place of Carpatho-Rusyns. After a spirited exchange on both sides, it seemed to me that Mr. Magocsi was open to compromise.

"I deeply regret that when having to leave this person I had feelings of sorrow and disappointment."

—Ivan Krasovs'kyi
Til'ky z ridnom narodom, 2nd rev. ed.
(L'viv, 2012), pp. 63-65

"I was asked . . . if I would be willing to visit Serbia and Republika Srpska [in Bosnia Hercegovina] as an independent observer. . . . [with] Professor P. R. Magocsi [who] was also invited. . . .

"From Belgrade we were taken to Novi Sad to showcase for us the support that various minority cultures received in Serbia. . . . Just prior to entering the Rusyn-Ukrainian club, an amusing conversation took place between me and Professor Magocsi. He insisted that no Ukrainians, and only Rusyns, were to be found in the region and that I was simply mistaken. We were . . . welcomed by the chair who was Ukrainian. Later on Professor Magocsi apologized for his exaggerated Rusyn nationalism."

—Peter J. Potichnyj
My Journey
(Ancaster, Ont. and L'viv, 2012), pp. 209-210

"As for the question of what he thinks about the Carpatho-Rusyn theory of Magocsi, Mykhailo Ramach responded: 'This is a fruitless effort. It does receive political and financial support among certain circles in Serbia and abroad. It is not, however, politics, but rather political speculation which may have some short-term impact but not any perspective in the long term'."

—Ivan Hvat
Duklia (Prešov)
Vol. LXI, No. 1 (2013), p. 86

"Professor Magocsi's *History of Ukraine* is a study written by an impartial historian without any preconceptions toward past events or personages; it is a work free of the kind of 'political correctness' that is so fashionable among various 'media-hungry' historians with a political agenda, in particular when they deal with events in the twentieth-century that were tragic for Ukraine. . . .

"Professor Magocsi's history is written from a state perspective; that is, it is based on the territorial principle normally used by historians writing about state peoples. . . .

"From the standpoint of present-day state building efforts in Ukraine, it is precisely this integrative approach toward the study of one's national past that is essential."

—Oleh Romanyshyn
"The Scholarly Activity of the Historian Paul Robert Magocsi"
Homin Ukraïny (Toronto)
12. III. 2013, p. 9

"In June 2013 Prešov University will award an honorary doctorate (*doctor honoris causa*) to the most renown scholar in the field of Carpatho-Rusyn studies—Professor Paul Robert Magocsi of the University of Toronto. We should stress that this is happening not only for the first time at Prešov University. It is the first time in the history of higher education, whether in Prešov, or Slovakia, or anywhere in the world, that a university is awarding an honorary doctorate to a person, who, through his scholarship has created the foundation and in various ways has enriched the new discipline of Carpatho-Rusyn studies. This very fact alone, we believe, will provide motivation for the further development of Carpatho-Rusyn studies in Slovakia and elsewhere in the world, and in particular serve as an inspiration for younger generations interested in uncovering the numerous unknown aspects of Carpatho-Rusyns and their culture."

—Anna Plïshkova
Rusyn (Prešov)
Vol. XXIII, No. 1 (2013), p. 4

"The granting of the prestigious title, *Doctor honoris causa*, is always an exceptional event not only for the university bestowing the award but also for the person who has achieved such honor. On 11 June 2013, at a celebratory session of Prešov University's Academic Council, this honor was bestowed upon the professor of history at the University of Toronto—Paul Robert Magocsi. This is a most worthy recognition, since Professor Magocsi is a renowned scholar of broad interests, including, among other matters, Carpathian studies. . . .

"Having been able to observe him at close hand, I have long been amazed by his style of work in resolving a given task, his endurance, his degree of intensity, and the precise allotment of time devoted to every research project. . . .

"Particularly important for research in Carpathian related matters is the *Encyclopedia of Rusyn History and Culture* (2002, 2005), prepared under his direction and without which present-day research in the field of Carpathian studies is inconceivable."

—L'ubica Babotová
"Tribute to a Canadian Historian"
Dejiny:časopis Inštitutu histórie Prešovskej univerzity (Prešov)
No. 2 (2013), pp. 123-126

"The Canadian scholar, Professor P. R.Magocsi, supported by the Carpatho-Rusyn Research Center in Pennsylvania, brought together

Rusyns at a World Congress in 1991. In 2002, the Transcarpathian Regional Assembly (Oblasna rada) turned to the central government in Ukraine with the request to recognize Rusyns as a distinct nationality. On 7 March 2007, the Regional Assembly adopted a resolution recognizing Rusyns as an indigenous nationality in Transcarpathia."

—Maksymilian A. Shepelev
"The Rusyn Question"
Heopolityka: entsyklopediia
(Kyiv, 2013), p. 665

"Why is this book [by Paul Robert Magocsi], *Ukraine: A History of the Land and Its Peoples*, truly so significant, and why should it be required reading for all those who are professionally interested in the history of Ukraine? It is because the work is not just another textbook, or yet another addition to the many existing historic syntheses, but because it is the first and up to now the most consistent and successful effort to write a territorial and multinational history of Ukraine."

—Volodymyr Sklokin
Drynovs'kyi zbirnyk, Vol. VI.
(Kharkiv and Sofia, 2013), p. 431

"Relatively weak in Transcarpathia is the 'Subcarpathian Rusyn' faction, whose leading ideologist is the Canadian historian and political scientist of Lemko origin, Paul Robert Magocsi. That movement is sometimes referred to as 'Magocsi-izm' (*magoczyzm*) and its followers 'Magocsi-ites' (*magoczysti*). The official goal of this faction of 'neo-Rusynism' is the creation of a separate people encompassing all 'Carpatho-Rusyns'. . . .

"The official 'neo-Rusyn' organization in Poland derives its views from the ideas of Paul Robert Magocsi. 'Magocsizm', however, is not adaptable to the realities in Poland. . . . For one thing, the concept of 'Carpatho-Rusyns' is not easy to accept, since the word *Rusyn* is what the Poles use to identify Ukrainians, which the autonomists do everything to convince Poles that they are not.

"The idea of a 'Fourth Rus',' which implies the existence of yet another Rus' people after Russians, Belorusans, and Ukrainians, is another problematic aspect of 'Magocsizm', since such a view undermines the tradition of a single All-Rus' world. Hence, in practice, 'neo-Rusynism' in Poland reminds one more of old-fashioned Lemko Muscophilism than it does the ideas of Paul Robert Magocsi."

—Bohdan Halczak
Dzieje Łemków od średniowiecza do współczesności
(Warsaw, 2014), pp. 255 and 263

"To begin, our *Urtext* for 'creation' is the Book of Genesis. With apologies to its author: Darkness was on the face of the deep. And Paul Robert came out of the Garden on the sixth day and he said: 'Let there be light!' And he saw that it was good. And the light continues to spread, as we have heard this afternoon from our presenters. And now, when Paul Robert looks out upon the world of Carpato-Ruthenica, he finds that things are getting even *better*."

—Thomas E. Bird
Comments at the 46th Annual Convention of
Association for Slavic, East European, and Eurasian Studies
San Antonio, Texas, 21 November 2014

"The head of the Union of Rusyns-Ukrainians [in Slovakia] Viktor Koval' spoke of two foreign centers of political Rusynism and their divisive role. . . . One is P. R. Magocsi, a half-Hungarian half-Ukrainian, who was educated with funds from the Ukrainian diaspora. His public statements suggest the need to create a borderland people on territory between Ukraine and Slovakia. Koval' based his opinion on the statements of P. R. Magocsi at the first World Congress of Rusyns in Medzilaborce (1991), where he called for the creation of a 'homeland called Rusinia' with appropriate state attributes. Magocsi also provided instructions on how to eliminate Ukrainianism in the Carpathian region."

—Michal Škurla
Hlas pamäti
(Prešov, 2014), p. 181

"When, as Andrij Timkovič [later the Basilian monk Gorazd], I was during Communist totalitarian times a long-time student in Rome, I received in 1989 a Rusyn religious newspaper published in Pittsburgh (USA) . . . which announced that someone named Magocsi would be giving a lecture in America about Subcarpathian Rusyns.

"I thought to myself: How can some kind of Magyar, and on top of that in far away America, know anything about Rusyns? Let me ask him for some information and see just how much he knows about us. . . .

"Not long after I was summoned from my monastic cell and told there was a phone call. . . . Professor Paul Robert Magocsi from the University of Toronto, while dealing with some other matters on a visit to Rome, would like to meet with me. As my heart was pounding and almost jumping out of my chest, we spoke and agreed to meet that very afternoon. . . .

"I, together with two other Redemptorists from Slovakia, were met by a very sympathetic and friendly middle-aged gentleman, who, from his very first words was clearly no Magyar as I had previously and wrongly surmised from the surname. . . .

"It was not long before all our fears and skepticism dissipated, so that we felt that with Magocsi we were meeting a long-time friend. His modesty was truly remarkable: he, a university professor, was dealing with us, plain students, as his equals. His knowledge of history was no less remarkable, and he was particularly well informed about the situation of Rusyns behind the Iron Curtain.

"From then on and for the next 15 years, Magocsi acted with seriousness and care toward us [me and my younger brother Iosafat] as if we were his own sons.

"The [ongoing] contacts with Professor Paul Robert Magocsi truly had an impact on both us Timkovič brothers and priests in our evolution to becoming fully conscious Rusyns. Following his example, we became particularly active in Greek Catholic church matters in Slovakia in the last years of the twentieth and beginning of the twenty-first century."

—Gorazd Andrij Timkovič, OSB
Narodný novynkŷ (Prešov, Slovakia)
19. II. 2015, pp. 1-2

"Ivan Vanat . . . writes that the Rusyn national revival is political Rusynism, a program spread among us from America by Paul Robert Magocsi. Rusyns themselves cannot agree with such a statement. We are not dependent on what Paul Robert Magocsi brings us from America. We know ourselves that we are Rusyns, just as we know from practice that political phenomena are the result of the work of political parties.

Magocsi is in no political party here. Rather, he attends our meetings as our guest and speaks to us as our guest, whose scholarly views on the strategic development of Rusyns we highly regard. It is only to the good that there is a scholar not burdened with totalitarian [Communist] views of the past century, who takes an active interest in Rusyns from a historical and contemporary perspective."

—Ian Kalyniak
Narodnŷ novynkŷ (Prešov, Slovakia)
19. II. 2015, p. 1

"Professor P. R. Magocsi is a name which is and will always be connected with the birth of the Rusyn movement in general. . . . Although not a linguist, this wise person knew at the time [of the 1995 codification]—and he still knows—that it is not possible for a people to develop and sustain itself without a literary language. He has given his all in the past and still does so in the present for the good of the Rusyn people and its language, and we sincerely hope that he will continue to do so long into the future."

—Vasyl' Iabur
"Celebrating the Rusyn Literary Language in Slovakia"
Rusyn (Prešov, Slovakia)
Vol. XXV, No. 1 (2015), p. 3

"The works by Paul Robert Magocsi [*A History of Ukraine: The Land and Its Peoples* and *Illustrated History of Ukraine*] are without doubt of interest not only for specialists but as much for the wider public interested in the history of Ukraine. Among books by Western scholars translated into Ukrainian, the works of Magocsi hold a very high and respected place."

—Elena Borisenok and Svetlana Lukashova
Belorussiia i Ukraina, Vol. 5
(Moscow, 2015), p. 533

"Paul Magocsi, the leading inspiration behind the worldwide Rusyn movement, has not won in the struggle for Transcarpathia. . . .

"Paul Magocsi has achieved the incredible: during the past quarter century he has created a variety of Rusyn institutions in different countries and has even found means to finance them. Rusynism has appeared on the scene in all central European countries, at the same time that it has undermined each of those countries' Ukrainian minorities, not simply dividing them into two groups but creating two antagonistic camps among them.

"And so we should say to the 70-year-old Magocsi and his retinue: 'Subcarpathian Rusyns, Arise from Your Deep Slumber'—or, more precisely: From Your Deep Reverie.

"Rusynism as a phenomenon has reached its peak and gradually it will decline."

—Oleksandr Havrosh
"One's Opinion"
Radio Liberty (Washington, D. C.)
20. XII. 2015

"From various sources I have learned that Iurii Bacha criticizes me for my participation in 'political Rusynism' and for ties with the Canadian professor, Paul Robert Magocsi. I have on more than one occasion stated that I respect P. R. Magocsi as a scholar, even though I do not agree with his political activity directed toward having the government of Ukraine recognize Transcarpathian Rusyns as a fourth East Slavic people. . . . The works about Ukraine by P. R. Magocsi are received positively in scholarly circles among Ukrainian historians. . . .

"Taking into consideration that during the last 2011 census 33,482 citizens of Slovakia identified themselves as Rusyns and that 55,469 stated their mother tongue is Rusyn, I, as a scholar cannot deny the existence of a Rusyn national minority in Slovakia."

—Mykola Mushynka
"Making Use of the Right of Self-Defence"
Duklia (Prešov, Slovakia)
Vol. LXIII, No. 3 (2015), p. 57

"Even people who do not have any specific ideological agenda are in danger of being regarded as ideologists the moment they write about anything that can be interpreted in terms of national identity. The most prominent example of this is Paul Robert Magocsi, whose books on Ukrainian history are considered among the best scholarly works available, but who is at the same time often accused of being a Rusyn nation-builder."

—Agnieszka Halemba
Negotiating Marian Apparitions
(Budapest and New York, 2015), p. 118

"An outstanding contemporary example of a scholar who is at the same time an ethnic activist is P. R. Magocsi, who is perceived and described as the chief ideologue behind the Carpatho-Rusyn movement."

—Tomasz Kosiek
"On Different Aspects of Identity"
Ukraïntsi i narody tsentral'no-skhidnoï Ievropy
(Uzhhorod, 2015), p. 343

"The enormous genocidal-like forced migration connected with World War II was followed immediately by a no less tremendous multiple process of flight and expulsion of populations. A few years ago the Canadian historian of eastern Europe Paul Robert Magocsi has, in his exemplary *Historical Atlas of Central Europe*, made a courageous effort to depict cartographically these phenomena in a map with the euphemistic title, "Population Movements, 1944-1948.""

—Stefan Troebst
"From Kokoschka via Magocsi to Modigliani"
Dekonstruieren und doch erzählen: polinische und andere Geschichten
(Göttingen, 2015), p. 311

"The name Magocsi is inseparably associated with the Rusyn national revival of the late nineteenth and early twentieth centuries in which the academic scholar has taken a direct part. . . . In that sense, we see the phenomenon of a scholar who, as a researcher of nationalism, has had a practical impact on the status and development of the contemporary Carpatho-Rusyn identity."

—Mikhail Dronov
Slavianskii al'manakh (Moscow)
No. 1-2 (2015), p. 466

"To a significant degree the success of the Dukla [Ukrainian Song and Dance Ensemble in the United States in 1971] was the result of exceptional promotional work. This included the publication of a beautiful program booklet filled with fall-color photographs . . . and a substantive history of Rusyns and Ukrainians in Czechoslovakia. The materials for this *Souvenir Program* were prepared by the past and present friend of Rusyns, Dr. Paul R. Magocsi, [then] of Harvard University. . . . One must emphasize here that the success of the Dukla Ensemble in Canada and the United States as well as the general awareness abroad of our Rusyn homeland is due largely to Professor Magocsi."

—Andrii Hnat
"My Years of Experience with Our Culture"
Info Rusyn (Prešov, Slovakia)
Vol. XIII, No 1-2 (2016), pp. 12-13

"When speaking of the general international context, the main 'guru' of Rusynism these days is the professor at the University of Toronto, the ever agile Paul Robert Magocsi. Many of us [Vojvodinian Rusyns] know him through his book, the representative survey of Rusynism, *Narod niodkadz* (The People from Nowhere)."

—Miron Džunja
"Strawberry Fields Forever"
Ruske slovo u shvetse, Vol. XI, No. 19, in *Ruske slovo* (Novi Sad)
Vol. LXXII, No. 31 (2016), p. 20

"I know Paul Robert Magocsi (b. 1945) since the late 1960s when he was a graduate student on a visit to the Ukrainian Research Center [at Šafárik University in Prešov]. He is a highly qualified specialist in the history of the East Slavs, especially in the history of Ukraine. . . . He is the author of numerous monographs. . . . which have been positively received in scholarly circles in Ukraine. . . . In short, he is recognized by the historical profession in Ukraine.

"No specialist in Carpathian Studies can avoid making use of his *Encyclopedia of the History and Culture of Carpatho-Rusyns* . . . , and this includes those who do not agree with his views on the nationality of Rusyns-Ukrainians.

"On several occasions in the press I have mentioned that I consider P. R. Magocsi an outstanding historian, even if I disagree with his theory regarding the existence of Rusyns as a fourth East Slavic people.

This does not, however, impede us from maintaining mutual scholarly relations which are advantageous to both of us."

—Mykola Mushynka
U vsiakoho svoia dolia: rozmova Iaroslava Shurkaly z Mykoloiu Mushynkoiu
(Prešov, 2016), pp. 250-252

"The manipulation and artificiality that characterizes the process of creating the 'Rusyn' [language] becomes evident in the name of the language and people in question. For this new Slavic people P. R. Magocsi has not chosen a new name, but instead he gives preference to the older ethnonym *Rusyn*, which, as is well known, was used not only by the inhabitants of historic Transcarpathia but also of other Ukrainian lands until the 18th and early 20th centuries. . . . In a manipulatory fashion Magocsi provides [this name] with the meaning of a distinct ethnic marker."

—Liubomyr and Les' Belei
"Rusyn Studies as a Form of Anti-Ukrainian Technology"
Naukovyi zbirnyk Muzeiu ukraïns'koï kultury (Svidník)
Vol. 28 (2016), p. 46

"Magocsi has devoted his life not only to scholarship, but also to Rusyn national activism, the latter task being particularly arduous, as formerly the Soviet and today Ukrainian authorities have not been welcoming of the idea. . . . His lifelong commitment to the weaker side is worthy of admiration, even if one has doubts concerning the chances of his project."

—Stanislav Holubec
Hungarian Historical Review
Vol V, No. 3 (2016), p. 42

"It was at the International Congress of Ukrainianists in Chernivtsi in the fall of 2002 that I first heard a rather unorthodox lecture by the Ukrainian-Canadian historian P. R. Magocsi. . . . Dealing with theoretical and methodological principles, the lecture was an eye-opener for scholars engaged in the current Ukrainian academic discussions. In short, P. R. Magocsi presented to our researchers something unknown to them until then: the concept of multiple loyalties versus mutually-exclusive identities as the key to explaining the complexities of the 19th century

national revival and, no less important, as a means to understand the
particular nature of the Ukrainian mentalité and national consciousness."
—Anatolii Filiniuk
Osvita, nauka, kul'tura na Podilli (Kamianets'-Podil's'kyi)
Vol. XXIII (2016), p. 429

"As is evident from our research, Ukrainian scholars in the humanities
who have actively engaged in discussions with the leading ideologist of
neo-Rusynism, P. R. Magocsi, have either not noticed or have ignored the
technological nature of his anti-Ukrainian doctrines, which have nothing
to do with scholarship, in particular linguistic, historical, ethnographic,
folkloric, and other data. . . . In response to the scholarly arguments
of Ukrainian scholars, neo-Rusyn ideologues respond by accusing
their opponents of being instruments of 'Soviet' totalitarian views that
supposedly are now combined with nationalistic convictions. Therefore,
P. R. Magocsi—the Western and impartial scholar—concludes that it
makes no sense to enter into discussion with representatives of Soviet
totalitarian scholarship."
—Liubomyr and Les' Belei
"Neo-Rusynism in the Context of Present Day Ukraine"
Stratehichni priorytety (Kyiv)
No. 1 [42] (2017), pp. 57-58

"Following the so-called recognition of the Rusyn nationality by the
Transcarpathian Regional Assembly in March 2007 there occurred
a new wave of technological steps to legitimize the so-called Rusyn
language. These steps took the form of the publication of dictionaries,
encyclopedias, and textbooks of Rusyn literature and the establishment of
Rusyn-language Sunday [extracurricular] schools. The initiator of these
activities has been P. R. Magocsi with the financial assistance of Steven
Chepa and Viktor Baloha as well as the support of the Transcarpathian
Regional Assembly and the Rusyns'ka Rodyna program on the regional
television station Tysa 1.
—Liubomyr and Les' Belei
"Neo-Rusynism in the Context of Present Day Ukraine"
Stratehichni priorytety (Kyiv)
No. 1 [42] (2017), p. 58

"The Transcarpathian neo-Rusyn movement is divided into a pro-Euroatlantic and a pro-Russian trend. To the first trend belong leaders connected with the World Council of Rusyns . . . and the Canadian-American scholar Paul Robert Magocsi of the Carpatho-Rusyn Research Center."

—Mykhailo Zan
"Neo-Rusynism in Transcarpathia as a Latent Factor and Disintegrative Threat to the Unity of the Ukrainian Ethnonational Space"
Stratehichni priorytety (Kyiv)
No. 1 [42] (2017), p. 69

"The [alleged] upcoming appearance in L'viv of the co-author [of the book *Jews and Ukrainians*] truly provoked surprise among L'viv civic circles. After all, Paul Magocsi is one of the ideologists of Transcarpathian separatism (so-called modern-day Rusynism). It is quite strange that the authorities of Ivan Franko National University of L'viv would invite such an odious person."

—Tetiana Mohinska
Forpost
6. VI. 2017

"Now in his later years Paul Robert Magocsi is at the height of his creativity and fame as a renowned historian.

"His scholarly interests are wide ranging. . . . Yet his works differ from the majority of his colleagues in Canada and other countries in that they present an innovative and unorthodox approach to research and the manner of presenting the history of various countries, including Ukraine, to which he has applied new ideas and methodological-conceptual principles that have undermined long held beliefs."

—L.V. Bazhenov
Visnyk Kamianets'-Podil's'koho natsional'noho universytetu: Istorychni nauky (Kamianets'-Podil's'kyi)
No. 10 (2017), pp. 9 and 11

"We have gotten used to [the Ukrainian journalist Oleksandr Havrosh] and how he and those like him have for years and years attacked names like Magocsi and Padiak, figures who on the international stage are closely tied to the Rusyn awakening. As 'public' figures these two are forced to be blackened by Rusynophobes whom they can only wave away dismissively but continue on with their own work."

—Petro Medvid'
"Breaking Out of the Depths"
InfoRusyn/Narodnŷ novynkŷ (Prešov)
Vol. XIX, No. 22 (2017), p. 12

"Taking note of various present-day scholarly monographs and books of conference proceedings dealing with the history of Carpathian Rus', with regard to those published outside of Ukraine, in virtually all of them Paul Robert Magocsi figures as their co-author or in which, at the very least, his works are cited over and over again. This indefatigable researcher, academic scholar, and civic activist has inspired numerous authors to reflect upon the following: in what way and to what degree his activity has contributed not only to an understanding of the past of Carpathian Rus', but also to the creation and support of a society whose inhabitants are known as the Carpatho-Rusyn nationality. . . .

"One may conclude, following the precepts of the renowned philosopher and sociologist Florian Znaniecki, that Magocsi should be considered a classic representative of an elite which, from a wide variety of regional artifacts, creates a national culture."

—Tomasz Stryjek
"A Central European First Nation?:
The Historical Past and Present of Carpathian Rus' according to Paul Robert Magocsi"
Kwartalnik Historyczny (Warsaw)
Vol. CXXIV, No. 4 (2017), pp. 773-774, 776

"The appearance in 2015 . . . of the fundamental work, *With Their Backs to the Mountains*, by the renowned Canadian historian and Slavist, university professor Paul Robert Magocsi, is the most outstanding event in the Rusyn world during the last decades. . . . The work is destined to become for the foreseeable future the basic source for all those who wish to study the history and culture of the indigenous population of Carpathian Rus'. . . .

"It is clearly no exaggeration to say that this book by Professor Magocsi is the most mature, profound, and professionally comprehensive work on the history of Carpathian Rus' and the Rusyns which is sure to warrant the attention not only of Slavs but of a much broader international audience."

—Kirill Shevchenko
Slavianskii al'manakh (Moscow)
No. 1-2 (2018), pp. 379 and 393

"Aside from P. Magocsi and P. Getsko there are today no other known Rusyn political activists. . . .

"Although P. Magocsi is described as a scholar, his activity clearly shows him to be a political activist who already many years ago shaped the direction of Rusynism; he is in effect one of the longest active figures in the new Rusyn movement both in Europe and in Ukraine. . . .

"There is no doubt that P. Magocsi is one of the realistic Rusyn political activists on the international scene, and until recently he was really the only one."

—"What is Political Rusynism Today?"
http://rusmatica.org/materials/politrusin.html
June 2018

"The ideologist of neo-Rusynism is the unfortunate Paul Magocsi. It is precisely he who put forth the theory of a 'fourth East Slavic nationality'. He has raised money in the United States and Canada for the development of the neo-Rusyn movement. Every year he travels to Ukraine where he presents his books. In other words a person, who is the leader of Transcarpathian separatism and who for decades has worked for the disintegration of the Ukrainian nation, freely moves about our country and propagates his ideas! He should have long ago been declared *persona non grata*. Already in the early 1990s, Ukrainian civic activists tried to prohibit his entry into Ukraine, but that did not happen. Instead he continues his destructive work."

—Oleksandr Havrosh
"Transcarpathia is One of Ukraine's Weak Links
and That's Why Our Enemies are Fighting Over It."
Vysokyi zamok (Uzhhorod)
04. 07. 2018

"Professor Paul Robert Magocsi . . . is the doyen of Carpatho-Rusyn Studies on the planet and absolutely, by far, the most prolific scholar

dealing with things Rusyn—and things Ukrainian. . . . He is accused
of inventing Carpatho-Rusyns. . . . Because Professor Magocsi doesn't
support either the Russian or Ukrainian cause he . . . has been accused of
being in the pay of foreign powers, working for various secret services
or, plain and simple being a failed researcher.

"Strangely enough, Professor Magocsi is supported by a good sized
cadre of academically trained scholars both here and abroad."

—Paul Best
Karpatska Rus' (Higganum, Conn.)
Vol. LXXXIX, No. 4 (2018), p. 21

"Imperialist and revanchist forces in the Soviet Union/Russia, Hungary,
and Czechoslovakia did everything in their power to create in historical
Transcarpathia a neo-Rusyn movement, whose ideologue became the
Canadian historian Paul Robert Magocsi. One can only guess at the
reason for this unexpected choice of the ideologue of present-day neo-
Rusynism. Perhaps an important factor was that P. R. Magocsi appeared
in the circles of American Sovietologists after the appearance in 1978
of his monograph, *The Shaping of a National Identity: Subcarpathian
Rus', 1848-1948*, which was directed at the disintegration of the Soviet
Union. One should also not dismiss the view that there is no basis to the
accusation that P. R. Magocsi cooperated with the security services of
the Soviet Union and [Communist] Czechoslovakia. In any case, during
the 1990s P. R. Magocsi was amazingly effective in creating neo-Rusyn
organizations in the Transcarpathian oblast of Soviet Ukraine as well as
in eastern Slovakia, Hungary, and Yugoslavia (Serbia)."

—Liubomyr Belei
"A Critique of the Technology of Carpathian Nation Creation"
Nove zhyttia (Prešov)
27. IV. 2018, p. 4

"I knew the University of Toronto professor Robert Magocsi going back
to the mid-1960s, when he was still a graduate student [doing research
in Czechoslovakia]. I even was supposed to be the *starosta* at his
wedding to the dancer from the Dukla Ukrainian Dance Ensemble Maria
Chuvan. . . . In the 1970s I was a frequent contributor to his journal, the
Carpatho-Rusyn American. . . . Later we became estranged because of

our [differing] views about the nationality question in Transcarpathia. Nevertheless, my relations with him did not end."
—Mykola Mushynka
Zibrani tvory/Collected Works, Vol. I
(Prešov, 2018), p. 129

"In 1989, after the fall of the Communist regime in Czechoslovakia, the people got greater possibilities for self-identity. . . . Thanks to a campaign by civic activists, in particular the Canadian historian of Rusyn-Hungarian origin Paul Robert Magocsi, gradually more and more people identified themselves as Rusyns. Today [in Slovakia] their number has officially reached more than 35,000."
—Anton Semyzhenko
"A People Without Roots"
Lokol'na istoriia (L'viv)
No. 3 [5] (2019), p. 76

"The main person who initiated the international summer school of Carpatho-Rusyn Studies was Professor Paul Robert Magocsi who proposed the name Studium Carpato-Ruthenorum."
—Mikhala Holubkova
Rusyn (Prešov)
Vol. XXX, No. 4 (2019), p. 8

"American and Canadian scholars look at the [language] question [in Galicia] from the concept of multiculturalism and the study of the phenomenon of ethnic borderlands.

"This approach is represented by the renowned specialist in Rusynism and the history of Slavic peoples, the Canadian historian Paul Robert Magocsi. Contemporary Ukrainian and Russian scholars have adopted in their work the schema proposed by him [Magocsi] of dividing the participants in the nineteenth-century language debates in Galicia into 'traditionalists' and 'modernists'."
—B.P. Savchuk and G.V. Bilavich
"The Alphabet War in Galicia (1830s-1850s) in Present-Day Scholarly Discourse"
Rusin (Chişinău, Moldava)
Vol. LVI (2019), p. 71

"Looking at how historical topics about Carpatho-Rusyns [have been treated in the Russian media 2010-2019], the most thorough accounts are those put forth by the eminent American-Canadian historian of Rusyn ancestry, Paul Robert Magocsi."

—M.V. Podrezov and A.V. Goldovskaia
"The Rusyn Question in the Russian Media Agenda (2010-2019)"
Rusin (Chişinău, Moldova)
Vol. LVIII (2019), p. 298

"We could . . . wonder whether Magocsi's contributions to Ukrainian scholarship are a gesture to court sympathy for the Carpatho-Rusyn cause? Or a shield to defend himself as a de facto Carpatho-Rusyn nation-builder against attacks that he is anti-Ukrainian? Or even as a reserve of intellectual capital that he could 'cash in' for scholarly recognition of Carpatho-Rusyns? . . .

"The attempt to make sense of the tension between what would seem to be the multicultural liberalism of *A History of Ukraine: The Land and Its Peoples* or his recently co-authored *Jews and Ukrainians: A Millennium of Coexistence* and the national-patriotic conservatism of *With their Backs to the Mountains* all too often transforms these studies into commodities within an economic transaction or, at worst, characters within a Faustian bargain taking place in the soul of its author: in exchange for promoting Ukrainian culture, Magocsi receives the power of a Carpatho-Rusyn nation-builder. Thus, formulations like 'the Magocsi problem' or 'the Magocsi paradox' are bound to reduce the existence or non-existence of Carpatho-Rusyns or Carpathian Rus' to an epiphenomenon of a single individual, a formulation which ignores the right of the hundreds of thousands of individuals who identify as Carpatho-Rusyns to have a history of their own.

"Thus, let us view the book [*With Their Backs to the Mountains*] as a deliberately provocative text, one that openly invites its readers to question its premises, something like the first musical phrase in a call and response."

—Nicholas K. Kupensky
"Tensions and Triumphs in the First History of Carpathian Rus' and Carpatho-Rusyns"
Nationalities Papers (New York and Cambridge, Eng.)
Vol. XLVII, No. 3 (2019), pp. 508-509

"Paul Robert Magocsi has been a familiar name ringing in my academic ears for more than three decades. . . . In the early 1980s . . . he was already speaking of a distinct society, a term that has a peculiar Canadian ring to it. In other words, a distinct society which had the potential to achieve the status of belonging to a particular nation or to an ethnic group that might form one (or even more) political nations. . . .

"Professor Magocsi has been unjustly censured for actively transforming sets of collected myths into historical facts and groupings of diverse dialects into a fully-codified Rusyn language, as if everything he has done runs counter to what has also often been carried out by the national patriotic schools of Russia, Ukraine and so forth."

—Harvey Goldblatt
Nationalities Papers (New York and Cambridge, Eng.)
Vol. XLVII, No. 3 (2019), pp. 512-513

"I should note my appreciation for Magocsi's promotion of Carpatho-Rusyn identity. I would even bolster his assertion that Carpathian Rus' is both 'real and imagined' by suggesting that precisely it is and has been imagined for so long—and not as a delusion but as a grounded aspiration—[therefore] it is real.

". . . certainly the most enduring religious, theological, and ethical dimension of Magocsi's book [*With Their Backs to the Mountains*] is its honesty. Every time that one begins to sense the author may be veering in the direction of partisan scholarship, he returns to the path of objectivity and fairness. An impressive feat indeed! This is typical of Magocsi—a Rusyn who has done more for the Ukrainian cause than many Ukrainian organizations. May you live long enough, Bob, to see your honesty fully reciprocated!"

—Peter Galadza
"An Historic History"
Nationalities Papers (New York and Cambridge, Eng.)
Vol. XLVII, No. 3 (2019), pp. 520 and 522

"Freedom to create and scholarly objectivity are the essence of Magocsi's academic credo, and this is reflected in the degree to which he is not subject to the dictates of an ideology. . . . [He] has systematically written about all the regions of Carpathian Rus'. . . . It is in this sense that Magocsi stands alone. He simply has no competitors."

—Valerii Padiak
Nationalities Papers (New York and Cambridge, Eng.)
Vol. XLVII, No. 3 (2019), p. 524

"Paul Robert Magocsi. . . . has on numerous occasions visited my institution [Max Planck Institute] in Halle, Germany and played the role of 'historian-in-residence' in a community of social anthropologists. . . .

"We have always disagreed on some rather basic issues concerning ethnicity and what makes a nation or nationality. As I read his latest *magnum opus*, I conclude that we are destined to forever disagree.

"Having said that, let me stress how much I have learned from Magocsi's academic work, even before getting to know him in person. It is surely healthy in this day and age that differences of opinion on scholarly issues need not be an obstacle to collegiality and friendship. He remains for me the gold standard in all matters Rusyn and I cite him often.

—Chris Hann
"Threats to Regional Identity: From Atheist Communists to the Virgin Mary"
Nationalities Papers (New York and Cambridge, Eng.)
Vol. XLVII, No. 3 (2019), pp. 526-527

"Paul Robert Magocsi [is] a person eminently qualified as professor of history of many years at the University of Toronto (something which also gives him the necessary distance from the politics resonating in Europe today). Known as the author of a number of studies of the history of Ukraine and Central Europe . . . as well as a number of historical and geographical atlases, . . . his name alone offers the assurance of a work of excellence."

—Jiří Martínek
Journal of Historical Geography (London)
Vol. LXV (2019), p. 106

"One must say that while [the three versions of the *Let's Speak Rusyn* phrasebook] are scholarly publications, they are really designed to introduce to Carpatho-Rusyns living in the United States and Canada who do not speak the language of their ancestors some knowledge about their ethnic roots. This has symbolic importance, namely to convey to the descendants of Rusyns living abroad that the [Rusyn] language in its present-day codified form has the functional capacity to be used in various spheres of life. In our view this is what is the most significant value of [P. R. Magocsi's] phrasebooks."

—Gleb P. Pilipenko
Slavianskii al'manakh (Moscow)
No. 1-2 (2019), p. 539

"Professor Paul Robert Magocsi is one of the best-known historians of Ukraine in the world. . . . His *History of Ukraine: The Land and Its Peoples* is considered a true revolution in the history of Ukraine. . . . He both personifies and to a large degree has initiated a 'methodological revolution', by proposing a territorial and multicultural instead of the standard ethno-national approach to Ukrainian history."

—Stepan Sikora
"On the 75th Anniversary of the American Historian of Carpatho-Rusyn Background"
http://www.mukachevo.net/ua/blogs/view-post/1577
25. 01. 2020

"The name of Professor P. R. Magocsi will forever be linked to the birth of the Rusyn literary language and the recent Rusyn movement in general. This is a person who stood at the beginning of the scholarly approach to the . . . codification process. We are particularly grateful for his incalculable assistance in the present-day development of the language and in promoting it throughout the world. Although he is not a linguist, this wise man was aware—and still is—that the development and on-going existence of a people is not possible without its having a language. He has done and continues to do everything in his power for the good of the Rusyn people and their language. We hope that he will continue to do so."

—Vasyl' Iabur
"On the 25th Anniversary of the Rusyn Literary Language in Slovakia"
Rusyn (Prešov, Slovakia)
Vol. XXX, No. 1 (2020), p. 4

". . . the term 'Rusyn' was in use long before Professor Magocsi had written a word; thus, Rusyn was not his or any particular person's invention. . . . To claim that Magocsi invented the Rusyns is simply false."

—Paul Best
"The Other Shoe Drops" and "Commentary"
Karpatska Rus' (Higgunam, Conn.)
Vol. XC (New Series IV), No. 4 (2020), pp. 4 and 7-8

"It is difficult for me to imagine who else among historians/Ukrainianists in the second half of the twentieth century has provoked such violent or excessive emotions on the part of his irreconcilable opponents and his admiring fans as has Professor Magocsi. Like [the Ukrainian historian and civic activist Ivan] Lysiak-Rudnyts'kyi, Magocsi has continually existed 'between history and politics', although his ideal, without question, is to remain within the scholarly 'ivory tower'."

—Volodymyr Kravchenko
Krytyka (Kyiv, Ukraine)
Vol. XXIV, No. 1-2 (2020), p. 20

"Paul Robert Magocsi is the most productive historian of Ukraine in the West. Magocsi's *History of Ukraine* (1996, 2010) fully reflects the subsequent research carried out by Ukraine's Institute of National Memory when it was under the direction of Volodymyr Viatrovych. Does this mean that Magocsi is the same kind of 'nationalist' as is Viatrovych? Magocsi's history and the publications of the Institute of National Memory adopt an inclusive approach to history, giving attention to all ethnic groups who have ever lived on the territory of Ukraine. In 2014 Magocsi published one of the first histories of the Crimean Tatars to appear in the West. Soon after, during the presidency of Petro Poroshenko, the history of Crimean Tatars began to appear in the country's school textbooks."

—Taras Kuzio
"Neither Objective, or Liberal—Georgii Kasianov's New Book, *Past Continuous*"
Zbruch (L'viv ?)
20 May 2020
https://zbruc.eu/node/97770

"The late civil engineer Alexander Herenchak, long time [chairman] of the Lemko Association . . . would, at the beginning of each and every executive meeting, rant for 15 minutes . . . and get very agitated and would repeat and repeat that he had told 'Bob' (Professor Paul Robert Magocsi) at several Carpatho-Rusyn meetings . . . that 'we [Lemkos] are Russians' and that we spoke the 'Russian Lemko dialect'."

—Paul J. Best
"The Great Argument—Who are We?"
Karpatska Rus' (Higganum, Conn.)
Vol. XCI, No. 3 (2020), pp. 11-12

"Before 1993 [Uzhhorod University professor] Volodymyr Fenych, like all of us born in the Soviet Union, did not care much about one's ethnic identity. . . . But in 1993 Fenych read Paul Magocsi's book, *The Shaping of a National Identity*. . . . From that moment Fenych returned to the national identity of his paternal [Carpatho-Rusyn] forebears, which, he felt did not conflict with his sense of patriotism to Ukraine.

"In 2008, the honorary chairman P. R. Magocsi issued a public proclamation that distanced the World Congress from all forms of extremism within the Rusyn movement. And yet Ukrainians do not mention the views of Magocsi but rather those of [the pro-Russian Orthodox priest Dymytrii] Sydor and [self-designated leader Petro] Hetsko'.

"Not only in Transcarpathia, but also Rusyns living in other countries are Russophiles. . . . When Paul Magocsi meets with them he always asks: 'What is wrong with you and your crazy leanings toward Moscow?' But even his words have little influence. That's because he is up against tradition. And [Putin's] Moscow is exploiting that tradition."

—Andrii Taranenko
"The Rusyn Card
Or, How We Looked for the Hand of Moscow Among Separatists in Transcarpathia"
Ukraïns'ka pravda (Kyiv)
II. XI. 2020, pp. 10, 12, and 20-21

"Robert Magocsi called [my contact in Toronto, Professor] Maksym Tarnawsky in order to invite me to lunch. Maksym immediately and ironically quipped that Robert Magocsi was certainly going to try to recruit me into his Rusyn faith. Robert and I immediately agreed we would not talk about political matters, with the result that our conversation focused exclusively . . . on his unique Carpatho-Ruthenica collection. I was simply enthralled by his love of books about the history and culture of the Silver Land [Carpatho-Ruthenia/ Ukraine], but I saw in his character two people: a thoughtful historian; and a person whose image built on rumor [is that of a devil] with horns on his head."

—Vasyl' Gabor
Hold your Tongue: Occasional Notes from the Years 1977 to 2015 [15.IX.2012]
(L'viv, 2020), pp. 380-381

"Any reader of Paul Robert Magocsi's cartographic works can only admire and commend the efforts and scholarship of the author. . . . [whose] work has already been helpful to an entire generation of students of Central Europe. . .

"One could only wish that the region had more historians like Paul Robert Magocsi. . . ."

—Anton Kotenko
Harvard Ukrainian Studies (Cambridge, Mass.)
Vol.XXXVII, No. 1-2 (2020), pp. 225 and 228

"The phenomenon—not the paradox or 'problem of Magocsi'—lies in the fact that he has at the same time succeeded in continuing the work of Mykhailo Hrushevs'kyi [Ukraine's national historian] and in completing the work of Mykhailo Luchkai [the Carpatho-Rusyn national historian]. . . . Like Hrushevs'kyi and his Ukrainian followers, who wished to be a full-fledged distinct people with its own history, culture, and language and not a part of the Russian historical, cultural, and linguistic discourse, Paul Robert Magocsi with his Carpatho-Rusyn followers has, in the footsteps of Luchkai, inevitably created an analogous historical narrative for a distinct (both from Russian and from Ukrainian) Carpatho-Rusyn people."

—Volodymyr Fenych
Historian Nation-Builder: The Scholarly and Civic Activity of Paul Robert Magocsi
(Uzhhorod and Prešov, 2021)

"Paul Robert Magocsi is at present one of the most productive Ukrainianists and Carpatho-Rusynists—a publisher, bibliographer, cartographer, and a figure of broad encyclopedic knowledge. Moreover, he has been the organizer of a wide range of scholarly and educational bodies, international conferences, editor and compiler of various scholarly collected works, and editorial board member of leading academic journals. . . . In short, this energetic, productively creative, unstoppable, and truly exceptional *One-Man Institution* is someone about whom it is at the same time easy and most difficult to write about.

—Volodymyr Fenych
Historian Nation-Builder: The Scholarly and Civic Activity of Paul Robert Magocsi
(Uzhhorod and Prešov, 2021)

Subject Index

Numbers and letters in **bold** typeface refer to entries in the Bibliography sections. Roman and Arabic numbers refer to pages in the Front matter and in the section, Commentaries in Periodicals and the Media.

Abaúj/Abov county, 204
Academy of Sciences of Canada.
  See Royal Society of Canada
Africa, 183
Aleksander Dukhnovych Society
  (Prešov), 185
Alekander Dukhnovych Theater
  (Prešov), **617, 714**; 185, 224-225
Almashii, Mykhailo/Mykhayl, **617, 714**
Alsace, xxiv
Amazon, 183
America, 206, 222, 260
American Association for the
  Advancement of Slavic Studies
  (AAASS), 232, 247
American Association for the Study
  of Hungarian History, xix
American Carpatho-Russian
  Orthodox Greek Catholic Church,
  144, 582, 617, 714
American Indians, 245
Amerikansky russky viestnyk
  (newspaper), **145, 582, 617, 714**
Anti-Semitism, **859**
Architectue: Carpatho-Rusyn, **32**;
  Ukrainian, **799, 800**
Armenians, **177**
Art: Carpatho-Rusyn, **32**; Ukrainian,
  799, 800
Ash, Timothy Garton, **539**
Assembly of Rusyn Intelligentsia
  (Uzhhorod), **613**

Austria, xxviii
Austria-Hungary, xxvii, xxviii
Autonomy: Carpatho-Rusyn, **288,
  582, 617, 710, 712, 714, 715, 722,
  778, 813**

Babota, Liubytsia/Babotová,
  L'ubica, **617, 714**
Babyn Iar, **796, 801, 802**
Bacha, Iurii/Bača, Juraj, **617, 714**;
  262
Bakhmetieff Archive, Columbia
  University, xiii
Balega, Iurii, 188
Baloha, Viktor, 266
Baludians'kyi, Mykhail, **53**
Banderites, 207, 223
Bazylovych, Ioannykii, **303**
Belgrade, 255
Belorussians, **70**; 258
Bereghy, Albert, 186
Best, Paul, J., **617, 714**
Bible, 226, 229
Bibliography: Carpatho-Rusyn, xiv,
  xx; **22, 27, 39, 52, 63, 87, 105,
  120, 123, 140, 154, 165, 185, 195,
  201, 227, 252, 399, 429, 458, 504,
  612, 636, 655, 703, 721, 738, 785**;
  Ukrainian, xvi, xvii, xx; **65, 108,
  129, 156, 187, 717**
Bicentennial, United States, **28**
Billington, James, xxiv
Bogatyrëv, Pëtr, **506**

Boikos, 243, 255
Bokshai, Emilian, 417
Boldyzhar, Mykhailo, 188
Bonkalo, Alexander/ Bonkáló,
   Sandor, 230, 582, 617, 714
Borsod county, 204
Bosnia-Hereogovina, 255
Bosnian Muslims, 517
Bratislava, 194, 200, 203, 206
Bretons, 403
Brodii, Andrei, 187, 190
Brooklyn Dodgers, xxiv
Budapest, xxviii; 203, 227
Bukovina, xxviii; 179
Byzantine Catholic World
   (newspaper), 146, 582, 617, 714

Canada, 136, 138, 202, 708; 178,
   181, 187, 189, 195, 206-209,
   215, 240, 246, 267, 273. See also
   Carpatho-Rusyns: in Canada;
   Ukrainians: in Canada
Carpathian Alliance (New York
   City), 168, 169
Carpathian Rus', 219, 225, 248-250,
   252, 255, 268, 272, 273
Carpatho-Rusyn American
   (magazine), xxii; 270
Carpatho-Russia, 167
Carpatho-Russians, 169, 249, 250
Carpatho-Rusyn Research Center,
   xxv; 114, 125, 143, 164, 196, 199,
   206, 221, 224, 226, 240, 250, 262,
   281, 284, 324, 368, 376, 489, 521,
   582, 602, 617, 714, 750; 172, 181,
   197, 208, 215, 222, 226, 250, 258,
   267
Carpatho-Rusyn Society
   (Pittsburgh), 617, 714, 857
Carpatho-Rusyns/Rusyns, xxi, xxiii-
   xxvii; 24, 42, 48, 82, 86, 152, 216,

228, 232, 233, 248, 249, 258, 264,
271, 275, 288, 290, 291, 294, 295,
298-301, 305, 306, 308-310, 312-
314, 318, 322, 323, 326, 327, 330,
332, 334, 338, 343, 346, 347, 353,
358, 362, 367, 385, 388-392, 396,
398, 407, 413, 415, 418, 420, 423,
428, 430, 439, 450, 451, 455, 460,
461, 463-465, 469, 474, 478, 483,
486, 492, 493, 495, 499, 501, 510,
515, 520, 522; 529-531, 533-536,
539, 541, 544-546, 552, 554-557,
559, 571, 572, 575, 576, 582-584,
589, 591, 592, 595, 599, 601, 604,
609, 617, 621, 624, 642, 644, 647,
652, 653, 666, 668, 672-675, 677,
685, 687, 689, 694, 696-698, 701,
705, 706, 710, 713-715, 720, 722,
723, 729-731, 737, 739, 740, 746,
754, 766, 767, 774, 784, 786, 790,
791, 806, 808, 820-824, 827, 830;
in Canada, 138, 202, 374, 518,
623, 708; in Czechoslovakia, see
below, Slovakia (Prešov Region);
in Hungary, 293, 561; 181, 198,
204, 220, 221; in Poland, see
Lemkos; in Romania, 865; 198,
204, 220, 231; in Serbia (Bachka,
Vojvodina), see Vojvodinian
Rusyns; in Slovakia (Prešov
Region), 17, 23, 25, 26, 100, 119,
220, 238, 279, 335, 341, 373,
410, 412, 443, 546, 577, 765,
776, 787, 847, 864; 185, 198; in
Ukraine (Subcarpathian Rus'/
Transcarpathia), 239, 242, 265,
289, 311, 325, 372, 490, 503, 505,
509, 511, 514, 528, 532, 549, 562,
597, 598, 613, 614, 659, 736; in
United States, 20, 27-30, 49, 55,
71, 102, 122, 133, 138, 144-148,

155, 175, 186, 209, 215, 217, 218, 244, 256, 261, 274, 285, 302, 339, 340, 361, 374, 401, 404, 480, 481, 543, 560, 623, 625, 629, 769, 844, 846; 171, 185, 197, 230, 245; in Yugoslavia, *see* Vojvodinian Rusyns. *See also* Art; Architecture; Bibliography; Congress of the Rusyn Language; Historiography; History; Language; Literature; Ukraine; World Academy of Rusyn Culture; World Congress of Rusyns
Carpatho-Ruthenia, 167, 253
Carpatho-Ukraine, 167, 168, 189
Cartography/Maps, xxi, xxvi-xxvii; **79, 109, 157, 342, 438, 492, 510, 533, 552, 559, 581, 616, 816, 847, 854**; 252, 278. *See also* Geography
Caves Monastery (Kyiv), 239
Cenko Prize in Ukrainian Bibliography, Harvard University, xx
Census, **177, 215, 319, 708, 829**; 177, 193, 238, 262
Chair of Ukrainian Studies (University of Toronto), xv, xviii, xx, xxv, xxvii, xxviii; **80, 84, 88, 89, 103, 180, 188, 189, 203, 447, 508, 839, 840**; 172-174, 176, 179, 190, 193, 196, 207, 226, 227, 247, 249, 251
Charles, Prince of Wales, **5**
Charles University, Prague, xiii
Chepa; Steven, **617, 714**; 266
Chmielnicki, Bogdan, *see* Khmelnyts'kyi, Bohdan
Chornock, Orestes, **163, 582, 617, 714**
Christianization of Rus', xxviii; **159, 193, 194**; 173

Church/Religion, **159, 192-193, 194, 211, 232, 290, 305, 330, 364, 444, 445, 453, 473, 481, 488, 494, 513, 527, 543, 593, 683, 748, 784, 799, 800, 810, 814, 822, 845.** *See also* Greek Catholics/Eastern Catholics; Mukachevo, Greek Catholic Eparchy; Orthodox Church; Prešov, Greek Catholic Eparchy of
Chuvan, Maria, 270
Cleveland, Ohio, **122**
Columbia University (New York City), xiii, 184
Congress of European Rusyns, 240
Congress of the Rusyn Language, **298, 316, 345, 520, 680, 789**
Communism/Communist party, 197, 202, 204, 216, 219, 232, 233, 235, 253, 254, 259, 261; in Czechoslovakia, 183, 270, 271; in the Soviet Union, 170, 189, 194; in Ukraine, 175, 187, 196, 213
Conquest, Robert, **176**
Coranič, Jaroslav, **811**
Cossacks, **8, 72**; 254
Cracow,
Crimea, **759-761, 831**;197
Crimean Tartars, **759-761, 831**; 276
Croats, 206
Cultural Society of Rusyns in Romania (Deva), **582, 617, 714, 864**
Czech Republic, 208
Czechoslovak Security Services (ŠtB), 191, 192, 195, 196, 213, 222, 253, 270
Czechoslovakia/Czecho-Slovakia, xiii, xxi, xxiv, xxvii; **6, 7, 17, 23, 24, 25-26, 119, 213, 217, 220, 242, 244, 261, 376, 382, 528,**

765, 776, 787, 817, 838; 187, 193, 204, 219, 236, 238, 270. *See also* Carpatho-Rusyns in Slovakia (Prešov Region)
Czechs, **582, 585, 596, 617, 714, 747, 817, 870**; 195, 200, 229

Deák, István, **149**
Debrecen, 176
Dee, Sandra, **81**
Demko, George J., **237**
De-ukrainianization. *See* Ukrainianization
Department of Ukrainian and Rusyn Studies (Nyíregyhaza), 206
Dnieper River, 214
Dobrians'kyi, Adol'f, **47**
Dovhovych, Vasyl', **128**
Dreisziger, Nandor, **276**
Duć-Fajfer, Helena/Duts'-Faifer, Olena, **617, 714, 871**; 224
Dukhnovych, Aleksander, **43, 582, 617, 714, 866**; 171, 176
Dukhnovych Society. *See* Aleksander Dukhnovych Society
Dukhnovych Theater. *See* Aleksander Dukhnovych Theater
Dukla Ukrainian Song and Dance Ensemble, 263-264, 270
Dyrud, Keith P., **381**
Dzhumba, Jerry, *see* Jumba, Jerry
Dziubai, Alexander, **147, 153, 582, 617, 714**

Eastern Catholic Life (newspaper), **148**
Eastern Catholics, **73, 810**. *See also* Greek Catholics
Emblem: Carpatho-Rusyn, **171**
Encyclopedia of Canada's Peoples, xxi, xxiv, xxvii; **516**

Encyclopedia of National Cultures in Slovakia, 203, 235
Encyclopedia of Rusyn History and Culture, xxvii; **617, 714**; 257, 264
Encyclopedia of Ukraine, 207
European Union, 218, 242, 249

Faessler, Peter, **475**
Farmer, Kenneth C., **135**
Faust, 272
Fedynyshynets', Volodymyr, **444, 476**; 182
Fekula, Paul M., xxviii
Fentsyk, Stepan, 187
Fenych, Volodymyr, **876**; 277
Firtsak, Gheorghe, **865**; 231
Flags: Carpatho-Rusyn, **171**
France, xxiv
Frank, Alison Fleig, **664**
Franko, Ivan, **168**; 172
Friesel, Evyatar, **349**
Frisians, xvi; **74**

Gajdoš, Marián, **617, 714, 741**
Galicia, xvi-xvii, xxvi; **36, 41, 45, 65, 83, 107, 108, 127, 129-130, 131, 234, 260, 272, 287, 377, 578, 579, 631, 632, 717**; 179, 188, 195, 214, 248, 252, 271
Galicia: A Historical Survey and Bibliographic Guide, xviii, xx, xxv; **129**
Gellner, Ernest, 212, 215, 237
Genesis, Book of, 259
Geography: Carpathian Rus', **44, 398, 499, 582, 609, 617, 624, 685, 714**. *See also* Cartography/Maps
Germans/Shvabs, **617, 714, 747**
Germany, xxiv, xxviii
Getsko/Hetsko, Petro, 269, 277
Gorazd, Andrij Timkovič. *See*

Timkovič, Andrij
Gorbachev, Mikhail, 182, 194, 227
Gorlice, Poland,
Grabar, Igor, **95**
Grabowicz, George,
Great Famine/Holodomor in
 Ukraine, **176**
Greek Catholic Church. *See* Church/
 Religion; Mukachevo, Greek
 Catholic Eparchy of; Pittsburgh,
 Greek Catholic Metropolia of;
 Prešov, Greek Catholic Eparchy of
Greek Catholic Union (Butler,
 Pennsylvania), **617, 714**; 212
Greek Catholics/Eastern Catholics,
 73, 683, 748, 810; 203
Grendzha-Dons'kyi, Vasyl', **115**
Guiness Book of World Records, 205
Gypsies/Roma, **617, 714, 747**; 228

Habsburgs, House of, **260, 287, 448,
 582, 617, 714**
Halasz, Mary, **548**
Halle an der Saale, Germany, 274
Hamm, Michael F., **383**
Hann, Chris/Christopher M., 211, 228
Hannan, Kevin, **496**
Hanulya, Joseph P., **158, 198, 582,
 617, 707, 714**
Haraida, Ivan, **454**
Haraksim, L'udovít, **617, 714**
*Harvard Encyclopedia of American
 Ethnic Groups*, xvi, xviii, xix,
 xxv; **70-77**
Harvard Ukrainian Research
 Institute, xviii, xxv; 169, 173, 190,
 196
Harvard University, xviii, xxv; **39**;
 167, 169, 172, 237, 264
Hattinger, Gabriel, **617, 714**; 204
Havel, Václav, **224**; 193

Havrosh, Oleksandr, 267
Hebrew language, 197
Herbenick, Raymond, **482**
Herenchak, Alexander, 276
Hetsko, Petro. *See* Getsko, Petro
Himka, John-Paul, **558**
Hirka, Bishop Ján, **221, 226**
*Historical Atlas of [East] Central
 Europe*, xxi, xxvii; **342, 581, 848**;
 198, 230, 232, 253, 263
Historiography, **605, 615, 627, 634,
 719, 727, 734, 807**; Carpatho-
 Rusyn, **22, 31, 93, 94, 110, 191,
 197, 205, 243, 315, 331, 536, 582,
 590, 617, 663, 690, 692, 714, 716,
 771, 783, 788, 808, 825, 835, 852,
 860, 862**; 278; Ukrainian, **83, 96,
 108, 129, 210, 257, 753, 841**; 252,
 262, 275, 277-278
History: Carpatho-Rusyn, **15, 32, 42,
 48, 100, 119, 372, 373, 418, 514,
 532, 533, 536, 577, 582, 595, 601,
 604, 609, 617, 621, 623, 639-640,
 641, 652, 653, 666, 685, 697, 698,
 714, 765, 766, 774, 776, 778, 790,
 806, 813, 817, 838, 853, 869, 870**;
 Ukrainian, **8, 34, 38, 96-99, 127,
 130, 157, 176, 210, 211, 234, 257,
 260, 272, 287, 337, 377, 447, 448,
 452, 508, 578, 579, 629, 631, 632,
 654, 661, 681, 718, 733, 735, 759-
 761, 786, 793, 799-802, 804, 809,
 816-818, 832, 838, 844**; 172
*History of Ukraine: The Land and
 Its Peoples*, xxvi; **718**; 207, 209,
 211, 213, 243, 244, 248, 251, 252,
 254, 256, 258, 261, 272, 275, 276
Hodinka, Antal, **321**
Hollywood, 239
Holodomor. *See* Great Famine in
 Ukraine

Homin Ukraïny (newspaper), 174-175
Horbal, Bogdan, **617, 711, 714**
Hořec, Jaromír, 186
Hranchak, Ivan, 188
Hrushevs'kyi, Mykhailo, 179, 238, 278
Hryniuk, Stella, **269**
Hungarian Kingdom, 228
Hungarians/Magyars, xxiv; **242, 265, 416, 441, 582, 617, 714, 747;** 200 201, 260
Hungary, **291**; 192, 204, 206, 210, 221, 223, 227, 229, 231, 244, 259, 270. *See also* Carpatho-Rusyns: in Hungary
Hutsuls, 243, 255

Iabur, Vasyl', **582, 617, 714, 803, 805, 812**
Illyés, Elemér, **273**
Immigration/Ethnic Studies, **177, 319, 371, 516, 580, 619, 742, 795, 797**
Institute of National Memory (Kyïv), 276
Institute of Rusyn Language and Culture (Prešov University), **850**
International Congress of Ukrainianists, 176, 178, 265
International Slavonic Academy (Kyiv), xxv
Iron Curtain, 260
Irshava, Ukraine, 195

Jabur, Vasil', *see* Iabur, Vasyl'
Jacyk, Peter/Petro, xxviii; **120**
Jagiellonian University (Cracow), 205
Janissaries, 203
Jason, Sonya, **688**
Jews, **8, 369, 582, 617, 631, 649, 662, 665, 700, 714, 747, 772, 773,** **796, 799, 800, 807, 827, 833, 859;** 205, 213, 214
Jews and Ukrainians; **799, 800**; 267, 272
John-Paul II, Pope, **136**
Jumba, Jerry, **582, 617, 707, 714**

Kachkovs'kyi Society, **272, 582, 617, 714**
Kann, Robert A., **118**
Karabelesh, Andrei, **121**
Karlowich, Robert A., **547**
Karpachova, Nina, 239
Kashubes, 228
Kasinec, Edward, **617, 714**; 176
Kennedy, Michael D., **570**
Kerensky, Alexander, **405**
KGB, 181, 187, 188, 192, 193, 196, 213, 270
Khmelnyts'kyi, Bohdan, **8, 626**
Khymynets', Iuliian, **150**
Kiev. *See* Kyiv/Kyïv
Kliuchevskii, Vasilii, 210
Kocisko, Stephen J., **262, 284, 582, 617, 714**
Kohanik, Peter, **707,**
Kolesar, Iuliian, **178, 304, 582, 617, 714**
Komlóska, Hungary, 204
Konečný, Stanislav, **617, 714, 741**
Koriatovych, Fedor, **104**
Kostel'nyk, Havriil, **172**
Kosyk, Wolodymyr, **236**
Kovach, Fedir, **617, 714**
Koval, Viktor, 259
Kozik, Jan, **229**
Krafcik, Patricia A., **582, 617, 714, 858**; 176
Krainiak, Frantishek/Krajňak, František, **617, 714**
Kralyts'kyi, Anatolii, **106, 582, 617,**

714

Krämer, Julius, **101**
Kravchuk, Leonid, 220
Krushko, Shtefan, **582, 617, 714, 741**
Krynica, Poland, 211
Krytyka (journal), 243
Kryvs'kyi, Ivan, 188
Kubek, Emilii A., **124, 582, 617, 684, 714, 875**
Kuchma, Leonid, 235
Kuras, Ivan, 239
Kuzmiak, Petro, **582, 617, 714, 863**
Kyiv/Kyïv, xxix; **16, 137, 141, 796**; 178, 200, 215, 221, 239
Kyivan Rus', 243

Ladizhyn'skyi, Shtefan, **582, 617, 714, 864**
Lajos Kossuth University, Debrecen, xiii
Language: Carpatho-Rusyn/Rusyn, **32, 33, 37, 46, 54, 56, 64, 82, 132, 152, 233, 264, 298, 316, 317, 345, 350, 384, 386, 393-394, 395, 400, 408, 414, 419, 421, 422, 432, 434-437, 440, 442, 520, 586, 608, 610, 611, 625, 637, 638, 646, 648, 669, 670, 680, 709, 781, 803, 805, 812, 815, 826, 837, 843, 849**; 167, 200, 220, 222, 224, 226, 231, 235-236, 248, 253, 261, 265, 266, 273, 274-275; Ukrainian, **36, 41, 45, 107, 131, 745, 799, 800**; 170, 222, 248; Vojvodinian Rusyn, **487**
Latin, xxix; **643, 772**
Latta, Vasyl', **617, 714, 873**
Legnica, Poland, 212, 224
Lemko Association/Lemko Soiuz,
Lemko Association/Stovaryshŷnia Lemkiv, 212, 224

Lemko Region, xxi; 178, 202, 248
Lemkos/Lemko Rusyns, **179, 235, 247, 344, 670, 837**; 178, 181, 190, 198, 201, 202, 211, 212, 217, 219, 220, 224, 229, 233, 234, 242, 243, 255, 258, 277; in Canada, 186
Let's Speak Rusyn, xix; **33, 64, 487, 781, 815**; 167, 274
Levine, Joseph, 2
Levyts'kyi, Ivan E., **65, 717**
Liber, George O., **375**
Library of Congress, xxiv; **491**
Liebich, André, **446**
Literature: Carpatho-Rusyn, **32, 49, 82, 169, 233, 411, 459, 568**
Little, David, **379**
Losten, Basil H., **305**
Luchkai, Mykhail Pop-, **166, 582, 617, 714**; 277
Luciuk, Lubomyr, **269**
Luckyj, George, **167**
Luczkiw, John, xxviii
Ludanyi, Andrew, **276**
Lukianenko, Levko, **352**
Luxembourg, xxii; **1, 5, 6, 50, 366**
Luxembourgers, xvi ; **75, 91**
L'viv, xxix ; 248, 267
Lysiak-Rudnyts'kyi, Ivan, 276

Macedonians, **319, 370**
Machievelli, 173
Magocsiana/Magocsi-izm, xvii; 191, 258
Magyarone, 236, 243
Magyars. *See* Hungarians/Magyars
Mahler, Raphael, **204**
Maltese, xvi, 76
Mandych, Olena Shinali, **445**
Maps. *See* Cartography/Maps
Markovych, Pavlo, **182, 582, 617, 714**

Markus, Vasyl', **94, 110, 582, 617, 714**; 171
Marton, Mykhailo, 240
Marx, Karl, 200
Masaryk, Tomás G., , 238
Masica, Peter V., , 167
Masons, 179
Matsyns'kyi, Ivan, **183, 582, 617, 714**
Max Planck Institute for Social Anthropology (Halle), 274
Maxwell, Robert, **214**; 205
May, Karl, 245
Mayer, Maria, **484, 485, 582, 617, 714**
Mazeppa, Ivan, 223
Mečiar, Vladimír, 235
Medzilaborce, Slovakia, 192, 259
Meshkov, Iurii, 197
Messiah, 182, 199
Mihalik, Peter, 167
Mikhlukho-Maklai, Nikolai, 201
Millennium of Christianity in Rus'. *See* Christianization of Rus'
Monaco/Monégasques, xxii; **208, 280, 512**
Moscow, 185, 200, 203, 227, 240, 247, 277
Moscow Patriarchate. *See* Russian Orthodox Church
Moses, 222
Mosný, Peter, **663**
Motyl, Alexander J., **117**; 251
Múcsony, Hungary, 204
Mukachevo, **665, 676**; 206
Mukachevo, Greek Catholic Eparchy of, **444-445, 446, 453, 473, 488, 494, 513, 527, 582, 617, 714**
Multicultural Historical Society of Ontario (Toronto), xviii-xxv; **181, 277, 286, 357**; 196, 227

Muscophiles/Muscophilism. *See* Russophiles/Russophilism
Museum of Modern Art (Medzilaborce), **281**
Museum of Ukrainian Culture (Svidník), **617, 714**; 185
Mushynka, Mykola, **617, 714**
Music, **134, 151, 582, 617, 714, 799, 800, 834**
Myshanych, Oleksa, 189

Narodnŷ novynkŷ (newspaper), 239
Nation-state, **263, 354, 365**; 218
National Inquirer (tabloid), 193
Neo-Rusynism, 181, 244, 245, 255, 258-259, 266, 267, 269, 270. *See also* Rusynism
Neverlý, Mikuláš, 223
New Jersey, xiii, xxiv
New York Times, xiv
Nod', Nikola/ Nagy, Nikolaj, **222, 617, 714**
Novi Sad, 255
Novyny Zakarpattia (newspaper), 185
Nyíregyháza, Hungary, 206

Of the Making of Nationalities There is No End, xx; **535, 536**; 228, 254
Old Ruthenianism/Old Ruthenians, xvii, xix; **127, 582, 617, 714**
Omel'chenko, O., 239
Ontario, **136, 202**
Organization of Rusyns in Hungary (Budapest), **561, 582, 617, 714**; 204
Orlai, Ivan S., **170**
Orthodox Church/Orthodoxy, **232, 748, 810, 814**; 171, 203, 223
Ottawa, 181
Our People: Carpatho-Rusyns and Their Descendants in North

America, xvi-xvii, xx; **138**; 175,
198
Padiak, Valerii, **582**, **617**, **627**, **679**,
695, **714**, **856**; 267
Papuga, Djura, **240**
Passaic, New Jersey, xxviii
Pavlovych, Aleksander, **92**
Pawliczko, Ann Lencyk, **507**
Pekar, Athanasius B. **296**, **582**, **617**,
714
The People from Nowhere, **641**; 239,
264
Perestroika, 194, 227
Periwal, Sukmar, 228
Perth Amboy, New Jersey, 198
Petrov, Aleksei L., **466**, **497**, **498**,
500, **582**, **617**, **714**
Pittsburgh, Greek Catholic
Metropolia of, 193
Plishkova, Anna, **582**, **617**, **648**,
702-704, **714**, **764**
Pochaïv, xxix
Poland, xxi, xxvii ; **235**; 175, 178,
192, 204, 205, 208, 211, 214, 217,
219, 220, 222, 224, 231, 254, 258.
See also Lemkos
Poles, **235**; 200, 258
Polish Academy of Sciences, 211
Polish Institute for the Study of
National Minorities, 205
Political Rusynism, **617**, **714**; 184,
187, 195-198, 204-208, 227, 229,
230, 236, 238, 244-246, 259, 260,
262, 269
Polynesia, 201
Poroshenko, Petro, 276
Potichnyj, Peter J., **448**
Polynesia, 201
Prague, xxv; **13**; 185, 194, 203, 227
Prague Spring (1968), xxix; **7**
Prešov, 176, 192, 203

Prešov, Greek Catholic Eparchy of,
593, **582**, **617**, **714**; 260
Prešov, Greek Catholic Teachers
College, **617**, **714**
Prešov Region, **238**, **335**, **582**, **617**,
714, **781**; 183, 185, 201, 207,
222, 227, 231. *See also* Carpatho-
Rusyns: in Slovakia
Prešov University, 256-257
Princeton University, xiii, xvii, xxiv
Pritsak, Omeljan, xxv; **242**; 174, 190
Proctor, Vermont, **20**, **155**
Protestanism, **784**, **822**
Provisional Government of
Subcarpathian Rus', 206, 221, 245
Pugh, Stefan M., **757**; 247-248
Puskás, Julianna, **297**
Putin, Vladimir, 277

Rakovs'kyi, Ivan, **268**
Ramach, Ianko, **617**, **714**
Ramach, Mykhailo, 256
Reagan, Ronald, 239
Redemptorists, 260
Reichlin, 197
Reinfuss, Roman, 220
Religion. *See* Church/Religion
Renaissance Carpatho-Russian
Student Society—Vozrozhdenie
(Prague), **617**, **714**, **872**
Renoff, Richard, 176
Reszler, André, **446**
Revay, Julian I., **58**; 168, 189
Revolution of 1989, **216**, **223**, **232**;
241, **251**, **255**, **266**, **270**, **291**, **323**,
362, **397**, **433**, **468**; 222
Roma. *See* Gypsies/Roma
Roman, Stephen B., **200**
Romania, 231, 240. *See also*
Carpatho-Rusyns: in Romania
Rome, xxviii; 259-260

Rosocha/Rosokha, Stepan, **126**, **173**
Rovt, Aleks, **728**
Royal Society of Canada/Academy
of Sciences of Canada (Ottawa),
xxx; 224, 240, 244
Rudé krávo (tabloid), 191, 193
RUKH, 239
Rusinia, 187, 236, 247, 259
Rusinko, Elaine, **380**
Ruski Kerestur, Serbia, 234
Rusnaks, 167, 169, 189, 199
Russia, xxix; **162**; 242, 244, 270,
273
Russian Orthodox Church—
Moscow Patriarchate, 172
Russians, xvi; **582**, **617**, **714**, **747**;
167, 169, 194, 213, 223, 229, 248,
258, 277; in the United States **77**,
177, **207**, **402**, **406**, **770**
Russophiles (Muscophiles)/
Russophilism, xvii, xix; **112**, **127**,
582, **617**, **714**; 194, 198, 224, 250,
259, 267, 277
Rusyn Cultural Foundation/Ruska
Matka (Ruski Kerestur), **617**, **714**;
234
Rusyn language. *See* Language:
Rusyn
Rusyn Renaissance Society in
Slovakia (Prešov), **378**, **582**, **617**,
714; 185, 192, 203, 222, 223
Rusyn Scholarly and Enlightenment
Society (Uzhhorod), **490**
Rusyn separatism, 181, 194, 199,
203, 267, 269
Rusyn Sunday School Program
(Transcarpathia), 241, 266
Rusynism, 176, 181, 182, 184-187,
190, 195, 202, 206, 208, 213,
222, 224-228, 231, 234, 238, 244,
245, 254, 261-264, 267, 269, 277.

See also Neo-Rusynism; Political
Rusynism
Rusyns. *See* Carpatho-Rusyns
Rusyns-Ukrainians, 178, 183, 192,
199, 203, 205, 236, 250, 264
Rutgers University, xiii
Ruthenes/Ruthenians, 167-168, 199,
201, 237
Ruthenia, 237

Saint Petersburg, Russia, 200
Šafárik University (Prešov), 264
SBU. *See* Ukrainian Security
Service,
Secretariat of Christian Unity (The
Vatican), 173
Sembratovyč, Josyf, **329**
Serbia, **650**; 220, 255, 256, 270
Shandor, Vincent, **564**, **582**, **617**,
714
Shaping of a National Identity, The,
xiv, xvix, xxiv; **42**; 168-171, 226,
229, 247, 270, 277
Sheptyts'kyi, Andrei, xx; **211**, **732**;
173, 174, 252
Shevchenko, Taras, 214
Shevelov, George, 184
Shtets', Mykola, **14**, **582**, **617**, **714**
Sighet, Romania, 240
Sigismund of Luxembourg, **50**, **366**
Silesia, 170-171
Sirka, Iosyf, 188
Slovak Academy of Sciences
(Bratislava), 203, 235
Slovak League of America, 235
Slovakia, xv, xxiv; **100**, **119**, **220**,
394, **435**, **574**, **600**, **765**, **776**, **787**;
175, 194, 201, 203, 205, 208, 219,
220, 222, 227, 231, 236, 244, 254,
257, 259, 260, 262, 270. *See also*
Carpatho-Rusyns: in Slovakia

(Prešov Region); Czechoslovakia
Slovaks, **217**, **261**, **336**, **528**, **582**,
617, **714**, **747**; 195, 200, 223, 235
Šmigel, Michal, **741**
Smiian, Petro K., **18**
Society of Carpatho-Rusyns in
Transcarpathia (Uzhhorod), **289**,
582, **617**, **714**, **874**; 183, 199
Society of Fellows, Harvard
University, xiii, xviii, xxv
Society of Friends of Subcarpathian
Rus' (Prague), **617**, **714**; 185
Soim/Parliament of Subcarpathian
Rusyns, 245
Sopinka, John, **225**
Sopoliga, Miroslav/Sopolyga,
Myroslav, **617**, **714**
Soviet Embassy: Canada, 175, 181
Soviet people, 180
Soviet Ukraine, 215, 270
Soviet Union, xxiv; **6**, **260**, **287**;194,
204, 221, 227, 232, 237, 247, 270.
See also Transcarpathia
Stalin, Iosif, 182
ŠtB. *See* Czechoslovak Security
Services
Stefan, Augustine, **90**, **173**
Stercho, Peter G., **184**, **582**, **617**, **714**
Stolarik, M. Mark, **775**
Struk, Danylo, 207
Studium Carpato-Ruthenorum
International Summer School
(Prešov University), 271
Subcarpathian Rus', **10**, **22**, **31**, **32**,
42, **416**, **582**, **617**, **662**, **663**, **665**,
710, **712**, **714**, **715**, **722**, **747**, **778**,
815, **817**; 172, 175, 179, 193, 207.
See also Transcarpathia
Subcarpathian Rusyns. *See*
Carpatho-Rusyns
Subcarpathian Ruthenia, 237

Subtelny, Orest, **449**; 212
Sugar, Peter, xxi; 253
Sukhŷi, Shtefan/Suchý, Štefan, **617**,
714
Suny, Ronald Grigur, **570**
Suslov, Mikhail, 185
Svaliava, Ukraine 206
Švorc, Peter, **582**, **617**, **663**, **714**
Sydor, Dymytrii, **617**, **714**; 277
Sysak, Myron, **467**
Szlonzaks/Silesians, 228

Takach, Basil, **161**, **582**, **617**, **714**
Tamash, Iuliian/Tamaš, Julijan, **617**,
714
Tarnawsky, Maksym, 277
Taylor, William, 242
Thomas, Brandon, **4**
Timkovič, Andrij (Gorazd), 259-260
Timkovič, Iosafat, 260
Tito/Josef Broz, 234
Tkach, Joseph W., **231**
Tomchanii, Mykhailo, **226**, **457**
Toronto, Ontario, 202, 215, 238
Toth, Alexis G., **142**, **356**, **582**, **617**,
714
Transcarpathia, xxviii; **239**, **416**,
441, **549**, **554**, **556**, **571**, **582**, **585**,
596, **601**, **617**, **635**, **649**, **659**, **714**;
169, 177, 181, 186-188, 192, 197-
199, 204-206, 210, 211, 213, 220,
224, 225, 228, 230, 231, 236, 243-
247, 249, 254, 258, 261, 265, 270,
271, 277. *See also* Subcarpathian
Rus'
Transcarpathian Regional Assembly/
Oblasna rada (Uzhhorod), 187,
237, 240, 241, 258, 266
Transcarpathian State
Administration, 241
Treadgold, Donald, xxi; 253

Turianytsia, Ivan M., **617**, **714**; 206
Turkey, **836**
Turok-Hetesh, Vasyl', **582**, **617**, **633**, **714**; 194, 203
Tyvodar, Mykhailo, 227

Ucrainica at the University of Toronto Library, xvii, xxviii; **156**
Udovenko, Hennadii, 239
Udvari, István, **617**, **714**; 206
Uhro-Rusyns, 169, 228, 249, 250
Ukraine, xxi, xxiii, xxv, xvii; **34, 38, 99, 157, 355, 364, 452, 455, 569, 594, 651, 654, 661, 672-674, 718, 733, 735, 758, 762, 763, 772, 779, 780, 793, 823, 824, 832, 836, 842, 859**; 183, 192, 194, 196, 200, 203, 204, 207, 213, 219, 220, 221, 225, 227, 230, 231, 235, 238, 240, 243, 244, 249, 252, 256, 259, 262, 264, 273-277. *See also* Carpatho-Rusyns: in Ukraine; Galicia
Ukraine: A Historical Atlas, xix, xxvii; 174
Ukraine: An Illustrated History, 252, 261
Ukrainian Catholic University (L'viv), 231
Ukrainian Institute (New York City), 189
Ukrainian National Theater (Prešov), 185, 203
Ukrainian Research Center (Prešov), 264
Ukrainian Research Institute. *See* Harvard Ukrainian Research Institute
Ukrainian Security Service (SBU), 240, 241
Ukrainian Students Club (University of Toronto), 193

Ukrainianization, 183, 193, 199, 203, 236
Ukrainians, **98**, **260**, **430**, **448**; 172-174, 176, 177, 186, 190, 195, 197, 198, 208 209, 219, 224, 227, 228, 252, 258; in Canada, xxviii; **134**; 172, 201; in Czechoslovakia, 17; 186, 193; in Poland, **235**; in Slovakia, 201, 203, 227, 231, 235; in Subcarpathian Rus'/ Transcarpathia, **582**, **617**, **714**, **747**, **818**; 169, 197, 229; in Ukraine; **799**, **800**; in the United States, xvi; **34**, **40**, **59-61**, **78**, **102**, **219**; 171, 189; in Yugoslavia, 194, 255. *See also* Architecture: Ukrainian; Art: Ukrainian; Historiography: Ukrainian; History: Ukrainian; Language: Ukrainian
Ukrainophiles/Ukrainianism, 186, 193, 194, 201, 223, 224, 229, 241, 259
Union of Lemkos in Poland (Gorlice), 211
Union of Rusyns-Ukrainians in Slovakia (Prešov), 259
Unionville, Ontario **136**
United Nations, 206, 239
United States, **28**, **40**, **59**, **102**, **138**, **209**; 178, 179, 181, 195, 196, 203, 215, 217, 224. *See also* Carpatho-Rusyns: in the United States; Ukrainians: in the United States
United States State Department, 242
University of Budapest, 190
University of Chernivtsi, 254
University of Copenhagen, 217
University of L'viv, Ivan Franko, 267
University of Poznań, 205

University of Toronto, xv; 172, 182, 186, 190-195, 199, 201, 202, 206, 211, 214, 223, 226, 227, 299, 254, 256, 260, 270
University of Warsaw, 233
University of Wrocław, 205
Ustinov, Peter, **162**
Uzhhorod, 180, 184, 200, 206, 220, 238, 247, 277
Uzhhorod State/National University, 181, 277

Vanat, Ivan, **617, 714**; 260
Vaňko, Juraj, **542, 582, 617, 714, 866**
Vatican, The, 173, 203
Veličko, Alexander, **240**
Velvet Revolution (Czechoslovakia), 238
Venelin-Hutsa, Iurii, **113**
Vermont, **20, 155**
Viatrovych, Volodymyr, 276
Vico, Fedor, **282, 566, 567, 582, 607, 617, 714**
Vienna, xxv, xxviii; **83**
Vojvodina, **617, 714**; 234
Vojvodinian Rusyns, **21, 35, 190, 320**; 175, 194, 198, 212, 264
Voloshyn, Avgustyn, **51**
Vozrozhdenie. *See* Renaissance Carpatho-Russian Student Society

Wales, **5**
Warhol, Andy, **67, 213, 283, 482, 563, 582, 617, 645, 714, 861**;
Warhol Museum of Modern Art (Medzilaborce), 180
Warsaw, 233
Warsaw Bloc, 177
Weller, Catherine Roberts, **582, 617, 714**

Wells, H.G., 199
Willebrands, Jan Cardinal, 173
With Their Backs to the Mountains: A History of Carpathian Rus' and Carpatho-Rusyns, **790, 806**; 268, 272, 273
World Academy of Rusyn Culture, **686**
World Congress/Council of Rusyns, **258, 409, 431, 462, 472, 479, 523-526, 565, 573, 582, 587, 617, 622, 628, 630, 656, 657-660, 671, 699, 714, 724-726, 750-752**; 180, 192, 204, 208, 211, 218, 221, 224, 237, 240, 241, 243, 245, 246, 249, 258, 259, 267, 277
World Federation of Ukrainian Lemko Organizations, 248
Wynar, Bohdan S., **307**
Wytrzens, Günther, **222**

Yugoslavia, **21, 35**; 181, 192, 198, 204, 224, 234, 270. *See also* Vojvodinian Rusyns
Yurcisin, John, **582, 617, 714**

Zapletal, Florian, **111**
Zaporozhian Cossacks, xxiv. *See also* Cossacks
Zarechnak, Dimitry, **212**
Zarechnak, Michael, 183, 186
Zhatkovych, Gregory I., **62, 582, 617, 714, 869, 877**; 238
Zhupan, Ievhenii, **456**
Zilyns'kyi, Orest, 207
Znaniecki, Florian, 268
Zobl, Engelbert, **139**
Zobl, Hertha A., 139
Zozuliak, Alexander, **224, 582, 617, 714, 743**

Personal Name Index (Authors, Commentators, Editors, Interviewers, Reviewers, and Translators)

Numbers and letters in **bold** typeface refer to entries in the Bibliography sections. Roman and Arabic numbers refer to pages in the Front matter and in the section, Commentaries in Periodicals and the Media.

AP, see Pilátová, Agáta
A.P., see Plishkova, Anna
A. Ka., see Kappeler, Andreas
A.S.Sh., see Sheptyts'kyi, Andrei
A.Z., see Zozuliak, Aleksander
Adamovych, Serhii, **TTa**
Adamski, Łukasz, **654**
Abramson, Henry, **665**; **AAA, JJJ**; 215
Alexander, J.M., **342**
Almashii, Mykhailo/Mykhayl, **372**, **617**; **714**; 245
Alvarez, Manuel B. García, **42**
Amato, Anthony J., **484**
Anderson, Alan B., **516**
Andrejčákova, Jarmila, 181
Andriewsky, Olga A., **713**
Anghelescu, Hermina G.B., **342**
Antalyk, Ivan, 201
Arel, Dominique, **734**; **YY**; 252
Arens, Meinorf, 233
Ash, Timothy Garton, **539**
Ashley, Leonard R. N., **579**
Arzhevitin, Stanislav, 168
Aydar, Ferit Burak, **831**
Aycock, Wendell M., **49**
Azzolina, D.S., **848**

B.K., **176**

Babota, Liubytsia/Babotová, Ľubica, **312, 376, 380, 390, 408, 437, 483, 511, 617, 714; EEE**; 257
Bach, Kim, **502**
Bacha, Iurai/Bača, Juraj, 203, 205
Bahan, Oleh, **LL**; 242, 243
Bakke, Elizabeth, **578**
Balabushevych, T.A., 157
Balcar, Miroslav, **532, 585, 592**
Balega/Baleha, Iurii, **DD**; 177, 185, 188, 249
Baludians'kyi, Mykhail, 53
Ban, D. András, **266**
Baran, Alexander, **119**
Barber, Tony, **342**
Bardyn, Ihor, **JJJ**
Barkan, Eliott Robert, **516, 563**
Barr, Brenton M., 157
Bartov, Omer, **746**
Basarab, Maria, **583**
Batsman, Marina, **799**
Bazhenov, L.V., **733**; 267
Bazylovych, Ioannykii, **303**
Belei, Les, **608**; 265, 266
Belei, Liubomyr, **608, 640, 652**; 253, 265, 266, 270
Belitser, Natalya, 222
Beller, Steven, **619, 665**
Belok, Michael V., **42**

Ben-Shlomo, Zev, **342**
Berendt, Ivan T., **581**
Berentsen, William H., **342**
Besier, Gerhard, **696**
Best, Paul J., **42**, **438**, **617**, **706**, **714**, **790**, **816**, **839**; 270, 276
Bihl, Wolfdieter, **42**, **129**, **156**, **157**, **195**
Bilak, Gaby, **809**
Bilak, Youry, **809**
Bilavich, G.V., 271
Bilenky/Bilenkyi, Serhii, **640**, **654**, **661**, **682**, **722**, **735**, **786**, **840**
Biletska, Yuliya, **759**
Bilocerkowycz, Jaro, **579**
Binder, Harold, **631**
Biondich, Mark, **619**
Bird, Thomas E., 259
Birnbaum, Henrik, **132**
Bister, Feliks J., **111**
Black, Jeremy, **Q**
Blanke, Richard, **108**
Blanutsa, Andrei, **786**
Bliakhars'kyi, Zynovii, 190
Bogatyrёv, Pёtr, **506**
Bohachevsky-Chomiak, Martha, **138**, **211**, **654**
Bokshai, Emilian, **417**
Boliubash, Volodymyr, **179**
Bonkáló, Alexander, **230**, **582**, **617**, **714**
Borisenok, Elena Iu., **733**, **735**; 261
Borisz, János, **427**
Borzęcki, Jerzy, **581**
Botík, Ján, **666**
Boxwall, James, **342**
Brězan, Simon, **177**
Browne, Wayles, **33**
Bryk, M.V., **168**
Budurowycz, Bohdan, xiii-xvii; **B**
Buchhofer, Ekkehard, **577**

Buckwalter, Donald W., **342**
Bulkina, Inna, **840**
Bunža, Bohomír, **244**
Burg, A., **119**
Burkut, Ihor, **42**, **714**; **NN**, **TT**; 247, 250, 254
Burns, Virginia M., **127**
Bytsko, Mykhal, **209**; 245

Calvi, Luca, **372**, **377**; 212
Caprio, S., **738**
Caps, Val'ter, 177
Carey, Stephen, **269**; 202
Carlson, Keith Thor, **580**
Carlton, T. R., **435**
Carynnyk, Marco, **89**, **241**, **257**
Časlavka, Jan, **390**
Čehulić, Lidija, **342**
Charles, Prince of Wales, **5**
Chelak, Ivan, **DDD**
Chepa, Steven, **674**
Cherepania, Bogdan, **635**
Chernigovstsev, Mikhail, 242
Chilaru, Elvira, **653**
Chirovsky, Andriy, **617**
Chodkiewicz, Andrzej, **235**
Chološnjaj-Matjijov, Michail, **111**
Choma, Vasiľ, *see* Khoma, Vasyľ
Chornock, Orestes, **163**, **582**, **617**, **714**
Chornovil, Viacheslav, 213
Chorváthová, Ľubica, **138**, **195**, **209**
Chrétien, Jean, 207
Christa, Boris, **197**
Chuchka, Pavlo P., 197, 200
Chvany, Catherine V., **435**
Chyrkov, Oleh, **760**
Clarke, Angus, **342**
Clemens, Walter C. Jr., **157**
Čobejová, Eva, 249
Cohen, Gary B., **108**
Cohn, Henry S., **661**

Comeau, Pauline, **516**
Cone, Edward B., **342, 581**
Conquest, Robert, **176**
Cook, Bernard A., **571**
Coranič, Jaroslav, **748, 776, 811**
Cordasco, Francesco, **218**
Cornis-Pope, Marcel, **606**
Crawley, Devin, **516**
Crowe, David M., **801**
Csáky, Pál, **574, 600**
Cśaszári, Eva, **813**
Cummins, George, **542**
Custer, Richard D., **581, 624**

Dabrowski, Patrice, M., **582**
Danta, Darrick, **342**
Danylenko, Andrii, **702, 781, 815,
    837**
Danziger, Edmund J. Jr., **580**
Dashkevych, Iaroslav, 253
Datsei, Vasyl'/Dacej, Vasil', 236
Davidzon, Vlad, **799**
Davies, Norman, 253
Dawson, Andrew, **342**
Daycock, Davis, **661**
Deák, István, **149, 548**
Debreczyn, Paul, **127**
Dee, Sandra, **81**
Demetria, Sr. M., **209**
Demko, George J., **237, 342**
Diakun, Nadia Odette, **156**
Diamond, Norma, **358**
Dickason, Olive Patricia, **580**
Dickie, Iain, **342**
Diuk, Nadia, **108**
Dmitriev, M. V., **452**
Dobrians'kyi, Adol'f, **47**
Doležalová, Antonie, **870**
Dombrovs'kyi, Oleksander, **159**
Donski, Michal, 178
Dovhei, Vasyl', 188

Dovhovych, Vasyl', **128**
Dragan, M.J., **194**
Dranichak, Julianna, 172
Dreisziger, Nandor F., **276, 374**
Dronov, Mikhail, **711**; SSS; 263
Duć-Fajfer, Helena/Duts-Faifer,
    Olena, **428, 615, 617, 670, 714,
    722, 737, 739, 853, 860, 869, 871**;
    KKK
Dudash, Natalia, **411, 459**
DuFeu, V.M., **132**
Dukhnovych, Aleksander, **43, 380,
    582, 617, 714**
Dulichenko, Alexander D., **500, 617,
    643, 646, 843**
Duplak, Mykola, 190
Dupont-Melnyczenko, Jean-Bernard,
    452
Durkot, Iurii, **723, 786**
Dushnyk, Walter, **96, 97, 98, 99**
Duts'-Faifer, Olena, *see* Duć-Fajfer,
    Helena
Dyczok, Marta, **452**
Dyrud, Keith P., **129, 341, 790**
Dyvnych, Vadym, **248**
Dziubai, Alexander, **147, 153, 582,
    617, 714, 806**
Džunja, Miron, 264

E. Hö., *see* Hösch, Edgar
Eddy, Eva, **748, 806, 858**
Ehnberg, Mårten, **842**
Einax, Rayk, **631**
Eisenstadt, Peter, **629**
Eley, Geoff, **42**
Ellison, Herbert J., **578**
Ember, Melvin, **480**
Eperessy, Ernő, **450**
Epp, George K., **157**
Ernő, Marton Gellért, **718**

Faessler, Peter, **475**
Faktor, Viktor, **553**
Farmer, Kenneth C., **135**
Fedaka, Serhii, **328**
Fedorovych, Mykhailo, *see* Rebet,
  Andreas
Fedynyshynets', Mykhailo, **477**,
  515, **562**, **584**, **701**
Fedynyshynets', Vladymyr/
  Volodymyr/ Fedinisinec,
  Volodimir, **248**, **438**, **444**, **452**,
  476, **582**; **K**; 180, 188, 189, 199,
  201
Fedyshyn, Oleh S., **119**
Feisa, Mikhailo, **360**, **487**, **559**, **685**,
  697
Felak, James R., **578**
Fenych, Volodymyr, **800**, **875**, **878**;
  QQ; 245, 278
Fiedler, W., **33**
Fielder, Grace E., **435**
Filiniuk, Anatolii M., **TTTa**; 266
Filippenko, Yana, **525**
Firtsak, Georghe/Firczak, Iulius,
  751, **865**
Fischer-Galati, Stephen, **42**
Fishman, Joshua A., **306**; 196
Fizer, Ivan/John, 183
Flynn, James T., **211**
Forostyna, Oksana, **800**
Frank, Alison Fleig, **631**, **664**
Frank, Andre Gunder, **342**
Franko, Ivan, **168**
Fras, Janina, 213
French, R.A., **157**
Fried, Alexander, **42**
Friedl, Jiří, **711**
Friedrich, Paul, **358**
Friesel, Evyatar, **349**
Frinta, Mojmír S., **111**
Frucht, Richard, **555**

Fulford, Robert, **516**

Gabor, Vasyl', 277
Gajdoš, Marian, **483**
Gajecky, George, **22**, **24**
Gal, Francisc, **783**
Gal, Lev, 205
Galadza, Peter, **452**, **631**, **732**, **790**;
  JJJ, **YYY**; 211, 273
Galens, Judy, **401**
Galloway, Julian, **456**
Galos, Adam, **108**
Gardner, Laura, **582**
Gąsowski, Tomasz, **631**
Gasparov, Boris, **330**
Gazdag, Vilmos, **797**
Gecse, Géza, **310**
Gegal'chii, Alexandr, 249, 250
Geissbühler, Simon, **799**
Geistlinger, Michael, **759**
Gelfand, Janet E., **207**
Gerrits, A.W.M., **342**
Gibson, Catherine, **795**
Glazier, Michael, **481**
Glisson, Peg, **581**
Goehrke, Carsten, **157**
Golczewski, Frank, **579**
Goldblatt, Harvey, **131**, **790**; **YYY**;
  273
Goldovskaia, A.V., 272
Goliat, Roman S., **129**
Good, David F., **287**
Görner, Franz, **568**
Górny, Grzegorz, 199
Gottsman, Andreas, **452**
Govlia, Anita, **697**
Grabar, Igor, **95**
Grabowicz, George G./Hrabovych,
  Hryhorii, **654**, **734**, **792**; **WW**;
  251
Grabowski, Jan, **580**

295

Graff, Sharon M., **516**
Grau, Conrad, 42
Gregorovich, Andrew, **42, 111, 119,
129, 157, 342, 351, 661**
Grendzha-Dons'kyi, Vasyl', **115**
Grod, Paul, 193
Grodziski, Stanisław, **129**
Gula, Nestor, **452**
Gulovich, Maria, **688**
Günaysu, Ekin, **759**
Gustavsson, Sven, **646**
Guthier, Steven L., 42
Gyidel, Ernst, **617, 654, 733, 790,
816**

H.D.D., **211**
H.R., **342**
Hainyk, Ivan, **33**
Halas, Borys, 187
Halasz, Mary, **548**
Halczak, Bohdan, 255, 259
Haleika, Ia., **70**
Halemba, Agnieszka, **790**; 263, 264
Halenko, Oleksandr, **654, 760**
Hamilton, Geoff, **580**
Hamm, Michael F., **383, 452**
Hamuliak, Ivan Ia., 172
Handlin, Oscar, **138**
Hann, Christopher M., **535, 631,
691, 790; J, S, YYY**; 202, 216,
217, 221, 237, 274
Hannan, Kevin, **496, 621**; 171
Hansen, Henrietta, **138**
Hanulya, Joseph P., **158, 198, 582,
617, 707, 714**
Haraida, Ivan, **454**
Haraksim, Ľudovít, **42, 342, 435,
617, 714**
Harasymiw, Bohdan, **59**
Härtel, Hans-Joachim, **111**
Häusler, Wolfgang, **129**

Hausmann, G., **631**
Havel, Václav, **224**
Havrosh, Oleksandr, **640, 654**; 246,
262, 269
Hebden, Ralph, **342**
Heineman, P. E., **661, 718**
Heppner, Harald, **342**
Herbenick, Raymond, **482**
Herbut, Djura, **31**
Herod, Charles C., **108**
Heuberger, Valeria, **364**
Heydenkorn, Benedykt, **129, 138,
211, 260**
Hill, John S., **342**
Himka, John-Paul, xviii-xxiii; **42,
119, 342, 558, 661, 740, 790; V,
YYY**; 212, 219, 232
Hirik, Serhii, **714, 790, 800, 848**
Hirka, Bishop Ján, **221, 226**
Hitchins, Keith, **42**
Hladnik, Mira, **350**
Hnat, Andrii, 264
Hocking, Barbara Ann, **580**
Hodinka, Antal, **321**
Hoerder, Dirk, **186**
Holiat, Roman S., **138, 211**
Holubec, Stanislav, **790**; 265
Holubkova, Mikhala, 271
Horak, Stephen M., **129**
Horbal, Bogdan, **341, 617, 693, 711,
714; X, II, JJ**; 233
Hordyns'kyi, Sviatoslav, **111**
Horčaková, Václava, **GG**
Hořec, Jaromír, **488**;
Hösch, Edgar, **342**
Hoshko, Iurii, 187
Hoshovs'ka, K., **452**
Hostyniak, Stepan, 192, 194, 203
Howard, Susan V., **342**
hr, *see* Ľudovít Haraksim
Hrachova, Sofiia, **654, 733**

Hrabovych, Hryhorii; *see*
  Grabowicz, George G.
Hroch, Miroslav, **870**
Hrushevs'kyi, Mykhailo S., **96**
Hrynevych, Vladyslav, **801**, **802**
Hryniuk, Stella, **129**, **211**, **269**
Hrytsak, Iaroslav, **377**, **452**
Hrytsyshchuk, Tetiana, **659**
Hudak, Gabrijela, **391**
Hudchenko, Z., **111**
Huk, Bohdan, 248
Hunczak, Taras, **631**, **661**
Hundert, Gershon David, **676**
Hurst, Michael, **108**
Hvat, Ivan, 256
Hvozda, Ivan, **235**
Hyidel', Ernest, *see* Gyidel', Ernst

I.Ia., *see* Iatskanyn, Ivan
Iabur, Vasyl'/Jabur, Vasil', **582**, **603**,
  617, **714**, **803**, **805**, **812**; 261, 275
Iadlovs'kyi, Iaroslav, **439**
Ias', O.V., **733**
Iatskanyn, Ivan, **415**; 187, 204
Iavornyts'ka, Stefaniia, 224
Ibler, Reinhard, **542**
Ibryamova, Nouray A., **536**
Il'chenko, Larysa, **655**, **785**
Illyés, Elemér, **273**
Il'nyts'ka, Luiza I., **717**
Ingrao, Charles W., **342**; 218
Iuryk, I., **372**
Iusova, Natalia, **640**, **652**
Ivanchenko, Raïsa, 197
Ivchenko, Anatolii, 186
Ïvha, Mrs., 182
Izady, Mehrdad, **342**; 198

Jabur, Vasil', *see* Iabur, Vasyl'
Jacková, Božena, **501**, **528**
Jackson, Kenneth T., **403**

Jacobs, A., **111**
Jacyk, Peter, **120**; 174
Jagiełło, Michał, 219
Jakešová, Elena, **261**, **263**, **373**, **516**,
  528
Jakubčionis, Algirdas, **342**
Jančář, Josef, **111**
Jason, Philip K., **799**
Jason, Sonja, **688**
Jawornicka, Aleksandra, 229
Jelinek, Yeshayahu, **617**, **665**
Jersild, Austin, **535**, **536**
Jiřičková, Hana, **662**
Jobst, Kerstin S., **435**, **504**, **579**, **582**,
  661
John-Paul II, Pope, **136**
Johnson, Daniel, **342**
Johnson, D. Barton, **582**
Johnson, Owen V., **42**, **119**
Johnston, Robert E., 195
Jordan, Neil, **342**
Jordan, Peter, **554**, **601**
Julius, Annette, **334**
Jumba, Jerry, **582**, **617**, **707**, **714**
Jurijčuk, J., **452**
Juščak, Peter, 180

Kachurovs'kyi, Vasyl', 168
Kalyniak, Ian, 261
Kamenïtski, Iuliian, 212
Kamusella, Tomasz, **504**, **535**, **536**,
  795; 229, 254
Kandler, H., **342**
Kanet, Roger E., **536**, **581**
Kann, Robert A., **118**
Kappeler, Andreas [A.Ka], **108**, **120**,
  452, **554**, **720**, **723**
Kapral', Mikhail, **435**
Karabelesh, Andrei, **121**
Karas', Hanna, **OOO**
Karavans'kyi, Sviatoslav, 231

Kardashinets', Imre, **560**
Karger, A., **374**
Karlowich, Robert A., **195**, **547**
Karmacsi, Zoltán, **797**
Karychak, Iaroslav, 206
Kasianova, Alla, **535**, **536**
Kasinec, Edward, **120**, **547**; 176
Katsaveiko. *See* Sirs'kyi, Vasyl'
Keleher, Serge R., **138**, **342**
Kelly, T. Mills, **435**
Kemin', Mykhailo, 209
Kennedy, Michael D., **570**
Kercha, Igor, **372**, **640**
Kerensky, Alexander, **405**
Kessler, Wolfgang, **88**, **182**
Khmel'nyts'kyi, Bohdan, **626**
Khmil', Ivan S., **42**; 170
Khoma, Vasyl', **582**; **W**; 225
Khomova, Mariia, **582**
Khorunzha, Tetiana, **652**
Khymynets', Iuliian, **150**; 181, 188, 190
Kiebuzinski, Ksenya, v-ix, xxiv-xxv; **ZZ**
Kimball, Stanley B., **119**
King, Francis, **848**
Kipel, Vitaut, **138**, **156**
Kiraly, Béla K., **42**
Kirschbaum, Joseph M., **119**, **138**
Kirschbaum, Stanislav J., **535**, **536**
Kis', Oksana, **855**
Kiss, Judit/Kishshova, Iudita, **478**, **557**
Kiunnap, A., **643**
Klein-Pejsová, Rebekah, **661**
Klemenčić, Mladen, **342**, **601**, **698**
Kletke, Kristen, **759**
Klid, Bohdan, **579**
Klippenstein, Lawrence, **342**
Kloss, Heinz, **54**
Knoll, Paul W., **341**, **790**

Knysh, George, **452**; 210
Kobal', Iosyp, 237
Kočík, René, **582**
Kocisko, Stephen J., **262**, **284**, **582**, **617**, **714**
Kodýtek, Vilém, **582**
Kohanik, Peter/Kokhanyk, Petro, **707**
Kohut, Zenon E., **713**
Kolesar, Julian, **178**
Kolesnyk, Iryna, **PPP**
Koliesar, Havriïl/Koljesar, Gabriel, **264**; 175
Kollmann, Jack E., **111**
Kolodiichyk, Vasyl', 198
Komaryns'kyi, Volodymyr, **42**; 169
Konečný, Stanislav, **483**, **652**
Kononenko, Natalie, **506**
Konstantinovich, Stevan, **255**
Kopecký, Miroslav, **644**, **766**
Koporova, Kvetoslava, **642**, **687**, **705**, **715**, **849**; **OO**, **TTT**; 246
Kordan, Bohdan S., **138**
Koriatovych, Fedor, **104**
Koropenko, Iryna, **316**, **389**, **415**, **426**, **447**, **473**
Kosiek, Tomasz, 263
Kostel'nyk, Havriil, **172**
Kosyk, Wolodymyr, **236**
Kotenko, Anton, **816**, **848**, 278
Kovačević, I. Ch./Kovachevich, I.H., **285**, **391**
Kovach, Fedir, **617**, **714**; 179, 183, 236
Kovach, Mikhailo, **387**
Koval, Peter, **806**
Koval's'kyi, Mar"ian, **235**
Kovtun, Jiří, **42**
Kozik, Jan, 229
Koźmiński, Maciej, **42**
Krafcik, Patricia A., **195**, **582**, **602**, **617**, **702**, **714**, **858**; **II**, **III**; 176

Krainiak, Frantishek, **617**, **714**, **QQQ**
Krainiak, Petro, **806**
Krainiak, Peter, Jr., **246**
Krajcar, Jan, **129**
Kralyts'kyi, Anatolii, **106**, **582**, **617**, **714**
Krämer, Julius, **101**
Krantz, Charles K., **108**
Krasovs'kyi, Ivan, **235**; **DDD**; 186, 191, 242, 255
Kravchenko, Volodomyr, **840**, **841**
Kravchuk, Olesya, **773**
Kresin, Oleksandr, **654**
Krieps, Roger, **42**
Król, Marek, **832**
Krups'kyi, K., **17**
Krushko, Shtefan, **582**, **617**, **714**, **741**
Krysachenko, Valentyn, **760**
Kubek, Emilij A., **124**, **582**, **617**, **684**, **714**
Kubijovyč, Volodymyr, **144**, **198**
Kučmaš-Klemens, Amalija, **541**
Kuffel, Józef, **860**
Kul'chyts'kyi, Stanislav, **654**
Kulke, Christine, **581**
Kundrat, Iurii, **338**
Kupensky, Nicholas K., **790**; **YYY**; 272
Kuropas, Myron B., **49**
Kushko, Nadiya, **640**, **643**, **645**, **646**, **693**, **714**, **722**, **728**, **733**, **737**, **739**, **745**, **753**, **760**, **761**, **763**, **786**, **787**, **788**, **794**, **797**, **798**, **809**; **MMM**
Kusin, Vladimir I., **342**
Kuzio/Kuz'o, Taras, **452**, **579**, **667**, **734**; **UU**, **LLL**; 251
Kuz'ma, Hanna, 195
Kuzmiak, Petro, **582**, **617**, **714**, **863**
Kuzmiakova, Anna, **557**

Kuznetsov, S. N., **643**
Kwoka, Tomasz, **608**, **670**
Laas, Natalia, **641**
Labrecque, Paul, **157**
Lacko, Michael, **22**, **30**, **42**; 169, 171
Ladizhyns'kyi, Shtefan, **582**, **617**, **714**, **864**
Lane, Hugo, **484**, **497**, **535**, **536**, **579**, **631**; 226
Latiak, Diura, **220**, **235**
Latko, Ivan, **501**, **527**, **528**
Łatyszonek, Oleg, **207**
Lavrincová/Lavrintsova, Magdaléna, **806**; **UUU**
Lazăr, Liviu, **783**
Lazar, Natalya, **617**
Lee, John, **138**
Leeming, H. **542**
Lefel'dt, V., **643**
Leff, Carol Skalnik, **374**
Legvold, Robert, **452**
Lehman, Jeffrey, **401**
Lemak, Vasyl', 185, 239
Lencek, Rado L., **342**
Lesiów, Michał, **22**
Levine, Joseph, **2**
Levinson, David, **480**
Leviţchi, Ioan, **586**, **649**
Levyts'kyi, Ivan E., **65**, **717**
Levyts'kyi, Myroslav, **235**; 196
Liavynets, Antonii, **545**; **RRR**
Liavynets, Marianna, **595**; 240
Liavynets'-Uhryn, Marianna, **712**, **852**
Liber, George O., **375**, **579**
Liebel, Aaron, **799**
Liebich, André, **446**, **790**
Litera, Bohuslav, **342**
Little, David, **379**
Liu, *see* Medješi, Ljubomir
Longworth, Philip, **129**, **342**, **579**

Lopata, Pavlo, 190
Losten, Bishop Basil H., **290, 305**
Low, Murray, **342**
Lowig, Evan, **42, 56, 59, 111, 119, 129, 138, 211**; 171, 175
Luchkai, Mykhail Pop, **166, 582, 617, 714**
Luciuk, Lubomyr Y., **202, 269, 355, 681, 762; JJJ**
Luckyj, George S.N./Luts'kyi, Iurii, **167**; 207
Ludanyi, Andrew, **276**
Lukan, Walter, **554**
Lukashova, Svetlana S., **733, 735**; 261
Lukianenko, Levko, **352**
Lupul, Manoly, **H**
Luts'kyi, Iurii. *See* Luckyj, George S.N.
Luzina, Myroslava, **777**
Lyko, Ivan, **235**
Lysinova, Silvia, **677**; 240

M.B., *see* Bystko, Mykhal
M.T., *see* Tejchman, Miroslav
Macek, Josef, **366**
MacKenzie, David, **157**
Mačuu, Pavel, **26**
Mahieu, Stéphanie, **683**
Mahler, Raphael, **204**
Mahowald, Teresa Tickle, **374**
Mair, Victor H., **342, 452**
Makeiev, Serhii, **R**
Makovyts'kyi, A., 209
Malets', Oleksandr, 210
Maľtsovs'ka, Mariia, **617, 695; JJ**
Mamatey, Victor S., **341**; 233
Manailo, Ivan, **652**
Mandych, Olena Shinali, **445**
Marchenko, Alla, **799**
Marcinkowski, Bartosz, **759**
Marinova, Marinela, **843**

Mark, Rudolf A., **129, 211, 338, 341, 631**
Markova, O. Ie., **157**
Markovits, Andrei S., **107**
Markovych, Pavlo, **182, 582, 617, 714**
Markus', Dariia, **707**
Markus', Vasyľ, **42, 94, 110, 177, 393, 535, 536, 582, 617, 707, 714**; 170, 193, 200, 204, 205, 206, 228
Marosi, Ernő, **366**
Marrus, Michael R., **JJJ**
Martínek, Jiří, **816**; 274
Martyn, Volodymyr, 241
Marunchak, Mykhailo H., **C**
Marvan, Jiří, 237
Maser, Peter, **111**
Mašir/Mashir, Tomislav, **698**
Maskevich, Aleksandr, **635**
Matejka, Ladislav, **137, 192, 327**
Mathews, Edward G., Jr., 157, 195
Matley, Ian M., **157**
Matlovič, René, **JJJ**
Matsyns'kyi, Ivan, **183, 582, 617, 714**
Matthews, Geoffrey J., **157**
Maxwell, Robert, **214**
Mayer, Maria, **484, 485, 582, 617, 714**
Mayer, Vera, **111**
Mayo, Olga K., **39**
McBride, Paul W., **138**
McConnell, Grant D., **54**
Meaufront, Marcel, **546**
Medieshii, Liubomir, *see* Medješi, Ljubomir
Medješi, Helena, **387, 534**
Medješi, Ljubomir/Medieshi, Liubomir, **42, 138, 338, 420, 438, 452, 461, 463, 464, 471, 535, 536, 582, 697, 708; D, M, HH**; 177, 197
Medve, Zoltan, **P**

Medvedovs'ka, Anna, **848**
Medvid', Petro, **806, 814, 817, 818,**
819, 822, 823, 825, 826, 827, 828,
829, 830, 834, 835, 845, 846; 268
Medwidsky, Bohdan, 182
Melnyk, Vasyl', **235;** 182
Mendelsohn, Ezra, **157, 452;** 214
Mestrovic, Stjepan G., **641**
Metzler, Wilhelm, **129**
Michaels, Philip, **66, 95, 104, 106,**
113, 115, 121, 124, 128, 140, 142,
158, 163, 166, 170, 172, 178, 212,
214, 225, 231, 232, 233, 236-238,
239, 258, 268, 282, 293, 303, 321,
329, 356, 417, 444, 454, 466
Micgiel, John S., **342**
Michalik, Sławomir, **582**
Michaud, Claude, **129, 157**
Michna, Ewa, 235
Mihaly, Orestes J., 171
Millar, James R., **599**
Miller, Michael L., **665**
Miller, Sally M., **175**
Miller, Stefania Szlek, **448**
Miller, T., **581, 582**
Mills, Judith M., **127**
Mironowicz, Antoni, 342
Miz, Roman, **42, 55, 110, 205, 391**
Mnich, Roman **747**
Mohinska, Tetiana, 267
Moisiuc, Ivan, **591**
Mokyr, Joel, **594**
Morley, Patricia, **516**
Moroz, Valentyn, 176
Morozowich, Mark, **641**
Moser, Michael, **435, 608, 631, 742**
Moskovich, Wolf/Moskovych, Vol'f,
747, 807, 833
Mosný, Peter, **663**
Motyl, Alexander J., **117, 734; VV;**
252

Mount, Ferdinand, 201
Moynihan, Daniel Patrick, **207, 209,**
560
Mudrak, Myroslava M., **111**
Mullen, Richard, **342**
Mund, Stephane, **582**
Murashko, Pavlo, **111, 119**
Murphy, Curtis, **790**
Mushynka, Mykola/Mušinka,
Mikola, **182, 300, 315, 438, 617,**
714; 185, 246, 262, 265, 271
Mushynka/Mušynka, Oles, **328, 360**
Myshanych, Fedir, **452;** 182
Myshanych, Oleksa, **I;** 196, 208,
227, 230

Nagy, Milada, **700**
Nagy-Nod', Nikolai, **222**
Naumescu, Vlad, **683**
Neubauer, John, **606**
Neumann, Hans B., **342**
Nevrlý, Mikuláš, 223
Newall, Veneta, **182**
Niederhauser, Emil, **42, 138, 157,**
195, 342, 372, 377, 452; 221
Nimchuk, Vasyl', **314**
Nomachi, Motoki, **795, 843**
Nota, Volodymyr, **33**
Novak, Michael, **138**
Nowak, Jacek, **U;** 220

Ofitsyns'kyi, Roman, 182
Okenfuss, Max J., **374**
Oliinyk, Borys, 238
Olynyk, Marta, **801**
Olszański, Tadeusz Andrzej, **299,**
452
Onyshkevych, Larissa, **380**
Orlai, Ivan S., **170**
Oros, Iaroslav, 239
Orton, Lawrence D., **129**

Osier, Jean-Pierre, **665**
Ostrowsky, E., **157**
Otriová, Jana, **544**

Padiak, Valerii, **582, 627, 635, 652, 679, 695, 714, 733, 785, 790, 806, 856; FF, HHH, III, YYY, ZZZ;** 274
Páll, Csilla, **392**
Panchuk, Ihor, **PP**
Panchuk, Mai, **415; R, MM;** 245
Pánek, Jaroslav, **GG**
Pan'ko, Iurii, **608**
Pankovič, Vasil, **528**
Panová, Katarína, **641**
Pap, Diura, **420**
Papazian, Dennis R., **452;** 210
Papharhaji, Djura, 234
Papuga, Djura, **240**
Parente, William J., **452**
Paul, Sebastian, **790**
Pauly, Matthew, **799**
Pavlovich, Frederika, **391**
Pavlovych, Alexander, **92**
Pavlychko, Dmytro, 195
Pawliczko, Ann Lencyk, **507**
Pekar, Athanasius B., **39, 296, 582, 617, 714**
Pelikan, Jaroslav, **211**
Pendzey, Luba, **B**
Penslar, Derek J., **JJJ**
Periwal, Sukmar, **J**
Perko, F. Michael, **374**
Pernal, Andrew B., **129, 157, 341**
Petrov, Aleksei L., **466, 497, 498, 500, 582, 617, 714**
Petrovsky-Shtern, Yohanan, **799, 800**
Petrovtsii, Ivan, **228, 493;** 176
Petryshche, Kh., 184
Petyo, Donald, **42**

Peyfuss, Max Demeter, **111**
Picchio, Riccardo, **131**
Pilátová, Agáta, **271, 372, 806**
Pilipenko, Gleb P., **781, 815, 837;** 275
Pinkerton, Daniel, **371**
Pirie, Paul S., **452;** 212
Piu, Stefan, *see* Pugh, Stefan M.
Plichtová, Jana, **300**
Pliouchth/Pliushch, Leonid, 194
Plishkova/Plišková, Anna, **343, 373, 460, 495, 503, 509, 510, 523, 530, 565, 574, 582, 588, 590, 603, 608, 617, 634, 637, 648, 657, 666, 669, 680, 702-704, 714, 756, 764; L, Y, RR, BBB, FFF, GGG, JJJ;** 257
Plokhii/Plokhy, Serhii, **713, 734, 804; XX;** 254
Podraza, Antoni, **615**
Podrezov, M.V., 272
Polchaninov, Rostislav, **42, 77, 133, 138, 207**
Polinsky, Maria, **742**
Polowy, Teresa, **582**
Pona, Steve, **452**
Ponomar'ov, Vitalii, **540**
Pop, Dmytro/Dymytrii, **572, 652**
Pop, Ivan, **342, 582, 617, 866**
Popovych, Mykhailo, **64**
Pospišil, Ivo, **766**
Potichnyj, Peter, J., **448;** 256
Potuľnyts'kyi, Volodymyr, **452**
Pries, Edmund, **157**
Priestly, Tom, **132**
Pritsak, Omeljan, **242;** 173, 174
Procko, Bohdan P., **119**
Prousis, Theophilus C., **211**
Prymachenko, Iana, **802**
Prymak, Thomas M., **452, 661, 718**
Pugh, Stefan M., **711, 757**
Puskás, Julianna, **297**

Pusztai, Bertalan, **338, 435, 497, 581, 582**

R.H.S., *see* Scott, Robert H.
Rackiewycz, Mark, **812a**
Rady, Martyn, **338, 342**
Raeff, Marc, **42, 452**; 213
Raevsky-Hughes, Olga, **330**
Rafal's'kyi, O., **MM**; 244
Raková, Svatava, **GG**
Rakovs'kyi, Ivan, **268**
Ramach, Ianko, **582**
Ramet, Sabrina P., **578**
Ramkema, Harm, **341, 582**
Ravlić, Aleksander, **537, 538**
Rawlyk, G.A., **59**
Razgulov, Valerii, 223
Rebet, Andreas, **42**
Rechcigl, Miroslav Jr., **209**
Rejzak, Jiří, **542**
Renner, Hans, **342**
Renoff, Richard, **30, 33, 42**; 176
Reshetar, John S., Jr., **42**
Reszler, André, **446**
Revay, Julian I., **58**;
Reynolds, Matthew J., 223
Reynolds, Stephen, **30**
Riasanovsky, Nicholas V., **452**
Riedl, Franz H., **138**
Riggs, Thomas, **769**
Righetti, John, **617**; **JJJ**
Risch, William Jay, **641**
Ristovska, Maja, **854**
Rodal, Alti, **807, 833**
Rolfe, Paul, **581**; 231
Roman, Bishop, **374**
Roman, Stephen B., **200**
Romanenchuk, Bohdan, **129**
Romanyshyn, Oleh, **733**; 256
Romeiser, John B., **581**; 230
Rosocha, Stepan, **126, 173**

Rothstein, Robert A., **542**
Rovt, Alex, **728**
Rudling, Per A., **801**
Rudnytsky, Ivan L., **42**; 168
Rudolph, Richard L., **287**
Rumpler, Helmut, **639**
Rundesová, Táňa, **551**
Rusek, Jerzy, **499**
Rusek, Zbigniew, **499**
Rusinko, Elaine, **380, 535, 536, 602, 617, 689, 693, 714**; **II**; 225
Rus'kyi, Iaroslav, 214
Rusnak, M., **389**; 200
Rusnak, Tim, **138**
Rusynko, Mykola, 192
Rutkowski, Alan, **156**
Rybotycki, W., **157**
Rychlík, Jan, **793**
Rynor, Michah, **516**

S.B., **111**
Sable, Thomas F., **374**
Sanfilippo, Matteo, **277**
Sapozhnikova, Galina, 241
Sasu, Aurel, **270**
Sasvári, László, **438**
Sauer, Serge A., **157**
Saunders, David, **157, 195, 380**
Savardii, Ivan, 168, 179
Savchuk, B.P., 271
Schaarschmidt, Gunter, **759**
Scheibert, Peter, **42, 59**
Schmidt, Albert J., **342**
Schobesberger, Nikolaus, **848**
Schreiber, Klaus, **582**
Schultze, Martin, **342**
Scott, Robert H., **342**
Seibt, Ferdinand, **366**
Sem, E., **342**
Sembratovyč, Josyf, **329**
Semczyszyn, Magdalena, **765**

Semeniuk, Sviatoslav, **621**; 243
Semyzhenko, Anton, 271
Senkus, Roman, **XXX**
Senyk, Sophia, **157, 211, 641, 661**
Sfetas, Spyridon, **342**
Shandor, Vikentii/Vincent, **42, 564,
582, 617, 714**
Shapira, Dan, **759**
Shatylov, Mykola, 231
Shchupak, Igor, **851**
Shebelist, Serhii, **733**
Sheets, Anna, **401**
Shelley, Thomas J., **481**
Shelton, Dinah L., **626**
Shen Yun, **189**
Shepelev, Maksymiliian A., 258
Sheptyts'kyi, Andrei, **211, 732**
Shevchenko, Kirill V., **790**; 269
Shevelov, George/Iurii, 184
Shimada, Tomoko, **579**
Shkandrij, Myroslav, **452, 579, 582**
Shkurla, Nykolai/Škurla, Michal,
193, 259
Shlepets'kyi, Andrei, **138**
Short, David, **435, 542**
Short, Elizabeth Chechur, 198
Shostak, Elizabeth, **342**
Shpontak, Mykhailo, 169
Shtefan, Avhustyn/Stefan,
Augustine, **42, 90, 173**
Shtets', Mykola, **14, 582, 617, 714**
Shtohryn, Dmytro M., **129, 156, 195**
Shurkin, Vlad, **342**
Siatkowski, Janusz, **499**
Siekierski, Maciej, **129**
Sigismund of Luxembourg, **50, 366**
Sikora, Stepan, 275
Simms, Brendan, 207
Simon, Constantin, 337, 341, 342,
579, 582
Simons, Thomas W., Jr., **108**

Sirka, Iosyf, 183, 188
Sirs'kyi, Vasyl'(Katsaveiko), 191
Skilling, H. Gordon, **265**
Sklokin, Volodymyr, **733, 736**; 258
Skuban, Helena, **471**
Skuban, Mikola, **311**
Skulimowska-Ochyra, Ewa, **30**
Škurla, Michal. *See* Shkurla,
Nykolai
Slančová, Daniela, **533, 552**
Slavutych, Yar, **156**
Slawinski, Ilona, **508**
Slavinska, Iryna, **772, 796**
Sloistov, Sergei M., **714**
Šmigel, Michal, **741**
Smiian, Petro K., **18**
Smith, Raymond A., 211
Smolii, Valerii, **654**; **CC**
Snow, G.E., **452**
Sochka, Vasyl', 180
Solchanyk, Roman, **452**
Soltés, Peter, **533**
Solynko, Dmytro, 186
Sopinka, John, **225**
Sopoliga, Miroslav/Sopolyga,
Myroslav, **617, 714**; 192, 204, 235
Sorokowski, Andrew, **452**
Sosnowska, Danuta, **579**
Stambrook, Fred, **338, 341, 374**
Stankiewicz, Barbara, **618**
Stauffer, Rachel, **641**
Stauter-Halsted, Kelly, **631**
Stebelsky, Ihor, **157**
Stebel's'kyi, Bohdan, **157**
Stefan, Augustine/Shtefan,
Avhustyn, **42, 90, 173**
Steffen, Gustaf F., **97**
Stefka, Joseph, **216, 217, 318**
Stepanov, G.V., **130**
Stępień, Stanisław, **513, 706**
Stercho, Peter G., **184, 582, 617, 714**

Stetsyk, Lidiia, **57**
Stirling, Andrew, **JJJ**
Stokłosa, Katarzyna, **696**
Stolárik, Imrich, **119**, **138**
Stolarik, M. Mark, **42**, **600**, **619**, **775**; **JJJ**; 235
Stolz, Benjamin, **137**
Stössl, Marianne, **182**
Strelka, Joseph P., **508**
Struk, Danylo Husar, **335**
Struve, Kai, **801**
Strumins'kyj, Bohdan, **33**, **37**
Stryjek, Tomasz, **654**, **790**; **KK**, **WWW**; 268
Stupp, J.A., **111**
Subtelny, Orest, **133**, **449**
Suda, Zdenek, **119**
Sukhŷi, Shtefan/Suchý, Štefan, **617**, **714**; 248
Šulc, Magdelena Veselinović, **205**
Suliak, Sergei, **652**; 240
Sulitka, Andrej, **806**
Sulyma, M., **42**
Sulyma, Petro, **176**
Suny, Ronald Grigur, **570**
Švagrovský, Štefan, **542**
Svoboda, Bohumil, **488**, **527**
Švorc, Branislav A., **755**
Švorc, Peter, **582**, **617**, **663**, **714**, **790**, **806**
Świątek, Adam, **832**
Switalski, John, **157**
Swoboda, Victor, **39**, **42**
Sword, Keith, **342**
Swyripa, Frances, **59**
Sydor, Dymytrii, **617**, **714**; 222
Sydorchuk, Oleksii, **727**, **733**, **734**, **760**; **AAA**
Sydorenko, Alexander, **799**
Syrnyk, Jarosław, **765**
Sysak, Miron, **467**, **577**

Sysyn, Frank E., **107**, **194**, **713**
Szabo, Franz A.J., **129**
Szabó, Miroslav, **665**, **816**
Szamvaj, Ruth, **119**
Székely, G., **373**
Szlanta, Wacław, 211

T.D.B., **342**
Taft, Robert, **32**, **138**, **182**, **374**; 168, 175
Takach, Basil, **161**, **582**, **617**, **714**
Takach, Havriïl, **190**
Talbot, Elizabeth, **207**
Talaga, Andrzej, 222
Tamaš, Julian/ Tamash, Iuliian, **617**, **714**, **737**; 186
Tambor, Jolanta, **JJJ**
Tanatar, Bülent, **759**
Taranenko, Andrii, 277
Tarasiuk, Renata, **747**
Tcaçiuc, Ştefan/ Tkachiuk, Shtefan, 231
Tejchman, Miroslav, **42**, **119**, **129**, **341**, **377**, **435**, **504**, **535**, **536**, **608**, **654**
Teslevych, Mykola, 189
Thernstrom, Stephan, **70**
Thomas, Brandon, **4**
Thurzo, Igor, **111**
Timkov, Oleksandr, **627**; 244
Timkovič, Gorazd Andrej, **617**; **NNN**; 260
Timkovič, Jozafát A., **617**
Tkach, Joseph W., **231**
Tkachenko, Bohdan, **540**
Tkachiuk, Shtefan. *See* Tcaçiuc, Ştefan
Tkacz, Edyta, **774**
Tokar, Marian Ia., **BB**
Tolstoj, Nikita I., **435**
Tomčanii, Mykhailo, **226**, **457**

Toops, Gary H., **608**
Torke, Hans-Joachim, **452**
Toth, Alexis G., **142**, **356**, **582**, **617**, **714**
Tóth, Enikő, **797**
Treptow, Kurt W., **342**
Trier, Tom, **529**, **531**, **536**; **T**; 218
Troebst, Stefan, **342**, **535**, **536**; 215, 221, 263
Trofimov, Valerii, **733**
Trokhanovskii, Petro, **582**, **588**, **654**, **743**, **774**, **806**, **812**, **816**; **III**
Tsitsak, Vasyl', 239
Tudlik, Ferencné, **754**
Turan, Ömer, **581**
Turii, Oleh, 231
Turok-Hetesh, Vasyl', **582**, **617**, **633**, **714**; 208
Tyvodar, Mykhailo, **439**; 215, 227-228

Udovenko, Hennadii, 209
Udvari, István, **373**; 176
Ueling, Greta, **759**
Ujj, Anna, **16**; **P**
Urbanitsch, Peter, **639**
Urry, James, **452**
Ustinov, Peter, **162**

V.M., *see* Markus Vasyl'
Van de Walle, André, **341**
Vangansbeke, Jeannick, **718**
Vaňko, Juraj, **542**, **582**, **617**, **714**, **866**
Varga, Béla, **767**
Varga, Boris, **617**, **820**, **821**
Varga, Mikhailo, **461**
Vegesh, Mykola M., **BB**
Veličko, Alexander, **240**
Venelin-Hutsa, Iurii, 113
Verešová, Timea, **813**

Verkholantsev, Julia, **631**
Veryha, Wasyl', **129**, **157**
Veszprémy, László, **342**
Vico, Fedor, **33**, **64**, **282**, **487**, **566**, **567**, **582**, **607**, **617**, **670**, **714**, **781**, **815**, **837**
Vidnians'kyi, Stepan, **CC**, **JJ**, **SS**
Vieter, Theodor, **129**
Vogl, Josef, **554**
Voloshyn, Avgustyn, **51**
Von Hagen, Mark, **452**
Von Werdt, Christophe, **790**
Vrabec, Eugenija, **698**
Vujačić, Ivan, **650**
Vushko, Emil, 188

W.B., **119**
Wagner, Francis S., **108**
Waligóra-Zblewska, Alicja, **832**
Walker, Christopher J., **342**
Wallace, Richard, 226
Walle, André van de, **342**
Warhol, Andy, **67**, **213**, **283**, **482**, **563**, **617**, **645**, **714**, **861**
Warner, E. A., **506**
Warzeski, Walter C., **42**
Washington, Idella, **209**
Watral, Marta, **869**
Weczerka, Hugo, **157**
Weitz, Eric D., **746**
Wendland, Anna Veronika, **338**, **341**, **452**, **535**, **536**
Wessel, Martin Schulze, **342**
Wexler, Paul, **42**
Whistance-Smith, Ron, **157**
White, Sanford, **824**
Wilczyński, Włodzimerz, **EE**
Wilke, Gundele, **580**
Wilms, Denise, **209**
Wilson, Andrew, **452**, **535**, **579**
Wilson, Sophia, **790**

Winokur, Marshall, **111**
Witkowski, Wiesław, **435, 504, 535, 536, 542**
Wojtaszczyk, Jakub, **592**
Woldan, Alois, **799**
Wolff, Larry, **713**
Wolowyna, Oleh, **177**
Woolfenden, Gregory, **374**
Worobec, Christine D., **42**
Wright, William E., **342**
Wróbel, Piotr, **582, 790**
Wynar, Bohdan S., **129, 156, 195, 307, 342**
Wynar, Lubomyr R., **157**
Wynnyckyj, Iroida L., **202**
Wytrzens, Günther, **42, 129, 195, 222**

Yekelchyk, Serhy, **631, 661**
Yevics, Philip, **133**
Young, Robyn V., **401**
Yun, Shen, **189**
Yurcisin, John, **582, 617, 714**

Zakharchuk, Iryna, **799**
Zakydalsky, Oksana, **582**
Zalevs'ka, Liliia, **724**
Zan, Mykhailo, 267
Zapletal, Florian, **111**
Zarechnak, Dimitry, **212**

Zaremba, O., **MM**; 244
Zayarnyuk, Andriy, **535, 536, 711**
Zavadiak, Mykhailo, 208
Zazuliak, M., **470, 628**
Żebrowski, Rafal, **665**
Zhatkovych, Gregory I., **62, 582, 617, 714, 869**
Zhenets'kyi, Stepan, **176**; 176
Zhuhai, Vitalii, **550**; 224
Zhuk, Sergei I., **790**
Zhupan, Ievhenii, **456**
Ziac, Martin Fedor, **Y**; 226
Zięba, Andrzej A., **138, 235, 302, 615, 832**; **VVV**
Zilynskyj, Bohdan, **793**
Zimmer, Kerstin, **661**; *see also* Jobst, Kerstin S.
Zlydnev, V.I., **234**
Zobl, Engelbert, **139**
Zobl, Hertha A., **139**
Zoltán, András, **722**
Zozuliak, Aleksander/Oleksandr, **224, 582, 617, 652, 714, 725, 743, 764, 780, 858, 863-868, 871-875**; **F, CCC**; 184, 234
Żurawski vel Grajewski, Przemysław, **338, 341, 579**
Zurowsky, Jaroslaw, **581**
Zyla, Wolodymyr T., **49, 129**